Supernaturalism in Christianity

Its Growth and Cure

MERCER
UNIVERSITY PRESS

Endowed by
TOM WATSON BROWN
and
THE WATSON-BROWN FOUNDATION, INC.

Supernaturalism in Christianity
Its Growth and Cure

by
WILLIAM E. PHIPPS

MERCER
UNIVERSITY PRESS

ISBN 978-0-88146-093-3 MUP/H748 (clothbound)
ISBN 978-0-88146-094-0 MUP/P372 (perfectbound)

Supernaturalism in Christianity:
Its Growth and Cure
Copyright ©2008
Mercer University Press
Printed in the United States of America
First edition

The paper used in this publication meets the minimum requirements
of American National Standard for Information Sciences—
Permanence of Paper for Printed Library Materials,
ANSI Z39.48-1984.

Quotations from the Bible are often the author's own translation,
but indebtedness to a variety of versions can be found.
Quotations from the New Revised Standard Version of the Bible
(NRSV), ©1989 by the Division of Christian Education
of the National Council of the Churches of Christ in the U.S.A.,
are used by permission.

Library of Congress Cataloging-in-Publication Data

Phipps, William E., 1930–
    Supernaturalism in Christianity : its growth and cure / by William
E. Phipps. — 1st ed.
        p.   cm.
    Includes bibliographical references and indexes.
    ISBN-13: 978-0-88146-094-0 (pbk. : alk. paper)
    ISBN-10: 0-88146-094-X (pbk. : alk. paper)
    1. Supernatural (Theology) I. Title.
BT745.P49 2007
231.7'3--dc22   2007044740

Contents

* * *

To Union Theological Seminary/ Presbyterian School of Christian Education

*Without that community during my formative years
and its excellent library during my professional years,
my life as a human and as a teacher
would have been greatly diminished.*

* * *

Preface

During the past generation, millions have watched the movie *Superman* and its sequels as well as the "Smallville" television series. Nostalgia attracted me to the extravaganzas because I grew up with *Action Comics*, which two Jewish artists created in 1938. The films triggered poignant memories of boyhood anxieties and fantasies. As a weakling who could not spring to the high bar on a playground, it was marvelous for me to behold the man who could leap over tall buildings and who was even more dashing than the Lone Ranger. In accord with his dual identity, he was sent by his father-god, Jor-El to save the earth. The incarnated infant grew up with adopted earth parents in Smallville. He was known as Clark Kent until he transformed himself from a fumbling, mediocre reporter into a bloodless, metallic force. "More powerful than a locomotive," Superman once pushed continental plates back together to remove an earthquake's effect. He also once raised his friend Lois Lane, who had died, by means of a titanic time-reversal of the earth. He could do naturally what is supernatural to earth creatures because he came from the more advanced planet, Krypton, where the force of gravity was much greater. The alien was invincible against Lex Luthor, his diabolical archenemy. Superman was vulnerable only if he exposed to mysterious kryptonite crystals from his homeland. After hearing my parents lament the Nazi invasions of other nations, it was reassuring to gaze at images of the indestructible Man of Steel zapping enemies of "truth, justice, and the American way." Never did it occur to me that his association of evil with people espousing values different from the majority of my fellow citizens, and his violent methods of destroying them, resembled the outlook and actions of Adolf Hitler.

The Kryptonian, whose native name was Kol-El, meaning "all that God is" in Hebrew, supplied me with myths that I transferred to the founder of Christianity. The Jesus of my youthful imagining was an almighty being who regarded heaven as his real home. Being omniscient, he knew everything about the world ages before he became veiled in flesh in order to rectify corruption and save the earth. His true procreator was Jah-El, that is, the Lord God, for Jesus only masqueraded as a son of carpenter Joseph after arriving miraculously from outer space to grow up in the small village of Nazareth. I usually referred to this deity in disguise as "Savior" because he specialized in rescuing the helpless. Since Lois Lanes were always getting themselves into difficulties, this clean and virginal prince charming was a gallant protector of women. Of course he would never marry one, for such human indulgence would compromise his single-minded devotion to smashing satanic forces. No fitting match was possible between Superman and the superficial human female, even though some later traditions claimed that Mary Magdalene was his intimate companion.

As I dredge up that Sunday school theology, I realize that other wires were crossed between Jesus and Superman. As a spy for the Kingdom of Heaven, the biblical Superman sent intelligence reports to his Father about the behavior of earthlings. Secrets could not be withheld from him, for his X-ray vision could penetrate brains. He did not work miracles most of the time, and usually he was thought to be a meek but charming preacher who dressed in white. While he sometimes allowed bad guys to treat him abusively as an ordinary mortal, he had two natures and could instantly switch on his supernatural energy. Without even changing clothes he could express omnipotence that he had imported from Glory Land. For example, while asleep on a boat cushion he was awakening by frightened fishermen who made him aware that the Sea of Galilee had become a raging tempest. By immediately causing the storm to cease, he saved his friends from drowning. Another time he amazed those fishermen by walking toward their boat on the surface of the sea and thereby defying the force of gravity.

Super-Jesus could vanish into thin air when the going got rough. Once when a hometown mob led him out of his synagogue to cast him off a cliff, he vamoosed. However, like Superman and Achilles, Jesus was vulnerable in one way: he was not protected by his Heavenly Father from a cross. His enemies made the most of this, killing him after a bloody ordeal. Their victory was temporary, however, for he soon slipped out of the cloth in which he was buried, arose, and pushed aside the massive stone sealing his tomb. After entering for a moment in eternity into the atmosphere of planet earth, this dazzling dynamo lifted off from a hill near Jerusalem into outer space. I presumed that Jesus was now gliding effortlessly with raised arms in the blue beyond, or sitting it out at the right hand of his Father's gleaming white throne in the heavens, awaiting a second entry. At the final Judgment Day he would descend from his orbit, knock out all Lucifer-like opposition, and gather up all reverential Christians to soar with him to heaven.

Robert Funk, who established the Jesus Seminar, wrote about the film *Superman*:

> In this cinematic epic, we have a fairly complete redeemer myth. . . . Mortal men and women are powerless within the framework of the myth because evil itself has cosmic dimensions. Spectator religion, morality, and politics are the

inevitable result. Human beings are pawns in the cosmic drama being played out on a stage wider than their own. We are encouraged to rely on the powers above us, alien to us. Myths in this category tend to tranquilize, to function as escapist fare. . . . God must intervene as the only way to right wrongs and guarantee rewards for the faithful.[1]

To relieve pent-up childhood emotions, many have yearned for a hero like the pretend human in blue tights. Thomas Wolfe, my contemporary, describes the outlook of boys then: "A glorious age, I tell you! . . . The myths that actually touched you at that time—not Hercules, . . . but Superman."[2] Some have attempted to blend the Superman mythology with the stories of a tragic but triumphant Jesus. A parody of this is seen in the musical *Godspell* where Jesus appears in a body shirt emblazen with a big "S."

Adults also occasionally take seriously the cosmic assumptions found in the Superman comic. The most famous of these is Erich von Daniken who believed that extraterrestrial creatures have visited in spaceships. He reported on a Russian scholar who has an even more outlandish outlook, "Dr. Vyatchealav Saitsev of the University of Minsk believes that Jesus came from outer space, that he was a representative of a higher civilization, and that that would partially explain his supernatural powers and abilities."[3]

* * *

The earliest Christian heresy was docetism, meaning that Jesus only *appeared* (Greek, *dokeo*) to be human because he was too holy to be a full earthling participant. A New Testament letter warns, "Many deceivers have gone out into the world, those who do not acknowledge Jesus Christ has come in the flesh."[4] Since these heretics presumed him to be the immortal God in the guise of a mortal, an apocryphal book of the New Testament claimed that he never made a footprint when he walked about.[5] Another ancient docetic writer alleged that Jesus disclosed:

> I am from above the heavens. I did not refuse them even to become a Christ, but . . . I revealed that I am a stranger to the regions below. . . . Some were

---

[1]Robert Funk, *Honest to Jesus* (San Francisco: Harper, 1996) 307-308.

[2]Thomas Wolfe, *The Electric Kool-Aid Acid Test* (New York: Bantam, 1969) 35.

[3]Erich von Daniken, *Miracles of the Gods* (New York: Delacorte, 1975) 109.

[4]2 John 7.

[5]*Acts of John* 93.

persuaded when they saw the wonders which were being accomplished by me. . . . I was not afflicted at all . . . and I did not die not in reality, but in appearance.[6]

Docetics viewed Jesus more as an immaterial angel than as a person with physical substance. Their simplistic propositions and logic were: since God is omnipotent, and since Jesus is God, therefore Jesus had unlimited power. Moreover, he was omniscient, knowing from the beginning the whole range of universal wisdom. Although he appeared to be a Palestinian peasant, underneath he was the infallible and almighty God.

In the fifth century, church leaders attempted to eliminate docetism by declaring the full humanity of Jesus, and the Chalcedon Creed that conveys the doctrine was accepted by all orthodox Christians. In spite of the claim made by those who recited, then as now, that "we all with one accord teach" the content of that creed, Christians have been more prone to praise Jesus' divinity than to appreciate his humanity, with its concomitant limitations. While docetism was the first heresy to be condemned, it still thrives because many Christians—as well as non-Christians—treat Jesus as though he was not really a male Jew who lived in an ancient Mediterranean culture. According to Anglican lay-theologian and scientist John Wren-Lewis, prior to the mid-twentieth century ordinary people generally did not envision Jesus as a human being; rather, he was "full of supernatural knowledge and miraculous power, very much like the Olympian gods were supposed to be when they visited the earth in disguise."[7] Subsequently, Catholic theologian Thomas Sheehan stated, "In official Church teaching this view of Jesus as a god who merely pretended to be human is a heresy, and the seriousness of the error is not mitigated by the fact that multitudes of the faithful, from catechists to cardinals, firmly believe and teach it."[8] Dale Allison, an eminent Protestant New Testament scholar, also observes that docetism is still prominent, "Much of the popular Christianity I have known seems to think that Jesus was at least three-fourths divinity, no more than one quarter human being."[9]

---

[6]*The Second Treatise of the Great Seth*, 52, 55.
[7]Dewi Morgan, ed. *They Become Anglicans* (London: Mowbray, 1959) 165.
[8]Thomas Sheehan, *The First Coming* (New York: Random House, 1986) 31.
[9]Robert Miller, ed. *The Apocalyptic Jesus* (Santa Rosa CA: Polebridge, 2001) 147-48.

Sociological surveys confirm that a disconnect exists between what Christians officially believe and what they actually accept. In the past generation a comprehensive study of all branches of American Lutheranism revealed that "a minority . . . fully acknowledge the humanity of Jesus." Most of those surveyed thought Jesus knew everything all the time, had command over the powers of nature, felt no sexual impulse, and had no sense of humor.[10] Another survey shows that the majority of American Christians agree with this statement, "It is completely true that Jesus walked on water."[11] One does not need to understand Archimedes' principle of specific gravity, discovered in the Greek culture before the Christian era, to realize that the density of any human body does not permit it to walk on the liquid state of water. Those accepting literally the Gospel's walking-on-water story must presume that at least on one occasion Jesus' body was altogether spiritual and had no physical weight. They may affirm that Jesus was a physical body from birth to death but they assume that he could at will become a fleshless phantom.

A song made popular by the Billy Graham Crusades causes many to fancy that being a Christian is putting "your hand in the hand of the man who walked on the water." Responding to this human impossibility that some think Christians must believe, New Testament authority E. P. Sanders comments:

> His [Jesus'] divinity neither combined with nor interfered with his humanity: he was not an odd mixture. It is heretical to say that his divinity buoyed him up while his human feet lightly grazed the water. The definitive [Chalcedon] statement on this issue is that he is "of one substance with us as regards his manhood; like us in all respects, apart from sin"—not, "apart from the ability to walk on water."[12]

Supernaturalism flourishes today because of the entertainment media as much as religious promotion. Due to special effects cinematography, paranormal wizardry is especially popular among those who would like to

---

[10]Merton Strommen et al., *A Study of Generations* (Minneapolis: Augsburg, 1972) 117, 367.

[11]Rodney Stark and William Bainbridge, *The Future of Religion. Secularization, Revival, and Cult Formation* (Berkeley CA: University of California Press, 1985) 55.

[12]E. P. Sanders, *The Historical Figure of Jesus* (New York: Penguin, 1993) 134.

believe that superhuman powers can magically be summoned to solve societal problems. The dazzling computer animation created for such movies as *Star Wars*, *The Matrix*, *Harry Potter*, and *Lord of the Rings* may entice many into believing that physical law can be defied. Children who consume an unbalanced diet of thaumaturgic television cartoons have difficulty distinguishing fiction from fact long past the appropriate age for comprehending what is really possible. Virtual reality technology sometimes hinders the development of critical judgment as to what acts or events are contrary to nature.

Many people persist in thinking that the clearest proofs of God's existence are when the Deity allegedly breaks the accustomed natural order. Correspondingly, when everything is rolling smoothly, little thought is given to God's greatness. Perennially recurring is the view that God's intervention is the cause of extraordinary disasters. God appears to be held more responsible for causing natural tragedies that damage and kill than for bringing about reconciliation and helping people build a more humane society.

Even catastrophes that are obviously due to human error, incompetence, or malfeasance have been defined as "acts of God" by employers, manufacturers, and insurance companies in order to escape liability. For example, in 1972 a rain soaked earth dam broke in West Virginia that had been poorly constructed by a coal company. As a result more than a hundred people who lived downstream on Buffalo Creek were killed. An official of the mining company called the disaster an "act of God."[13]

Virtually unquestioned for two millennia were the Psalter's songs about bolts of lightning being a direct manifestation of God's power. They declared that "the Lord flashes forth flames of fire" during a thunderstorm to accomplish some purpose.[14] This representation of the Hebrew God is similar to the way Baal was described by the Canaanites, Zeus by the early Greeks, and Thor by the early Germans. By means of a kite experiment, Benjamin Franklin discovered in 1752 that lightning is an electrical discharge from clouds. He then demonstrated that a wire attached to the highest point on a building could conduct electrical charge to the ground without damage. But some Christians refused to place lightning rods on

---

[13]Kai Erikson, *Everything in the Path* (New York: Simon and Schuster, 1976) 178.

[14]Psalm 29:7.

steeples, considering it blasphemous to attempt to interfere with God's sphere of activity. They were popularly called "heretic rods" in Germany.[15]

Charles Darwin wrote, "I dare say when thunder and lightning were first proved to be due to secondary [scientific] causes, some regretted to give up the idea that each flash was caused by the direct hand of God."[16] He realized that many humans, aware that their actions—often irrational—express their own desires, found it satisfying to project that erratic acts in nature are caused by a whim of God. But Darwin thought that the dignity of God is enhanced when weather, health, and other spheres are governed by rational law and not by the unpredictable anger of a deity or by the touch of an angel.[17]

People in developed nations, as well as in simple tribes, believe that nature usually operates regularly without the assistance of gods or God. But in times of individual or tribal emergency, a sky deity may interrupt the general pattern, often after prayer petitions. The tendency to treat God as an alien power who is can inflict or remove bad events continues to be widespread in contemporary culture:

> If a young person receives a diagnosis of terminal cancer, or if a tornado destroys a man's home and family, we hear dour complaints: "Why has God done this?" For every misery in human experience, from the Holocaust to a devastating flood, people speak of good and evil more than of social or scientific causes, and (like Job) they ponder how God could cause or allow things so horrific.[18]

More religious harm than help may have resulted from the assurances given sufferers that they will become physically cured if they firmly believe in God. Theologian Jeffrey Eaton writes:

> If person is told that God works miracles on behalf of the faithful and is offered as paradigm cases the stories of miraculous healings in the New Testament, and further, is promised that this sort of thing continues to be possible in Christ's name, what is the person to think when, beset with physical affliction,

---

[15]Ernst and Marie-Luise Keller, *Miracles in Dispute* (Philadelphia: Fortress, 1969) 32.

[16]Frederick Burkhardt and Sydney Smith, eds. *The Correspondence of Charles Darwin* (Cambridge: University Press, 1992) 7:381.

[17]William Phipps, *Darwin's Religious Odyssey* (Harrisburg: Trinity, 2002) 37.

[18]Donald Spoto, *The Hidden Jesus* (New York: St. Martin's Press, 1998) 115.

he/she finds no physical relief forthcoming from the hand of God? Is this not the addition of theological insult to physical injury?[19]

In the wake of the catastrophic 9/11 attack on America, fresh questions have been raised by those who have been taught that God, being almighty, can prevent or permit anything to happen. Since the terrorist hijackers were convinced that they were agents of the one God, and since those fanatic fundamentalists were not stopped by divine intervention, many have wondered if God: (a) lacks omnipotence, or (b) wants to punish severely the United States, or (c) tolerates the killing of innocent noncombatants, or (d) is uninterested in averting evil. Belief in the control of God over everything has been shaken, and some would list God among the missing persons at "ground zero."

Others have resolved the theological issue prompted by catastrophes by conceiving of God as the creator of good but not of evil. Terrorists are seen as misusers of freedom, one of the good and unique potentialities of all humans. Some responses to the al-Qaeda attack can be viewed as America's finest religious hour. Hundreds of firefighters, using their freedom in a divinely sanctioned way, gave their lives because of their dedication to rescuing victims. Some congregations have given attention to diminishing bigotry by engaging in interfaith dialogue and by expressing the *agape* of Christ in other nonsupernatural ways.

In 2004, waves rose up from the deep and obliterated many villages on the coast of the Indian Ocean. That tsunami was often reported as a devastation of "biblical" magnitude. The reference might have been to a psalmist's claim that "the earth quaked, . . . the channels of the ocean were exposed, and the earth's foundations were laid bare."[20] That writer, living along the geological fault line of the Jordan Valley, attributed cataclysms to the Lord's anger. Shlomo Amar, Israel's chief Sephardic rabbi, conveyed the Hebrew Bible's affirmation of an interventionist God when he commented that the tsunami was "an expression of God's wrath with the world; the world is being punished for wrongdoing."[21] He presumed that even the drowning of thousands of babies can be justified by the collective guilt of humans. But thanks to modern geology, the cause is now known to be a shift of tectonic plates because of pressure from the earth's molten

---

[19]*Modern Theology* (April 1985): 215.
[20]Psalm 18:7, 15.
[21]*Blogcritics* (8 January 2005).

core. Consequently, many religionists no longer think of earthquakes as due to a capricious deity; rather, they marvel that so many in the global community have been divinely inspired to launch a huge wave of relief for millions of desperate victims.

When calamity strikes the innocent, many ask, "Why did God let this happen?" Theologians who champion monotheism bear some responsibility for the angst prompting the question. Recognizing the nonexistence of a second and evil deity who can be blamed for catastrophes, they have to confront the dilemma that Job personally faced. Leaders of Judaism, Christianity, and Islam have often presumed an absolute determinism by the Omnipotent who can do anything, including interfering in the natural order. Atheism often results from the questionable assumption that a good God causes bad things to happen.

* * *

As a boy I strenuously resisted giving up the comfort of supernaturalism, beginning with the tale of Santa's sled moving through the sky. But I came to agree with my skeptical elementary schoolmates and set aside home indoctrination about a literal Santa. Even so, for the next decade I did not question the supernaturalism of the Bible. Having been raised in a family and congregation that interpreted biblical stories literally, I accepted, and was especially fascinated by, such miracle stories as Eve being made from Adam's rib and Jonah praying in the belly of a huge fish.

When I entered Davidson College, the atomic era that was just beginning attracted me to a major in physics. It became apparent that supernaturalism did not mesh with what I was learning about the forces of nature. Fortunately, the four semesters of Bible study required for graduation were taught from a historical-literary perspective. I came to realize that the essential message of the most investigated book in history can withstand critical scrutiny, and that science does not clash with a nonsupernatural vital religion. It became apparent to me that the scientific method need not clash with biblical teachings about love, justice, and God.

For more than fifty years I have engaged in an intense study of the writings of the apostle Paul, beginning with the doctoral dissertation I researched at a European university. Two decades ago some of that research resulted in *Paul against Supernaturalism*, published by Philosophical Library. Unfortunately, that press, which had produced quality academic books, went bankrupt shortly after my study was published; consequently, the book had very limited circulation. In the 1990s, graduate students who wanted to use it as that basis of seminar discussion had difficulty locating a few copies. That situation prompted me to engage in this much more extensive probe of the conflict between authentic Christianity and supernaturalism.

Recovering the elusive gospel of Jesus may not be fully possible, but Paul's understanding of it, which is distinguishable from the subsequently written Gospels, may in some ways provide a better access to the authentic Jesus. That apostle refused to pander to seekers of unnatural happenings, and never wrote about Jesus working miracles. Moreover, the views of Paul on such supernatural topics as angels, the resurrection, and hell differ remarkably from those of the Gospels. He acknowledged giving up thinking like a child as he grew to maturity, and his letters indicate that much of what he discarded was a magical view of the universe.

Paul has been my theological and ethical lodestar, but my admiration for the first great Christian thinker is not uncritical. I have argued in print that Paul's views on celibacy and homosexuality were shortsighted.[22] Also, his statement that "man is the image of God and mirrors his glory but woman reflects man's glory" misinterprets Hebrew theology and is inconsistent with his acceptance elsewhere of gender equality.[23] Although Paul was in some ways a man of limited vision, in other ways he has been a liberating influence to Christians of every generation.

Like all Christians, I value many well-established religious traditions, beginning with those associated with ancient Judaism onward. I think of myself as a champion of the fundamental beliefs of original Christianity, but I reject the five doctrines that "fundamentalists" have declared to be "essential": the inerrancy of the Bible, the virgin birth of Jesus, his supernatural works, his substitutionary atonement, and his physical resurrection.[24] Even so, I think of myself as an evangelical in the literal meaning of the term, for I accept and "publish glad tidings" of Jesus. However, I deplore a number of the positions—such as theological exclusiveness and gay

---

[22]William Phipps, *Clerical Celibacy* (Harrisburg: Continuum, 2004) 64-69; William Phipps, "Paul on 'Unnatural Sex,'" *Currents in Theology and Mission* (April 2002): 128-31.

[23]Genesis 1:27; 1 Corinthians 11:7; Galatians 3:28.

[24]George Marsden, *Fundamentalism and American Culture* (New York: Oxford, 1980) 117.

bashing—of many Americans who call themselves evangelicals. Again, as the chapters ahead show, I shun the acids of secular modernity and am eager to conserve the best of the Christian heritage.

* * *

Someone has said that research and plagiarism differ in that one involves copying from many texts and the other from a single source. I am indebted to many writers, and often I prefer to preserve their style and authority by quoting rather than paraphrasing their ideas. I can identify with Montaigne who admitted, "I have here made a bouquet of flowers that others have picked, and have contributed nothing but the ribbon to tie them together."[25]

---

[25]Michel Montaigne, *Essays* (1595) 3:12.

Chapter 1
Introduction

Defining Terms

What is a miracle, and how is it related to supernaturalism? Those who affirm or deny miracles usually do so without specifying what they mean by "miracles." Are miracles events in accord with nature that naive persons, who are unaware of the full possibilities of nature, claim to be unnatural? Are they really unnatural and inexplicable occurrences that God used in ancient times to convince people of religious truth but discontinued after Christianity became established? Are they strange things that are passed down in folklore but have now been proven to be sheer fantasies? Or, are they any unexplained happenings that awaken in individuals a realization of divine power and beneficence?

Even though "miracle" continues to be commonly used in American culture today, modern English translations of the Bible have generally exchanged its use in older translations for terms that better convey the particular meaning of the original Hebrew and Greek. The New Revised Standard Version has replaced the King James Version's use of "miracle," as indicated by the following italics: Pharoah challenges Moses, "Perform a *wonder*"; Jesus speaks of someone "who does a *deed of power* in my name"; and his changing water to wine is referred to as "the first of his *signs.*"[1]

There are several basically different meanings of the term "miracle." Minimally defined, it expresses a "marvel," which is what is connoted by its Latin root *miraculum*. From that same root comes "admire," which pertains to something causing wonder and appreciation. Augustine of Hippo, one of the most influential of all Christians, gave this definition, "I call a miracle whatever appears arduous or unusual that exceeds the expectation or abilities of the one who marvels at it."[2] Thinking in that manner, specialists in English literature have called miraculous the feat of a committee of ordinary scholars who produced the King James Version of the Bible. Jerome, in his Latin translation of the Bible that was unrivaled for a thousand years, employed *miraculum* to translate biblical terms that desig-

---

[1]Exodus 7:9; Mark 9:39; John 2:11.
[2]Augustine, *The Advantage of Believing*, 34.

nate an astonishment, and usually it did not carry an overtone of the super-natural. For example, he writes about the *miraculum* that will soon be pre-cipitated when Jewish exiles in Egypt are destroyed by sword, famine, and pestilence.[3]

Advertisers have appropriated "miracle" to hype whatever they deem extraordinary, from foods to fertilizer. It is also frequently used to express a response to an unusual happening that has no obvious explanation. For example, "Considering the traffic, it was a miracle that I got here on time." A casual remark like that is probably not intended to describe something happening contrary to the laws of nature, nor is it evoked to convey religious gratitude for a desired outcome. Coincidences are viewed by some as miracles because they satisfy certain hopes.

"Miracle" is used more seriously to designate something that arouses profound amazement in the beholder. Penicillin was called "a miracle drug" when first developed because it effected the healing of very sick persons. A recent science article, entitled "Development of Egg is Miraculous Process," tells about the intricacies of shell formation and about the yolk separating from a hen's ovary. When the Boston Red Sox overcame a presumed Bambino curse that had beset them for generations and won the 2004 World Series after being behind 3-0 games in the league pennant race, the feat was widely heralded as a miracle. The creative process in biology and in becoming baseball victors after decades of losses are awesome events even though no interference with natural processes is presumed.

What strikes an ignorant person as a miracle might have a quite different effect on someone who is educated. For example, the ancient Hebrews, unaware that the rainbow is naturally caused by the refraction of sun rays on rain drops, thought of it as a special "sign" that God hangs in storm clouds to remind him not to cause another Noachian flood.[4] Medieval philosopher Aquinas commented: "The word miracle . . . arises when an effect is manifest, and its cause is hidden, as when a man sees an eclipse of the sun without knowing its cause. . . . The cause of an effect which makes its appearance may be known to one, but unknown to others . . . as an eclipse is to a rustic, but not to an astronomer."[5]

---

[3]Jeremiah 44:12.
[4]Genesis 9:13-15.
[5]Aquinas, *Summa Theologica* 1:105:7.

In equatorial Africa I talked with a student about my home in the West Virginian highlands. To test his understanding of nature I told him that occasionally I have walked on water. At first he assumed I was not being serious and affirmed that only Jesus could do that. I explained about water in its frozen state, something he had never experienced because there were no freezers or high mountains in his region, and he had never traveled more than a few miles from home. Moreover, he had no exposure to books that contained descriptions of ice, nor to television that might show skaters on lakes. But slowly he became aware that I was not deceptive or deluded and that he had not been aware of a marvelous way in which nature functions.

Miracles as amazing happenings capable of scientific understanding, might be interpreted as providential rather than fortuitous. The renowned Jewish spiritual writer Martin Buber viewed a miracle as "an abiding astonishment" but insisted that it is "an incident, an event which can be fully included in the objective, scientific nexus of nature and history."[6] Linguist Robert Johnson comments: "In the biblical sense, a miracle is an unusual, marvelous event which testifies to God's active presence in the world. This does not mean, however, that the miracle is a disruption of the natural order."[7] A miracle is often an "Oh-my-God!" exclamation on the part of a somewhat reverent beholder that refers to naturally explicable happenings. "Miracle" as used by many is simply a religious designation for a wonderful event, as river town inhabitants might describe their deliverance when flooding rose only to the top of a levy.

Consider a teenage recipient of two cornea transplants who marveled over her transformed life in a "Dear Abby" letter: "I want to address my unknown donors: . . . You died, yet a part of you still lives. . . . My life is so different because of you. . . . With the help of God you created a miracle—the miracle of sight." Scientific miracles of this type have done more than the curative actions of biblical persons in saving many from physical blindness. They illustrate a saying attributed to Jesus in John 14:12 that his followers will do "greater works" than he did.

Often I think it is a miracle that I am now alive. As a boy I once explored the inside of a nineteenth-century railroad tunnel near my hometown. Thinking that its sixteen-foot width could not accommodate the behe-

---

[6]Martin Buber, *Moses* (Oxford: Phaidon, 1946) 75-76.

[7]Robert Johnson, "Signs and Wonders," *The Interpreter's Dictionary of the Bible* (Nashville: Abingdon, 1962).

moth modern locomotives, I assumed that trains had already been shifted to a nearby new tunnel. When I heard a rumble and saw a headlight coming toward me, I threw myself down and was unscathed by the train that roared over me. Fifty years later, after a cardiac arrest, I was briefly "clinically dead" (no pulse, no breath). Although few in that condition are revived, within several minutes my normal heart rhythms returned. Serendipitously, savvy paramedics were near at hand and they jump-started my heart with a defibrillator. I recognize a sign of God's grace in those extraordinary but in no way unprecedented or supernatural situations. Although my recovery was not scientifically inexplicable, the experience has caused me and my friends to irresistibly think of divine deliberance. A propos here is biblical scholar John Crossan's comment that a miracle is "a marvel that someone interprets as a transcendental action or manifestation" and that "to claim a miracle is to make an interpretation of faith, not just a statement of fact."[8]

Among the most longed for miracles are those that can reverse the course of a crippling or fatal disease. Occasionally individuals vouch that God has miraculously cured them of cancer because they had been given a prognosis years earlier that they had only months to live. The pious prefer to state their recovery in this way rather than to say that a physician's initial judgment was wrong. The doctor may not have given sufficient recognition that spontaneous remissions lasting for years may occur because of the body's complex immune system. In addition to, or independent from, religious faith, a patient's positive attitude and caregivers' support can effect a change in outcome.

Believers in miraculous healings tend to focus on deliverances and overlook the failure of prayer for a return to health that some encounter. Should it be presumed that God arbitrarily favors one situation and not another, even if both seem to be equally worthy of consideration? While busily ameliorating a crisis at one place in the universe, does God neglect crises elsewhere? Why would God see to it that most of the passengers on a bus are rescued after it plunged into a river while, in a similar accident, allowing most passengers to drown? Is God responsible only for accidents that turn out well in the judgment of the observers? The apparent divine injustice from presumed miracles can compound the problem of evil in the world.

---

[8]John Crossan, *The Birth of Christianity* (San Francisco: Harper, 1998) 303-304.

A basically different category of miracle is an alleged event that is contrary to the established order known by common sense or by scientists. Corn that produces ears of cats when planted rather than ears of corn would qualify as such a miracle, which some would call magic. Another example here would be an account occasionally found in folklore of a charismatic person reviving a decomposing corpse. Such a happening cannot be understood as just a remarkable coincidence.

Descriptive natural law is easily confused with prescriptive cultural law. To the latter there are occasional unpredictable exceptions. For example, the United States Constitution requires that Congress declare all wars, even though the nation has fought several wars without that formal approval. Again, Jesus was a notorious sabbath lawbreaker because he worked on that Jewish holy day.[9] But no one breaks laws of physics. A person who jumps without a bungee cord from a tenth-story window to refute the law of gravitation only confirms the law. If it can be shown that there are exceptions to a natural law, then it is no law.

Modern philosophers generally accept David Hume's definition of miracle. In his brief treatise on the topic, which is the most influential part of that most famous English-speaking philosopher's writing, he states that a miracle is "a transgression of a law of nature by a particular volition of the Deity, or by the interposition of some invisible agent."[10] Due to Hume's awareness of the incompleteness and defectiveness of empirical reports even by honest people, he was not convinced that any claim of a miracle could be substantiated. *The Oxford English Dictionary* amplifies Hume's classical discussion by defining "miracle" as "a marvellous event occurring within human experience, which cannot have been brought about by human power or by the operation of any natural agency, and must therefore be ascribed to the special intervention of the Deity or of some supernatural being."

* * *

The term "supernatural" has also been used with little discrimination, designating anything from a haunted house to the hallowed Trinity. What is translated from Greek as "supernatural" compounds *hyper* (beyond) with *physin* (physical) and was used in the ancient Mediterranean culture to refer

---

[9]Mark 2:23–3:4.
[10]David Hume, *An Enquiry concerning Human Understanding* (1748) 10:1.

to events contrary to the regular order. It was not used in the New Testament nor in the ancient church. In the medieval era Aquinas gave prominence to the Latin term *supernaturalis* by having it refer to the theologically "infused" virtues—faith, hope, and love—that supplement the "acquired" natural virtues of justice, prudence, fortitude, and temperance championed by Plato and Aristotle.[11]

New Testament scholar Frederick Grant argued, "If by the supernatural one is designating that universal reign of divine power in this world, . . . then all Christians of the modern mind are devout believers in the supernatural."[12] For liberal theologian William Brown, the "supernatural" is the sine qua non of religion. In his Yale University lectures he defined "supernatural" as belief that God, "the transcendent reality," is at work throughout the cosmos, and he stated that "religion stands or falls with the supernatural." He conceived of religion as concerned with an aspect of reality distinct from science, but he viewed them as working together in harmony.[13]

Yet for many other moderns "supernatural" and "superstitious" are synonymous; current titles in book stores for the general public show that this has become the prevailing association. Philosopher Peter Forrest, in his book entitled *God without the Supernatural*, defends a theocentric understanding of the world without involving any violation of natural law as claimed by the superstitious.[14] *The Dictionary of the Supernatural* carries this subtitle, *An A to Z of Hauntings, Possession, Witchcraft, Demonology, and the Occult Phenomena*.[15] Following this popular usage, "supernatural" is used in this study to describe alleged happenings that are contrary to natural law, whether physical or psychical. Supernaturalism is the belief that a divine intervention is necessary to explain such happenings because they cannot be, even potentially, verifiable scientifically.

While the natural is distinguished from the spiritual in the Bible, they do not belong to opposing realms.[16] Many centuries later Christians introduced "supernatural" to describe acts of the omnipotent God that intervened

[11]Aquinas, *Summa Theologica* 2:62, 65.
[12]*The Christian Century* (14 December 1922): 1545.
[13]William Brown, *God at Work* (New York: Scribner, 1933) 25, 31-32.
[14]Peter Forrest, *God without the Supernatural* (Ithaca NY: Cornell, 1996).
[15]Peter Underwood, *The Dictionary of the Supernatural* (London: Harrap, 1978).
[16]1 Corinthians 15:44.

in the scientific order. William Jennings Bryan, a famous American super-naturalist, was convinced that everything happened just as literally stated in the "Word of God." At the Scopes trial in 1925 he testified that one miracle was as easy for him to believe as another and that he would have no difficulty believing that Jonah swallowed a whale, if the inerrant Bible had said so. Bryan may have been aware of Thomas Paine's quip; he remarked that since a whale might be large enough to swallow a human "it would have approached nearer to the idea of miracle if Jonah had swallowed the whale."[17] Bryan could have labeled his religious viewpoint as "supernatural-ism" if the term were given this dictionary definition: "The theological doctrine that the divine is fundamentally different from the temporal order and cannot be approached through its categories. . . . In this view, faith, revelation, and the authority of Scripture take the place of reason."[18]

Traditional Western philosophy and religion has often posited a meta-physical dualism composed of higher and lower compartments. The superior divine sphere is separated from the natural realm, but occasionally the former interrupts the regular course of the latter. That dichotomy is quite different from the religion that accepts homogenization of life forces in the religious experiences of many peoples around the globe. Creating, sus-taining, and liberating are perceived in most of the world's religions as the outcome of the thought and will of God, the ultimate reality. In the Abra-hamic faiths, God's revelation percolates through the spatiotemporal realm. This brand of causality works through the laws of nature rather than around them. Intrinsic to Judaism, Christianity, and Islam is the doctrine that God is beyond (Latin, supra) nature, but that belief in transcendence need not include the notion that the divine functions against (Latin, contra) nature.

Wonder-Workers in Religious History

Charismatic figures of biblical history were remembered not as much by what they actually said and did in their lifetimes as by the expanded records of their less inspired hagiographers. After those bigger-than-life hero stories, told by adoring disciples, got into common circulation, the humanity of particular historical characters became devalued. Inflation is a problem for interpreters of religious literature as well as for economists studying the

---

[17]Thomas Paine, *The Age of Reason* (1795), near the end of part 1.

[18]William Reese, *Dictionary of Philosophy and Religion* (Atlantic Highlands NJ: Humanities Press, 1980).

marketplace. Just as coins of base metal alloys drive out of circulation coins of pure substance, so the authentic earliest accounts of religious figures were alloyed with wondrous later exaggerations that were transmitted by folk culture.

The retellings of the story of Moses illustrate the inflation that occurs with succeeding generations. The first two chapters of Exodus, which record mainly early traditions about Moses, contain no reference to unnatural happenings. There the Israelite slave resistance is portrayed as instigated by five women who are armed only with compassion and cleverness. To save the lives of some infants, two Hebrew midwives and an Egyptian princess, along with Moses' mother and sister, engage in nonviolent civil disobedience against a Pharoah.[19] Providence is expressed through the resourcefulness of those women, not through direct divine intervention.

The Book of Exodus is an editorial mosaic of Mosaic traditions. Recorded there are several fragmentary accounts of different vintage that had been circulated orally for many generations. The literary structure of the entire Pentateuch resembles the mound left by an ancient town. The different levels of artifacts reveal to the archaeologist the succession of peoples who lived there over the centuries. Likewise, textual scholars have painstakenly probed the layered pentateuchal documents in search of chronological development. The earlier recorded traditions are less about supernatural happenings than are the supplements made by the priestly editors of the Pentateuch who lived about seven centuries after Moses.[20] Just as the top strata in a dig provides the most recent and least valuable materials, so the latest redaction in the composite Mosaic literature displays the most recently written and least authentically historical part.

In what may be the earlier version of the Israelite crossing the water separating Egypt from the Sinai peninsula a natural explanation is given for the event: "a strong east wind all night" caused a body of water to part.[21]

----

[19]William Phipps, *Assertive Biblical Women* (Westport CT: Greenwood, 1992) 31-41.

[20]Martin Noth, *Exodus* (Philadelphia: Westminster, 1962) 74; Walter Harrelson, *Interpreting the Old Testament* (New York: Holt, 1964) 82; Richard Friedman, *The Bible with Sources Revealed* (San Francisco: Harper, 2003) 130-43.

[21]Exodus 14:21.

According to the Hebrew text, the Israelites walked through a "reed lake,"[22] that is, a shallow marsh with fresh water growth, after a forceful wind shifted its waters. The Egyptian charioteers became stuck in the wet sand, amid papyrus and cattails, and were unable to continue their pursuit. Nuclear physicist and Episcopalian priest William Pollard, comments that this extraordinary event does not "violate any known scientific laws." Even so

> The miracle of the exodus from Egypt was a central turning point in the history of Israel, and a crucial act in the sequence of historical events through which God's revelation of Himself to Israel was made. . . . If a miraculous event could only happen outside the natural order of things, then it would necessarily imply that it would be unnatural for God to exercise providence over his creation.[23]

In the later traditions pertaining to the exodus of Hebrew slaves from Egypt, emphasis is placed on plagues wrought by the magical powers of Moses and his brother Aaron.[24] Aaron's staff is turned into a snake at a performance in Pharoah's palace. However, "the magicians of Egypt did the same by their secret arts" by using their own wands, "but Aaron's staff swallowed up theirs." The story sinks to a boasting that the Israelite deity will best any Egyptian deity by doing more fantastic supernatural deeds. To top the snake "sign" of divine power, the Nile is turned to blood: Aaron's rod strikes the river and all the fish die.[25] That is just the first of ten incredible plagues. After they have caused havoc, the Israelites flee to the east but are halted by a body of water. Inserted here is a song of Moses containing the anthropomorphic figure of the Lord blowing his nose, causing the waters "to pile up in a heap." After the Israelites escape to freedom, the Omnipotent One permits the waters to return and drown Pharoah's army.[26]

-----

[22]Exodus 13:18; 15:4. According to the Greek mistranslation, the setting is at the "Red Sea," a designation repeated in later European versions. (The Red Sea is about 2,000 feet deep.)

[23]William Pollard, *Chance and Providence* (New York: Scribner, 1958) 106-107, 118.

[24]Robert Pfeiffer, *Religion in the Old Testament* (New York: Harper, 1961) 46-48; David Tiede, *The Charismatic Figure as Miracle Worker* (Missoula MT: Scholars Press, 1972) 317-24.

[25]Exodus 7:3-24.

[26]Exodus 15:8-10.

The later elaborators were Jerusalem priests who had a "tendency to make the calamity more severe,"[27] so they embellished already inflated tradition. In Judeo-Christian history, more have been impressed by superman Moses and his brother than by the courageous women who actually started the rebellion against the Egyptian government. Moses's "status as a powerful magician was exalted" by Jewish spokesmen in the Hellenistic era.[28] Artapanus records a popular legend that depicts Moses escaping from prison when "the doors of the prison opened of their own accord." Some of the magical power associated with Aaron in the Exodus text is transferred to his brother. Now it is Moses's staff that becomes a snake before Pharoah, turns the waters of Egypt into blood, and brings the plagues of frogs and insects.[29] Thus Moses became more of a wand-wielding wonder-worker than a believable human.

In cases where biographical information is written by Hebrew charismatic personalities themselves or by their contemporaries, the absence of supernaturalism is notable. With the exception of Isaiah's making a sun dial's shadow move back ten "steps" as proof of what God would do,[30] no supernatural miracles are attributed to the latter prophets in the Hebrew canon (authoritative scriptural writings) during the several centuries from Amos to Malachi. By contrast, Moses and other earlier prophets, Elijah and Elisha, were especially remembered by supernatural stories recorded more than a century after they died.

The subsequent course of Israelite religion was much affected by the latest level of the Mosaic literary "mound," where appeal is made to signs as proof. Those with little depth of faith looked for what seemed supernatural in visual manifestations. To illustrate, consider the story of Jesus' trial in the Jerusalem palace of his king. This confrontation is alleged, "Herod was delighted to see Jesus because he had heard about him and had long desired to meet him, in the hope of seeing a miracle performed by him."[31]

---

[27]Coert Rylaarsdam, "Exodus," *The Interpreter's Bible* (Nashville, Abingdon, 1952) 1:838.

[28]John Gager, *Moses in Greco-Roman Paganism* (New York: Abingdon, 1972) 164.

[29]Artapanus, *Concerning the Jews*, 23-32; quoted in Eusebius, *Praeparatio Evangelica* 9:27.

[30]Isaiah 38:8.

[31]Luke 23:8.

The outlook of Herod has been well depicted for contemporary audiences by the rock opera *Jesus Christ, Superstar*. The Jewish king urges Jesus to walk on his swimming pool and thereby provide a spectacular demonstration of his ability. The Jews eagerly wanted a miracle-man messiah who could perform supernatural tricks like the legendary Moses.

* * *

What has happened to central figures in the Judeo-Christian tradition is commonplace in other world religions that also originated in Asia. Further understanding of postmortem enlargements of pivotal personalities can be gained by examining their parallel process of oral and literary transmission. Zoroastrianism, Buddhism, and Islam have in their traditions a growth of miracles attributed to their founders. In the *Gathas*, the only source of historical information about Zoroaster, there is no supernaturalism. But fantastic legends infiltrated the tradition later, including an account of his "confining of hail, spiders, locusts, and other terrors."[32]

Earlier stories of the Buddha contain no suggestion of supernatural powers. Levitation claims by gurus in his parent Indian religion caused this reaction by historical Buddha, "I command my disciples not to work miracles."[33] While approving "the miracle of instruction," he judged appeals to supernaturalism as devoid of spiritual significance as conjurers' tricks. In one story the Buddha meets an ascetic who claims he can cross a river by walking on water. But the Buddha judges this feat a waste of effort because riding a ferry is inexpensive. In spite of the Buddha's distaste for the miraculous, legends arose regarding his ability to vanish and reappear, to pass through walls, and to fly like an eagle.[34]

The saga of the life and times of Muhammad also shows the way in which factual data about a dead hero bloats over time. When he was asked to prove his prophethood by doing supernatural acts, the earliest source conveys his criticism of those who demand such, affirming that performing signs and wonders was not a part of his mission. According to the *Qur'an*, the Meccans challenged him in these ways: "Let him show us some sign as

---

[32]Max Muller, ed. *Sacred Books of the East* (Oxford: Clarendon, 1879–1910) 47:76.

[33]*Dhammapada* 18:254; Muller 10:1:64.

[34]"Miracle: Buddha," *Encyclopedia Britannica* (Chicago, 1974).

did the apostles of old,"[35] and "We will not believe in you until you make a spring gush forth from the earth for us." But, unlike the legendary Moses, Muhammad refused to pander to the rabble's appetite for the spectacular. He humbly announced, "I am only a mortal messenger."[36] He recognized that miracle workers tend to seek worldly approval rather than serve as a divine agent.[37] For him the natural regularities were such a marvelous witness to God that no unnatural portents were needed.[38] The superlative wonder was the internal disclosure that God has given his messengers across the centuries.[39] A Muslim scholar explains why early Islam claimed no miracles for Muhammad, "What proves Muhammad's prophethood is the sublime beauty and greatness of the revelation itself, the Holy Quran, not any inexplicable breaches of natural law which confound human reason."[40]

In spite of Muhammad's candid acknowledgement that he was no wizard, his followers soon claimed that he possessed supernatural powers. Pious Muslims were not content with a wholly human prophet and within a century of his death fantastic stories were accepted as part of Islamic orthodoxy. Muhammad's earliest biographer, Ibn Ishaq, who wrote a century after the prophet lived, told about his providing an abundant lunch for his troops by taking a few dates in his hand and multiplying them. Also, when diggers on a battleground were having difficulty removing a large rock, Muhammad caused it to pulverize by spitting on it.[41] Al-Bukhari's ninth-century collection of Muhammad's activities includes a report on his praying for rain during a drought in Medina. Suddenly it rained for a week, causing the mud brick houses to collapse. The prophet then pleaded: "O God! Round about us and not on us." So the sky became clear in his city but there was rain in the surrounding region.[42] According to Tabari's biography, Muhammad proved that he was a prophet by summoning to himself a

[35]*Qur'an* 21:5.
[36]*Qur'an* 17:90-93.
[37]*Qur'an* 7:113-18.
[38]*Qur'an* 10:5-6.
[39]*Qur'an* 6:110; 10:221; 13:30; 21:5-6; 29:49-51.
[40]Isma'il Faruqi, *Islam* (Niles, IL: Argus, 1984) 20.
[41]Alfred Guillaume, trans., *Ibn Ishaq's Sirat Rasul Allah* (Lahore: Oxford, 1955) 451-52.
[42]Muhammad Khan, trans., *Sahih Al-Bukhari* (Chicago: Kazi, 1979) 17:13.

cluster of dates from where it was hanging. With a magical snap of his fingers the cluster came to him and then, at his command, reattached itself to the tree.[43] Ali Dashti, who studied in Iran to be an imam, explains what many Muslims have done to Muhammad: "They have continually striven to turn this man into an imaginary superhuman being, a sort of God in human clothes. . . . As the years advanced, myth making and miracle mongering became more and more widespread and extravagant."[44]

* * *

Compare the life of Francis Xavier, the pioneer Catholic missionary to East Asia, as he and his contemporaries recorded it, with what is contained in subsequent biographies. Letters by and about him dating before his death in 1572 tell of his modest manner, not his supernatural acts. For example, he rejected the advice that a Jesuit should take along a servant, saying that the way to acquire respect was to wash one's own underwear.[45] However, two decades after Xavier's death, his earliest biographer told how he instantly cured various diseases by making the sign of the cross over the afflicted, and how he changed sea water to drinking water on a voyage from Japan to China. Another pious biographer, after a lapse of two more decades, portrayed him as stilling a tempest and halting a plague in Japan. Six decades after his death, Cardinal Monte described ten miracles worked by Xavier, including levitating, causing an earthquake, raising the dead, and destroying a town by calling fire down from heaven. Pope Gregory XV was so impressed by the wonders accredited to Xavier that he had him canonized as a saint.[46]

Chronologically, the charismatic founder of Christianity belongs between Moses and Xavier. The story of Jesus' life and of the church's beginning have been subject to inflationary tendencies similar to those that transformed the life stories of his illustrious predecessors and followers. New Testament specialist Milo Connick has written: "Miracle stories clustered like grapes about the stem of historical personages. Their aim was

---

[43]Ehsan Yar-Shater, ed., *The History of al-Tabari* (Albany NY: SUNY, 1988) 6:67.

[44]Ali Dashti, *Twenty-Three Years* (London: Allen and Unwin, 1985) 1, 26.

[45]Edith Robertson, *Francis Xavier* (London: SCM, 1930) 96.

[46]Georg Schurhammer, *Francis Xavier* (Rome: Jesuit Historical Institute, 1982) 4:126, 294-95, 598, 617.

to inflate the personal status of the hero. It was even considered legitimate to manufacture miraculous tales for this purpose."[47]

In pursuit of the most authentic information about Christian beginnings, it is necessary to disentangle the relevant strands of tradition. Because of the scarcity of ancient sources it is more difficult to write as precisely about the growth of legendary material concerning Jesus than it is for Xavier. But more source material exists for Jesus than for Moses or Buddha. This study, as in some of this author's previous works,[48] will be anchored in Paul's understandings, found in the oldest surviving Christian documents.

Beginning with parts of the New Testament, the unhealthy growth of supernaturalism in Christianity will be examined. The probe will continue through Euro-American church history, including its residual impact today in cultures dominated by scientific inquiry. But merely diagnosing the causes and resulting damage of this insidious disease is not enough. Attention will also be given to a tested and reliable cure for this cancer in the body of Christ. The deviant type of Christianity that has established a dichotomy between religious revelation and natural processes can be restored by a generous application of Paul's theology and ethics.

Questers for the historical Jesus are like art restorers of an old master. Consider the painstaking surgery that Leonardo da Vinci's most famous mural has undergone. *The Last Supper* was completed in 1497 on a plaster wall of a refectory in a Milan monastery, but it soon began to deteriorate. For centuries, adoring but insensitive painters overlayed the original in an effort to preserve it—making it almost as gross as its glossy copies now found in discount stores. Some who had not examined the artist's preliminary sketches thought that the soft colors and simple lines were due to fading, so they added garish hues to recover its original luster. Because of such unintended abuse, the painting that I viewed in Milan fifty years ago was largely the invention of uninspired painters who lived long after Leonardo. Subsequently, skilled restorers, aided by microscopic analysis and special solvents, have worked for years on his fresco. Scalpels have been used to

---

[47]C. Milo Connick, *Jesus, the Man, the Mission, and the Message* (Englewood Cliffs NJ: Prentice-Hall, 1963) 281.

[48]William Phipps, "The Attitude of the Apostle Paul toward Scripture" (diss., University of St. Andrews, Scotland, 1954); *Encounter through Questioning Paul: A Fresh Approach to the Apostle's Life and Letters* (Washington: University Press of America, 1983).

flake off layers of overpainting and to clean off the grime that had obliterated the original details. As a result, the grandeur of some of the figures of
Jesus and his disciples has come to light. But after appearing bearded for
centuries, some may judge Leonardo's shaven Peter to lack sanctity!

In a parallel manner, interpreters of the figure of Jesus have added a
supernatural coloring that misrepresents the earliest cameo recorded by
Paul. Even as artists have encircled Jesus' head with a halo to enhance his
holiness, storytellers in the New Testament era and afterwards have
attributed supernaturalism to him to make him into something other than
human. For example, Jesus' role at his last supper has for centuries been
seen by most Christians as that of a magician who transformed the "substance" of bread and wine into flesh and blood. The task of seekers of
earliest gospel stories is to peel away the various layers of redaction that
have accumulated over the course of oral and written transmission in hopes
of recovering the original nucleus. Finding acceptance for what can be
recaptured is difficult because many people have become devoted to later
hagiographic distortions that can be found even in the Gospels.

A historical approach has been used as far as possible in discussing the
gospel interpreters in the chapters ahead. This involves disregarding the
traditional arrangement of the New Testament "books." To enter the New
Testament by way of the Gospels is like entering a house by way of a
second floor opening and overlooking the door on the ground floor. Analysis will begin with the authentic letters of Paul, because they were written
significantly earlier than the rest of the New Testament.[49] Paul's letters were
mostly written in the 50s, earlier than the four Gospels. Mark was probably
written around 70 CE and the other Gospels a decade or two after Mark.
Momentous happenings occurred in the period between Paul's letters and
the Gospel writings that affected the message conveyed by the latter: in 64
the persecution of Christians began with Emperor Nero in Rome and in 70
the center of Jewish Christianity was lost when Romans destroyed
Jerusalem. I agree with Paula Fredriksen who, after examining each of the

----

[49] A scholarly consensus has emerged that eight letters were penned by Paul and
his amanuensis: 1 Thessalonians, Galatians, 1 and 2 Corinthians, Romans, Colossians, Philippians, Philemon. Five others can be designated as Pauline, because
they most likely were written after the apostle's death by his followers: 2 Thessalonians, Ephesians, Titus, 1 and 2 Timothy.

four canonical Gospels, states, "The Pauline letters are the primary sources for the Christian tradition par excellence."[50]

Supernaturalism was accentuated by the patristic editors of the New Testament, who placed the Gospels before Paul's letters. Moreover, when Athanasius, Archbishop of Alexandria, first listed in 367 the completed canon of twenty-seven books, he placed the Gospel of Matthew before the earlier Gospel of Mark.[51] The original Mark contains no account of a physically resurrected Jesus as well as no supernatural birth narrative.[52] The arrangement of the New Testament books without regard to the approximate time when they were written makes the miraculous appear to be more prominent than it was in the earliest Christian community.

In the chapters that follow I will deal with hot-button New Testament issues pertaining to the theme of this book. The way alleged supernaturalism is, in my opinion, properly interpreted by critical biblical scholarship is contrasted with the usual way it has been understood in church history: Jesus' conception in chapter 2; astrology and angels in chapter 3; his miracles in chapters 4 and 5; his resurrection in chapters 6 and 7. Chapter 8 deals with interpreters over the millennia who have rejected literalistic treatments of these issues and who have outlooks compatible with modern science. The relevancy of the apostle Paul to my theme, which is touched on repeatedly throughout the book, is brought back into focus in the last chapter.

---

[50]Paula Fredriksen, *From Jesus to Christ* (New Haven CT: Yale University Press, 2000) 53.

[51]Athanasius, *Festal Letters*, 39.

[52]Mark 16:9-20 is a spurious ending from the second century.

Chapter 2
From Sexual to Asexual Conception

Few matters related to the Bible have provoked more rancorous disputes in modern society than the question of how Jesus' life began. Many Christians first become aware of New Testament literary-historical scholarship—often called "higher criticism"—as they examine arguments pertaining to Jesus' alleged virginal conception, commonly but less accurately called his "virgin birth." Christians have generally assumed that Mary was physically affected with the usual pangs of childbirth and that the delivery from her uterus was normal.

Scholars first intensely investigated the traditional assumptions about Jesus' conception in the nineteenth century. That discussion has subsided, but unfortunately not because Christians have reached a general consensus on the issue. In 1965, opinion surveyors Charles Glock and Rodney Stark found that approximately half of the Protestants and three-quarters of the Roman Catholics in the United States accept as completely true the statement, "Jesus was born of a virgin."[1] At that time the suggestion by a Spanish Jesuit that Jesus' alleged virginal conception could be treated as a legend "brought indignant petitions by over 10,000 Spaniards."[2] According to a recent United States opinion poll, ninety-one percent of Christians, as well as forty-seven percent of non-Christians, say they believe in Jesus' "virgin birth."[3] It is unlikely that the percentage of Christians accepting the virginal conception doctrine will decline this century because it is an article of faith among those denominations with the most rapid growth. On this volatile issue, memories of harsh fundamentalism-modernism fights, and an eagerness to avoid more discord in the church, may explain the current paucity of public debate on the manner by which Jesus was conceived.

The battle lines of the long conflict between the Christian supernaturalist and the reductive naturalists can still be distinguished. The supernaturalists believe that Jesus was not conceived in the same manner as other humans by the biological union of a male sperm with a female ovum. Rather, Mary of Nazareth, a virgin, became pregnant when the Spirit of God

---

[1]Charles Glock and Rodney Stark, *Religion and Society in Tension* (Chicago: Rand McNally, 1965) 95.

[2]Raymond Brown, *The Birth of the Messiah* (Garden City, NY: Doubleday, 1993) 701.

[3]*New York Times* (15 August 2003) A29; Harris poll (12 August 1998).

acted miraculously in her uterus. By contrast, the naturalists regard any reference to God in explaining biological processes as irrelevant because the only necessity they see is chromosomes supplied equally by a man and a woman. They tend to explain away the traditional birth stories of Jesus as little more than enchanting fairy tales and argue that Jesus must have been sired either by a human male, or else he could not have been a historical and human person. Spokespersons for both parties continue to marshal the same traditional arguments to justify their positions. For a good sample of the supernaturalists, see the scholarly tomes of Catholic exegete Raymond Brown and German theologian Hans von Campenhausen.[4]

Both sides of this dispute have fallen into the fallacy of false disjunction, that is, thinking that a proposition must be *either* true *or* false, and little progress has been made toward a common understanding. Seldom heard is a third position, gained from an understanding of the outlook on conception that permeated ancient Mediterranean cultures. This viewpoint, which might be called "dual parenthood," avoids the either/or mode of thinking and assists in understanding the outlook of the earliest Christians.

Dual Parenthood

The dual parenthood concept is arrived at by combining on the human level the father and mother as one component, and having the androgynous divine being as the other one. The Hebrews combined male and female metaphors in conceptualizing deity. In spite of the profuse use of masculine imagery in their Bible, feminine imagery is not lacking. For example, the Song of Moses says of the Lord, "Is not he your father, who created you?" but it also extols divine motherhood in praising "the God who gave you birth."[5] Again, Isaiah is bold in theological word pictures that cannot be interpreted literally. The prophet declares, "Your Creator is your husband," but he also portrays Yahweh as a suffering and sympathetic woman. Wishing to convey to Jewish exiles that they are not godforsaken, he proclaims in Yahweh's name, "I will comfort you as a mother comforts her child."[6]

In their more mystical moods, ancient people thought of human procreation as involving both deity and human parents. The etymology of "procre-

---

[4]Brown, *The Birth of the Messiah*; Hans von Campenhausen, *The Virgin Birth in the Theology of the Ancient Church* (Naperville, IL: Allenson, 1964).

[5]Deuteronomy 32:7, 18.

[6]Isaiah 54:5; 66:13.

ate" suggests their theology of generation. A *pro*creator is one who acts on behalf of a creator, just as a prophet speaks for God and a *pro*noun represents a noun. The ancients commonly believed that the male/female Creator worked through human agents in the conception of a baby. Realizing that pregnancy does not occur in most instances of human intercourse, they explained fertilization by referring to the divine will as well as to the activity of sexual partners. Acknowledging the role of the deity conveyed their humble gratitude for the wonderful gift of new life. This wholesome and reverential belief, however primitive it may seem today, pervaded traditional cultures.

Dual parenthood is an appropriate label for the inclusive way in which African and Asian cultures have recognized the presence of a god or goddess in any human conception. In Egyptian mythology, pharoahs were viewed as conceived from the spirit of god Amon-Re in the form of the ruling king and his queen.[7] Also, the Bantu of have this saying, "We should not boast, 'I have begotten,' for it is God who begets."[8] Ku-liang Chaun, a classic commentator on Confucius's teachings, said: "The female alone cannot procreate; the male alone cannot procreate; and Heaven alone cannot produce a child. The three collaborating, a person is born. Hence, anyone may be called the son of his mother and the son of Heaven."[9]

Some eminent persons of the patriarchal Greek culture were said to have had two fathers. Odysseus is acknowledged in an epic as both the son of King Laertes of Ithaca and the son of Zeus.[10] The deity's activity was perceived as supplementing, not supplanting, the copulation of husband and wife. Pious Athenians had a story of how Plato's mother became pregnant. After Ariston had no success in producing a child with Perictione, he had a vision of Apollo when she became pregnant. Consequently the philosopher's sublime wisdom could be credited to the god of wisdom, while his political prominence could be attributed to having Solon, the first prominent Athenian patriarch, as an ancestor.[11] According to Roman writer Suetonius, the conceptions of Alexander the Great and Caesar Augustus also involved

---

[7]Hans Küng, *Credo* (New York: Doubleday, 1993) 42.

[8]Alexis Kegame, *La Philosophie Bantu* (Brussels, 1956) 351.

[9]Miles Dawson, ed., *The Basic Thought of Confucius* (New York: Garden City Publishing, 1939) 145.

[10]Homer, *Iliad* 10.144.

[11]Diogenes Laertius, *Lives of the Philosophers* 3.1-2.

both Apollo and human parents. Instrumental in accomplishing the conception of Alexander was a light ray from Apollo that penetrated Olympia as she slept with her husband, Philip of Macedonia. Centuries later, Apollo acted similarly with Atia, who became Augustus's mother "ten moons" later. Suetonius also calls Caesar Augustus the son of Octavius, Atia's husband.[12] To explain the greatness of individuals, both the Greeks and the Romans accepted myths pertaining to their beginnings. Post-humously they told of divine-human couplings to differentiate heroes from ordinary mortals.

Parallels between stories of the lives of Jesus and religious teacher Apollonius are instructive. The latter's mother, according to Philostratus's biography, lived with her husband during the reign of Caesar Augustus. She was informed by means of a theophany that she was carrying an incarnation of Proteus. After the god-man was born and learned the wisdom of his culture, he taught and performed miracles as he traveled from town to town.[13]

The presence of God in human conceptions is also recognized in Hebrew Scriptures. A clear illustration of the former is found in the story of Ruth: "Boaz took Ruth and she became his wife. When he had intercourse with her, the Lord caused her to conceive and she bore a son."[14] The divine presence was considered even more significant when a wife who had been presumed barren became pregnant. The most prominent example of such is found in the story of Isaac's birth: "The Lord visited Sarah as he had said, and the Lord did to her as he had promised. She conceived and bore Abraham a son in his old age."[15] This dual parenthood is described by John Otwell:

> The new life given the people of God came into being because the Lord worked in the woman's womb, bringing to fruition the sexual relations of husband and wife. Thus the woman was uniquely the locus of the basic manifestation of the benign presence of God in the midst of the people, for without new life the people would soon cease to exist.[16]

---

[12]Suetonius, *Lives of the Caesars* 2.94.
[13]Philostratus, *Apollonius* 1.4-9.
[14]Ruth 4:13.
[15]Genesis 21:1-2.
[16]John Otwell, *And Sarah Laughed* (Philadelphia: Westminster, 1977) 192.

In some other Hebrew birth accounts, the human father is implicitly assumed but not explicitly mentioned. As a way of expressing piety, it is said of Leah and other women, that God "opened her womb."[17] A psalmist likewise thought of God as the prime cause of his conception. Without intending to deny the role of a human father, that poet addressed God in poetic parallelism, "You formed my inward parts;/ you knit me together in my mother's womb."[18] Jewish scholar Geza Vermes points out that "such divine intervention was never interpreted as divine impregnation."[19]

As part of their belief in a continuously creative God, the Hebrews held that organic life could not be adequately explained in a physiological manner. Acting as a life force was one function of God's Spirit (*ruach*, female gender).[20] She produced land and animal fertility, and animal as well as human offspring.[21] Job affirmed, "The Spirit of God has made me."[22] Accordingly, humans were sometimes dignified as "children of the living God."[23] God said to David, through Nathan's oracle, regarding a child that his wife bore: "I will raise up your son. . . . I will be his father and he shall be my son."[24]

Ancient Jewish tradition made more explicit the theory of dual parenthood suggested in Hebrew Scriptures. Eve's exclamation, "I have brought a boy into being with the help of the Lord,"[25] is the basis for this talmudic deduction, "There are three partners in the production of any human being: the Holy One, . . . the father, and the mother."[26] According to Jewish scholar Israel Abrahams, "the rabbinic theory of marital intercourse is summed up" in the belief that God participates as a third parent in every act of procreation.[27] A Genesis midrash, an expression of Jewish folklore, declares: "In

---

[17]Genesis 29:31; 30:22.

[18]Psalm 139:13.

[19]Geza Vermes, *Jesus the Jew* (London: Collins, 1973) 217.

[20]E.g., Genesis 6:3; Job 27:3.

[21]E.g., Isaiah 32:15, 44:3-4; Psalm 104:30.

[22]Job 33:4.

[23]Hosea 1:10; Deuteronomy 14:1; Isaiah 43:6.

[24]2 Samuel 7:12, 14.

[25]Genesis 4:1.

[26]*Kiddushin* 30b.

[27]"Marriage (Jewish)," *Encyclopaedia of Religion and Ethics* (New York: Scribner's, 1928).

the past Adam was created from the dust of the ground and Eve was created from Adam. Henceforth it is to be 'in our image and after our likeness'— meaning, man will not be able to come into existence without woman, nor woman without man, nor both without the Shekinah."[28] "Shekinah," literally "One-who-dwells-within," is a postbiblical circumlocution for Yahweh and is often used interchangeably with "Holy Spirit" (*ruach hakodesh*).[29] Juxtaposing those terms that are feminine in Hebrew, along with the masculine imagery for deity in that language, conveys that meta-phors from both genders assist in understanding God. The immanent deity might be called androgynous or psychically bisexual.[30] The Spirit or the Shekinah is present with assembled worshipers,[31] and with marital partners, "When husband and wife are worthy, the Shekinah is with them."[32]

Philo of Alexandria, a Jewish contemporary of Jesus, shared the rabbinical belief that procreation resulted from divine-human cooperation.[33] He stated that Isaac was a son of Abraham and Sarah, yet also a "son of God" because he was begotten by God.[34] Philo drew allegorical significance from the fact that there is no overt mention of that Hebrew patriarch engaging in marital intercourse. Figuratively that meant the children of Isaac and Rebekah were sired by God.[35]

This probe of ancient non-Christian literature shows that pious Jews and Gentiles alike thought in terms of dual parenthood. No historical data indi-cates that they believed babies could be conceived without human insemination. The Hebrews held that the Torah's first command, "Be fruitful and multiply," was obeyed when God's blessing was coupled with the male-female union of those made in the divine image.

---

[28]*Genesis Rabbah* 8, 9.

[29]George Moore, *Judaism in the First Centuries of the Christian Era* (New York: Schocken, 1971) 1:437; Joshua Abelson, *The Immanence of God in Rabbinical Literature* (New York: Hermon, 1969) 207.

[30]See William Phipps, "The Sex of God," *Journal of Ecumenical Studies* (July 1979): 515-18.

[31]*Aboth* 3:2; cf. Matthew 18:20.

[32]*Sotah* 17a.

[33]Philo, *On the Decalog*, 107; *On the Special Laws* 2.2.225.

[34]Philo, *On Abraham*, 254; *On the Change of Names*, 131, 137.

[35]Philo, *On the Cherubim*, 40-47.

* * *

What does the New Testament say about dual parenthood and the marital relationship between Mary and Joseph? Paul, who provides the earliest historical reference to Jesus' birth, states merely that he was "born of woman."[36] That phrase is a biblical idiom meaning the offspring shared the human condition,[37] and does not imply the apostle believed that a human father was precluded from Jesus' conception. He did not use here the Greek term *parthenos*, meaning "virgin," but *gune*, meaning "woman" or "wife." Paul brought divine and human parentage together when he referred to Jesus as the "Son of God" who was born "of David's sperm according to the flesh."[38] Since it was through the male line that the patriarchal Jewish culture traced descent, Paul's claim would have been nonsense if Jesus had no human father. Also, when Paul made the theological comment that Isaac was born "according to Spirit,"[39] he was not declaring that the Holy Spirit alone caused the pregnancy; the affirmation was not intended to exclude the role of his biological parents, Abraham and Sarah. Moreover, the apostle refers to seminally generated Christians as "children of God" who are privileged to call God *Abba*. Jesus favored that affectionate Aramaic name for father, which might be translated as "Daddy."[40] It is likely that one of his earliest words was *Abba*, addressed to Joseph. I came to a realization of this when I heard a lost two-year-old crying "*Ab! Ab!*" in a Jerusalem marketplace.

Mark, the earliest Gospel, calls Jesus the "Son of God" but that designation is not associated with the way he was conceived, which is never mentioned. Rather, it pertains to his first special awareness of God at his baptism and his last at his crucifixion.[41] "Son of man" is also used by Mark to designate Jesus, and his Nazareth family of brothers and sisters are mentioned.[42] No New Testament writer asserts that Joseph was only Jesus' legal or foster father. Since Jesus' father is not mentioned in the stories of his adulthood in any Gospel, one might plausibly assume that he had died.

---

[36]Galatians 4:4.
[37]Job 14:1; Luke 7:28.
[38]Romans 1:3-4.
[39]Galatians 4:29.
[40]Galatians 4:5-6; Romans 8:14-15; Mark 14:36.
[41]Mark 1:11; 15:39.
[42]Mark 6:3; 14:61-62.

Mark refers to Jesus as the "son of Mary," the way in which a widow's son would be designated.[43] She is not part of the inner group of followers in the only story about her in Mark.[44]

The only New Testament books that appear to state that Jesus was virginally conceived are Matthew and Luke, which were written nearly a century after it supposedly happened. Matthew begins with genealogy; Mary's husband Joseph and many of Jesus' paternal grandfathers are named, starting with Jacob. The best text for the conclusion of this genealogy is probably the Syriac version of Codex Sinaiticus, which forthrightly states, "Joseph, the father of Jesus." In that patriarchal culture, tracing Jesus' paternal ancestry legitimized him as a royal descendant of David. The extensive branching of a family tree over the course of a millennium, especially since David and Solomon had many wives, probably meant that every Jew in Palestine could claim kin to David!

But Matthew then states that Mary, his betrothed, became pregnant before she and Joseph lived together. We are told that he did not think that he was responsible for the pregnancy, but his consternation was placated by an angel. The messenger informed him that the conception was "from a holy spirit" and he should not fear to take Mary as his wife. If the opening chapter of Matthew is taken literally, the genealogy in the first part contradicts the last part, which presumes that Jesus had no paternal family tree. Vermes reasons: "If Joseph had nothing to do with Mary's pregnancy, the intention prompting the reproduction of the (genealogical) table is nullified, since Joseph's royal Davidic blood would not have been passed on to Jesus. . . . The logic of the genealogies demands that Joseph was the father of Jesus."[45]

Various attempts at understanding this matter have been suggested. Jane Schaberg speculates that Mary was a rape victim, but she admits that "we have no evidence from the late first and the second centuries C.E. to indicate that Jewish or Gentile Christians ever entertained the possibility that Jesus was illegitimately conceived."[46] John's Gospel may hint of sexual irregularities because Jesus' adversaries contemptuously say to him, "We were not born of fornication,"[47] implying that he was. Historian Donald

---

[43]Mark 6:3; Luke 7:12.
[44]Mark 3:31-34.
[45]Vermes 214-15.
[46]Jane Schaberg, *The Illegitimacy of Jesus* (San Francisco: Harper, 1987) 192.
[47]John 8:41.

Akenson states what he considers to be the most plausible hypothesis to explain Mary's conceptions: "Yeshua [Jesus] was the product of a woman who, while betrothed to a man named Joseph, became pregnant by another man. Yet Joseph stayed with her, loyal, though mortally humiliated by this cuckholding, and later his union with Miriam [Mary] was fruitful, producing several brothers and sisters of Yeshua."[48] Joseph's forgiveness is commendable in that scenario, but evidence for Mary's unfaithfulness is weak.

Consider what textual research has to say about the process by which Matthew's Gospel was completed and the effect it might have had on this nativity story. Charles Davis gives a probable reconstruction of its content before a later redaction was made that became the Gospel of Matthew a half-century after Jesus' death. He concludes that the pre-Matthean story read:

> The engendering of Jesus was in this fashion. When his mother Mary was engaged to Joseph, before they came together she was discovered to be pregnant. Now Joseph, her husband, had decided to divorce her, but after he had reflected upon these things, behold, the angel of the Lord appeared to him through a dream saying: "Joseph, do not be afraid to take Mary as your wife; for that which is begotten in her from the Spirit is holy. She shall bear a son, and you shall call his name Jesus, for he shall save his people from their sins." Rising from his sleep, Joseph did as the angel of the Lord directed him. He took his wife, and she brought forth a son, and he called his name Jesus.[49]

The pre-Matthean tradition did not claim that divine activity was substituted for the act of a human progenitor.[50] Borrowing the Hebrew outlook on conception, the account affirmed that Mary's child was ultimately caused by God. While dual parenthood was assumed by Jewish Christians, the role of a human male was explicitly excluded in the expansion now called the Gospel of Matthew. The Evangelist (the upper case refers to one the four canonical writers of the good news—*euangelion*) shared with Plutarch, who lived about the same time, the notion that babies destined to be heroes could be conceived without semen. The Roman writer said, "I do not find it

---

[48]Donald Akenson, *Saint Saul* (New York: Oxford, 2000) 209.

[49]*Journal of Biblical Literature* (December 1971): 412-13.

[50]Rudolf Bultmann, *The History of the Synoptic Tradition* (New York: Oxford, 1968) 291.

strange if it is not by a physical approach, like a man's . . . that a god alters mortal nature and makes it pregnant with a more divine offspring."[51]

New Testament specialist Lane McGaughy has noted the way the infancy narratives about Jesus conform to the usual structure for heroic stories in Hellenistic literature. To establish human and superhuman status, six elements were mixed together: a genealogy of illustrious ancestors, a divine/human conception, an angelic annunciation or vision of the impending birth, unusual birth circumstances, a supernatural sign pertaining to the infant's special destiny, and responses by human bystanders expressing fear or praise.[52]

According to Matthew, Joseph dreamed of an angelic messenger and this resulted in his having no intercourse with Mary until Jesus was born. This is similar to a dream in which Apollo appeared to Ariston, as we have seen, and in consequence of it he abstained from marital intercourse until Plato was born.[53] Matthew indicates that sexual abstinence did not continue long for Joseph and Mary, for he probably recognized that in Judaism nonconjugal marriage was a contradiction in terms. According to the Torah, it was the husband's sacred duty to give his wife her marital rights.[54] Regarding this, Marcus Cohn has stated, "The most important common obligation of the married couple is the performance of the marital act."[55] Paul introduced that Jewish custom into Christianity when he defended the right and duty of all married couples, "Do not withhold sexual intercourse from one another unless it is only temporary and by mutual agreement in order that you may devote yourselves to prayer."[56]

Matthew's use of the Greek mistranslation of a Hebrew word is another source of confusion. Jesus and his mother are associated by Matthew with a passage in Isaiah that had no messianic connection. The prophet, living in the eighth century BCE, had announced to Ahaz, his king, that due to the unfaithfulness of their nation Judah, God would bring severe judgment to the region. It would be devastated by the Assyrian army, he said, before an

---

[51]Plutarch, *Table-talk*, 8.1.
[52]*The Fourth R* (September 1992); 1.
[53]Matthew 1:20, 25; Laertius 3.2.
[54]Exodus 21:10.
[55]"Marriage," *The Universal Jewish Encyclopedia* (New York: Ktav, 1948).
[56]1 Corinthians 7:5.

unspecified expectant woman can bear and raise a child.[57] This was Isaiah's dramatic way of saying that the invasion would soon happen, and indeed, the prophecy was fulfilled by military action a few years later. *Almah* (young woman) is used in the Hebrew text, not *bethulah* (virgin). But there was a mistranslation here in the Septuagint, produced centuries later for the edification of Jews dispersed in the Greek culture. Some New Testament writers also could not read the original Hebrew text. The Septuagint scholars should have used the present tense and *neanis*, meaning girl, so that controversial phrase under consideration would have been properly translated, "A young woman is pregnant."

Matthew's annunciation story quotes the Septuagint's rendering of *almah* as *parthenos*, which usually refers to a virgin.[58] Matthew is innovative in his claim that Mary's conception is a fulfillment of Isaiah's prophecy that "a virgin shall conceive" because there is no record of anyone else in the Jewish or Christian communities who believed that the messiah's birth would come about in that manner. The mistranslation of a single word gave the final editor of Matthew the basis for introducing into Christianity the pagan Greco-Roman notion that sexual abstinence was prerequisite to exceptional holiness.[59]

The ancient Jewish definition of a *bethulah* or *parthenos* assists in understanding how the term could apply to a young woman who was engaged in conjugal relations. The Mishnah includes in the definition of a virgin "a girl who has never seen blood even though she is married."[60] The Talmud comments that this means that in a prepuberty marriage, a "virgin" might become pregnant and give birth without prior menstruation. Catholic theologian Rosemary Radford Ruether, with her usual perspicacity, comments:

> It is possible that in the earliest Christian traditions the idea that God specially intervened in Jesus' birth also did not exclude the fatherhood of Joseph. The young Mary might have been thought of as a girl who is betrothed at too early an age to be fertile (a not uncommon practice at this time) and who conceives before menstruation gives the first evidence of her fertility. Rabbinic writings

[57]Isaiah 7:11-17.
[58]Matthew 1:22-23; but see Genesis 34:3 and Joel 1:8 for atypical occasions when *parthenos* does refer to a woman who has engaged in sexual intercourse.
[59]William Phipps, *Clerical Celibacy* (Harrisburg: Continuum, 2004) 13-15.
[60]*Niddah* 1.4.

refer to such births as "virgin births." So God's miraculous intervention does not need to exclude Joseph's biological role. At least some of the traditions that shaped the New Testament clearly believed Joseph to be Jesus' biological father.[61]

Due to the fact that a girl was customarily married near the age of puberty, and that social sanctions protected unwed Hebrew daughters from seduction, she would usually not be sexually experienced prior to betrothal. In the Hebrew culture, betrothal legally constituted a marital relationship.[62] It was sealed by a transaction in which the boy's guardian paid an agreed sum to the girl's guardian. Breaking a betrothal was so serious that it involved obtaining a bill of divorce.[63] There was no wedding service conducted by a priest or by a state officer in the biblical era. Not long after the betrothal was contracted, the husband had the privilege and responsibility of cohabitating with his bride. Tobias, a devout ancient Jew, slept with Sarah in her home on the night following their betrothal. Jews would not have been greatly surprised had she become pregnant before the wedding feast, which was held later.[64] The Mishnah, the prime codification of ancient Jewish legal traditions, indicates that marital consummation occasionally occurred while the betrothed girl was still residing in her parents' home, and any resulting pregnancy was considered legitimate that was accepted by the husband.[65]

Rudolf Bultmann, noted for his "demythologizing" of stories in the New Testament, finds in the claim that Jesus was born of a virgin this meaning, "It is the legendary expression for faith's claim that the source of the meaning of the person of Jesus is not to be seen in his natural this-worldly origin."[66] Anglican Bishop John Robinson, who was much influenced by Bultmann, focuses on the theological purpose of the New

---

[61]Rosemary Radford Ruether, *Mary, the Feminine Face of the Church* (Philadelphia: Westminster, 1977) 34-35.

[62]Deuteronomy 22:23-24; 2 Samuel 3:14; Philo, *On the Special Laws* 3.12; Ephraim Neufeld, *Ancient Hebrew Marriage Laws* (London: Longmans, 1944) 144.

[63]Matthew 1:18-19; *Kiddushin* 3.8.

[64]Tobit 7:12–9:6.

[65]*Kethuboth* 1:5; Louis Epstein, *Sex Laws and Customs in Judaism* (New York: Ktav, 1967) 126.

[66]From an interview in Werner Harenberg, *Der Spiegel on the New Testament* (London: Macmillan, 1970) 230.

Testament treatments of Jesus' conception. "It is not concerned with gynecology any more than Genesis is concerned with geology," he states.[67] Elsewhere he provides this amplification:

> Clearly the men of the first century did not intend the genealogies to be set against the assertion of Jesus' heavenly conception, or vice versa. They were affirming *both* in the closest juxtaposition, just as the early formula had conjoined the statements [of Paul] that "on the human level he was born of David's stock, but on the level of the spirit—the Holy Spirit—he was . . . Son of God." In other words, each is true—at its own level. The purpose of the nativity story is not to deny something at the level of flesh asserted in the genealogy, but to affirm something at the level of spirit—namely, the initiative of God in and through it all. The significance of Jesus is not to be understood solely from the point of view of heredity and environment.[68]

Matthew's main message pertaining to the birth of Jesus can be missed by focusing on the Evangelist's treatment of "virgin." At the beginning of his good news, Matthew appropriately takes "Immanuel" from the Isaiah passage under consideration and associates the name with forthcoming mercy, not doom. His Gospel ends with assurance that with-us-God (*immanuel*) will never leave the peoples of the earth. When Jesus is in Galilee after his crucifixion, he commissions his apostles to make disciples internationally and gives them this promise, "I am with you always, to the end of time."[69] Matthew emphasizes divine immanence, thereby diminishing the overemphasis in Judaism on God's transcendence. All transcendence and no immanence is deism, while all immanence and no transcendence is pantheism. Matthew's balanced mixture is a vibrant theism, which assures that the God of creation is not remote. Rather, the divine agent who was incarnate is now not taken away to another place, but is ultimately near and abiding.

* * *

Luke's Gospel begins with the story of Elizabeth conceiving a baby after the normal years of childbearing had passed, which is markedly similar to the conception story of Samson's mother.[70] In both, an angel announces

---

[67]*The Christian Century* (21 March 1973): 340.

[68]John Robinson, *The Human Face of God* (Philadelphia: Westminster, 1973) 46.

[69]Matthew 1:23; 28:20.

[70]Judges 13:3-25.

that a previously barren wife will have a child. God's role in the divine-human triangle is emphasized without denying that both wives were impregnated by their spouses. Pertaining to the one who would be called John the Baptist, Gabriel informs husband Zechariah that "even before his birth he will be filled with a holy spirit." After Elizabeth conceives, she says, "The Lord has done this to me and has taken away the disgrace I have endured from people."[71]

Gabriel then similarly announces to a young woman "espoused" (*mnesteuo*) to Joseph that she will bear a son who will be named Jesus. Luke uses the verb *mnesteuo* to refer to Joseph's relation to Mary at the time of Jesus' conception as well as at the time of his birth.[72] The angel again states that deity will be active during Mary's pregnancy, "A holy spirit will come upon you, and highest power will come over you; therefore the holy one being born will be called a son of God."[73] As we have seen, participants in the biblical culture believed that, for all people, God opens wombs or withholds "the fruit of the womb."[74] It would do violence to biblical literature and theology to interpret that poetic verse literally as pertaining to a physical union between Mary and God *the* Holy Spirit. The Spirit as a part of the threefold Godhead pertains to a debate among theologians after the New Testament era. In Luke, God's spirit works through the interaction of human agents, although the process by which this occurs is not fully expressed.[75] G. B. Caird perceptively comments, "It would never have occurred to a Jew to consider the overshadowing of Mary by the Holy Spirit as a substitute for normal parenthood."[76] Luke is not saying that the Spirit performed the male role in sexual intercourse.

After Gabriel's annunciation of a future conception, Mary is represented as inquiring, "How can this be since I am not married?"[77] Her puzzlement is puzzling, for why would a betrothed woman in a culture without birth control not expect to become pregnant soon? Since the rest of

[71]Luke 1:15, 24-25.
[72]Luke 1:27, 2:5.
[73]Luke 1:35.
[74]Genesis 30:2, 22.
[75]Luke 1:13-15; Acts 13:2, 15:28.
[76]G. B. Caird, *The Gospel of St. Luke* (New York: Seabury, 1963), 31; see Niddah 31a.
[77]Luke 1:34.

Luke's nativity story assumes that Joseph was Jesus' father, it seems likely that Mary's question was the final editor's interpolation into an earlier non-supernatural tradition. Both of the beautiful nativity stories in Luke and Matthew that emphasize Jesus' dual parenthood were probably altered by Gentile redactionists or copyists who wished to inject the pagan idea that sublime purity involves no consummation of the marital union. Ancient copyists of the Gospels were not noted for their accuracy; indeed, early Christian scholar Origen complained that some of them audaciously "make additions or deletions as they please.[78] For example, on the basis of altered Greek texts, the King James translators of Jesus' birth story twice refer to "Joseph and his mother." Older manuscripts show that the translation should be "his father and his mother" or "his parents."[79]

Jesuit Joseph Fitzmyer, a distinguished New Testament exegete, comments on Luke's nativity story, "When this account is read in and for itself . . . every detail of it could be understood of a child to be born to Mary in the usual human way."[80] Again, in a commentary bearing the Catholic imprimatur declaring it free of doctrinal error, he writes that the annunciation passage should not be viewed as "the affirmation of Mary's virginity, which is never presented in any biological sense."[81] Biblical mythology was not about God copulating with women, human or divine. Consequently, Luke's account of divine parenthood should be understood as a metaphor depicting God's activity in bringing Jesus into the world. After the generation was symbolically accomplished by the Creator and biologically by the husband, the fetus in Mary's uterus developed normally.

Luke's genealogy of Jesus also follows the male line, as is characteristic of all biblical genealogies. The composer of the family tree was not interested in publishing historical records he had gathered but, as his conclusion shows, in making this theological point: all humans share kinship with Jesus, a descendant from the titular head of humanity, Adam, who is God's son. It appears that an early scribe recognized the problem of including this genealogy in a nativity story featuring Mary being recognized as a virgin when Jesus was conceived. To diminish this inconsistency, a

---

[78]Origen, *Commentary on Matthew* 15.14.

[79]Luke 2:33, 43; Tatian, *Diatessaron* (Edinburgh: Clark, 1894) 49.

[80]*Theological Studies* (December 1973): 567.

[81]Joseph Fitzmyer, *The Gospel according to Luke 1–9* (New York: Doubleday, 1981) 340.

parenthetical phrase was added, "He was a son (as was supposed) of Joseph."[82] The insertion, by expressing doubt over Jesus having paternal ancestors, attempts to void the purpose the original compiler had in mind, namely the tracing of Jesus' lineage through Joseph to noted Jewish forefathers. Unfortunately, no autograph manuscript for any part of the New Testament is extant so it is impossible to show evidence of where the original Greek text was doctored by copyists in the second or third century.

The virginal conception stories are poetic expressions, to be interpreted seriously but not literally. Similar to the conception stories of Sarah and Abraham, Hannah and Elkanah, Ruth and Boaz, and Elizabeth and Zechariah, the story of Mary and Joseph highlights the role of God in the biological process. Robert Funk presided over a think tank that published precious few certainties about Jesus' life, yet he issued this firm statement:

> The Fellows of the Jesus Seminar were certain that Mary did not conceive Jesus without the benefit of human male sperm. . . . The birth stories of Isaac, Samson, and Samuel provided the evangelists [Matthew and Luke] with models for their own versions of the birth of Jesus. . . . Mary was not impregnated by some god masquerading as a human lover.[83]

Some of the lore about the mothers of Jesus and Muhammad is similar. When Abdullah came to have sex with Amina, one of his wives, he was noticed to have a white blaze between his eyes. This brightness was transferred to Amina's conception, resulting in this comment, "As she was pregnant with him, she saw a light come forth from her by which she could see the castles of Busra in Syria."[84] In Muslim mysticism, God creates Muhammad from a handful of light prior to the creation of the world.[85] The motif of Muhammad's birth story is somewhat parallel to Luke's story of Simeon, wherein a devout man recognizes in baby Jesus the fulfillment of Isaiah's prophecy of the coming of a radiant "light to the nations."[86]

Consider similarly the writing of Clement Moore's "Visit from St. Nicholas," the most widely read and memorized Christmas poem in

---

[82]Luke 3:23.

[83]Robert Funk et al., *The Acts of Jesus* (San Francisco: Harper, 1998) 499.

[84]Alfred Guillaume, *The Life of Muhammad: A Translation of Ibn Ishaq's Sirat Rasul Sahih* (Lahore: Oxford University Press, 1955) 69.

[85]Cyril Glasse, "Nur Muhammadi," *The Concise Encyclopedia of Islam* (San Francisco: Harper, 1989).

[86]Isaiah 49:6; Luke 2:25-32.

America. Its composer had no interest in persuading fellow New Yorkers that a jolly elf literally soared from roof to roof in a snow sleigh, making chimney entrances into homes. Moore, a seminary professor, knew that the Bishop of Myra lived in the ancient Roman empire and had a reputation of providing unexpected gifts. He wished to add merriment for children to the story of the saint who allegedly died in December 343. In no way was Moore attempting to establish an Arctic rather than a Mediterranean origin for Nicholas, or to persuade children that someone could miraculously defy gravity and float through the air with reindeer. He presumed that his readers would not confuse flights of the imagination with matter-of-fact truth. Accordingly, most Americans recognize that Santa stories should not to be understood literally but are significant nonetheless for providing a delightful explanation for the anonymous gifts left in stockings hung by a chimney. Luke was likewise not intending to deny a human male's participation in Jesus' conception; rather, he was adding a theological dimension to biology.

Evidence that the notion of a virginal conception is a later interpolation to the original data about the historical Jesus can be shown by considering the effect if the eight verses pertaining to it were removed from Matthew and Luke.[87] Were they absent, nothing would be lost in understanding the rest of those Gospels. Apart from the annunciation stories, the rest of the writings of Matthew and Luke unambiguously support a theory of dual biological and theological parenthood. Following Matthew, Christians should all think of themselves as primarily children of God. Jesus, with his characteristic hyperbole, instructed his disciples to call no earthly man father because the new surrogate family has one Father—the one in heaven.[88] He affirmed for himself the ultimate allegiance he advocated for others. In Luke's Jerusalem temple episode, Mary is represented as scolding boy Jesus, "Your father and I have been searching for you anxiously." In responding, their son asserts that he has been in his "Father's house."[89] Luke is not suggesting here that Joseph was not biologically Jesus' father but rather that the maturing boy had come to recognize a more important spiritual relationship beyond his nuclear family.

---

[87]Matthew 1:18-20, 23-25; Luke 1:34-35.
[88]Matthew 23:9.
[89]Luke 2:48-49.

Along with frequent assertions in the Gospels that Jesus is God's son, there are other references to his being the son of a human father. Matthew refers to Mary's impregnation as coming "from a holy spirit" but also reports that Jesus was known as "the carpenter's son."[90] Episcopal theologian Gardiner Day comments:

> There are certain instances recorded in the Gospels which are hard to explain convincingly if Jesus were miraculously born. If the latter had been the case, surely his parents and fellow townsmen would have known about it. This is the kind of news that would have spread by word of mouth very rapidly throughout the countryside. Yet when he returned to Nazareth and preached for the first time in the synagogue, the people were astounded . . . [and asked,] "Is not this the carpenter's son?" Or as St. Luke's Gospel renders it, "Is not this Joseph's son?"[91]

The prologue of John's Gospel also states that the life of Christians originates from more than the physical desire of human parents. All "children of God" join Jesus in being "born of God."[92] According to the Fourth Gospel, the complete life includes being born of the Spirit in addition to natural fleshly conception.[93] One's significance should not be interpreted solely on the organic level of heredity and environment. Disciple Philip calls Jesus, "Joseph's son from Nazareth," and disciple Nathanael responds by acknowledging that the person so identified is also "the Son of God."[94] Some other Jews assert: "Is not this Jesus, Joseph's son? We know his father and mother."[95]

Elsewhere in the Johannine literature, dual paternity is also assumed. A letter of John states, "Everyone who loves was fathered by God" and "Everyone who does justice is fathered by him."[96] The Johannine writings and Paul's letters account for most of the New Testament references to Jesus as "the Son of God," but neither hints at a virginal conception. On recognizing the way in which Jewish tradition meshes with the Gospels' accounts of Jesus' sonship, New Testament scholar Walter Wink has

---

[90]Matthew 1:18, 20; 13:55.
[91]Gardiner Day, *The Apostles' Creed* (New York: Scribner's, 1963) 56.
[92]John 1:12-13.
[93]John 3:6-7.
[94]John 1:45, 49.
[95]John 6:42.
[96]1 John 4:7; 2:29.

endorsed my position that "the earliest view of Jesus' birth was that of a 'dual paternity,' in which procreation was conceived of as a triad of God, husband, and wife."[97]

Jesus calls God his Father in all four Gospels but he accepts Joseph as his earthly father. The luminaries in the Acts of the Apostles, the first book of church history, do not refer to Jesus' birth. The lateness of the nativity stories is suggested by the fact that no reference is made to them in the rest of the New Testament. None of the Gospels record any comment by Jesus pertaining to a miraculous conception. Had the "son of man" spoken of his biological beginning, he might have expressed himself in a manner similar to the earthy testimony of a Jewish contemporary:

> Like everyone else, I am mortal, a descendant of the first earthling. I was molded into flesh in a mother's womb, where, for ten moons I was compacted in blood, the result of male semen and sexual pleasure. When I was born, I breathed the common air and was laid on the earth that bears us all. My first sound was a scream, like everyone else; I was wrapped in swaddling cloths and nursed with care. No king begins life differently; for there is only one way into life and one way out.[98]

Mary's Sexuality in Church History

Ignatius, Bishop of Antioch in the early second century, was the first "church father" to write about Jesus' conception. To combat the current docetism, Ignatius stressed that Jesus was physically like other humans from womb to tomb. In one letter he advises Christians, "Be deaf to any talk that ignores Jesus Christ, of David's lineage, of Mary; who was really born, ate, and drank."[99] In another letter the bishop affirms dual parenthood, "Our God, Jesus the Christ, was conceived by Mary in accordance with God's plan—being sprung both of the sperm of David and from the Holy Spirit."[100] Sometimes Ignatius refers to mother Mary as a *parthenos*,[101] which probably does not connote a woman who is sexually inexperienced.[102] Clearly virginity is excluded from the meaning of the word when

---

[97]*Journal of the American Academy of Religion* (June 1975): 440.

[98]Wisdom of Solomon 7:1-6.

[99]Ignatius, *Trallians* 9.1.

[100]Ignatius, *Ephesians* 18.2.

[101]Ignatius, *Ephesians* 19.1; *Smyrnaeans* 1.1.

[102]After careful examination of *parthenos* in ancient Jewish and Christian

he refers to "*parthenoi* who are called widows."[103] It would have gone against Ignatius's desire to show Jesus' genuine humanity to claim that his conception was only half human and thereby unlike other mortals.

The other most influential Christian in the first half of the second century was Marcion, from the Greco-Roman culture, who had an opposing view of the physical body. Recognizing that sex is described in Genesis as a product of the Creator, he deemed that deity inferior to the God of Jesus. Since for Marcion physical contact with a woman was defiling, Jesus could not have come from a uterus. Avoiding reference to Jesus' conception, birth, and maturation, Marcion's gospel began with an adult descending angel-like from heaven.[104] In orthodox Christianity Marcion was condemned as an archheretic.

In the New Testament the circumstances pertaining to Jesus' birth were peripheral, but that outlook soon shifted. Catholic theologian Uta Ranke-Heinemann observes, "Christians did not invent reverence for virginity, which in no way comes from Jesus. Rather, Christians adapted themselves to their environment." The culture to which she refers was predominantly influenced by the Stoics, and also by other body-hating ascetics.[105]

Justin Martyr, who lived a century after the time of Jesus, was the first postapostolic church leader on record to state unambiguously that Jesus was virginally conceived. He had a strong Hellenistic background and correspondingly little understanding of Hebraic culture. Having studied under neo-Pythagoreans and Neoplatonists, he introduced their ascetic philosophy into his biblical interpretations.[106] By associating coitus with the satanic serpent of a Genesis, Justin assumed that Jesus would have been defiled

---

literature, Josephine Ford concludes: "The term 'virgin' is not necessarily confined to one who has not experienced coitus, but, on the one hand, may be used of a minor who has married and been widowed, and, on the other, of people who have only taken one spouse during their lifetime." *New Testament Studies* (July 1966): 298.

[103]Ignatius, *Smyrnaeans* 13.1.

[104]Tertullian, *Against Marcion* 4.7.

[105]Uta Ranke-Heinemann, *Eunuchs for the Kingdom of Heaven* (New York: Penguin, 1990) 47-48.

[106]Justin, *Dialogue*, 2; *Apology* 2.13.

were he conceived through a sensual union.[107] The death brought by "virgin Eve" when she had intercourse with "the logos [wisdom] of the serpent" is contrasted by Justin with the benefits of virgin Mary who was impregnated by the overpowering logos of God.[108] In subsequent church teaching, ordinary women were identified with Eve who "fell" because of lustfulness. A play was made on Latin words in claiming that Gabriel greeted Mary with *Ave* because she, the antithesis of *Eva*, had no sexual desire.[109] Had Justin comprehended the Hebraic concept of dual parenthood he would not have glibly presupposed that physical passion and spiritual power cannot coexist in a person.

Citing a verse from Isaiah about a virgin conceiving, and relying on the Greek translation for his authority,[110] Justin declared, "Christ is not man of men, begotten in the ordinary course of humanity."[111] But rabbi Trypho, with whom he was debating, pointed out that such a mode of birth was contrary to Jewish messianic expectations; that Isaiah was referring to an occurrence in the immediate future of his nation; and that the terminology pertained to a young woman, not particularly to one who was sexually inexperienced. Trypho told of the Jewish understanding that Isaiah was referring to the mother of the successor of Ahaz, the king to whom the prophet was speaking.[112] Hezekiah succeeded his father Ahaz and reigned during the era when Assyria destroyed most of Judah. Trypho expressed the common Jewish hope for the future, "We all await the messiah who will be a man of human birth."[113]

Justin's argument for a virginal conception came from Matthew's eisegesis of a Hebrew text, as we have seen. Trypho accused Christians of adapting pagan birth stories of demigod heroes to aid in propagandizing their religion. He said, "In Greek mythology there is a story of how Perseus was born of Danae while she was a virgin when the one whom they call Zeus descended upon her in the form of a golden shower." Also, the

---

[107]Erwin Goodenough, *The Theology of Justin Martyr* (Amsterdam: Philo, 1968) 181, 238.

[108]Justin, *Dialogue*, 100.

[109]Susan Haskins, *Mary Magdalen* (New York: Harcourt Brace, 1994) 140-41.

[110]Isaiah 7:14.

[111]Justin, *Dialogue with Trypho*, 54.

[112]Justin, *Dialogue*, 66-67; *Apology* 1.33.

[113]Justin, *Dialogue*, 49.

prevailing myth of the begetting of Hercules involved Zeus copulating with mortal mother Alcmene, causing Zeus's wife Hera to become jealous.[114] Trypho then chided, "You Christians ought to be ashamed of telling the same stories as the heathen. It would be better to say that Jesus was a man of human parentage. . . . If you do not want people to say you are as foolish as the Greeks, you must stop speaking of these things."[115] But Justin, far from being ashamed of the parallel, used it in defense of his doctrine. Calling on the prologue of John's Gospel, which describes the Logos, the wisdom of God, as becoming infleshed in Jesus, Justin wrote, "When we declare that the Logos, who is the first offspring of God, was born without sexual intercourse . . . we introduce nothing different from your view about those called sons of Zeus." Justin thought he was strengthening the appeal of Christianity in the Gentile world by demonstrating that accounts of virginally conceived persons are not unique. Actually he was placing Christianity on a level with superstitions that many reasonable persons had rejected. Justin did concede, "Jesus, even if only a man by ordinary generation, on account of his wisdom is worthy to be called the Son of God."[116]

Justin admitted, "Some people of our kind acknowledge Jesus to be Christ, but at the same time declare him to have been a man of human birth. I, however, cannot agree with them, and will not do so, even if the majority were to insist on that opinion." He was probably referring to Jewish Christians, initially led by James, the brother of Jesus, who led the church in Jerusalem.[117] Because they had lived in Palestine, their perception of nascent Christianity holds more historical value. The belief that Jesus was not the child of a union between a man and a woman had overtones of pagan mythology and was abhorrent to those Christians.[118] Here is telling evidence that the virginal conception mythology was a late addition by Gentile Christians.

Bishop Irenaeus of Lyons in Gaul, who lived in the latter part of the second century, became the most formidable defender of what had come to be recognized as orthodox Christianity. He did much to entrench the dogma

---

[114]Euripides, *Madness of Hercules*, 798.
[115]Justin, *Dialogue*, 67.
[116]Justin, *Apology* 1:21-22.
[117]Galatians 1:18-19; Acts 15:13.
[118]Justin, *Dialogue*, 48.

of the asexual conception of Jesus by developing Justin's tortured typology, treating Jesus and Mary as Adam and Eve in reverse. Irenaeus drew this parallel: "While it was still virgin, God took dust of the earth and fashioned the man, the beginning of humanity. So the Lord, summing up afresh this man, reproduced the scheme of Adam's incarnation, being born of a virgin by the will and the wisdom of God."[119] Jesus, like Adam, was made from "untilled and yet virgin soil."[120] But neither Jesus nor his mother, unlike Adam and Eve, engaged in sex and thereby they restored corrupt mankind to the good graces of God.[121]

Irenaeus took issue with the Jewish Christians or Nazarenes, whose first leader was James the brother of Jesus. He called them Ebionites and judged them to be heretics, in part because they believed their crucified and risen Jesus had been conceived in the normal human manner.[122] Contained in a third century church manual is a condemning reference to "the Ebionites who will have the Son of God to be a mere man, begotten by human pleasure and the conjunction of Joseph and Mary."[123] Unfortunately, none of the four Evangelists wrote about Jesus from a Jewish perspective and in the Aramaic language of Palestine, so the Ebionite outlook on Jesus' life was almost completely lost.

The notion of dual parenthood for Jesus was lost after the structure of Christian belief jelled in the latter part of the second century, and the doctrine of Jesus' virginal conception became part of the basic creed. The last trace of dual parenthood for Jesus in early Christian literature is found in the *Gospel of Philip*, which was written down in the third century. It was buried some time later in upper Egypt, not to be rediscovered until 1945. The authors of that Gospel state that they were Hebrews prior to becoming Christians.[124] Jesus is declared to be the son of Joseph the carpenter, yet "the Father of everything united with the virgin" to produce Jesus. Moreover, dual parenthood is an appropriate designation for all baptized Christians for they have what might be called a virgin birth by being born again through

---

[119]Irenaeus, *Proof of the Apostolic Preaching*, 32.

[120]Irenaeus, *Against Heresies* 3.21.10.

[121]Irenaeus, *Against Heresies* 3.22.4.

[122]Irenaeus, *Against Heresies* 5.1.3.

[123]*Constitutions of the Holy Apostles* 6.6.

[124]*Gospel of Philip*, 52.

the Spirit.[125] Knowing that "spirit" came from the feminine Hebrew word *ruach*, those authors of Philip chide, "Some say, 'Mary conceived by the Holy Spirit.' . . . They do not know what they are saying! When did a woman ever conceive by a woman?" The *Gospel of Philip* claims that Jesus would not have said "My Father in heaven" unless he were distinguishing God from his earthly father.[126]

Orthodox Christians no doubt believed they were doing a service to the faith by removing holy Jesus from the defilement they thought would ensue had he been generated on a bed soiled by erotic passion. Around 200 CE a Christian gave this explanation, "Our Lord Jesus Christ was born of a virgin only, for the following reason: he was to bring to naught the begetting that proceeds from lawless appetite, and show the ruler of this world that God could form man even without human sexual intercourse."[127] Here is stated the anti-Hebraic outlook that sexual desire and its fulfillment is contrary to the law of God and that those who are immaculately pure must renounce it completely. Both female and male sexuality is besmirched by linking the exalted status of Mary and Jesus with their alleged lifelong rejection of sexual intercourse.[128]

The "books" that came to be known as the New Testament were among numerous Christian writings over a one century era, ending in the middle of the second century. Many years were to follow before disputes were settled over exactly which ones to include in the Bible. Among the redactions that the canoners accepted were those made by Gentiles on the nativity stories of Matthew and Luke. Tatian, a second-century ascetic who believed that sexual intercourse was an invention of the devil,[129] deleted from the gospel story references to Joseph as Jesus' father.[130] By the late fourth century there was general agreement on the 27 books that would compose the New Testament canon. Apostolic authorship was the main test of canonicity, but we know now that Paul was actually the only apostle whose writings are included. As we have seen, on the basis of that one

---

[125]*Gospel of Philip*, 71, 73.

[126]*Gospel of Philip*, 55.

[127]Pseudo-Justin, *On the Resurrection*, 3.

[128]Phipps, *Clerical Celibacy*, 20-53.

[129]Clement of Alexandria, *Miscellanies*, 3:12:80-81.

[130]Theodoret of Cyrrhus, *Compendium of Heretical Fables* 1:20.

apostolic author of the New Testament, there are no grounds for claiming that Jesus was virginally conceived.

Tertullian, writing around 200 CE, insisted that Mary was Jesus' only human parent, "Otherwise he had two fathers, a divine and a human one, the thought of which is ridiculous."[131] He had been trained as a lawyer to champion either/or dichotomies rather than both/and modes of thinking. That Latin father followed Justin's line of defense by establishing a tie with Hellenistic legends of unnatural liaisons. Tertullian described the manner of Jesus' birth in this way: "The Son of God has a mother touched by no impurity. . . . When a ray is projected from the sun, it is a portion of the whole. . . . This ray of God . . . entered into a certain virgin, and, in her womb fashioned into flesh, is born, man mingled with God."[132] He was probably influenced by the myth of sun god Apollo siring Alexander the Great. A divine ray penetrated his mother's womb, according to Plutarch, causing her pregnancy.[133]

Origen, another third-century theologian, defended Jesus' alleged virginal conception differently. He explained that the pagan Greeks invented myths of gods having a special role with human women in order to enhance the wisdom and power of the offspring they conceived, but he was unwilling to accept that Christian nativity stories were similarly motivated.[134] Rather, he used Scripture in a quirky way to prove that Jesus' virginal conception was prefigured in Isaiah's prophecy of the suffering servant. Origen interpreted "Like a root out of dry ground" to refer to Mary's virginal womb that was not moistened with semen.[135]

The view of those ascetic church fathers prevailed in subsequent centuries, for Christians came to believe that in the unique case of Jesus, male-female parentage and divine-human parentage were mutually exclusive. The pillars of orthodoxy in the patristic era twisted the earliest Christian testimony by claiming that Jesus was discontinuous with humanity because his mother's ovum was not fertilized by the sperm of a male. By treating Mary's conception as an unnatural occurrence, they magnified out of proportion the significance of Jesus' nativity in the life of earliest Christianity.

---

[131]Tertullian, *Against Marcion* 4:10.
[132]Tertullian, *Apology* 21.9-14.
[133]Plutarch, *Life of Alexander*, 2.
[134]Origen, *Against Celsus* 1:57.
[135]Isaiah 53:2; Origen, *Genesis Homilies*, 17.

In the creeds of the postapostolic church, the mode of Jesus' birth usually has as significant a place as his sufferings and resurrection. In the New Testament the uniqueness of Jesus is bound up with his way of life, which incarnated love, justice, and freedom; but orthodoxy has emphasized his being born in a manner that was removed from the so-called tainted sensual pleasures and the corrupted sperm of Adam. Archbishop Athanasius, the most powerful theologian of the fourth century, articulated the settled ecclesiastical outlook when he stated that the Logos took a human body "directly from a spotless, stainless virgin, without the agency of human father—a pure body, untainted by intercourse with man."[136] In all major branches of Eastern Orthodoxy and Latin Catholicism, the Athanasian position on Mary has been declared to be an obligatory belief for Christians.

Some of the later church fathers went so far as to refuse to accept the New Testament assumption that Joseph had sex with Mary even after Jesus was born.[137] To justify their contention, they drew on the *Infancy Gospel of James*'s portrayal of Joseph as an old widower who has sons from an earlier marriage. After Mary's pregnancy begins to show, she and Joseph are charged with fornication, but they prove their innocence by the poison ordeal. Mary survives after drinking a potion, verifing her claim not to have engaged in sexual intercourse with anyone. The story goes on to allege that physical evidence proves that Mary's virginal hymen was unruptured during her delivery. Salome enters the cave where Mary gave birth, submits her to a gynecological examination, and concludes that Mary has remained an intact virgin. But Salome is penalized for having been skeptical by having her hand burned by a miraculous flame.[138] It could be said that if Mary had an unruptured hymen after giving birth, she surely could have retained such after having had intercourse.

A letter that Bishop Ambrose wrote to Pope Siricius in 390 gives the first indication of the church's approval of the doctrine of Mary's perpetual virginity. The Bishop justified the Milan Synod's condemnation and exiling of monk Jovinian, who had maintained that Mary did not remain a virgin after the birth of Jesus. Ambrose supported his position by allegorizing a biblical prophecy. Ezekiel, in describing the new temple in Jerusalem, explained why the outer east gate will be kept closed: "No one may pass

---

[136]Athanasius, *The Incarnation of the Word of God* 8.5.

[137]Matthew 1:25; 13:55.

[138]*Infancy Gospel of James* 9, 15-16, 19-20.

through it, for the Lord, the God of Israel, has entered by it. Therefore, it must be kept shut."[139] Ambrose asked, "Is not Mary the gate through whom the Redeemer entered the world?"[140] Siricius, writing to Bishop Anysius in 392, gave additional explaination why Mary's virginity was necessarily lifelong, "Jesus would not have chosen birth from a virgin had he been forced to look upon her as so unrestrained as to let that womb, from which the body of the Lord was fashioned, that hall of the eternal king, be stained by the presence of male seed." For semen contaminated by Adam's sin to ooze into Mary's holy of holies uterus was unthinkable.

At this time, when the old Roman empire was falling, church doctrine was greatly influenced by men who fled wilderness areas to live ascetic lives. In his classic *History of European Morals*, William Lecky writes:

> To an ordinary layman the life of the anchorite [hermit] might appear in the highest degree opposed to that of the Teacher who began His mission in a marriage feast; who was continually reproached by His enemies for the readiness with which He mixed with the world, and who selected from the female sex some of His purest and most devoted followers; but the monkish theologians avoiding, for the most part, these topics, dilated chiefly on His immaculate birth, His virgin mother, His life of celibacy, His exhortation to the rich young man. The fact that St. Peter, to whom a general primacy was already ascribed, was unquestionably married, was a difficulty which was in a measure met by a tradition that he, as well as the other married apostles, abstained from intercourse with their wives after their conversion.[141]

In an attempt to make a supernatural birth of Jesus more plausible, monk Jerome told of a tradition pertaining to Siddhartha, the founder of Buddhism, which he accepted as true. Prior to the Christian era, some Buddhists recorded a story about Queen Maya, claiming that she was void of sexual desire even though married. She became impregnated by a divine power when the tusk of a white elephant penetrated her right side. The fetus was later miraculously born from the same place, and the infant grew up to become the Buddha.[142] Jerome thought skeptics would be persuaded by this

---

[139]Ezekiel 44:2.

[140]Ambrose, *Letters* 44.

[141]William Lecky, *History of European Morals* (New York: Appleton, 1870) 2:111.

[142]*Lalitavistara*, 6; see Alfred Foucher, *A Life of Buddha according to the Ancient Texts* (Middletown CT: Wesleyan University Press, 1963) 23-30.

parallel attestation that a woman could conceive and deliver in an unnatural manner.[143]

The closest parallel in Christian lore to this story of Queen Maya conceiving in a nonvaginal manner can be found in Augustine's theology. So as to avoid any suggestion of a passion arousal in Mary, he stated that Gabriel used one of her ears as the orifice for impregnating her.[144] In medieval art that fanciful thought is illustrated by a dove, representing the Holy Spirit, depositing *sperma* in her ear. Karl Barth found that point of contact "essentially right" since the ear is the customary organ into which God's revelation is implanted.[145] He said: "Here there is no question of a sexual event. . . . Procreation was realized rather by way of the ear of Mary, which heard the Word of God. . . . The male has nothing to do with this birth."[146]

Comparative religions specialist Geoffrey Parrinder notes a common bias in ascetic interpreters of traditions pertaining to founders of religions: "The work of celibate theologians in formulating distortions of attitudes to sex and marriage can hardly be overestimated. A similar process can be observed in Buddhist stories, also compiled by celibate monks, first of the miraculous and then of the virginal conception of the Buddha."[147] When Mark Twain compared stories showing similar origins of Buddha, Krishna, and Jesus, he was "struck with the fact that virgins are not as fertile now as they used to be."[148]

Jerome was offended by the nerve of Helvidius, a scholarly contemporary, who contended that marital sexuality was as holy as virginal abstinence. Jesus' mother was cited as proof, for the New Testament suggests that she had a number of normal pregnancies.[149] Helvidius pointed out that Luke referred to Jesus as Mary's "firstborn" (*prototokos*), while the Evangelist uses another term (*monogenes*) to refer to a person who procreates only one child.[150] In response, Jerome alleged that the Bible

[143]Jerome, *Against Jovinian* 1:42.

[144]Augustine, *On the Birth of the Lord*, 121.

[145]Karl Barth, *Church Dogmatics* (Edinburgh: Clark, 1936) 1.2.201.

[146]Karl Barth, *Dogmatics in Outline* (London: SCM, 1949) 99.

[147]Geoffrey Parrinder, *Son of Joseph* (Edinburgh: Clark, 1992) 122.

[148]Quoted in William Phipps, *Mark Twain's Religion* (Macon GA: Mercer University Press, 2003) 241.

[149]Mark 6:3.

[150]Luke 2:7; 7:12; 8:42; Jerome, *Against Helvidius*, 8.

contains a prophecy of Mary's unbroken hymen because the bride in the Song of Songs is described as "a fountain sealed."[151] On this subject, his innovative mind produced another perverse interpretation. The passing of Jesus supernaturally through a closed vagina is linked with his moving through a closed door after his resurrection.[152]

Realizing that even an old man with sexual experience would probably try to have sex with a young wife, Jerome rejected the claim of the second-century apocryphal *Infancy Gospel of James* that Joseph was a widower with children by his former marriage. He declared that Joseph was a lifelong virgin and consequently Jesus did not have even step-siblings; the brothers and sisters of Jesus who are referred to in the Gospels were really cousins![153] Had Jerome's contention been correct, the Greek New Testament would have used *anepsios,* its word for cousin, not *adelphos,* its word for brother.

In honoring Mary, Catholics have attempted to deprive her of daughters, and all but one son. The current Catholic catechism endorses Jerome's eisegesis by stating as a matter of "fact" that the "brothers of Jesus" mentioned in the New Testament are sons of another Mary.[154] Such fabrications to uphold the defunct doctrine of Mary's postpartum virginity win little respect for Christianity. Jesus' younger male and female siblings are always associated with his mother in the New Testament, not with some other Mary.[155] Although historical grounding is totally lacking, Catholicism affirms a tripartite hymen intactness of Mary: before, during, and after the birth of Jesus; her sexual parts were always like new. Mary's perpetual virginity was declared by the Chalcedon Council, and in 649 the Lateran Council made it a main doctrine of Roman Catholicism. This doctrine epitomizes the medieval church's hostility to sex even in holy wedlock.

In Catholic tradition, Jerome has long been respected as an authoritative interpreter of the Bible. Even though he often read his own presuppositions into the text, Catholics have, at least until recently, regarded him as not only

---

[151]Song of Solomon 4:12; Jerome, *Letters* 48.21.

[152]Jerome, *Against the Pelagians* 2.4; John 20:19, 26.

[153]Jerome, *Against Helvidius*, 14, 17, 21.

[154]*Catechism of the Catholic Church* (Washington DC: Catholic Conference, 2000) 126.

[155]Mark 3:32; Acts 1:14.

an excellent Latin translator but as a preeminent exegete.[156] *The Jerome Biblical Commentary* editors, for example, refer to him as "the foremost Scripture scholar among the Church Fathers, a pioneer in biblical criticism."[157] However, John Kelly notes in his biography of Jerome, "At the heart of his teaching lay the conviction that chastity was the quintessence of the gospel message, and that its supreme exemplification and proof was Mary, the virgin mother of the virgin Savior."[158]

From the fifth century onward, a principal title for Mary among Catholics has been "God-bearer" (*Theotokos* in Greek). That designation was given at the ecumenical council held in 431 at Ephesus. Gordon Laing argues convincingly that the worship of Artemis (Latin, Diana) as both virgin and mother at the grand Ephesian temple contributed to the veneration of Mary. Artemis had been called "the virgin goddess and the immaculate one."[159] Nestorius, the Patriarch of Constantinople, was deposed as a heretic because he advocated the title *Christotokos* and rejected *Theotokos*. With sound judgment he thought that to call Mary the "mother of God" (as usually translated into English) was incompatible with Jesus' humanity. But the title *Theotokos* continues to be prominent in Eastern Orthodoxy, which presumable makes Mary's parents the grandparents of God!

Specimens of Mary's presumed milk are deposited in many churches of Europe. Medieval Catholics believed that her milk not only nourished Jesus but fed adoring churchmen. Mary was alleged to have rewarded Bernard of Clairvaux for his eulogies to her by visiting his cell and allowing him to be refreshed by her breast. Other monks were allegedly cured of sickness when she appeared and breast-fed them.[160] Paralleling the "our Lord" designation for Jesus was "our Lady" for Mary from this era onward.

The hyperveneration of Mary contains overtones of a pagan cult originating in Asia Minor (modern day Turkey) that had become entrenched in

---

[156]William Phipps, *Influential Theologians on Wo/Man* (Washington DC: University Press of America, 1980) 37-55.

[157]Raymond Brown et al., eds., *The Jerome Biblical Commentary* (Englewood Cliffs NJ: Prentice-Hall, 1968) xx.

[158]John Kelly, *Jerome* (New York: Harper, 1975) 335.

[159]Gordon Laing, *Survivals of Roman Religion* (New York: Longmans, 1931) 92-93.

[160]Benjamin Warfield, *Counterfeit Miracles* (New York: Scribner's, 1918) 94-96, 269-70.

the Roman empire. The religion was centered in Cybele, who was worshiped as the mother of the gods and as the provider of the earth's fertility. Attis, her associate, was sometimes regarded as her virginally conceived son. The most distinctive feature of the myth of Attis is that he slashed off his testicles to show abhorrence toward Venus and devotion toward Cybele.[161] Accordingly, priests of the "Magna Mater" were expected to attain perfection by emasculating themselves.[162] Beginning in the third century after Christ, the bloody death of Attis as a result of castration was annually commemorated at the spring equinox. On the day following was the *Hilaria*, a joyful celebration of Attis's resurrection.[163]

The beliefs and practices of the Cybele-Attis cult can be related to the spiraling asceticism in Christianity during the latter years of the Roman era:

> There is a similarity between the goddess Cybele with her eunuch priests and the later worship of the Virgin Mary sustained by a celibate clergy. The widespread worship of Mary retained the all-giving earth mother but removed the dangerous sexual qualities by making her a permanent virgin. And indeed the carefully desexualized figure of Christ is more than a little reminiscent of Attis.[164]

Islam has been affected by Eastern Catholicism, where veneration for Mary has been even stronger than in the West. Mariolatry in Ethiopia, the nearest Christian nation to Mecca, caused Muhammad to conclude that Jesus' mother was a member of the divine family that Christians worshiped. He was scornful of Christians because he thought they believed in three different deities, one being the goddess Mary who was impregnated by intercourse with the father God. Over against that, the *Qur'an* asks, "Jesus, son of Mary, did you ever say to people, 'Worship me and my mother as gods beside God?' 'Praise to you,' he will answer, 'How could I say that to which I have no right?' "[165] Muhammad, like many Christians, could not fathom the complex monotheism of the Nicene triunitarian formula which begins simply, "We believe in one God. . . ." His perception that Christian-

---

[161]Catullus, *Poem* 63.5-17.

[162]Ovid, *Fasti* 4.240.

[163]John Ferguson, *The Religion of the Roman Empire* (Ithaca NY: Cornell University Press, 1970) 29; Franz Cumont, *The Oriental Religions in Roman Paganism* (Chicago: Open Court, 1911) 56-57.

[164]Hoffman Hayes, *The Dangerous Sex* (New York: Putnam, 1964) 107.

[165]*Qur'an* 5:116.

ity is another version of the pagan polytheism he opposed in Arabia provides some understanding of why Islam arose as Christianity's chief rival.[166] But the *Qur'an* has no problem with Mary having a supernatural conception: " 'How can I bear a son,' she said, 'when I am a virgin, untouched by a man?' 'Such is the will of your Lord,' He replied. 'That is easy for Me.' "[167] Also, Jesus acts in a miraculous way as an infant that goes beyond anything in the New Testament. When Mary is accused of unchastity, she points to her son's cradle from which he speaks out like a mature man in her defense.[168]

Aquinas, some centuries later, affirmed regarding Mary that there was no "unlocking of the enclosure of virginal purity," in spite of the reference in Luke to Jesus "opening the womb."[169] That "chief custodian of Catholic antisexuality"[170] shared Jerome's anger toward Helvidius:

> Without any hesitation we must abhor the error of Helvidius, who dared to assert that Christ's mother, after his birth, was carnally known by Joseph, and bore other children. . . . This error is an insult to the Holy Spirit, whose shrine was the virginal womb, wherein he had formed the flesh of Christ. Thus it was unbecoming that it should be desecrated by intercourse with man.[171]

Aquinas borrowed Greek biological theory in explaining how virginal conception saved Jesus from original sin.[172] The ancient Greeks believed that the *sperma* (meaning "seed") alone conveyed the nonmaterial intelligible form of humanness to offspring and that women merely provided the moist matter and receptacle for its incubation.[173] A drama of Aeschylus, for example, contains these lines: "The so-called offspring is not produced by the mother. She is no more than the nurse, as it were, of the newly conceived fetus. It is the male who is the author of its being."[174] According to Aquinas, a virginally conceived Jesus could not have inherited sin

---

[166]William Phipps, *Muhammad and Jesus* (New York: Paragon, 1996) 209-12.

[167]*Qur'an* 19:20-21.

[168]*Qur'an* 19:29-30.

[169]Aquinas, *Summa Theologica* 3.28.2; Luke 2:23.

[170]Uta Ranke-Heinemann, *Putting Away Childish Things* (San Francisco: Harper, 1995) 198.

[171]Aquinas 3.28.3.

[172]Aquinas 3.28.1.

[173]Aristotle, *On the Generation of Animals*, 729a.

[174]Aeschylus, *Eumenides* 11.661-63.

because a woman cannot transmit character qualities to an embryo. She can supply only food and a warm environment for the microscopic human contained in the male seed implanted in her uterus. Since the defining human characteristics of a man's preexisting baby are generated in his testicles, Aquinas thought that the wasting of precious human life by masturbation, sodomy, or *coitus interruptus* was a graver sin than adultery, rape, or incest.[175]

Cardinal Roberto Bellarmino, the lead prosecutor at Galileo's trial, argued that it is as erroneous to claim that the earth revolves around the sun as to assert that Jesus was not born of a virgin.[176] Consider his statement in reverse: it is as erroneous to assert that Jesus was born of a virgin as to claim that the sun revolves around the earth. The cardinal's logic, which is cogent but factually false, expresses well the historic blunders that the Vatican has even today only partly acknowledged. Centuries later it acknowledged that the sun is the center of our planetary system, but recognition may never be given of its biological, historical, and theological errors pertaining to the desexualized mother of Jesus.

* * *

With the discovery of ovulation in 1827, scientists have recognized that the female contributes equally with the male to the genetic characteristics of their offspring. That new knowledge may have had some influence on Pope Pius IX, who announced in 1854 the Dogma of Mary's Immaculate Conception. The "infallible" declaration is interpreted to mean that all taint of original sin was miraculously removed from Mary at the moment of her conception, that she was liberated from sexual desire, and that she was made incapable of sinning.[177] Being more pure than angels, this unique woman could not infect the fruit of her womb, even though all other mothers and fathers transmit sinfulness to their children. Pius attempted to rewrite history by stating that his dogma "always existed in the church." Ironically, what is now a mandatory belief in Roman Catholicism was rejected as unsound by Aquinas, the most influential medieval contributor to the adoration of Mary.[178]

---

[175] Aquinas 2-2.154.12.

[176] Letter from Roberto Bellarmino to Paolo Foscarini, 12 April 1615.

[177] See Marina Warner, *Alone of All Her Sex* (New York: Knopf, 1976) 236-38.

[178] Mary was "wholly conceived in original sin" according to Aquinas 3.31.7.

On the surface, the Immaculate Conception may appear to exalt womankind, but by removing Mary's feet of clay it accentuates the innate sinfulness of the rest of Eve's children. Not only does it deprecate women who participate in normal marital sexuality, but it also slurs the purity of virgins. While Catholicism continually praises to high heaven virgins who are "unblemished," it nevertheless assumes that they are, in comparison to Mary, defiled. As Friedrich Nietzsche put it, the dogma of the "Immaculate Conception" has "maculated" conceptions of ordinary humans.[179] It would be more in accord with the biblical ethic for the church to declare that the libido is without sin when serving the companionable, recreative, and procreative purposes of holy marriage, and that all infants born from such a union are "immaculate" conceptions.

Pope Pius XII issued the Assumption of Mary bull in 1950 that claimed she was "preserved from the corruption of the tomb" and physically ascended into heaven. Ironically, this notion had been condemned in the fifth century by Pope Gelasius.[180] The doctrine is a modification of a church tradition that no bodily decay ensues when an exceptionally holy person dies. Such supernaturalism is the chief sign of a saint in Russian Orthodoxy.

Then, in 1954, Pius added a sixth step to the exaltation of Mary. Whereas in the earliest historical source Jesus rebukes her mildly,[181] and in Luke he rejects giving her special praise,[182] before the end of the first Christian century she was presumed to have had been uniquely honored by supernaturally conceiving Jesus. Perpetual virginity and the "God-bearer" title were second and fifth century developments for Mary. Nineteenth- and twentieth-century dogmas allegedly exempted her from sinning during life and from bodily decay after death. The last step so far has been Pius's proclamation that Mary was crowned "Queen of Heaven" after her Assumption. The biblical source for that title is Jeremiah who denounced Jewish refugees from Egypt that were worshiping a deity so named.[183] Further identification of that goddess is provided by Apuleius, writing in the second century CE. He prays to the "Queen of Heaven" and she replies that her divinity is adored by many names, but the Egyptians "call me by my true

---

[179]Friedrich Nietzsche, *The Anti-Christ*, 34.
[180]Giovanni Miegge, *The Virgin Mary* (Philadelphia: Westminster, 1955) 86.
[181]Mark 3:31-35.
[182]Luke 11:27-28.
[183]Jeremiah 44:15-17.

name, Queen Isis."[184] Representations of Isis, the wife of god Osiris, with infant god Horus on her lap, are precursors of the medieval Madonna and Child art. The Christian concept of God, assisted by pagan transfers, appears to have become a quarternity by Vatican decree!

Maude Royden, a noted Anglican lay preacher in the 1920s, was one of the first women of a mainline denomination to reject Jesus' alleged virginal conception. She had no problem in accepting even the miracle of Jesus' walking on water, but judged the virginal conception doctrine defective quite apart from its supernaturalism. Influencing the development of that doctrine, Royden recognized, were the sentiments of this psalmist, "I was shapen in iniquity, and in sin did my mother conceive me."[185] She found that moral stance revolting:

> One cannot resist an uneasy suspicion that it arose in the minds of men out of a sense that there is something fundamentally base about sex. . . . To assume that God could not come to his people through the love of a man and woman is to assume that in love, when it is expressed in sex, there is something that is degrading.

Royden advocated that parents should view the Holy Spirit as "over-shadowing" the birth of *every* child that is born and reject the tradition that imputes shamefulness to the generation of human beings.[186] Robert Mullin recognizes her perspicacious contribution, "The view that human sexuality was somehow low and tawdry permeated the idea of the virgin birth and its presupposition that God could not enter the world through the normal love of a man and woman but only in an unnatural way."[187]

In that 1920s era, the virginal conception controversy reached its crescendo in America. Gresham Machen was then the academic leader of Protestant fundamentalism. His agenda was to cleanse Christianity of those who do not believe that God, at his pleasure, contravenes the natural order. He labeled such persons as "liberals" and describes them as "un-Christian."[188] Claiming that it was difficult to find any real Christian who

---

[184]Apuleius, *The Golden Ass* 11.2, 4.

[185]Psalm 51:5.

[186]*Christian Century* (20 October 1921): 12-15.

[187]Robert Mullin, *Miracles and the Modern Religious Imagination* (New Haven CT: Yale, 1996) 231.

[188]J. Gresham Machen, *Christianity and Liberalism* (New York: Macmillan, 1923) 7.

rejected "the virgin birth," he used it as the litmus test of orthodoxy. He accurately wrote, "The question of the virgin birth brings us sharply before the question of the supernatural, and . . . a man who accepts the virgin birth has taken his stand squarely upon supernaturalistic ground." Machen asked, "If we believe, as the Bible teaches, that all mankind are under the awful curse, then . . . how, except by the virgin birth, could our Saviour . . . have been from the very beginning no product of what had gone before, but a supernatural Person come into the world from the outside to redeem the sinful race?" Had Jesus been conceived by ordinary human sexuality he would have been one "in whom the divine life merely pulsated in greater power than in other men."[189]

More recently, Henry Morris, a polemicist for American fundamentalism, has attempted to resolve the Christological dilemma precipitated by modern genetics. To prevent the transmission of a sinful nature into Jesus, he claims the zygote that was implanted in Mary's womb was "formed neither of the seed of the man nor the egg of the woman."[190] To save Jesus from the alleged corruption of fallen humanity that would have been conveyed by the chromosomes of either male or female parent, Moore presumes that God directly created *ex nihilo* the perfect zygote for the second Adam. Even though Jesus lacked real human parents, Mary provided the surrogate uterus for nurturing God's fertile implant.

Nikolas Berdyaev, a leader of Russian Orthodoxy, writes that he read Emil Brunner's *Mediator* with great appreciation until he discovered that the author of a variety of theological tomes did not believe that Jesus was born of a virgin. On learning that, he said, "It seemed to me as though everything had now been cancelled, as though everything else [written by Brunner] was now pointless." Barth, the bellwether Protestant theologian of the twentieth century, quoted that disdainful criticism of his Swiss colleague, and gave it his endorsement.[191] The imperative to accept the virginal conception of Jesus is stressed in some commentaries. For example, Charles Briggs, in discussing the so-called Apostles' Creed, devotes six

---

[189]J. Gresham Machen, *The Virgin Birth of Christ* (New York: Harper, 1930) 390, 395.

[190]Henry Morris, *The Battle for Creation* (San Diego: Creation-Life, 1976) 308.

[191]Karl Barth, *Church Dogmatics* (New York: Scribner's, 1956) 1.2.184.

times as many pages to defending it as to considering the forgiveness of sins clause,[192] which reverses the emphasis of the New Testament.

Significance of the |ssue

The apostles held that Jesus was without sin because of his godly decisions and actions throughout his ministry. Judging from the New Testament, Paul and the other early missionaries never mentioned virginal conception, and accordingly it is not in the confessional statements of the apostolic church.[193] Catholic scholar John Noonan expresses a common error in stating that "one of the central facts of the New Testament [is] that Christ was born of a virgin."[194] Actually, as we have seen, the several verses that pertain to virginal conception have differing interpretations. Anglican theologian Claude Moss is also outspoken in asserting that anyone who does not believe that fact "cannot be a Christian at all."[195] But the alleged "virgin birth of Christ" is neither factual history nor germane theology. Significantly, the "Brief Statement of Faith" approved by the Presbyterian Church (USA) in 1991 affirms that Jesus was "fully human, fully God" but does not mention anything about his birth. Mennonite Gordon Kaufman rightly evaluates the virginity doctrine as a threat to the foundational Christian claim that God became human; a being cannot be truly called human without a biological father. That Harvard theologian shows how the doctrine deviates from the main purpose of the fifth-century Chalcedon Creed:

> It does not portray Jesus as either truly God or truly man: he is apparently half and half. A kind of pasted-together being, he not unreasonably is taken by many moderns to be simply a piece of fantastic and incredible mythology, rather than the one point within human history which is a genuine clue to ultimate reality, the very *man* who is the revelation of the very *God*.[196]

To make the alleged virginal conception of Jesus more palatable to reasonable Christians, furtive attempts have been made in the course of church history to interpret it in a nonsupernatural manner. Origen recog-

---

[192]Charles Briggs, *The Fundamental Christian Faith* (New York: Scribner, 1913).

[193]Philippians 2:11; 1 John 4:2.

[194]George Frein, ed., *Celibacy* (New York: Herder, 1968) 143.

[195]Claude Moss, *The Christian Faith* (London: SPCK, 1943) 115.

[196]Gordon Kaufman, *Systematic Theology* (New York: Scribner's, 1968) 203.

nized that parthenogenesis is a scientific fact for some animal species. If God has created vultures who can reproduce asexually, the Christian apologist argued, it is not incredible for such to happen in the human species.[197] Contemporary zoology provides additional evidence of eggs developing independently of sperm fertilization. Not only can insects and lizards reproduce without males, but scientists discovered in 2004 that parthenogenesis extends even to the mammalian classification that includes the human species.[198] Even though parthenogenesis is a natural though rare occurrence for some animals, how is this relevant to the doctrine of Jesus' virginal conception? Do not those who advocate it want to show that his conception was unique and unlike that of any other creature? Also, only female offspring have been found to be genetic possibilites in fatherless reproduction because only males can contribute the Y chromosome.

Mormon scholar Stephen Robinson has come up with another pseudo-scientific way of of explaining the status of Jesus. He "has 46 chromo-somes, like everyone else"—23 from God, and 23 from the Virgin Mary."[199] Since for the Church of the Latter-day Saints, God is a physical being, chromosome production presumably containing his DNA poses no diffi-culty to its doctrine.

Scientific objections to facets of Jesus' nativity stories in the Gospels can be reduced by understanding the biblical view of dual parenthood. That ancient outlook joins modern biology in rejecting human conception without physical male insemination. Its revival would result in a fuller recognition that divine activity does not exclude human cooperation. A rapprochement might be accomplished between the supernaturalist and the naturalist stances if both sides could accept the Hebrew idea that the dynamic Spirit of God need not circumvent the natural processes of creation in generating nature in its totality, or in generating Jesus in particular. This should be corrective to the supernaturalists who find the divine mainly in that which violates the Creator's work, as we know it. Those who can find nothing spiritual in carnal intercourse need to recall that the first blessing in the Bible is on marital sexuality. The frowning disapproval of sexual passion in the history of Western civilization has been influenced by those who have wrongly given an asexual interpretation to the relationship

---

[197]Origen, *Against Celsus* 1.37.
[198]*Discovery* (January 2005): 51.
[199]*The Week* (16 April 2007): 13.

between Mary and Joseph, and then have exalted them as models of holiness. Portraits of Joseph and Mary embracing are virtually absent in European iconography. He is pictured as an elderly gentleman who is literally out of touch with his young wife.

Conversely, the naturalist should see in a theory of dual parenthood that human endeavors need not exclude the divine presence. The theory illustrates a central claim of Paul, that "in all things God works for good with those who love him."[200] The God of the Bible is found more in the warp and woof of ordinary human life than in inexplicable extraordinary events. Human sexuality can be an arena for discerning God's love and mercy as well as a means of hedonistic gratification. The dual parenthood theory provides understanding that is more theologically adequate, more scientifically plausible, more literarily imaginative, and more historically sound than the polar positions that all too often have been evoked regarding Jesus' nativity. Those who champion this theory view his conception not as a case of *either* the Spirit giving life to Mary's ovum *or* a man's sperm fertilizing it. Rather Jesus was *both* the pure enfleshment of God *and* the complete human that was formed by the union of male and female genes.

The original purpose of the story of Mary conceiving Jesus with divine assistance was to make a positive claim about the Spirit, not a negative assertion about the flesh and biological reproduction. The story is on as different a level from the science of genetics as Genesis is from geology. The literary-historical investigation of Jesus' generation can be compared with the scientific treatments of human genesis. Until organic evolution was defended by Charles Darwin and others, the consensus judgment in Western civilization was that the birth of humankind came about a few thousand years ago when God specially intervened in nature to create Adam and his spouse.

Most well-educated Christians, Jews, and Muslims have come to realize that Darwin's theory of natural selection is compatible with the doctrine that God created the universe. Indeed, the origin of humanity as a distinct species by development from some lower form was regarded by Darwin himself as a beautiful expression of the Creator's order. Darwin, who graduated from Cambridge with a degree in theology, touches on this in the conclusions of his two major works. In rejecting the claim that God directly functions as a biochemical provider, he writes, "To my mind it accords

---

[200]Romans 8:28.

better with what we know of the laws impressed on matter by the Creator, that the production and extinction of the past and present inhabitants of the world should have been due to secondary causes." Drawing on philosophical theology, Darwin acknowledges God as the primary cause of life but dignifies scientific causation as the way in which God works in the world. He finds "grandeur" in the view that the Creator acts through biological regularity rather than by abrogating the natural order.[201] When God wants a great happening, fearsome thunderbolts are not released but a baby is naturally born to humble parents and grows up to express the divine will.

Darwin should be viewed as doing a service to religion by assisting in freeing the opening chapters of Genesis from a literalistic interpretation. The Creator can better be thought of as an immanent Spirit who is perennially creative through the chemical elements of nature rather than one who during six days actually spoke a few momentous words that formed all the present species. A *dual causality* is operative: God is understood as the ultimate cause of the universe and the distinctive spirit of man, but evolutionary process is recognized as the method by which life is created.[202] An adaptation of the postscript to Darwin's *Descent of Man* is in order:

> I am aware that the conclusions arrived at in this work will be denounced by some as highly irreligious; but he who denounces them is bound to show why it is more irreligious to explain the conception of Jesus through the laws of ordinary reproduction. The birth of individuals and species are equally part of that grand sequence of events that our minds refuse to accept as the result of blind chance.

The problems of reconciling evolutionary theory with the myth of the formation of the first humans have paralleled in time and place the attempts to harmonize science with the birth of the one whom Paul calls the "last Adam,"[203] the Hebrew idiom for the "ultimate human." The traditional theory of Jesus' conception, which was discussed intensely by European scholars in the nineteenth century, caused shock waves that hit fundamentalists in America during the first part of the twentieth century. Over the past generation the discussion and the accompanying heresy trials have

---

[201]Charles Darwin, *Origin of Species* (London, 1859) chap. 15; *Descent of Man* (London, 1871) chap. 21.

[202]William Phipps, *Darwin's Religious Odyssey* (Harrisburg PA: Trinity, 2002) 125-26, 197-99.

[203]1 Corinthians 15:45.

subsided, but unfortunately this is not due to Christians having become reconciled on the issue. A survey several decades ago of American Lutherans, not noted for extreme conservative views, discloses that belief in the virgin birth of Jesus was the most firmly held belief of the denomination. Only eight percent agreed with this dual parenthood statement: "Jesus is the supreme revelation of God to men, but he was conceived like anyone else. In a sense any child is divinely conceived."[204] According to a 2004 *Newsweek* poll, seventy-nine percent of adult Americans "say they believe in the virgin birth" of Jesus.[205]

Literalists trained in Western technology presume that for something to be a fact and not a fabrication it must be publicly observable to all present, whether religious or nonreligious. The categories of interpretations of the Gospels' virginal conception stories parallel those of Genesis' creation stories. About one-third of Americans (but only seven percent of Britons)[206] treat those accounts about all organic species being created in several days as factual history, to be taken seriously and literally. A similar proportion treat them as primitive fairy tales, not to be taken seriously or literally. They find it silly to think of God strolling in Eden to talk with creatures he had made of mud. The other third treat the stories as imaginative treatments of timeless concerns, to be taken seriously but not literally.[207] Surveys of contemporary Americans cause one to wonder if Americans should generally be thought of as a scientifically oriented culture because more believe in the nonbiological conception of Jesus than in biological evolution. But some shift in the comprehension of biblical texts is evident; in 2006, twenty-eight percent of Americans polled by Gallup expressed belief that the Bible is literally true, down from thirty-eight percent thirty years earlier.[208]

The comprehension of religious and poetic literature is perennially distorted by those who equate thinking seriously with thinking literally. To them, myths are necessarily false because they are fictions. Truth is equated

---

[204]Merton Strommen et al., *A Study of Generations* (Minneapolis: Augsburg, 1972) 379.

[205]*Newsweek* (13 December 2004): 51.

[206]*The Public Perspective* (August 1998): 41.

[207]George Gallup and D. Michael Lindsay, *Surveying the Religious Landscape: Trends in U.S. Beliefs* (Harrisburg PA: Morehouse, 1999) 35-36.

[208]*Time* (12 June 2006): 21.

with matter-of-fact prosaic data that can actually or potentially be sensed. The literalist is the ancestor of the mechanical computer; both process, store and retrieve information but are incapable of responding to figurative nuances. Literal-minded persons, whether they live in a prescientific ancient culture or in a technological modern culture, presume that words make sense when they point to what is out there in physical world. Thus, devils, hell, paradise, and the like have reality to the extent that they are objective and external. Teachers of "dead poets" struggle continually with students who relegate imaginative thinking to the closet of outgrown childhood things.

Robinson comments on the birth story of Jesus:

> Myth has its perfectly legitimate, and indeed profoundly important, place. The myth is there to indicate the significance of the events, the divine depth of the history. And we shall be grievously impoverished if our ears cannot tune to the angels' song or our eyes are blind to the wise men's star. But we must be able to read the nativity story without assuming that its truth depends on there being a literal interruption of the natural by the supernatural, that Jesus can only be Emmanuel—God with us—if, as it were, he came through from another world.[209]

If Christians do not understand the way in which the Bible presumes a dual view of origins, much theological confusion can result. Consider the way in which the Bible is declared from pulpits to be the "Word of God." A child might imagine that the book is composed of occasional sound bites from heaven booming down to scare or to direct people. The scriptural collection might better be explained as the outcome of both human and divine viewpoints. In the child's catechism I memorized, "God" is the one word answer to the first question, "Who made you?" I believed this but also realized that my parents were involved in my creation, and no attempt was made by them to direct me to think otherwise. They dignified my existence by teaching me that every child was a special gift from God, but they did not deceive me by asserting that they did not have an essential part in my creation. Unless children are encouraged to juxtapose the different ways of expressing theological and biological meaning, when they grow up they may come to think of either religious or scientific statements as false.

---

[209]John Robinson, *Honest to God* (Philadelphia: Westminster, 1963) 67-68.

To separate Jesus' life either before birth or after death from the general human condition poses a core Christological problem. If there was a unique conception and resurrection for Jesus that was categorically different from those of other mortals, how can it be said that Jesus was fully human like us? Was the one who called himself the "Son of Man" actually the son of no man? Isaiah observed that all flesh perishes like grass, but was Jesus' flesh uncorrupted by the grave? The earliest Christians had little difficulty in accepting Jesus as both the son of Joseph and the Son of God, but later theologians, influenced by pagan asceticism, engaged in historical fabrications to eliminate Joseph from the God-husband-wife triangle.

The attempt to exclude the male participation in conception did not thereby raise the stature of women. Catholic theologian Jane Schaberg treats the asexual Mary of church history as a manifestation of entrenched sexism. Perceptively she writes:

> Defined as wholly unique, she is set up as a model of womanhood that is unattainable. As the male projection of idealized femininity, a patriarchal construction, she is the good woman, stripped of all dangerous elements; she receives worship, not equality. . . . The shadow side of the glorification of the passive and dependent Virgin Mary is the denigration of women. Carl Jung comments that the consequence of increasing Mariolatry in the later Middle Ages was the witch hunt. The Mary myth reduces woman to something less than a whole human being.[210]

* * *

Two outstanding Americans have envisioned the outcome of this virginal conception idea in different ways, reflecting the range of opinions still in circulation. Mary Baker Eddy, the founder of the Christian Science church, believed that physical sexuality is metaphysically unreal. She admired the "virgin mother" of Jesus, and called him "the offspring of Mary's self-conscious communion with God." Eddy thought of his parthenogenesis as a step toward all people becoming exclusively God's incorporeal children.[211] She wrote, "When we understand man's true birthright, that he is 'born, not . . . of the will of the flesh, nor of the will of man, but of God,' we shall . . . regard him as spiritual, and not material."[212]

---

[210]Schaberg, *The Illegitimacy of Jesus*, 12-13.

[211]Mary Baker (Glover) Eddy, *Science and Health with Key to the Scriptures* (Boston: First Church of Christ, Scientist, 1875) 29-30, 64-69.

[212]Mary Baker Eddy, *Miscellaneous Writings* (Boston, 1896) 181; John 1:13.

While president of the United States, Thomas Jefferson extracted and pasted in a notebook the teachings of Jesus from the Gospels that he thought were authentic, and discarded obfuscating supernatural stories. America's prime exemplar of the Englightenment era sanguinely asserted, "Had the doctrines of Jesus been preached always as pure as they came from his lips, the whole civilized world would now have been Christian."[213] He wrote John Adams: "In the New Testament there is internal evidence that parts of it have proceeded from an extraordinary man; and that other parts are the fabric of very inferior minds. It is as easy to separate those parts, as to pick out diamonds from dunghills."[214] He also expressed to Adams his hope for the end of the long night of superstition that is exemplified by what he considered to be the virgin mother oxymoron:

> The truth is, that the greatest enemies to the doctrines of Jesus are those, calling themselves the expositors of them, who have perverted them for the structure of a system of fancy absolutely incomprehensible, and without any foundation in His genuine words. And the day will come when the mystical generation of Jesus, by the Supreme Being as His Father, in the womb of a virgin, will be classed with the fable of the generation of Minerva in the brain of Jupiter. But we may hope that the dawn of reason, and freedom of thought in these United States, will do away all this artificial scaffolding, and restore to us the primitive and genuine doctrines of this most venerated Reformer of human errors.[215]

---

[213]Letter to Benjamin Waterhouse, 26 June 1822, in Allen Jayne, ed., *The Religious and Moral Wisdom of Thomas Jefferson* (New York: Vantage, 1984) 32.

[214]Letter to John Adams, 24 January 1814, in ibid., 18-19.

[215]Jefferson to Adams, 11 April 1823, in ibid., 31.

Chapter 3
Astral and Angelic Agencies

For at least as long as recorded history, humans in many global cultures have been fascinated by alleged astral deities and angelic messengers. The assumption has been that those spirits have the power to forecast and control the successes and disasters of earthlings. Since warmth and rain are essential for organic life—but too much of either can result in catastrophic droughts or floods—sky gods have been especially associated with weather phenomena. Christianity has been among those religions affected by astrology and the frequently related angelology.

Astrology and Magic

Like all ancients, the Sumerians believed that circumstances making for human happiness and unhappiness were masterminded from above. They shared the common ancient geocentric cosmology in which a firm astrodome rested on the mountains at the earth's perimeter. That first Mesopotamian civilization presumed that the resplendent objects seen in the sky willfully controlled happenings in their valley. Consequently they made celestial observations and established what they believed to be a causal relationship between the positions of those heavenly bodies and particular happenings in the lives of individuals. Anthropomorphic characteristics were attributed especially to the sun, moon, and five visible planets. Their continual movement in the firmament was believed to be due to their self-determining personalities.

Some four thousand years ago, the Babylonians became the dominant civilization in Mesopotamia, adopting much of the Sumerian culture. The Babylonians continued the fascination with the alleged astral deities who could determine human destiny.[1] Their tall ziggurat temples served as observatories for priests to trace celestial movements. The earliest concerns of the trained skygazers centered on what was most obvious, the sun and the moon, but the planets and the more prominent fixed stars also captured their attention. God *Shamash* was associated with the sun, *Yarah* with the moon, *Marduk* with Jupiter, and *Ishtar* with Venus. Divination was made after some data from of these personified bodies was obtained by careful obser-

---

[1] Morris Jastrow, *The Religion of Babylonia and Assyria* (Boston: Ginn, 1898) 356-73.

vation. For example, one omen text states that a lunar eclipse will bring destruction if it takes place in the first month of the year, but prosperity if it happens in the fourth month.[2] Out of simple predictions such as this, a complicated zodiacal system of mapping the firmament developed. The Babylonians made detailed horoscopes, believing that the position of the heavenly bodies at the time of an individual's birth determined that person's destiny. One horoscope, found inscribed on stone, reads, "Mercury in [the constellation] Gemini means that he will have sons and daughters."[3]

When the Persians conquered Mesopotamia in the sixth century BCE, they carried on the astrology of the earlier local cultures. The military success of the Persians against the Babylonians drove them to fight their way further westward, all the way to Greece. Mesopotamian astrology then entered into European civilization by way of the Greeks. Athenian philosopher Plato, who lived shortly after the Persians occupied countries of the eastern Mediterranean, learned from them the astral speculations that Mesopotamians had evolved over millennia. In setting up his three-tiered heaven, Plato placed the capricious Olympians first in the chain of beings, in deference to his Hellenic tradition. They actually function as emeriti deities because the second-ranked divine spirits who animate the celestial bodies are "the greatest, most worshipful and clear-sighted of them all." The orderly way they act signified for Plato their sublime intelligence.

From Plato's third rank come "the spirits and the creatures of the air" that flit about the earth. He advised that they "should be peculiarly honored in our prayers so they may transmit comfortable messages." Since each airy spirit (*daimon*) is "intermediate between the divine and the mortal," it "interprets between gods and men, conveying and taking across to the gods the prayers and sacrifices of men, and to men the commands and replies of the gods."[4] "God has no contact with man," Plato affirmed, so the diverse spirits are "mediators who span the chasm that divide them."[5]

Plato's doctrine of reincarnation also involves astrology. The universe has souls equal in number to stars, so each soul is assigned before birth to

---

[2]Jastrow, *The Religion of Babylonia and Assyria*, 458-59; S. H. Hooke, *Babylonian and Assyrian Religion* (Norman: University of Oklahoma Press, 1963) 94-95.

[3]*Journal of Cuneiform Studies* (1952): 60.

[4]Plato, *Epinomis*, 984.

[5]Plato, *Symposium*, 202-203.

a star. At death, the soul of the good person returns to its native star to prepare for recycling.[6]

After the Greek conquest of much of Asia, led by Alexander of Macedonia, "the conqueror was conquered." A torrent then developed from the trickle of Mesopotamian astrology that had affected the cogitation of earlier Greeks. Classicist Gilbert Murray describes its impact in this way, "Astrology fell upon the Hellenistic mind as a new disease falls upon some remote island people."[7] Compared with the irrational conduct of the traditional Greek Olympian pantheon, the star gods appeared to behave more reasonably and they seemed to provide persons a key for unlocking their destiny. Chaldeans (or Babylonians), originally a designation of people in an empire west of the Persian Gulf, now became identified by Greek writers only with Mesopotamian astrologers. Theophrastus, a disciple of Aristotle who lived at the beginning of the Hellenistic era inaugurated by Alexander, stated that "the most extraordinary thing of his age was the lore of the Chaldeans, who foretold not only events of public interest but even the lives and deaths of individuals."[8] In the third century, access to Babylonian astrological texts was simplified by Berossus, a Babylonian priest, who translated them into Greek. He popularlized astrology in the Greco-Roman culture when he set up a school on the Aegean island of Kos.

Among the several Hellenistic schools of philosophy, Stoicism was the most affected by the foreign astral virus. The Stoics admired astrology because it provided a universal framework for their philosophical theology. Zeno, the Stoic founder, and his successors found in it a reinforcement of their belief in pantheism and fate. No longer did they need to appeal to local city gods, as had been done in the traditional Greek culture. In his study of the relationship between astrology and religion in the Greco-Roman culture, Franz Cumont states:

> Beneath the lowest sphere, that of the moon, the zones of the elements are placed in tiers: the zones of fire, air, water, and earth. To these four principles, as well as to the constellations, the Greeks gave the name of *stoicheia*, and the Chaldeans already worshipped the one as well as the other. The influence of Oriental religions, like that of Stoic cosmology, spread throughout the West the

[6]Plato, *Timaeus*, 41-42.
[7]Gilbert Murray, *Five Stages of Greek Religion* (New York: Doubleday, 1955) 177-78.
[8]Proclus, *On Timaeus*, 285.

worship of these four bodies, believed to be elements, whose infinite variety of combinations gave rise to all perceptible phenomena.[9]

The astrology that had been a spoil of war imported into Greece from western Asia became, centuries later, a spoil that the Romans brought back from their conquest of Greece. John Ferguson states that "this tyranny of superstition," which flourished in pagan Rome during the empire era, was fostered by the Stoics and Platonists.[10] On celestial movements, asserted leading Roman Stoic Seneca, "depend the destinies of peoples; the greatest and the smallest events are shaped by their malign or favoring influence."[11] The Caesars had astrologers among their advisers whom they frequently consulted on public and private matters. After receiving a favorable forecast from one astrologer, "Augustus had such confidence in his destiny that he made his horoscope public and issued a silver coin featuring the symbol of the Capricorn sign under which he was born."[12] Emperors Tiberius and Nero were similarly convinced, and "Titus was haunted by his horoscope."[13] Domitian worried throughout life about the precise prediction by an astrologer of the hour of his death. When that day approached he executed some of his servants in order to avert his doom by those possible agents. However, conspirators assisted the doctrine of fate by assassinating that Caesar just at the hour he most dreaded.[14] Lawrence Jerome writes, "It was the Romans who most developed and believed in fatalistic astrology, so by the middle of the second century A. D. emperors of the Roman Empire literally lived and died according to the 'dictates of the stars'."[15]

Senator Cicero, who lived a century before Christianity arrived in Rome, was one of the few Roman leaders scornful of astrology. He separated it from rational religion in his essay entitled *Divination*, "Just as it is a duty to extend the influence of true religion which is closely associated

---

[9]Franz Cumont, *Astrology and Religion among the Greeks and Romans* (New York: Dover, 1960) 121.

[10]John Ferguson, *The Religions of the Roman Empire* (Ithaca NY: Cornell University Press, 1970) 154.

[11]Seneca, *Consolation to Marcia*, 16.

[12]Suetonius, *Lives of the Caesars* 2.94.12.

[13]Dio Cassius, *History* 57.15.7-9; Jack Linsay, *Origins of Astrology* (London, 1971) 293.

[14]Suetonius, *Lives* 8:14-17.

[15]Lawrence Jerome, *Astrology Disproved* (Buffalo NY: Prometheus, 1977) 30.

with the knowledge of nature, so it is a duty to weed out every root of superstition."[16] After showing the futility of a number of other popular superstitions—such as necromancy, dream revelation, forecasting from entrail examination, and prophesying by frenzied seers—he turned to an examination of astrology. Cicero respected the infant science of astronomy, which had predicted eclipses, but "incredible madness" was his judgment of the pseudoscientific claim that an individual's temperament and career is determined by the position of planets on that person's birthday. Cicero concluded his devastating criticisms of astrology with this observation:

> Is it no small error of judgment that the Chaldeans fail to realize the effect of the parental seed? . . . No one fails to see that the appearance and habits, and generally, the carriage and gestures of children are derived from their parents. This would not be the case if the characteristics of children were determined, not by the natural power of heredity, but by . . . the condition of the sky. . . . The fact that men who were born at the very same time are unlike in character, career, and in destiny makes it very clear that the time of birth has nothing to do in determining man's course in life.[17]

Tacitus, who lived in the first century CE when astrology was at its peak in Rome, indicates that it affected ordinary citizens as well as Caesar's court. "Most people," he admitted, "cannot part with the belief that each person's future is fixed from his very birth."[18] He had in mind astral fixation, not determination by genes or by wealth and influence of family. Historian Karl Baus writes that both low and high class Romans, "even in the simple and commonplace affairs of everyday life, . . . consulted the stars with an almost slavish fear . . . and sooner or later fell victims to a gloomy fatalism, which found expression in many an epitaph of the time."[19] Even Claudius Ptolemy, whose geography was the most scientific of ancient times, wrote a treatise in which astrological lore is presented as fact. He asserted that one's character is determined by the planet in ascendancy at the time of one's birth, "Mars causes men to spit blood, makes them melancholy, weakens their lungs, and causes the itch or scurvy."[20] Vettius

---

[16]Cicero, *On Divination* 2.72.

[17]Cicero, *On Divination* 2.149.

[18]Tacitus, *Annals* 6.22.

[19]Hubert Jedin, ed., *Handbook of Church History* (New York: Herder, 1965) 1:94-95.

[20]Ptolemy, *Tetrabiblos* 3.12.

Valens, another writer at that time, stated, "Fate has decreed as a law for each person the unalterable consequences of his horoscope."[21]

Mithraism, a cult steeped in astrology, was one of the more popular religions in the Roman Empire. It was centered in solar deity Mithras, who had been worshiped by the Persians before the rise of Zoroastrianism. According to Mithraic doctrine, a devotee's soul ascends by means of a seven-rung astrological ladder in this order: Saturn, Venus, Jupiter, Mercury, Mars, the Moon, and the Sun. Each day of the week was marked by the adoration of one of those spheres.[22] A vestige of Mithraism is found in some of the names in European languages for the days of the week. Contemporary English terms such as sunny, lunatic, jovial, venereal, martial, saturnine, and mercurial are rooted in the Roman belief that the sun, moon, and the planets affect human temperament and behavior.

Christianity moved into Rome at the time when astrology was most pervasive. Certain days or periods were presumed to have been designated by star powers as times when certain kinds of actions were approved or forbidden. "The fear of these world rulers, particularly the Sun, the Moon, and the five planets, lay heavy on the old world. The Mysterious Seven held humanity in the mechanism of iron necessity."[23] This pagan fatalism caused people to attempt to transfer decisions about the future to forces separated from the human condition. A flight from responsibilities, and an authoritarian reliance on prognosticators, accompanied the belief that destiny is predetermined by divine spirits who make celestial bodies their abodes. Ernst Zinner comments:

> Christianity was founded at a time when it was customary to consult astrologers and other fortune tellers about any important decision. Men were caught up in a network of interrelations between heaven and earth and only the astrologers knew the correct relation. The latter for their part maintained that human activities were predetermined by the stars in their courses. Accordingly it was impossible for man to alter his fate.[24]

* * *

[21]Vettius Valens, *Anthologies* 5.9.2.

[22]Henry Chadwick, *Origen: Contra Celsum* (Cambridge: University Press, 1953) 334; Jerome, *Letters* 107.2.

[23]Edwyn Bevan, *Hellenism and Christianity* (London: Allen, 1921) 77.

[24]Ernst Zinner, *The Stars above Us* (New York: Scribner, 1957) 85.

Shifting attention now from pagan to Hebrew culture, we find that star powers are adamantly rejected in the Bible of the Israelites. They believed that "the heavens declare the glory of God,"[25] but that revelation was in natural appearances such as the orderliness of the seasons and the regular movements of the moon. The status of the celestial bodies is suggested by the symbolic opening chapter of Genesis. There the radiant Creator makes the sun, moon, and stars to provide additional light, but God does not get around to forming them until the latter part of the creative week. The low priority luminaries have only a physical function, and are no more divine than the plants created on the day before or the fish the day after. They are controlled by the one God who hangs them as lanterns on the sky vault, and they do not have power to control human destiny. Most other ancient peoples would have regarded this theology as radical, and would have been offended by its slighting of their primary deities. But the most basic tenet of the Hebrew religion from its very beginning and onward was their covenant with and allegiance to the one invisible God.

The Torah condemns consultation with diviners who predict events by gazing at the positions of planets.[26] Expressions of contempt for Mesopotamian star-god devotion found elsewhere in the Hebrew Bible include an indictment against Manasseh, a king of Judea, because he "worshiped all the host of heaven."[27] Living during the Babylonian dominatation of western Asia, he participated in augury that was internationally popular but prohibited by Jewish law. Later, a prophet to the Babylonian exiles taunted his captors, "Let your astrologers come forward and save you, those who gaze at the stars, who tell you from month to month what is going to happen to you."[28]

The second-century BCE Book of Daniel shows disdain for "the magicians, the enchanters, the Chaldeans, and the diviners" on whom a Mesopotamian king relied for wisdom.[29] Jewish literature during that Hellenistic era claimed that Abraham of Ur rejected his Chaldean astrology heritage and recognized the futility of looking for signs in the sky.[30]

---

[25]Psalm 19:1.
[26]Deuteronomy 4:19.
[27]2 Kings 21:3.
[28]Isaiah 47:13.
[29]Daniel 4:7.
[30]*Jubilees* 12:16-18.

Because he pledged homage to God alone who controls celestial phenomena, Abraham was scorned in his native country. "It was in fact owing to
these opinions that the Chaldeans and the other peoples of Mesopotamia
rose against him, and he, thinking it fit to emigrate, at the will and with the
aid of God, settled in the land of Canaan."[31] The boast was made that the
descendants of that patriarch have also refrained from "such things as
witless men are searching out day by day" in "Chaldean astrology."[32] Greek
philosopher Celsus, in the second century of the Christian era, wrote a
diatribe against biblical "superstitions" yet he faults the Jews because "they
reject paying homage to its [heaven's] most sacred parts, namely the sun,
moon, and the other stars—both fixed and mobile." He believed that they
are "beings who foretell the future so clearly" by telling "all the productivity of nature." But the Jews treat as worthless "the clearest proof of the
divinity above us."[33]

In spite of the polemics against astrology in the Hebrew Bible and in
subsequent Jewish literature, some Jews did accept the dominant pagan
Greco-Roman belief that planets influence earthly affairs. James Charlesworth, an expert on intertestamental Palestinian culture, tells of several
excavated synagogues that contain prominent zodiac mosaics. A Jewish
writing of the first century BCE asserts, "Everyone born in Scorpio will
survive birth, but will be killed at the end of the year."[34] Charlesworth states
that "astrology had become attractive to, and made an impression upon,
numerous Jews during the Hellenistic and Roman periods."[35]

The earliest Christians were in accord with their Hebrew heritage in
rejecting the prevailing focus on astrology. Georg Luck, after a detailed
study of the occult in the Greco-Roman world, concluded that he found "no
evidence that Jesus and his disciples believed in the power of the stars."[36]
The first code of Christian ethics states: "Do not be an enchanter or an

[31]Josephus, *Antiquities* 1.155-57.
[32]*The Sibyline Books* 3.219-36.
[33]Celsus, *True Doctrine* (New York: Oxford University Press, 1987) 85-86.
[34]*Treatise of Shem*, 8.
[35]*Harvard Theological Review* (July 1977): 193, 200.
[36]Georg Luck, *Arcana Mundi* (Baltimore: Johns Hopkins University Press, 1985) 314.

astrologer or a magician. Moreover, have no wish to observe or heed such practices, for all this breeds idolatry."[37]

Paul regarded astrological phenomenon perilous because it was thought to determine destiny. He referred to the Galatians' bondage to the "cosmic elements" (*stoicheia*) prior to their liberation by Christ. The apostle was chagrined that some gullible Christians were regressing into hallowing auspicious days and thereby serving *stoicheia* they presumed to be divine. As we have seen, many pagans believed that each of the seven known astral bodies in the solar system had power to determinine events on one of the seven days of a week. Paul writes chidingly about such constricting astrology:

> When we were immature we were enslaved to the cosmic elements. . . . But now that you know God . . . how can you turn back to those weak and pitiful elements? Why do you want to serve them again? You are scrupulous about certain days, months, seasons, and years. I am afraid that my work with you has been wasted.[38]

Paul would have been unperturbed by the "ides of March," associated with the predicted assassination of Julius Caesar, or by any other alleged ominous day on the Roman calendar. He was acutely aware of the presence of evil in the world, but he maintained that its source was human misuse of freedom. The apostle's stance is articulated by the trenchant words Shakespeare put on the lips of Caesar, "The fault, . . . is not in our stars, but in ourselves."[39] The main theme of the Galatian letter continues to have relevance for the many Christians who have been captivated by perennially popular astrology. "For freedom, Christ liberated us," the apostle declared; "Stand firm, then, and do not submit again to the yoke of slavery."[40]

The fatalism that holds that future events have been destined to occur by transcendent forces strips humans of self-determination. The early Christians recognized the futility of calling people to repent if they are not mainly responsible for their own character and conduct. The New Testament is abundantly supplied with praise for those who make moral choices, and with criticism of those who neglect to do their Christian duty. This, of

---

[37]*Didache* 3:4.
[38]Galatians 4:3, 9-11.
[39]Shakespeare, *Julius Caesar* (1599) 1.2.18, 139.
[40]Galatians 5:1.

course, presumes that people have free will and that their every act has not been previously decided.

* * *

Magi, a Greek term that has been transliterated into English, is the root of "magician," but ancient magicians should be distinguished from modern entertainers who share their name. Sleight-of-hand artists today only pretend to believe in supernatural forces that they can coerce, and their audiences look to them for no more than mystifying tricks. But the original magicians usually believed that such forces were real, as did their clients.

Greek historian Herodotus traces the term "magic" to one of the tribes of the Persians, the *magoi*, who flourished several millennia ago.[41] They belonged to Persia's Zoroastrian religion and were deemed wise by those who believed that they could describe causal connections between configurations of heavenly bodies and human happenings. Their continued prominence centuries later is displayed in one of the earliest charming Christmas stories. According to Matthew, "*magoi* from the East" followed a moving star to Palestine in search of the Jewish king it portended. Christians generally have a sentimental attachment to ancient magi because of that New Testament passage. Jacques Duquesne explains:

> The Jews had long hated astrologers because God and the prophets had condemned them, and what is more, these came from the East, as had the Chaldean troops who had frequently invaded Judaea, pillaging and murdering. But opinions had altered somewhat. Astrology was so seductive, and the desire to know the future so strong. . . . Over the years, and especially at the time that Matthew's Gospel was composed, astrologers of every sort had begun to get a better press.[42]

The ancient Jews were aware of magi and comet stories. One of their legends (*midrashim*) tells about a Pharoah and his magi in the generation before the Israelite exodus. The Egyptian magi predicted that the child of a then pregnant woman would save the people of Israel and subdue the king of Egypt. Pharoah became alarmed and ordered every male drowned who was born during the next year.[43] Another story is about a Gentile sage and

---

[41]Herodotus, *History* 1.140.
[42]Jacques Duquesne, *Jesus* (Liguori MO: Triumph, 1996) 49.
[43]Midrash, Exodus 1:18; Josephus, *Antiquities* 2:205.

a star. The book of Numbers tells of a diviner named Balaam "from the East," who predicted that a "comet will arise from Israel."[44] In the second century BCE, a Jewish writing contains this oracle pertaining to Maccabean priest John Hyrcanus, "Then shall the Lord raise up a new priest, and to him all the words of the Lord shall be revealed; . . . and his star shall rise in heaven as of a king."[45] Shortly before the coming of Christianity, the scripturally forecasted astral body was associated in Judaism with a messianic teacher.[46] Thus, the Jews, despite their long tradition of rejecting astrology, were influenced by surrounding cultures to think of strange heavenly apparitions as heralding the birth of someone destined to be prominent. During the Roman era especially, Jews tended to interpret unusual appearances in the sky as signs that a righteous leader would replace their treacherous Jewish rulers.

The unknown writer of the Gospel known as Matthew skillfully wove magi into a story that blended a comet with religion and royalty. Living some decades after Jesus, he or she was probably stimulated by two remarkable happenings in the year 66, namely the sighting of a bright comet and a visit of Asian magi to Caesar. Those events were combined with Jewish lore to produce a nativity narrative imbued with religious meaning. During the last decades of the first century this story was placed near the beginning of Matthew's Gospel, and has ever since been for many a source of wonder.

Astronomers agree that what has come to be called Halley's comet, with its period of 75 to 79 years, orbited near the earth in 66 CE and 77 years earlier. Roman writer Dio Cassius described the way Halley's comet looked when viewed from Rome in 12 BCE, "The star called the hairy one hung for several days over the city."[47] When Seneca wrote about astronomy near the time of Halley's appearance in 66, he observed that comets caught the attention of people who were blind to other unusual stellar phenomena. The Roman statesman wrote, "They are not quite sure whether to admire or fear the celestial newcomer; some people inspire terror by forecasting its grave import."[48] It was widely viewed that year because there are both Chinese

[44]Numbers 24:17 REB.

[45]*Testament of Levi* 18:3.

[46]Qumran, *The War of the Sons of Light* 11:6.

[47]Dio Cassius, *History*, 54.

[48]Seneca, *Natural Questions*, 7:1.

and Jewish records of the apparition. At the outset of the Jewish rebellion against Rome, Josephus described "a comet resembling a sword hanging over Jerusalem."[49] After a lengthy siege, Jerusalem was destroyed in the year 70. It is understandable that Josephus, writing shortly after its fall, would interpret the comet's luminous trail of gases and dust as an ominous sign that his capital city would be put to the sword. The writer of Matthew's nativity story may have recalled his grandparents telling him of the previous appearance of that flamboyant comet during the reign of Herod the Great prior to Jesus' birth.

Christians have presumed over the centuries that the Christmas "star" was a comet. Origen, a leading scholar of the early church, was the first to take what was then known of astronomy and relate it to the star story at the beginning of the New Testament. Writing some years after the appearance of Halley's comet in the year 218, which he may have seen, he suggests that "the star which appeared in the east . . . is to be classed with the comets which occasionally occur."[50] Italian artist Giotto was so stimulated by the 1301 appearance of Halley's comet that he featured it when he painted a Bethlehem nativity scene. A comet with a fiery beard dominates the sky in his "Adoration of the Magi" fresco at the Padua chapel. Joseph Lagrange reported in 1910 on what was seen in Jerusalem, "When Halley's comet passed from East to West, everyone was able to observe how its light dispersed over to the West where, after a day or two, it began to shine again." This phenomenon caused that Dominican biblical scholar to speculate that the Christmas star was "probably a comet" and that ancient people would have considered it to presage "some glorious reign that was about to take place."[51]

The terrestrial event in the year 66 that may have inspired the Christmas storyteller was a journey of magi from the Middle East to Rome. Their westward trek was motivated at least as much by politics as by their interpretation of an appearance of Halley's comet. Suetonius, Pliny, and Dio Cassius regarded the trip of these magi important enough to record in their Roman histories.[52] According to their accounts, "Tiridates the magus"—

[49]Josephus, *Wars* 6:289.

[50]Chadwick, *Origen: Contra Celsum*, 53.

[51]Joseph Lagrange, *The Gospel of Jesus Christ* (Westminster MD: Newman, 1938) 1:44.

[52]Suetonius, *Nero*, 13; Pliny, *Natural History* 30.3; Dio Cassius, *History*, 62-

along with a retinue of other magi—went to visit Emperor Nero. Writing a decade after this event, Pliny explained that the journey to Italy was overland because "the magi hold it a sin to spit in the sea or wrong that element by other necessary functions of mortal creatures." Claiming descent from the founder of the Persian empire, Tiridates hoped Nero would recognize him as the rightful ruler of the Asian nation. To obtain this favor, Tiridates paid homage to images of Nero. Then, falling at Nero's feet, he said, "I have come to you, my god, to worship you as I do Mithras." In appreciation of this fawning reverence, Nero replied: "By meeting with me face to face, you enjoy my grace. I now declare you to be the King of Armenia." Afterward there was a lavish banquet at which Nero played his lyre and sang. The magi then boarded a ship to return to Asia, in spite of their taboo against sea travel. "Matthew" may well have known about this visit of magi from Iran to Rome. Both the Gospel and the Roman accounts conclude by reporting that magi "fell down and worshiped" the ruler they had traveled far to find, and that they then returned by another route to their own country.

Tacitus attributed to Nero the first Roman persecution of Christians. Using them as scapegoats to transfer the blame he was receiving for burning buildings at his capital to provide space for his own constructions, he accused them of arson. Consequently, in the year 64 many of the nonconforming Christians were tortured while being executed.[53] In Palestine, meanwhile, the festering revolt of the Jews against Roman oppression was coming to a head. Among both Jews and Christians there was then an enormous longing for a leader who would overthrow the oppressive Romans. Hermann Usener suggests, "The reign of Nero may have been exactly the period at which the legends of the divine birth of Jesus began to take shape in the Christian world, and it is very possible that tidings of the Neronic persecution spread from Rome may have had their share in bringing about the introduction of the picture of a bloodthirsty tyrant into the story of the childhood."[54] "Matthew" was probably also aware of scriptural forecasts of Israel's restoration. Isaiah had told of foreign visitors from Asia to Jerusalem, "Nations shall come to your light,

63.

[53]Tacitus, *Annals*, 15:44.

[54]"Nativity," *Encyclopaedia Biblica* (New York: Macmillan, 1902).

and kings . . . shall bring gold and frankincense, praising the Lord."[55] The Gospel writer likewise may have regarded Jesus as the fulfillment of Psalm 72, which tells of tributes being brought internationally to a Jewish king who is an advocate for the poor. A king from Arabia, who brings gold, is among kings who come to Israel to bow down before a fellow monarch.

The legend about Egyptian magi prophesying the rise of a Jewish deliverer who would overpower an oppressive Pharoah might also have been known by the Christian nativity writer. Occasionally Jesus is viewed in the Gospels as a Moses-like liberator, so it would be as fitting for a story of Jesus—as it was for a story of Moses—to tell of a child arising from outside the court nobility who is destined to triumph over "the powers that be." The ruthless opposition to the promised redeemer is graphically depicted by the story of Herod's "slaughter of the innocents," an action that echoes Pharoah's attempt to destroy every male infant born to the Israelites.

The writer who blended these strands into the variegated infant Jesus story was not concerned with historical literalism. At Jerusalem the magi were informed that the village of Bethlehem, a few miles away, was the forecasted place for the messiah's birth, so the star's only directional function was to point out the precise place where Jesus was housed. It is unlikely that the Evangelist expected his readers to believe that a star actually moved out in front of the magi and then "came to rest over the place where the child lay."[56] This account belonged then to the realm of poetry even as the tale of Santa's sleigh stopping on the roofs of all good children does now. Also, had Herod actually "killed all the male children in Bethlehem and in all that region who were two years old or under" after Jesus' birth,[57] it is incredible that contemporary historians would not at least have alluded to that atrocity. Josephus records Herod's reign rather fully, including some cruel acts motivated by jealousy of possible rivals. However, that Jewish historian tells of nothing approaching the madness that would cause, or the civil unrest that would result from a regional massacre of many infants among his own subjects over many months.

Of course, historicity is not intrinsic to truth. For example, Shakespeare's "Julius Caesar" may reveal the emperor's character better than Plutarch's factual chronicle of his life. A subtle religious and political

---

[55]Isaiah 60:3, 6.
[56]Matthew 2:9.
[57]Matthew 2:16.

message seems to be hidden beneath the fascinating Christmas story in Matthew. Its creator apparently found Nero repulsive, along with some other Roman emperors, not only because they arrogated to themselves divine status, but because they persecuted those who refused to participate in Roman civil religion. This storyteller saw those rulers as contemporary expressions of the tyrannical Pharoahs and the sinister Herods of the past. The moral is transparent: sovereigns worthy of a heavenly sign and earthly adoration are altogether different from the haughty rulers of history. They rise from humble circumstances and triumph over persecution with a gospel of love.

Not long after Jesus' death, efforts were made by Christians to ascribe a higher social status to the former Galilean. Attempts at such elevation can be detected in the Gospels, for Jesus' nativity legends display a desire to identify him with Jewish royalty. Luke declares that Mary's son "will reign over the house of Jacob forever."[58] In Matthew's lore, foreign astrologers come to Judea, asking "Where is the child who has been born king of the Jews?" That Evangelist was satisfied that the answer to the magi's question could be found in Micah's prophecy that a new ruler would come from King David's town.[59]

Both nativity stories in the Gospels are more about political theology than about supernatural portents. Matthew, by portraying those presumed to be scholars as bowing before Jesus, seems to be making a statement that sages internationally recognize that a true ruler is not to be found among the tyrants who dominanted contemporary governments. Similarly, Luke begins his story with the only reference to Octavian Caesar in the New Testament. Wielding the greatest secular power of any ruler in ancient history, his birthday in August (the month named for the reverential title given him by the Roman Senate) was commemorated as "the beginning of the good news" in the world. He was known as the "Savior of mankind."[60] But Luke transfers the title "Savior" to one who would become a deliverer and king of a different type. In a not so subtle way, the Evangelist also associates

---

[58]Luke 1:33.

[59]Matthew 2:1-6.

[60]Josephus, *Antiquities* 16.105; "Augustus," *The Interpreter's Dictionary of the Bible* (Nashville: Abingdon, 1962).

birthday "good news" with one born in a culture that the Romans despised.[61]

* * *

The outlook on astrology in church history has varied from complete rejection to total acceptance. The last biblical book is the one that most delves into astrology. Jack Linsay notes:

> Early Christians could not easily disentangle themselves from the elements of astrology pervading their environment, especially those elements that had become imbedded in popular culture. Revelation is full of astrological ingredients as shown by the frequency of astral images and the stress on numerology, with seven and twelve especially prominent.[62]

In Revelation, "star" (Greek, *aster*) is used more frequently than in all other New Testament books combined. "A great star" named Wormwood falls from the sky, causing catastrophic poisoning of waters, but evenually Jesus, "the bright morning star" will triumph.[63]

Church father Tertullian found no truth in astrology and taught that the magi of the nativity story should not be honored as its patrons. According to Matthew, after they worshiped Jesus they had a dream warning them to avoid the route by which they came to Bethlehem. Tertullian interpreted that dream to mean that God directed them to forsake the ancient path of astrological studies.[64] Hippolytus wrote a chapter about astrologu in his book pertaining to false beliefs, saying that "the futile art is calculated both to deceive and blind the soul."[65] A century later, the first Christian emperor officially ousted astrology, along with some other features of pagan Roman culture. Constantine issued an edit in 321 threatening all astrologers with death.

As a youth, Augustine had been a follower of Mani who believed that stars controlled humans, but after converting to Christianity he developed an antipathy toward the prognostications of astrologers. Late in life he devoted nine chapters of *City of God*, his magnum opus, to excoriating

---

[61]Luke 2:1, 10-11.
[62]Linsay, *Origins of Astrology*, 395-96.
[63]Revelation 8:10-11; 22:16.
[64]Tertullian, *On Idolatry*,   9.
[65]Hippolytus, *The Refutation of All Heresies* 4.2.

astrology. He came to realize that the presumed wisdom of astrologers is due to the chance occurrence of a few of the many things they foretell.[66] The Bishop of Hippo advised worshipers to reject the deceptive claim that one's fate is determined by the particular position of the stars at the time of conception or birth. Twins who are generated at the same time often display great differences in their achievements, illnesses, and deaths. To illustrate this, he told of Jacob and Esau—"twins born so near together that the second held the first by the heel; yet the difference in their lives, manners, and actions made them enemies of one another."[67] Augustine rejected the astrology that Stoics had championed, finding it particularly odious because it posits that even God is controlled by blind and impersonal forces. Also, human responsibility is incompatible with the astrological dogma that destiny is fixed by fate.[68] His attack on astrology resulted in its condemnation by the Councils of Toledo and Graga, and in its loss of influence for some centuries.

Interest in astrology revived in the Middle Ages when Muslims brought philosophy from the Eastern Mediterranean into Spain.[69] Although astrology has not been a major theme in church history, it has had some distinguished supporters. English scholastic Roger Bacon believed that horoscopes legitimately associated the rise of the Hebrew religion and the Christian church with conjunctions of planets.[70] Aquinas, a thirteenth-century contemporary of Bacon, found no certainty in horoscopes but he did claim that astrology contained truth:

> The majority of men, in fact, are governed by their passions, which are dependent upon bodily appetites, in these the influence of the stars is clearly felt. Few indeed are wise enough to resist their animal instincts. Astrologers, consequently, are able to foretell the truth in the majority of cases, especially when they undertake general predictions.[71]

Some of the Renaissance popes were enchanted by astrology. It became "the regulator of official life" during the pontificate of Sixtus IV, Julius II,

---

[66]Augustine, *Confessions* 4.5.

[67]Augustine, *City of God* 5.1-4.

[68]Augustine, *City of God* 5.8-9.

[69]Gary Ferngren, ed., *The History of Science and Religion in the Western Tradition* (New York: Garland, 2000) 530.

[70]Roger Bacon, *Major Works* 1:266.

[71]Aquinas, *Summa Theologica* 1.115.4.

Leo X, and Paul III.[72] Through the practice of astrology, Urban VIII predicted the death dates of some of his cardinals. When they retaliated by doing the same for the holy father, Urban issued a *bulle* condemning the use of astrology in forecasting the time of death of popes and other rulers.[73]

Comets were widely regarded by Christians as predictors of slaughter and plague.[74] Callistus III was disturbed by a "hairy and red" object that blazed across the sky—Halley's comet. He set aside several days for prayer and fasting to shift the fated destruction toward enemies of the church at Constantinople.[75] Having unsuccessfully launched a fleet of ships to save that city from the 1456 Turkish invasion, the pope hoped that the heavens would fight against the Muslims.[76]

Renaissance scholars, who were devoted to reviving classical learning, often championed the astrology that was a part of the ancient Roman culture. There were professors of astrology in the Italian medieval universities under church control.[77] Some of the theologians who were attracted by rational and scientific approaches to knowledge nevertheless endorsed astral fatalism. Bertrand Russell writes regarding that era: "Astrology was prized especially by free thinkers; it acquired a vogue which it had not had since ancient times. The first effect of emancipation from the Church was not to make men think rationally, but to open their minds to every sort of antique nonsense."[78]

During that period, the magi of the Christian nativity story came to be called "wise men,"[79] even though they were not necessarily wise or men. The Revised Standard Version carries on the "wise men" mistranslation of the King James Version, although the Revised English Bible accurately

---

[72]"Astrology," *The Catholic Encyclopedia* (New York, 1907).

[73]P. T. Naylor, *Astrology* (London: Maxwell, 1967) 56-57.

[74]Theodore Wedel, *The Medieval Attitude toward Astrology* (New Haven CT: Yale, 1920) 28-29.

[75]William Phipps, "Heaven's Alarm to the World," *Natural History* (August 1985): 8.

[76]Bartolommeo Platina, *Lives of the Popes* (London: Griffith, 1865) 2:250.

[77]Wedel, *The Medieval Attitude toward Astrology*, 77.

[78]Bertrand Russell, *A History of Western Philosophy* (London: Allen & Unwin, 1946) 502.

[79]Mark Powell, "The Magi as Wise Men," *New Testament Studies* 46 (January 2000): 3, 18.

calls them "astrologers." Those magi become saints in church tradition, and three in number because of the three gifts they were alleged to have brought to Bethlelem. They were presumed to have gone to Europe after their visit to Bethlehem, and Cologne Cathedral claims to house their relics.

John Calvin applied to Christians the advice Jeremiah gave Jews, that they should not be influenced by the false astrological signs. The Protestant Reformer said, "When unbelievers transfer the government of the universe from God to the stars, they fancy that their bliss or their misery depends upon the decrees and indications of the stars, not upon God's will."[80] The Bible showed him that astrology has been destructive to both faith and morals. But Calvin accepted Matthew's diagnosis that epileptic seizures result from a person becoming moonstruck, and commented: "Those persons are called lunatic who suffer from fits when the moon waxes and wanes. . . . For experience teaches us with certainty that these sicknesses grow better or worse with the course of the moon."[81]

Regarding the stars, Calvin said that humans "are not ruled by them, as lying and boastful astrologers think."[82] He thought there was great difference between having one's true destiny determined by a loving God than by impersonal fate. Modern religious leaders also reject astrology in part because the fatalism on which it rests is incompatible with free will. In *Religion and the Decline of Magic*, Keith Thomas states: "Theologians could not accept that men were so much the victims of their own inherited dispositions as to be unable to break out of this astral bondage, and exercise independent moral choice."[83]

* * *

In spite of the opposition of some world religions to astrology, it is now followed to some extent by approximately one billion people on the globe. The modern revival of astrology began in 1930 when the London *Sunday Observer* began featuring horoscopes regularly. Thousands now make a living out of it by writing horoscopes, which may give an individual diametrically opposed forecasts. Major newspapers are much more likely

---

[80]Jeremiah 10:2; John Calvin, *Institutes* 1.16.3.

[81]Matthew 17:15; John Calvin, on Mark 9.17-18.

[82]John Calvin, on Isaiah 19.12.

[83]Keith Thomas, *Religion and the Decline of Magic* (New York: Scribner, 1971) 361.

to have daily columns on astrology than on astronomy. There is more interest in those who attempt to manipulate the universe so that it will cater to the subjective whims of humans than in those who attempt to describe the universe as it objectively is. As Will Durant put it, astrology has always been more popular than astronomy because simple folks "are more interested in telling futures than in telling time."[84] Precision of temporal measurement by astronomers is lame stuff when compared with information about events yet to come in one's own life, which can allegedly be supplied by forecasters claiming godlike omniscience.

Millions of astrology believers also claim to be members of the Jewish or Christian religions, in spite of the Bible's condemnation of astral divination. Abraham left behind the star-gods of the Chaldeans more than 3,500 years ago to become the father of the Hebrew, Christian, and Muslim religions. Jewish exiles separated themselves from Mesopotamian paganism more than 2,500 years ago, yet there are still many in the Judeo-Christian culture who remain in Babylonian captivity. Concluding his survey of belief in "paranormal phenomena," George Gallup states: "A high proportion, even among regular churchgoers, believe in astrology. At times it seems that Americans are prepared to believe almost everything."[85] He reports that 26% of those who claim to be "born again" believe in astrology, a higher percentage than those who do not so claim.[86]

In a twenty-first century publication, Phillip Lucas has written:

> According to recent national surveys, roughly one-fourth of all Americans ascribe some validity to astrology. Believers talk about "thanking one's lucky stars" for fortuitous happenings, much like religious devotees express gratitude to God for happy circumstances. As many as eleven thousand professional astrologers are at work in the United States, serving more than twenty million clients.[87]

Membership in the American Federation of Astrologers has more than doubled in the past generation, to 3500 at the beginning of this century.

---

[84]Will Durant, *The Story of Civilization: Our Oriental Heritage* (New York: Simon and Schuster, 1935) 80.

[85]George Gallup, *Religion in America* (Princeton, 1982) 6.

[86]George Gallup and Michael Lindsay, *Surveying the Religious Landscape* (Harrisburg PA: Morehouse, 1999) 40.

[87]"Astrology," *Contemporary American Religion* (New York: Macmillan, 2000).

Whole sections of major bookstores are filled with astrology publications, and computers have been programmed to produce horoscope printouts.

A generation ago, distinguished historian of religion Mircea Eliade observed regarding Euro-American astrology, "Never in the past did it reach the proportions and prestige it enjoys in our times." In former centuries, he asserted, it was popular with the rich and powerful, but now the zodiac business has hit the mass market. Eliade notes that this lucrative neopaganism persists in spite of the fact that the dominant theology of Western civilization has supported human freedom and has opposed astrological fatalism. He suggests that the fantastic enterprise has arisen in our technological culture among rootless individuals who long to become related to the entire universe. They seem to find grandeur in being part of a cosmic plan that is incomprehensible and preestablished, even thought this makes them puppets pulled by invisible strings.[88] The eminent Harvard psychologist Gordon Allport perceived that belief in astrology "is more readily accepted in times of disruption and crisis when the individual's normal safeguards against gullibility are broken down." He deplored this "magical practice" that pervades American culture because "it encourages an unwholesome flight from the persistent problems of real life" and evades the taking of responsibility for one's own actions.[89]

The perennial popularity of astrology in scientific cultures is difficult to fathom. For thousands of years there has been no essential change in the way the sky is divided for the drawing of horoscopes, in spite of the enormous increase in empirical observations. Since this activity is pseudoscientific, astronomy's rejection of the geocentric model on which astrology is based does not disturb it. What is bewildering is the way in which otherwise intelligent and educated people throughout the course of history have accepted zodiac readings that are simply fraudulent and scientifically inane.

* * *

Apart from astrology, how has Christianity responded to other expressions of the occult? The Torah treats the magic expressed in sorcery

---

[88]Mircea Eliade, *Occultism, Witchcraft, and Cultural Fashions* (Chicago: University of Chicago Press, 1976) 59-61.

[89]*Presbyterian Outlook* (27 October 1975): 7.

and seances as a capital offense.[90] Following that tradition, but in a less severe manner, the apostles denounced renegade Jews who operated as magicians in various cities.[91] In Ephesus, they sold small parchments or papyri on which formulas were written that were guaranteed to do wonders for their possessors.[92] One manual from the postbiblical era contains directions for making a Jewish amulet for curing fever. First, a sentence from Numbers 11:2 was to be written on parchment, "Moses prayed to God and the fire abated." Those words were then wrapped with leather and worn around the neck of a feverish patient during sleep.[93]

Ancient Christian Magic documents the ways in which the Copts of the first millennium continued the charms and curses that pre-Christian Egyptian socerers used to empower their clientele. That text contains a plethora of rituals that pertain to amulets and incantations. For example, fisherfolk repeat:

> O you who came to his apostles upon the sea . . . [and] said, "Cast your nets to the right side of the boat and you will find something." They cast them and discovered 153 (John 21:6-11). . . . So you must ordain Raphael the archangel for me, and he must collect every species of fish for me to the place where your figure and your amulet will be.[94]

Valerie Flint tells how European Christians were also involved in invocations aimed at obtaining supernatural benefits and protections. Her scholarly treatment of this topic concludes:

> Pagan magical beliefs and practices sneaked through into the early Christian West because too few of Christianity's adherents were alert or astute enough to stop them at the borders. . . . Skilled hagiographers preserved the type of religious leader who had been prominent in the non-Christian magical scene. . . . Certain birds and beasts, and woods, and writings, and medical specifics

---

[90]Exodus 22:18; Leviticus 20:27.

[91]Acts 8:9-24; 13:6-11; 19:13-19.

[92]Frederick J. Foakes-Jackson and Kirsopp Lake, eds., *The Beginnings of Christianity* (London: Macmillan, 1922–1939) 4:243.

[93]"Charms and Amulets (Jewish)," *Encyclopaedia of Religion and Ethics* (New York: Scribner's, 1928).

[94]Marvin Meyer and Richard Smith, eds., *Ancient Christian Magic* (San Francisco: Harper, 1994) 281.

were, because they were favored in the competing systems, actively chosen to mediate a supernatural message in the Christian one too.[95]

In the Roman era, a person who wore an amulet on a headband or neck chain was presumed to be fortified against evil powers.[96] The Rosetta stone refers to golden *phylaktaria* worn by Egyptian kings to safeguard them from malign influences. Jews adapted the phylactery (from the Greek verb *phylatto*, meaning "to protect") for their rituals. In excavating Qumran, a phylactery (Hebrew, *tefillin*) was found with compartments containing scriptural sentences.[97] The one reference to phylacteries in the New Testament is in words attributed to Jesus. He criticized the Pharisees who wore them to show off their special status.[98]

The *Shema*, the Hebrew confession of faith that was composed of texts from the Torah, was intended to have an inward theological and ethical significance, but it became a fetish. A tiny piece of parchment containing the *Shema* was placed in a little cube, with a leather covering and straps to bind it to the body. One of the boxes was bound on the left arm above the elbow so that the *Shema* message of loving God would be "upon the heart" as commanded by Moses! Another box was strapped to the brow at the hairline; unseen by the wearer, it reminded others of the wearer's religiosity. The main purpose of this object is explained in the Talmud, "Whoever has phylacteries on his body, fringe on his garment, and the mezuzah on his door may be presumed to be safe from committing sin."[99]

The Jewish practice of attaching phylacteries to the body has its parallel in church history. Jesus' cross-carrying command was a figurative way of urging disciples to dedicate themselves to his cause, even at the cost of martyrdom.[100] Paul gave it high significance when he wrote, "May I never boast of anything except the cross of our Lord Jesus Christ,"[101] but neither he nor any other New Testament writer advocated using the cross as an

---

[95]Valerie Flint, *The Rise of Magic in Early Medieval Europe* (Princeton NJ: Princeton University Press, 1991) 394, 398.

[96]Plutarch, *Moralia*, 377-78.

[97]"Tefillin," *Encyclopaedia Judaica* (Jerusalem: Keter, 1972).

[98]Matthew 23:5.

[99]*Menahoth* 43b.

[100]Mark 8:34.

[101]Galatians 6:14.

amulet. The earliest Christians focused on the symbolism of the cross, but they did not wear small facsimiles of it to ward off demonic forces.

In postbiblical church history, Jesus' imperative pertaining to taking up the cross resulted in external observances as literal as what is found in Orthodox Judaism. In a second-century apocryphal book, Thecla makes the sign of the cross when she is condemned to be burned for becoming Paul's disciple. Consequently, when she is placed on the pyre, the fire blazes up but does not burn her. God then sends a thunderstorm to quench the flame.[102] The fourth-century Roman emperor Julian informed Christians of a practice he disliked, "You adore the wood of the cross and draw its likeness on your foreheads."[103]

Constantine dreamed of a cross in the sky bearing a "conquer by this" inscription prior to winning a battle that would establish him as emperor.[104] Subsequently the cruciform banner became a fetish and it was presumed that victory over "infidels" would be assured if warriors carried it with them. From the fifth century onward, the cross has been widely worn as an amulet, and the novel *Dracula* treats it as a protection against vampires. Accounts can be found in folk literature of the ill being cured and the dead being raised by the power of a cross. Demons were said to vanish into thin air when a cross was placed in their paths. "Saint Leoba could still a tempest that was . . . snatching roofs from houses by making the sign of the cross."[105]

Many Christians continue to hang polished miniatures of the cross around their necks. Ironically, some treat the representation of an ancient torture device as a protecting charm. Starcrest of California advertised their "Good Luck Cross" in this way: "Lead a charmed life with this pretty pendant! . . . You can trust it to begin attracting love, success, and financial reward the moment you put it on. . . . Friends will surely admire its exquisite beauty—as well as your newly found fortune!"[106]

Most Christians who have worn crosses have probably not trivialized a core teaching of Jesus about renouncing self-centeredness, figuratively described as carrying one's cross. For them the symbol is perceived not as

---

[102]*Acts of Paul* 22.

[103]Julian, *Against the Galileans* 194d.

[104]Eusebius, *Life of Constantine* 1:28-29.

[105]Flint, *The Rise of Magic in Early Medieval Europe*, 176, 188.

[106]Quoted in *Christian Century* (16 October 1991): 951.

powerful magic, or as a lovely decoration to impress others, but as a reminder primarily to themselves of their commitment to one who laid down his life in love for friends and enemies. Likewise, most Jews who have worn phylacteries have probably not thought of them as fetishes but as a reminder of their allegiance to the Lord.

* * *

Jesus' metaphors were usually not misinterpreted until after the era of early Christianity. The most notorious example of such is the literalism applied to some words he spoke at the Last Supper, before his body was torn by crucifiers. After breaking a loaf of bread, he said, "This is my body."[107] There is no more reason for assuming that the bread distributed to the disciples at a house in Jerusalem was actually Jesus' body than that he became transformed into a grapevine when he allegedly said on that same occasion, "I am the vine."[108] When literally interpreted, the historical occasion is similar to the ceremony of cannibals who commemorate the death of a tribal elder by dividing a portion of his flesh and swallowing their leader.

The Fourth Lateran Council introduced in 1215 the doctrine that the substance of the bread and wine used in the Eucharist is transformed into the actual body and blood of the crucified Christ. This allegedly happens in the consecration of the elements whenever the priest intones "*Hoc est corpus meum*," the Latin translation of words attributed to Jesus at the supper with his disciples. That belief, called transubstantiation, was developed in the medieval era as a miracle counter to nature. Over the past millennium, the supernatural interpretation of those words of Jesus in Jerusalem has been a major cause of schism among Christians.

In 1651, English philosopher Thomas Hobbes gave a Protestant criticism of the preeminent Catholic sacrament. He compared the rite to the manipulations of Pharaoh's magicians at the time of Moses:[109]

The Egyptian conjurers, that are said to have turned their rods to serpents, and the water into blood, are thought but to have deluded the senses of the spectators by a false show of things. . . . And yet in this daily act of the priest, they do the very same, by turning the holy words into the manner of a charm, which

---

[107]1 Corinthians 11:24; Mark 14:22.
[108]John 15:5.
[109]Exodus 7:10-11, 21-22.

produceth nothing new to the sense; but they face us down, that it hath turned the bread into a man; nay, more, into a God. . . . The words, "This is my body,' are equivalent to these, "This signifies, or represents, my body"; and it is an ordinary figure of speech; but to take it literally is an abuse. . . . Nor did the Church of Rome ever establish this transubstantiation till the time of Innocent the Third [1215] . . . when the power of Popes was at the highest, and the darkness of the time grown so great, as men discerned not the bread that was given them to eat, especially when it was stamped with the figure of Christ upon the cross.[110]

The words by which Jesus instituted the Eucharist have had the most powerful influence on subsequent history of any he ever uttered. Magicians, recognizing folk's fascination with the appearance of supernatural power changing physical substance by means of a sanctimonious incantation, garbled the Latin words of the rite and uttered "hocus pocus" to make their acts appear more mysterious. "Hoax," its contraction, has come to mean tricking people into believing or accepting as genuine something false and often preposterous.

Much of what is called New Age spirituality, with its attention to self-deification, horoscopes, crystal gazing, seances, and other irrational magic, is but a current phase of Old Age superstition. Many people, longing for simple ways of guaranteeing outcomes that will make them feel satisfied, find reality too complex, too demanding, and too tragic. The continual human dilemma has not been primarily about choosing to be religious or nonreligious; rather, it has been about choosing a religion that focuses on learning to live within the Creator's order and to assist the vulnerable, or choosing one that presumes that individual agendas can be accomplished by manipulating ritual objects. Muhammad and Jesus opted for the former, but many of their followers have preferred the latter.

Celestial Messengers

Aggelos, transliterated as "angel" in English, was commonly used in early Greek literature to refer to a human messenger, and the New Testament occasionally illustrates that usage. For example, the Evangelists call wingless and featherless John the Baptist an aggelos because his role was to herald, to announce, the coming of Jesus. Also, when John was imprisoned and unable to go to Jesus personally, he sent aggeloi to convey his

---

[110]Thomas Hobbes, *Leviathan* 4:44.

concerns and to obtain a reply.[111] But throughout the Bible, an angel usually refers to a celestial spirit.

In the Hebrew Bible, an angel is sometimes a circumlocution for God, and at other times the Lord uses angels for communication with mortals rather than confronting people directly.[112] The Hebrews accepted much of the folklore about angels that was common in Mesopotamian literature.[113] They conceived of them as attendants of God, having sometimes a human form and sometimes an animal form. Occasionally they are called "sons of God" or "sons of gods," which appears to be a remnant of polytheism.[114] Since God was often thought of as a king, it was deemed appropriate for the heavenly court to function like earthly courts, with a number of celestial administrators in attendance to advise the king and to convey his decisions to those of lower status in the material realm. Angels were not objects of worship and were not usually associated with astral bodies.

After the Babylonian exile of the Jews, mediating angels were given a larger place because of "the increasingly austere transcendentalizing of Yahweh."[115] Since God was viewed as exceedingly remote, a hierarchy of angels and demons were introduced with protective and destructive duties. Jewish speculation on angels arose as an attempt to bridge the wide gap between God and humans. In biblical literature, narrators adopted the Zoroastrian notion that angels are assigned to guard the life of the righteous.[116] In contrast to the story in which God tests Abraham by commanding him to sacrifice Isaac, a book of the Jewish Pseudepigrapha assigns the testing to a demon.[117]

In the Apocrypha and the Pseudepigrapha, emphasis is placed on named angels who have a high rank. For example, Raphael describes himself as "one of the seven holy angels who present the prayers of the saints and

---

[111]Mark 1:2; Matthew 11:10; Luke 7:24, 27.

[112]Genesis 16:7, 13; 21:17, 19.

[113]"Angel," *The Interpreter's Dictionary of the Bible* (Nashville: Abingdon, 1962).

[114]Genesis 6:1-4; Psalm 29:1; Job 1:6.

[115]"Aggelos," *Theological Dictionary of the New Testament* (Grand Rapids MI: Eerdmans, 1964) 1:79.

[116]*Yasht* 13:1; Genesis 22:11; Matthew 18:10; Acts 12:7-11.

[117]Genesis 22:1-2; *Jubilees* 17:16.

enter into the glorious presence of the Holy One."[118] Like a monarch's principal ministers, an archangel has direct access to the King of Glory. In that role he acts as an intercessor for subordinate immortals and as a means through which the King reveals his purposes to mortals. The *Book of Enoch*, written in the first century BCE, tells of archangels who are positioned close to God's throne; they are encircled by "angels who could not be counted, a thousand thousands and ten thousand times ten thousand."[119]

Some angels were thought to be personifications of nature. A psalmist gives this praise to God, "You make winds your angels,/ Flames of fire your messengers."[120] The Book of Jubilees lists "angels of the spirit of the winds, and the angels of the spirit of the clouds, and of darkness, and of snow and of hail and of hoar frost, and the angels of the thunder and of the lightning, and the spirits of cold and of heat, and of winter and of spring and of autumn and of summer."[121] The Jews who lived at Qumran praised God for nature angels:

> When you stretched out the heavens . . .
> You also made potent spirits to keep them in bounds;
> Spirits immortal took on the form of holy angels.
> You assigned them to bear rule over divers domains:
> Over the sun and moon, to govern their hidden powers;
> Over the stars, to hold them to their courses;
> Over rain and snow to make them fulfill their functions;
> Over meteors and lightnings, to make them discharge their tasks.[122]

Angels, far from being sweet and fluttering cherubs, functioned as much to punish the vicious as to help the virtuous. The Bible opens with terrifying angels guarding Eden with flaming swords, and closes with them destroying the Satanic dragon.[123] In the Hebrew Bible, God is frequently called "the Lord of Hosts." "Hosts" is a military term, so the reference is to the Commander who leads an army of heavenly angels as well as Israelites into holy war.[124] Those scriptures tell of an angel who destroyed thousands

---

[118]Tobit 12:14-15.
[119]*First Enoch* 71:10.
[120]Psalm 14:4.
[121]*Jubilees* 2:2.
[122]Qumran, *Book of Hymns*, 1.
[123]Genesis 3:24; Revelation 20:1-3.
[124]E.g., Genesis 32:1-2; 1 Samuel 15:2.

of Israelites because King David took a census, and several centuries later the claim is made that an angel slaughtered 185,000 Assyrians who were besieging Jerusalem.[125]

At the dawn of the Christ1an era, Jewish philosopher Philo posited that the aloof God communicates with humans by means of mediating angels. This arrangement enables humans to withstand the "shuddering dread of the universal Monarch and the exceeding might of his sovereignty,"[126] while protecting the Holy One from being defiled by direct contact with creatures of clay. Philo interprets a Genesis account of human creation to mean that God made the spiritual soul while angels fashioned the physical body.[127]

* * *

Paul usually referred to angels as demonic forces in conflict with God, although theologian Alan Richardson exaggerates in claiming that he recognized no good ones.[128] In contrast to the good attributes usually associated with angels in the literature of his era, he was remarkably ambivalent. Only in his earlier letters did use the term *aggelos* positively. Drawing on his understanding of apocalyptic Judaism, he pictured an archangel announcing with a trumpet blast the Lord Jesus' descent from heaven for a second coming.[129] Also, in a nonmythical manner, he expressed appreciation to the Galatians for receiving him as "an angel of God."[130] He did not mean that they treated him as a discarnate spirit from another realm, but that they showed special consideration for him and were open to his disclosure of God's will.

The Jewish religious thought of Paul's day distinguished between the angels of darkness and of light.[131] In discussing the deceptions of "pseudo-apostles," he commented that "even Satan disguises himself as an angel of light."[132] The psychological insight here can be expressed less figuratively

---

[125]2 Samuel 24:16; 2 Kings 19:35.

[126]Philo, *On Dreams* 1.22, 142.

[127]Philo, *On Flight* 69.

[128]Alan Richardson, *An Introduction to the Theology of the New Testament* (London: SCM, 1958) 209.

[129]1 Thessalonians 4:16.

[130]Galatians 4:4.

[131]Qumran, *Rule of the Community* 3.

[132]2 Corinthians 11:14.

by saying that evil can be rationalized to look lovely. The apostle probably learned from earlier Jewish sages not to take demonology literally. One of them, Jesus ben Sirach, made this demythologizing comment, "When a godless person curses Satan, he really curses himself."[133] The apostle once used the phrase "angel of Satan" in reference to something that was tormenting him.[134] Satan is there a picturesque personification of some particular evil, and is not a courier with a distinctive supernatural personality who rivals God in power. When Paul profoundly describes the civil war between his higher self and his evil impulses in Romans 7, he makes no mention of Satan or the Devil. Neither in that introspective analysis nor elsewhere in his letters does he utilize the apocalyptic mythology of Judaism that Satan led some angels in opposing God.

As Paul's Christology developed, he moved away from the Pharisees' belief that angels are a good feature of religion.[135] In advising women to cover their hair "because of angels,"[136] it appears that he thought women should shelter themselves from exposure to beings who have the capacity for malevolence and lechery. As names for angels such as Gabriel and Michael indicate, they were conceived of as males in the biblical era. Genesis 6:2 was interpreted to refer to lustful angels who fornicate with human women.[137]

In relegating angels to an inferior position Paul did not regard them as nonexistent, as did the Sadducees.[138] But angelic folklore was treated by him as a cultural vestige and was largely superfluous for Christian doctrine. The apostle recognized that attention to angels stressed the distance between God and humans rather than the potential bonding of the two. He regarded his direct understanding of God as superior to what "an angel from heaven" might preach.[139] Far from having a status above humans, angels will be judged by Christians.[140] In order to indicate the inferiority of the Mosaic law and the superiority of direct guidance by God, Paul made use of a legend in

---

[133]Sirach 21:27.
[134]2 Corinthians 12:7.
[135]Acts 23:8.
[136]1 Corinthians 11:10.
[137]*First Enoch* 6-7.
[138]Acts 23:8.
[139]Galatians 1:8; 1 Corinthians 13:1-3.
[140]1 Corinthians 6:3.

which the giving of the law is associated with angels.[141] Angels previously may have been mediators for transmitting revelation from God to humans, he contended, but they no longer have that role.[142]

After alluding to a retinue of mythological beings that were accepted during his era, Paul affirmed that there is only one Lord through whom all exists.[143] He gave this assurance, "I am convinced that nothing in life or death, in the realm of angels or rulers . . . nor supernatural powers in height or depth, nor anything else in all creation can separate us from the love of God in Christ Jesus, our Lord."[144] "Height" and "depth" refer to astrological magnitudes determined by how near the earth's horizon a planet appears to be. The "rulers" pertain to cosmic forces that control human destiny, according to pagan belief.

Christians have been liberated from the clutches of such fate, Paul claimed, for Christ has delivered "the kingdom to God the Father after abolishing every rule and every authority and power."[145] Rather than interceding angels, Paul writes about the indwelling Spirit of Christ interceding for Christians.[146] He advocated an unbrokered access to God, so attempts to use heavenly angels as mediating channels to reach God was a hindrance to true piety. At the climax of his Christological discussion in his Romans letter, it is significant that angels are including in his triumphant hymn as among the demonic powers that are being vanquished. Pertaining to the role of angels in Paul's letters, Johannes Weiss notes, "Almost everywhere they are presented as powers hostile to God and his elect and stand as opposed to both, and only very seldom do they appear as devoted followers of God or of the Messiah."[147]

In his mature theology, Paul rejected any cosmological entity that might impose a barrier between the Christian and God. In writing to the Colossians, Paul criticized those who speculate about angels and thereby lose hold on Christ.[148] For him, Jesus satisfied a longing that was inadequately

---

[141]*Jubilees* 1:27.
[142]Galatians 3:19-20; Acts 7:53.
[143]1 Corinthians 8:5-6.
[144]Romans 8:38-39.
[145]1 Corinthians 15:24.
[146]Romans 8:9, 26.
[147]Johannes Weiss, *Earliest Christianity* (New York: Harper, 1937) 2:600.
[148]Colossians 2:18-19.

met by angel mythology. Job cried in desperation: "If only I knew how to reach God, how to enter his court."[149] "There is no umpire between us who might lay his hand on us both."[150] But now that God has become personified in Jesus, Paul was convinced that Christians need not believe that God is inaccessible, or one who issues commands by means of angelic subordinates. For the apostle, angels are superfluous, for their mediating function has been replaced by Christ. Paul's view is similar to that of the unknown writer of the letter to the Hebrews. He or she affirms that the Son of God, being a human rather than an angel, is superior to angels. This is counter to a verse in the Greek translation of a psalm, which states that humans are inferior in rank to angels.[151]

The Bible's only use of "philosophy" (Greek, *philosophia*) occurs in the Colossian letter to designate "angel worship" and devotion to other "cosmic elements."[152] Paul bluntly evaluated that pursuit as "empty deceit" and scorned its concomitant self-mortifying prohibitions. A rigid and unhealthy moral discipline resulted from this assumption: that which is upward and heavenly, in geocentric cosmology, is pure while that which is downward and earthly is contaminated. Paul asked those who found that philosophy appealing, "If with Christ you have died to cosmic elements, why should you be bound by rules that say 'Do not handle this, do not taste that, do not touch the other'?"[153]

Those accepting the religious philosophy that Paul denounced, believed that the "fullness" (Greek, *pleroma*) of God equaled the summing up of many divine emanations.[154] They held that divinity was distributed among celestial spheres known as "thrones, dominions, rulers, or authorities." Plato

---

[149]Job 23:3.

[150]Job 9:33.

[151]Hebrews 1:4; 2:7; Psalm 8:5. The Hebrew text of Psalm 8:5 (Hebrews 2:7 quotes the Septuagint, Greek, text) may be translated "lower/less than the gods/ heavenly beings." Early English translations (through the KJV) render "angels"; some later English translations—ERV and following (RSV, NRSV)—render "God." Notably, the current Jewish English translation (NJV, *TaNaKh*, 1962–1985) renders "little less than divine."

[152]Colossians 2:8, 18.

[153]Colossians 2:20-21.

[154]"Pleroma," *Theological Dictionary of the New Testament* (Grand Rapids MI: Eerdmans, 1968) 6:305.

had written about divine spirits animating the closer sun and the more distant planets.[155] Against that chain of beings, Paul boldly declared that "in Christ all the fullness of Deity is embodied."[156] Thus, Christians should reject the notion that planets and the moon embody mediating spirits.[157] Since the powers of divinity were fully expressed in the earthly Christ, there is no need to focus on heavenly angels, or even on Jesus' coming again from heaven. During his final decade of life, the apostle no longer expected an immediate reappearance of Christ. The "glory" of Christ shifts from a heavenly spectacle to be disclosed to Christians and becomes a phenomenon *within* Christians.[158] Paul thought that understanding of God could better be found inside humans than in the spirits alleged to be in the outside cosmos.

Theologian Harold DeWolf, in questioning the credibility of the existence of angels, reasons in a Pauline manner:

> If God is everywhere active, if He is concerned with the innermost life of every one of His children and if He immediately confronts the human person in divine-human encounter, there is little occasion for interest in messengers between heaven and earth. If "he is not far from each one of us," if "in him we live and move and have our being," (Acts 17:27-28) we have no need to communicate with Him from afar through intermediaries, nor is there need to believe in such intermediaries to account for experiences of divine illumination.[159]

The defeat of angelic power by Jesus' resurrection was an important part of Paul's eschatology, according to Albert Schweitzer. He recognized, as few other scholars have, that "Paul sees the Kingdom of God as meaning the overcoming through Jesus Christ of the Angelic beings who exercise a dominion alongside of and contrary to God's."[160] Schweitzer realized that

---

[155]Plato, *Timaeus* 38.

[156]Colossians 1:15-18; 2:8.

[157]Colossians 2:16.

[158]1 Thessalonians 4:16-17; Colossians 1:27.

[159]Harold DeWolf, *A Theology of the Living Church* (New York: Harper, 1968) 128.

[160]Albert Schweitzer, *The Kingdom of God and Primitive Christianity* (New York: Seabury, 1968) 157; see also his *The Mysticism of Paul the Apostle* (New York: Holt, 1931) 65-74.

Paul denigrates angels because they were associated with legalism, with his personal physical sufferings, and with the sexual abuse of women.[161]

* * *

Shirley Case begins his book on *The Origins of Christian Supernaturalism* with a vivid description of the Mediterranean culture:

> The sky hung low in the ancient world. Traffic was heavy on the highway between heaven and earth. Gods and spirits thickly populated the upper air, where they stood in readiness to intervene at any moment in the affairs of mortals. And demonic powers, emerging from the lower world or resident in remote corners of the earth, were a constant menace to human welfare. All nature was alive—alive with supernatural forces.[162]

As Christianity developed, Gnosticism to a large degree and orthodoxy to a small degree accepted the cosmic dualism that Paul rejected. Gnostics believed in a series of intermediaries between the spiritual God and the material creation. For example, Basilides and Saturninus held that the "unknown Father" created a long chain of archangels and angels and assigned them spheres of dominion. The rebellious lowest ranking angels in that hierarchy created the earth, under the leadership of the Jewish God. Consequently, the Father sent Christ to liberate believers from the dominion of the matter makers and to guide their souls up the cosmological ladder to the spiritual realm.[163]

The last two books of the New Testament canon illustrate both the strong influence of apocalyptic Judaism and the slight influence of Paul's Christology in the church that developed a generation after his death. Jude is principally indebted to the bizarre book of Enoch, which contains an embellishment on the mythology in Genesis about divine beings siring giants by means of human women.[164] Enoch interprets the myth as referring to the primeval rebellion and fall of some angels from Paradise. Because they left their proper heavenly home, defiling themselves with lust and engaging in unnatural divine-human intercourse, their punishment has been

---

[161]Albert Schweitzer, *Paul and His Interpreters* (London: Black, 1912) 56; 1 Corinthians 11:10.

[162]Shirely Case, *The Origins of Christian Supernaturalism* (Chicago: University of Chicago, 1946) 1.

[163]Irenaeus, *Against Heresies* 1:24.

[164]Genesis 6:1-4.

continuous imprisonment and fiery torture. The demons that have infiltrated the natural and social order are children of that illicit union.[165] Picking up on some of that Jewish folklore, Jude tells about archangel Michael contending with the Devil, and quotes as authority what Enoch records about the coming fierce judgment by the Lord.[166]

The Book of Revelation, written about the same time as Jude, contains dozens of references to angels—far more than any other book of the Bible. Myriads of angels surround God's heavenly throne, and mighty angels stand at the four corners of the flat earth below, holding back its winds.[167] Angelology is associated with astrology, "The mystery of the seven stars . . . are the angels of the seven churches."[168] A complex mythology is presented in Revelation in which Satan, formerly among the sons of God in the overworld, becomes, for a millennium, the chief of the underworld kingdom of evil.[169] According to Eric Dodds, most Christians in the era when Revelation was composed acknowledged the power of pagan deities, but in deference to their doctrine of the Godhead, they called them fallen angels.[170]

None of the esteemed theologians of Christian orthodoxy have followed Paul in depreciating angels. Ignatius boasts that he can "grasp heavenly mysteries, the ranks of angels, the array of principalities, things visible and invisible."[171] Justin includes angels among those persons whom Christians "worship and adore." To them God committed "the care of humans and of all things under heaven."[172] Origen calls angels "the highest rational creatures" and claims that they direct nations. These aerial creatures also animate heavenly bodies.[173] The tendency to exalt angels was checked in the fourth century by the Council of Laodicea, which prohibited invocations to angels, calling it idolatry.[174] Even so, Bishop Ambrose, writing after that

---

[165]*First Enoch* 10:4-12; 12:4-6; 16:1.

[166]Jude 6-9, 14-15; *1 Enoch* 1:9.

[167]Revelation 5:11; 7:1.

[168]Revelation 1:20.

[169]Revelation 12:7-10; 20:1-3; cf. Job 1.

[170]Eric Dodds, *Pagan and Christian in an Age of Anxiety* (New York: Norton, 1965) 117.

[171]Ignatius, *Trallians* 5.2.

[172]Justin, *Apology* 1.6; 2.5.

[173]Joseph Trigg, *Origen* (Atlanta: John Knox, 1983) 105-106.

[174]Council of Laodicea, canon 35.

Laodicea ruling, advises Christians to "pray to the angels, who are given to us as guardians."[175]

Angelology received a mighty boost with the publication of *Celestial Hierarchy* in the sixth century. It was authored by a Neoplatonic Christian who deceptively backdated his fantasy to a first-century man named Dionysius the Areopagite. Karl Barth rightly calls Pseudo-Dionysius "one of the greatest frauds in Church history."[176] The medieval treatise quickly attained high authority because Christians presumed that its writer was a biblical character who had obtained his ideas from an apostle. According to Luke, Paul converted an Athenian leader named Dionysius, but nothing more is known about him.[177] Pope Gregory the Great accepted *Celestial Hierarchy* as authentic, so from the seventh century until the modern era it was mined for its presumed theological treasure, and the author was acclaimed as *Saint* Dionysius. Catholic scholar Andrew Bialas acknowledges that the work "is largely responsible for angelic cult becoming firmly and universally established in the Church."[178] Its impact contributed to the Seventh Ecumenical Council giving approval to the veneration of angels in 787, and centuries later it inspired the adoration of angels in the scholastic theology of the Middle Ages. Adolph Harnack, a leading church historian, comments, "As the Deity was farther and farther removed from ordinary Christian people by speculation, there gradually arose, along with the thought of the intercession of the angels, a worshiping of them."[179]

Celestial Hierarchy teaches that God reveals himself only to the cherubim in the top triad of spiritual beings. Then, in a chain of revelation, truth is disclosed to the seraphim and thrones of the inner sanctum. From them knowledge of the divine descends in succession to the dominions, powers, and authorities of the second triad, and then to the principalities, archangels and ordinary angels of the lowest level. To approach God in the highest realm, humans must move up the bureaucratic chain of command, "Inferior beings are to rise spiritually toward the divine through the intermediary of beings who are hierarchically superior."[180]

---

[175]Ambrose, *On Widows* 9.

[176]Karl Barth, *Church Dogmatics* (Edinburgh: Clark, 1960) 385.

[177]Acts 17:34.

[178]"Angels," *New Catholic Encyclopedia* (Detroit: Gale, 2003).

[179]Adolph Harnack, *History of Dogma* (London: Williams, 1899) 3:252.

[180]Pseudo-Dionysius, *Celestial Hierarchy* 4.

Supernaturalis was introduced into Christian vocabulary when *Celestial Hierarchy* was translated from Greek. The Greek equivalent for that Latin term had been employed in the ancient pagan culture, but early Christians managed to explain their religion without using the word. After Catholic scholastics popularized the term, it became basic for theological discussions in subsequent centuries.[181]

Aquinas, who lived at the height of the Middle Ages, was entranced by *Celestial Hierarchy.* Accordingly, he wrote a lengthy and subtle treatise that enlarged on Pseudo-Dionysius's treatment of the substance and function of angels. Its popularity resulted in Aquinas being designated "the angelic doctor." His discussion of "whether several angels can simultaneously occupy the same place"[182] may have been stimulated by the ultimate trivia question of the scholastics, "How many angels can dance on the head of a pin?"[183] Due primarily to the discussion by that outstanding medieval theologian, Mortimer Adler, editor of the influential Great Books of the Western World, ranked "angel" as one of the hundred outstanding topics in the history of our civilization. Catholic philosophers such as Aquinas and Adler seem to have aspired to become bodiless intelligences, the way in which they define angels. They marvel at a sky filled with winged seraph squadrons. Dante, who gave a literary rendering of Aquinas's theology, tells in *Paradise* of touring the seven heavens of classical astrology and of coming to three triads of angelic choirs. In that monumental poem he acknowledges that he was following the angelic arrangement set down in *Celestial Hierarchy.*[184]

With the Protestant Reformation came a deescalation in the adoration of all figures who might compete with trinitarian monotheism, be they earthly saints or heavenly angels. Although Protestant theologians accepted the reality of angels, they were generally treated as having little significance. Regarding *Celestial Hierarchy*, John Calvin makes this satirical comment, "If you read that book, you would think a man fallen from heaven recounted . . . what he had seen with his own eyes!" Calvin advises his readers to "leave those empty speculations which idle men have taught apart

---

[181]"Supernatural," *New Catholic Encyclopedia.*

[182]Aquinas, *Summa Theologica* 1.52.3.

[183]A Puritan who thought dancing was sinful, answered, "An infinite number could, but no self-respecting one would."

[184]Dante, *Paradise* 28.98-138.

from God's Word, concerning the nature, orders, and number of angels."
That Reformer contrasts the writer of *Celestial Hierarchy* with Paul, who
refused to comment on the content of his celestial vision.[185] Calvin
concludes his discussion of angels with this dismissal, "Farewell, then to
that Platonic philosophy of seeking access to God through angels, and of
worshiping them with intent to render God more approachable to us."[186]

Most modern scholars would regard it silly to attempt to study angels
seriously, and few theologians now give much attention to the subject. Even
so, there lingers a great deal of belief in supermundane beings who are
complete with halos, wings, and white robes. A bibliographical resource
shows that in the 1990s more than 400 works were published on angels.[187]
A Gallup sampling shows that more Americans believe in angels than in
any of the rest of the wide range of paranormal phenomena.[188] In 1979
Gallup found that 54% of American adults believe that angels are real and
not imaginary; among persons who claim to take their religion seriously,
68% believe in angels.[189] In 1993, a *Time* poll discovered that only one-
quarter of Americans do not believe in the existence of angels or in having
their own guardian angel.[190] In 1997, a survey by Opinion Dynamics found
that 76% personally believe in angels.[191] Lynn Clark provides this data, "In
the last decade of the millennium, more than three hundred web sites were
devoted to angels; an average of eighteen million Americans a week
watched the televised series *Touched by an Angel*; and more than five
million books on angels have been sold."[192] Scientist Chet Raymo observes:
"Angels are hot properties. . . . Hollywood has given us a slew of angel
movies. Angelology has moved from theological texts to the supermarket
newspapers." He finds the proliferation of publications about angels in
tabloids and devotional books to be "symptomatic of our civilization's rift
between knowing and believing."[193]

---

[185]2 Corinthians 12:2-4.

[186]John Calvin, *Institutes* 1.14.4, 12.

[187]George Marshall, *Angels* (Jefferson NC: McFarland, 1999).

[188]George Gallup, *The People's Religion* (New York: Macmillan, 1989) 75.

[189]George Gallup, *Emerging Trends* (Princeton, 1979) 1:3.

[190]*Time* (27 December 1993): 56.

[191]*Public Perspective* (May 2000): 27.

[192]"Angels," *Contemporary American Religion* (New York: Macmillan, 2000).

[193]Chet Raymo, *Skeptics and True Believers* (New York: Walker, 1998) 265.

The mass appeal of alleged intervening beings from out of the blue is displayed by the several million copies of Billy Graham's *Angels* that have been sold. Interpreting the Bible literally, he states that angels are essentially sexless spirits but sometimes they "manifest themselves in physical form."[194] Graham has revived the notion of angelic warfare that is featured in the Qumran scrolls and in the book of Revelation. He assures those who are preparing for Armageddon: "Millions of angels are at God's command and at our service. The hosts of heaven stand at attention as we make our way from earth to glory, and Satan's BB guns are no match for God's heavy artillery." Yet, "Lucifer, our archenemy, controls one of the most powerful and well-oiled war machines in the universe. He controls principalities, powers, and dominions. Every nation, city, village, and individual has felt the hot breath of his evil power."[195] Graham tells of ten grades in the angelic hierarchy and claims that these hawkish and supernatural beings travel with an infinite velocity as "God's secret agents" to engage in surveillance of earthlings.[196]

Bishop John Robinson may speak for his English constituency but not for Americans when he writes, "For most ordinary people angels merely add to the cocoon of fantasy and unreality in which the Christian Gospel is wrapped."[197] Literary critic Harold Bloom observes, "An American angelology is developing among us, and not just among the Mormons and the Pentecostals, the New Age networks, but among Roman Catholics, Southern Baptists, Jews, and across the religious spectrum." In spite of biblical admonitions, Bloom states, "even devout Christians seem to have repressed Paul's incessant distrust of the angels."[198] Our culture commonly presumes that angels are altogether good; thus an American founding father wrote, "If men were angels, no government would be necessary."[199]

It has been shown that Paul, the ablest spokesman for original Christianity, had little regard for superstition and magic. He rejected the residual animism that was found in some Hellenistic philosophies. Although he did not have the privilege of understanding the cosmos as astronomers now

---

[194]Billy Graham, *Angels* (New York: Doubleday, 1975) 31.

[195]Graham, *Angels*, 15, 164.

[196]Graham, *Angels*, 49, 55, 92.

[197]John Robinson, *But That I Can't Believe* (London: Collins, 1967) 12.

[198]Harold Bloom, *Omens of Millennium* (New York: Riverhead, 1996) 69, 76.

[199]*The Federalist*, 51.

know it, he shared their presumption that the "celestial" spheres are void of divine substance. The material world was for Paul a good creation of God and not a work of the Devil, so it would have been a slur on the Creator had he speculated about an army of good spirits fighting to free humans from the shackles of physical existence. The apostle pushed aside Jacob's ladder with ascending and descending angels who were prominent in the religious outlook of Judaism. Also, he was not in sympathy with the pagan need for a hierarchy of spirit powers to gyrate the heavens, to control the natural elements, and to determine human "disasters" (literally, unlucky stars). The focus of Paul's concern was on the bloody flesh of Christ Jesus, and he believed that he was the only connecting link with Ultimate Reality.

Chapter 4
Authentic Signs and Wonders

In Paul's Letters

What terms did Paul use in discussing miracles? Throughout the Greek New Testament, "miracle" is occasionally used to translate *dynamis*. William Ramsay writes, "The word 'power' (*dynamis*) was technical in the language of religion, superstition, and magic, and was one of the most common and characteristic terms in the language of pagan devotion."[1] The divine was commonly associated with controlling power, not persuasive power. But there was a distinct difference between the usual employment of *dynamis* and the way Paul used the term in writing to communities where he had been working. He conceived of God as the source of inspiration that causes people to respond, rather than as one who forces things to happens. He wrote, "We know that in everything God works for good with those who love him."[2]

In several letters (dating from ca. 50–63) Paul referred in a general way to powerful expressions of God's Spirit.[3] These were not external marvels but internal manifestations of change within the members of the church. *Semeia* and *terata,* meaning "signs" and "wonders," are also terms that the apostle used in tandem with *dynamis* to describe the same phenomenon, and he claimed that he was an agent of Christ for their accomplishment.[4] *Semeia* points to the divine authority of the happenings, whereas *terata* emphasizes their unusual quality. Paul did not use *terata* apart from *semeia*, implying his unwillingness to divorce astonishment from theological significance.

In none of Paul's words for "miracle" did he suggest that miracles are disruptions of physical regularities. William Sanday, an eminent Pauline exegete, asserted that Paul's terms for miracles refer to "remarkable spiritual gifts, which included the gifts of healing." In his essay on miracles, Sanday stated, "The witness of St. Paul is no doubt the best that we have. That of the rest of the New Testament is not quite so immediate."[5] The

---

[1]William Ramsay, *The Bearing of Recent Discovery on the Trustworthiness of the New Testament* (London: Hodder and Stoughton, 1915) 118.

[2]Romans 8:28.

[3]Galatians 3:5; 1 Corinthians 12:10, 28-29.

[4]Romans 15:18-19; 2 Corinthians 12:12.

[5]William Sanday et al., *Miracles* (London: Longmans, 1911) 5-9.

miracles that Paul mentions can be accounted for "by the presence in the world of a unique Personality, and by that wave of new spiritual force which flowed from it."[6]

Paul ranked teachers and preachers above healers,[7] and lauded the expression of love (*agape*) as the hallmark of all authentic Christians. To convey its value, he followed his listing of personal gifts (*charisma*) with his ode to that ethical ideal, which he called a "more excellent way." Robert Grant, a specialist in early Christianity, states: "He rigorously subordinates wonder-working faith to love. . . . The creative activity of God is better expressed in works of love than in signs and wonders."[8] To Christians in Rome, Paul also conveyed that "signs and wonders" have their place to the extent that they proclaim "the good news of Christ."[9] The apostle may have been aware of some faith healings involving Jesus, but their importance paled, in his opinion, in comparison to Jesus' embodiment of *agape*.

Rudolf Bultmann is in accord with Paul when he writes that "wonder" pertains to God's forgiveness, not to marvels that violate the regular sequence of nature. Accordingly, that leading New Testament exegete of the last century argues that scriptural authority is not relinquished when supernaturalism is abandoned.[10] In support of that stance, Bultmann writes: "The idea that Jesus proved himself to be God's Son in his earthly life by miracles is really contradictory, as Philippians 2:6-11 shows. It is correspondingly foreign to Paul himself to conceive of Jesus' life as filled with the miraculous."[11] In describing for the Philippians the qualities of Jesus that he most admired, the apostle alluded to Jesus' role as a suffering servant but wrote nothing about his performance of supernatural feats.

For Paul, the superlative demonstration of the "dynamis of God" is the gospel.[12] He found the implosion of Christ's amazing grace to be God's

---

[6]William Sanday, *Bishop Gore's Challenge to Criticism* (London: Longmans, 1914) 24.

[7]1 Corinthians 12:8-10, 28.

[8]Robert Grant, *A Historical Introduction to the New Testament* (New York: Simon and Schuster, 1972) 331.

[9]Romans 15:19.

[10]Rudolf Bultmann, *Faith and Understanding* (London: SCM, 1969) 249-54.

[11]Rudolf Bultmann, *Theology of the New Testament* (New York: Scribner, 1951) 1:131.

[12]Romans 1:16.

mightiest work. Grace operates within the depth of alienated personalities, liberating them from destructive tendencies. He wrote that those who share the suffering of Christ "will live with him by the *dynamis* of God."[13] Paul would probably have agreed with Rene Descartes's judgment that God's three essential miracles were the created order, human freedom of will, and the revelation of the divine nature in Jesus.[14] Frederick Grant, an outstanding New Testament scholar, comments:

> Every miracle could be dropped from the biblical list and the authority of the gospel and Lord whose message it is would not be lost. . . . All words and works of power in the lives of Jesus and the prophets were signs and wonders. But they need not be regarded as violations of those laws in accordance with which all life moves.[15]

Using a verbal form of *dynamis*, Paul commented to the Philippians on his relationship with Christ, "I can do anything through him who empowers me."[16] The context of that affirmation displays the apostle's ability to cope with imprisonment that he might not survive, and be joyful whether he faced deprivation or an ample supplying of his needs. He did not mean that he could engage in supernaturalism and cause the prison door to unlock by prayer or reverse the aging process.

Paul disappointedly acknowledged that "Jews demand signs," that is, they expected God to accredit himself by supernatural performances. Fascinated by the legends of such acts by Moses, Elijah, and Elisha, they longed for a new prophet would perform likewise. A Palestinian contemporary of Jesus and Paul, who promised to produce a confirming sign that he was the messiah, exemplifies the kind of person many Jews followed in hope that he would be their savior. Josephus provides this historical information: "A certain impostor named Theudas persuaded the majority of the populace to take up their possessions and follow him to the Jordan River. He stated that he was a prophet and that at his command the river would be parted and would provide easy passage."[17] In effect Theudas announced that he would

---

[13]2 Corinthians 13:4.

[14]Genevieve Rodis-Lewis, *Descartes* (Ithaca NY: Cornell University Press, 1998) 54-55.

[15]Frederick Grant, "The Miraculous," *Christian Century* (14 December 1922): 1545.

[16]Philippians 4:13.

[17]Josephus, *Antiquities* 20.97. Another Jewish sign promiser was Jonathan of

repeat the Jordan River nature miracle that scripture alleges of Joshua and Elijah.[18] The New Testament also makes reference to Theudas who, around 50 CE, persuaded hundreds to follow him before he was killed.[19]

One of the earliest surviving writings attacking Christianity contains what was probably the typical reaction of outsiders who had become aware of the religion. In the second century, Celsus states: "Jesus permitted himself to be mocked and bedecked with a purple robe and crowned with thorns. Why did this son of a god not show one glimmer of his divinity under these conditions? Why did he refuse to deliver himself from shame—at least play the man and stand up for his own or for his father's honor?" Celsus also fired another broadside:

> What is God's purpose in undertaking such a descent from the heights? Does he want to know what is going on among men? If he doesn't know, then he does not know everything. If he does know, why does he not simply correct men by his divine power? A fine god indeed who must pay a visit to the regions below, over which he is said to have control. Yet the Christians maintain that he is unable to correct men by divine power without sending someone who is especially adept at saving people from their sins.[20]

Celsus declared that "God does not suffer,"[21] but Paul found the wonder-working of God displayed in Jesus' suffering humanity, not in erratic marvels. Howard Kee, in his thorough study of miracles in the ancient Mediterranean culture, notes the distinctiveness of Paul, "The essence of divine power, he declares, is not to be seen in the manifestations of human wisdom or charismatic gifts but in the death of Jesus."[22] The apostle proclaimed the crucified Christ as "the miracle [*dynamis*] of God and the wisdom of God." That true "miracle" was "scandalous" to many, he admitted, because it portrays one who did not supernaturally zap those who would crucify him.[23] The Jewish authorities of Jesus' day associated divine approval with the occurrence of something presumed to be impossible, such

---

Cyrene, according to Josephus, *Jewish Wars* 7.438-39.

[18]Joshua 3:10-16; 2 Kings 2:8.

[19]Acts 5:36.

[20]Celsus, *True Doctrine* (New York: Oxford, 1987) 65, 76.

[21]Celsus, *True Doctrine*, 107.

[22]Howard Clark Kee, *Miracle in the Early Christian World* (New Haven: Yale University Press, 1983) 172.

[23]1 Corinthians 1:22-24.

as a man escaping from crucifixion by tearing out the binding nails and subduing the armed executioners surrounding him.[24]

Catholic theologian Hubert Richards understands what is at the heart of Paul's religion, "The object of faith is not a number of mind-boggling prodigies which the Christian is asked to accept *quia absurdum*, but the foolishness of the cross, the scandalous reversal of values represented by the claim that God is revealed and the world saved in the shameful death of one rejected by political and religious authorities alike."[25] Anti-Christian philosopher Friedrich Nietzsche was also aware that, by associating God with submission and suffering rather than with worldly might, Paul had championed a startlingly different theology:

> Modern people, deadened to Christian language, no longer have a feeling for . . . the paradox of the formula, "God on the Cross." Previously there had at no time or place been such a bold reversal, nor anything at once so dreadful, questioning, and questionable as this formula: it ushered in a transvaluation of all ancient values.[26]

Paul paradoxically found potency in what was commonly regarded as impotent. He revered the modest person who, like Stephen, died praying for the forgiveness of those who persecuted him.[27] Paul was convinced that God chooses the weak and despised, not those who are strong by ordinary standards.[28] His model of true humanity is the "last Adam" who, unlike the first representative human, steadfastly lived in humble obedience to God.[29] Paul's Jesus transformed religious expectations by showing that God's action is best seen in situations of lowly oppression, not lofty splendor: "The message of the cross is moronic [Greek, *moria*] to those who are perishing, but to us who are being saved it is the miracle of God. . . . For God's foolishness is wiser than human wisdom, and God's weakness is stronger than human strength."[30]

Classical historian Charles Freeman comments on the way Christianity subverted the Roman culture, "The original message of Christianity, set in

---

[24]Mark 15:32; Luke 23:8.
[25]Hubert Richards, *The Miracles of Jesus* (London: Mowbray, 1975) 18.
[26]Friedrich Nietzsche, *Beyond Good and Evil*, 46.
[27]Luke 23:34; Acts 7:60.
[28]1 Corinthians 1:26-28.
[29]1 Corinthians 15:45; Philippians 2:6-8.
[30]1 Corinthians 1:18, 25.

a framework in which power, wealth, even conventional social ties were renounced, and proclaimed as it was by a spiritual leader who had suffered the most humiliating punishments the empire could administer, could be seen as a threat to that empire."[31] The absurdity of the adoration of a crucified person, as viewed by pagan Romans, is illustrated by graffiti scratched on a plaster wall in Rome around 200 CE. It shows an ass-headed person on a cross, and beneath this oldest crucifix in existence is the sarcastic inscription, "Alexamenos worships his god." Unlike Paul, most early Christians had difficulty reconciling the brutal Roman method for execution with their criminal leader. Only after their religion was officially accepted by Rome in the fourth century did Christian art show Jesus on a cross.

Paul discerned the inconsistency of appealing to supernatural signs as evidence of God's power and then preaching that Jesus did not intervene to use them to rescue himself before he was nailed to a cross. Paul was confronted with a Roman government that thought of power in terms of building armies, crushing enemies, levying taxes, constructing roads, and erecting impressive monuments to their "divine" Caesars. Power continues to be a basic word in the secular vocabulary of every nation and it is displayed in military power, electrical power, nuclear power, cyber power, political power, industrial power, and the like. Taking over a widely revered concept that is worldwide and history-long, Paul's Jesus radically transformed it to refer to what most would call powerless. In addressing the Corinthians, Paul associated "the extraordinary power of God" with withstanding these trying conditions: "We are often troubled, but not crushed; bewildered, but not despairing; persecuted, but not forsaken; knocked down, but not knocked out. . . . We are continually in danger of death on account of Jesus, in order that his life may be made visible in our mortal flesh."[32] Whereas great "power" has usually been associated with "power *over*," for Paul it was "power *within*."

Paul was aware of unworthy leaders who claimed they could do miracles, so any attempt to prove the preeminence of Jesus by appeal to similar phenomena was of no value.[33] Those who pretend to engage in

---

[31]Charles Freeman, *The Closing of the Western Mind* (New York: Knopf, 2003) 216.

[32]2 Corinthians 4:7-9, 11.

[33]Tertullian (*Contra Marcion* 3.3), in contrast to Marcion, was later to reiterate

supernatural sorcery are judged by Paul as lacking "the fruits of the Spirit."[34] Practitioners of magic arts are motivated by a love of power that blinds them to the self-authenticating power of *agape*.

Paul's disdainful outlook on supernaturalism provides a clue for understanding the viewpoint of some Jewish Christians whom he sarcastically labeled "superapostles."[35] Those adversaries whom he encountered in Corinth featured "signs and wonders" to legitimize their status, but he accused them of preaching about "another Jesus."[36] "This other Jesus," James Robinson suggests, "is a power-laden glorious miracle worker."[37] Helmut Koester, another outstanding New Testament scholar, explains why Paul was distressed by his Corinthian opponents, "Paul realized that the emphasis upon the supernatural elements denigrates the normal human experiences, because divine presence is not found in the common, everyday occurrences, events, actions, and tribulations of men."[38]

Focus on the supernatural was, in Paul's opinion, a liability rather than an asset to Christianity. E. P. Sanders notes, "When pressed for signs of his apostolic authority Paul appealed more to 'weakness' than to miracles."[39] To those who challenged him, he replied, "I will all the more gladly boast of my weaknesses, so that the power of Christ may dwell in me."[40] Paul found his personal deficiencies to be a helpful context for witnessing the grace of God. In writing that Corinthian letter, Paul first cited Jesus as the premier example of God's power misconceived by his opponents as weakness, and near the end of that correspondence the apostle pointed to himself as a lesser example. He was comforted by receiving the revelation of the divine modus operandi, that "power is fully expressed in weakness." Accordingly, he affirmed, "For Christ's sake I am content with a life of

---

that supernatural portents are, for the same reason, of no apologetic value.

[34]Galatians 5:19-22.

[35]2 Corinthians 11:5, 22-23; 12:11.

[36]2 Corinthians 11:4; 12:12.

[37]James Robinson and Helmut Koester, *Trajectories through Early Christianity* (Philadelphia: Fortress, 1971) 60.

[38]Robinson and Koester, *Trajectories through Early Christianity*, 218.

[39]E. P. Sanders, *Paul* (New York: Oxford University Press, 1991) 25.

[40]2 Corinthians 12:9.

weakness, insult, hardship, persecution, and distress; for whenever I am weak, then I am strong."[41]

Dieter Georgi argues that Paul's opponents in Corinth claimed to work miracles like those ascribed to Moses, Elijah, and Jesus in order to promote themselves, but the apostle deplored such marketing devices.[42] He depreciated the haloed Moses who charmed Hellenistic Judaism. While recognizing him as a principal figure in the "old covenant," Paul told of his "fading splendor" in the new covenant, or new testament.[43] The apostle extolled "the glory of God in the face of Jesus Christ"[44] but he did not try to find miracles Jesus may have performed in which that glory shone. Paul criticized those who smugly thought they were more evangelical because they attributed supernatural acts to Jesus.

The letters of the apostle Paul do not suggest that God interferes with the natural order. Those earliest Christian writings contain no supernaturalism, that is, happenings that can only be explained by divine causation interrupting the regular operation of nature. Supernatural stories about Jesus, from conception to resurrection, are absent from Paul's gospel. One would never guess from reading Paul's letters that Jesus was to become recognized as the greatest worker of miracles in world religions. The apostle does not mention any of the many particular miracles that, according to the later written Gospels, Jesus performed. That significant fact is rarely pointed out, since most New Testament interpreters are devoted to affirming that the varied writers shared basically the same religious outlook.

How can Paul's silence on Jesus' miracles be explained? In the time when he wrote, supernatural stories may not yet have been widely associated with Jesus, or, if they were circulating orally, he may not have found them credible. Anthony Harvey suggests that Paul's Jesus "who 'took the form of a servant' could hardly at the same time have been capable of performing supernatural feats."[45] Ernst and Marie-Luise Keller correctly

---

[41]2 Corinthians 12:9-10.

[42]Dieter Georgi, *The Opponents of Paul in Second Corinthians* (Philadelphia: Fortress, 1986) 278; "Corinthians, Second Letter to the," *The Interpreter's Dictionary of the Bible*, Supplementary volume (Nashville: Abingdon, 1976).

[43]2 Corinthians 3:13-14.

[44]2 Corinthians 4:6.

[45]Philippians 2:7; Anthony Harvey, *Jesus and the Constraints of History* (Philadelphia: Westminster, 1982) 99.

assert that Paul was "not interested in physical miracles; they do not fit into the picture which he gives of the earthly Jesus, and they are meaningless for the Christology that he preaches."[46]

In the ancient Mediterranean culture, there were stories galore of shamen and wizards doing spectacular things. Experiencing the divine in supernatural occurrences was commonly expected in folk religions. In his excellent book on miracles, Gerd Theissen documents that there was "a renaissance of belief in miracles" in the time of Jesus.[47] Had he been one more wonder-worker—whom the Greeks called *thaumatourgos*—he would not have been revolutionary. E. P. Sanders and Margaret Davies state: "People in the first century would not have thought that attributing miracles to Jesus made him divine in the sense of 'superhuman.' They knew about too many other miracle workers to make such a connection."[48]

In the Gospels

There is little doubt that Jesus was regarded as some type of miracle-worker, a claim that was not made for every charismatic figure in the New Testament. Both Josephus and the writer of the Fourth Gospel credit Jesus with miracles, but state that they were not performed by John the Baptist.[49] According to Mark, Jesus requested that one healing be confirmed by Jewish priests.[50] The Talmud, a medieval recording of rabbinic traditions, claims that Jesus' performace as a miracle-working magician was one main reason for his execution. Rabbi Joseph Klausner tells about the polemical accounts, "There are reliable statements to the effect that his name was Yeshu'a of Nazareth; that he "practiced sorcery"; . . . that he was hanged as a false teacher and beguiler; . . . and that his disciples healed the sick in his name."[51]

---

[46]Ernst Keller and Marie-Luise Keller, *Miracles in Dispute* (Philadelphia: Fortress, 1969) 190.

[47]Gerd Theissen, *The Miracle Stories of the Early Christian Tradition* (Philadelphia: Fortress, 1983) 274.

[48]E. P. Sanders and Margaret Davies, *Studying the Synoptic Gospels* (Philadelphia: Trinity, 1989) 163.

[49]Josephus, *Antiquities* 18:16-19, 63; John 10:4.

[50]Mark 1:44.

[51]Joseph Klausner, *Jesus of Nazareth* (New York: Macmillan, 1925) 46.

Jesus' Jewish opponents did not question that he could perform exorcisms, but they insinuated that the source of his power was sinister, not godly. They accused him of healing by means of "Beelzebub,"[52] a scornful name for the prince of demons, meaning "lord of flies." Moreover, they criticized him for breaking the sabbath law that did not permit the healing he was providing on that holy day.[53] To discredit Jesus, some Jews also charged him with engaging in witchcraft.[54]

Leading critical New Testament scholars during the past century have accepted the historicity of Jesus' healing role. Healings comprise more than half of the several dozen miracle stories found in the Gospels. Bultmann argued that little can be known of the historical Jesus, but he had "no doubt" that he "healed the sick and expelled demons" and that such actions were "attributable to natural causation."[55] The Jesus Seminar, although predominantly composed of biblical scholars with highly skeptical judgments, states that "the evidence is overwhelming that Jesus was regarded as a folk healer during his public career."[56]

God is viewed as a healer in the Hebrew history,[57] and Jesus considered himself to be an agent for deity. Hebrew scripture contains one exorcism story: David, while serving in Saul's court, used music from his lyre to expel an evil spirit from the king.[58] Disease-causing demons were talked about in the Jewish culture after Zoroastrian beliefs in such became prominent during period of Persian occupation of Palestine around the fifth century BCE.

Without intending his action to be a sign of his supernatural power, Jesus assisted some demoniacs. The Gospels contain more stories of his exorcizing demons than of any other kind of healing. In addition to Mark's record of eight such incidents, Matthew and Luke each have two others. The close relation between exorcizing and healing is expressed in these words attributed to Jesus, "I am casting out demons and performing

---

[52]Mark 3:22.

[53]Mark 3:1-6; Matthew 12:27.

[54]Justin, *Dialogue with Trypho* 69.

[55]Rudolf Bultmann, *Jesus* (Tubingen: Mohr, 1926) 146; Hans Bartsch, ed., *Kerygma and Myth* (London: SPCK, 1957) 1:4-5.

[56]Robert Funk et al., *The Acts of Jesus* (San Francisco: Harper, 1998) 59.

[57]Exodus 15:26; Psalm 103:3; Hosea 11:3.

[58]1 Samuel 16:14-23.

cures."[59] Nor can they be separated in the Greco-Roman culture, for sickness was usually presumed to be caused by some kind of demon possession, even as it continues to be with many Africans today. Pertaining to exorcism in Jesus' day, Josephus said, "This ability to cure remains a very strong power among us."[60] That historian, who lived in the first century CE, personally witnessed a Jew named Eleazar "cure" a man possessed by demons, by drawing them out of his body and commanding them never to return.[61] Jesus pointed out that his exorcisms were not unlike what Jewish contemporaries were administering, and he commended those outside his band who were engaged in such therapy.[62]

The first exorcism account in the Gospels pertains to a demoniac in the Capernaum synagogue where Jesus was functioning like a rabbi on the sabbath. Those gathered "were astounded at his teaching, for he taught them as one having authority, and not as the scribes." While Jesus was so engaged, he was interrupted by "a man with an unclean spirit." Revealing his divided personality, he denounced Jesus loudly, "Have you come to destroy us? I know who you are, the holy one of God." To the demons who were causing convulsions Jesus commanded, "Be quiet and come out of him!"[63]

Jesus' technique was one hypnotherapists have used for dealing with possessed sufferers. This Capernaum episode is analogous to one associated with Apollonius, a charismatic Greek who lived in the first century CE. While the philosopher was teaching, his voice was drowned out by the coarse laughter of a youth who was presumed to be the mouthpiece of a devil. Apollonius ordered the evil spirit out, and the youth returned to his senses.[64]

The best historical examples of Jesus' exorcisms are those pertaining to some women who journeyed with him in Galilee, because the account does not have bewildering elaborations such as is found in the case of the Geresene demoniac. The Jesus Seminar rates only six percent of the events described in the Gospels as "virtually certain" to have happened, but the

---

[59]Luke 13:32.
[60]*Antiquities* 8.46.
[61]*Antiquities* 8.46-47.
[62]Mark 9:38-40; Luke 11:19.
[63]Mark 1:21-26.
[64]Philostratus, *Apollonius* 4.20.

cure of Magdalene is included in that category.[65] Luke writes that she was among those "who had received therapy to release them from evil spirits and diseases" and that "seven demons had gone out" from her.[66] "*Seven demons*" suggests that she was treated by Jesus for a severe mental disorder. The Greek term *therapeuo* that is used here is usually translated, misleadingly, as "heal," rather than transliterated, probably to heighten the effectiveness of Jesus. But only a portion of therapy patients in any age have the outcome of becoming healed either temporarily or permanently. Aware that exorcisms might not have positive results, Jesus realistically warned of relapses of demon-cleansed persons in which they end up in a worse condition than ever.[67] To effect the permanent expulsion of an evil spirit, he suggested, a good spirit needs to be brought into one's psyche as a replacement. Magdalene's subsequent unwavering devotion to Jesus until, and beyond, his death suggests that having the Holy Spirit within gave her protection from the return of "demons."

Across history, picturesque descriptions for neurological illnessess have been created, such as a devil possessing the mind, or the id dominating the superego. The common ancient reference to "demons" displays that people once believed the air was populated with unclean spirits that could enter humans, causing physical and mental illness. This social construction of reality provided a way for dealing with deviant conduct; toleration could be justified on the belief that an individual was behaving involuntarily while under Satan's power. Ancient people had no concept of germs, viruses, psychoses and other medical discoveries of recent origin. But they were convinced that something beyond individual control was causing sickness and that certain gifted persons could assist in the restoration of health. Since many ancient people commonly believed that disease was due to demons invading their bodies, Jesus worked to expel them. To say that he was a psychotherapist or physical therapist might be the demythologized equivalent of claiming that he "cast out demons." Physicians now also use drugs to exorcise illnesses that bedevil patients.

Donald Spoto perceptively notes that

[65]Funk et al., *The Acts of Jesus*, 1, 36, 292.
[66]Luke 8:1-2.
[67]Luke 11:24-26.

As a man of his time, Jesus shared the anthropology as well as the religious language of that day—in other words, he was limited by all the myths and metaphors that then expressed perceptions of reality. Hence, when Jesus commanded an evil spirit to quit someone's body, he addressed what was *behind* the symptoms—the situation of a disordered personality. . . . We may choose to say that the ancient talk about a "possessed person" was really naive, and that the poor soul was actually suffering from . . . an inherited mental illness or from chemical psychosis.[68]

Exorcism may not be as prevalent now as it once was, but the nonsupernatural marvel is still more practiced than most scholars recognize. John Crossan comments on demon possession:

I . . . do not believe that there are personal supernatural spirits who invade our bodies from outside and, for either good or evil, replace or jostle for place with our own personality. But the vast, vast majority of the world's people have always so believed, and according to one recent crosscultural survey, about 75 percent still do.[69]

Michael Cuneo supplies more data on this subject:

During the last quarter of the twentieth century, exorcism was more widely preached in the United States than perhaps ever before. . . . The demon-expulsion front got some unexpected reinforcements. . . . By the early 1990s several hundred evangelical-based exorcism (or deliverance) ministries had sprung up across the country. . . . The majority of exorcism ministers are men; the majority of subjects are women.[70]

Jesus did not assume that there was anything unique in his ability to perform miracles. Never did he suggest that he alone had the power of healing. He taught his disciples to heal/exorcize because he believed that his piety and skills could be assimilated by those ordinary folk.[71] Accordingly, "they cast out many demons, and anointed with oil many who were sick and cured them."[72]

Jesus was disappointed when his disciples were unable to cast out "a spirit" that caused a boy to have convulsions. The story of that ill boy

---

[68]Donald Spoto, *The Hidden Jesus* (New York: St. Martin's, 1998) 114-15.
[69]John Crossan, *Jesus* (San Francisco: Harper, 1994) 85.
[70]"Exorcism," *Contemporary American Religion.*
[71]Matthew 10:8.
[72]Mark 6:13.

illustrates well the way in which descriptions of symptoms change, while the reality of diseases remains constant. What would now be diagnosed as an epileptic seizure was then reported in an unscientific manner. The original language of Matthew states that the boy was moonstruck; accordingly, the King James Version borrows *luna*, the Latin word for "moon," to translate the Greek as "lunatic."[73] In Mark, a demon possesses the boy, making him speechless: "He has a spirit that makes him unable to speak. Whenever it seizes him, it throws him down; he foams at the mouth, grinds his teeth, and becomes rigid."[74]

* * *

The effectiveness of Jesus' therapy was dependent on qualities in both the giver and the receiver. The curative power was primarily in sick persons who desired to be healed. Coupled with that was Jesus' complete faith in God, which was contagious. He passed on to those with whom he came into contact his profound trust in the victory of good over evil. Jesus recognized his powerlessness to facilitate healing for those who lacked confidence that they could regain health through the help of God.[75] It is a medical fact that some mental or physical illnesses are relieved by autosuggestion while some patients are benefited by following the advice of therapists. Jesus tried to make people aware of the psychosomatic causation of some illnesses, and occasionally he informed those who felt healed that their faith was the cause.[76] His giving prominence to the faith factor should not be interpreted to mean that he thought that other factors had no place in dealing with the cause and treatment of diseases. An important New Testament caveat here is the that individual health restoration and life continuance needs to be in accord with the will of God, which may conflict with the hope of the ill person.[77]

Consider one type of faith healing: Jesus encountered individuals with a skin disorder that could have been psychogenic in nature. What was misleadingly called "leprosy" in the Bible pertained to dermatological ailments such as boils, psoriasis, eczema, vitiligo, ringworm, or other fungal

---

[73]Matthew 17:15.
[74]Mark 9:17-18.
[75]Mark 6:5-6.
[76]Mark 5:34; 10:52.
[77]Mark 14:36; 2 Corinthians 12:7-9.

infections. Moreover, evidence is lacking that the Bible refers to what is labeled leprosy in modern science, known as Hansen's bacillus, which can result in wretched disfigurement.[78] The levitical law states, "The person who has the leprous disease shall wear torn clothes and let the hair of his head be disheveled; and he shall cover his upper lip and cry out, 'Unclean, unclean.'"[79] Those whom Hebrew priests declared to have various forms of dermatosis were quarantined and humiliated, but the biblical record indicates that their problems usually, in time, disappeared. In antiquity, visual symptoms were largely the basis for diagnosing the severity of an illness. There was little knowledge of—and hence concern over—the real killers, such as cancer and cardiovascular diseases. Before practitioners could become aware of those malfunctions, medical refinements were needed to enable them to inspect internal organs.

Jesus' stories of providing therapy seem to have both a historical kernel and embellishments from subsequent retellings. For example, Mark's statement that the leprosy "immediately" left the man can be attributed to the redaction process over several decades. Personal changes that developed over time would probably not be recorded as stages by the Evangelist because his interest was more in the completed event than in the gradual way by which it happened.

In the story of Simon the leper, Jesus identified with the outcast by entering his dwelling and dining with him.[80] That friendly gesture became a strong healing force, because being a pariah until symptoms disappear was probably more detrimental to Simon's well-being than the surface ailments. A similar disregard for conventional standards is displayed in the story of another so-called "leper" (Greek, *lepros*) who came to Jesus believing that he could be cleansed. Far from shunning him as contaminated and repulsive, Jesus was "moved with compassion" and laid his hand on the man.[81] The therapy in this case appears to have been the assurance communicated by Jesus that he was not polluted regardless of what the Jewish law stated about ceremonial defilement. Providing the excluded man a means for becoming restored to his community could have been pro-foundly curative.

---

[78]John Pitch, *Healing in the New Testament* (Minneapolis: Fortress, 1999) 156.
[79]Leviticus 13:45-46.
[80]Mark 14:3.
[81]Mark 1:40-41.

Contemporary stress-related illnesses provide an instructive analogy to Jesus' treatments of skin maladies. Consider the situation of Nancy Rosanoff, who had exceptional talent as a pianist. When she studied seriously to become a concert pianist, eczema broke out on her hands. Recognizing that their cracked and bleeding condition could ruin her career ambition, she consulted a psychological healer. She came to understand that her skin condition was caused by her fear of expressing herself creatively before others. As soon as she overcame that phobia, her eczema disappeared.[82]

Catholic theologian Hans Küng comments on the miracle narratives of the Gospels:

> More important than the . . . wonderful deeds is the fact that Jesus turns with sympathy and compassion to all those to whom no one else turns: the weak, sick, neglected, social rejects. . . . Everyone keeps his distance from lepers and "possessed." . . . [For example, the Qumran monks of Palestine in that era declared,] "no madman . . . or fool, no blind man, or maimed, or lame, or deaf man, and no minor, shall enter into the Community." . . . Jesus does not turn away from any of these. . . . To all those whose life is impoverished and hopeless he gives hope, new life, confidence in the future.[83]

* * *

The psychotherapeutic nature of Jesus' healing is also conveyed by a number of other stories. One example deserves close scrutiny because it discloses essential ingredients in authentic Gospel therapies. It pertains to an unnamed woman with a chronic uterine hemorrhage who had spent all that she had on physicians, but medical treatments had not helped. Her community viewed her as a total loser: incurably sick, financially destitute, and culticly polluted. Her illness may have been due in part to her religion. Women who believe menstruation to be God's "curse" display more symptoms of cramps and distress than others.[84]

Jewish priests regarded even regular menstruation as defiling, so continual bleeding compounded the impurity. Women during their periods were presumed to have an uncleanness so contagious that it could be transmitted indirectly without their being present. Special body bathing and

---

[82]Dan Wakefield, *Expect a Miracle* (San Francisco: Harper, 1995) 73-74.
[83]Hans Küng, *On Being a Christian* (New York: Doubleday, 1976) 235.
[84]*Psychology Today* (September 1973): 46.

clothes washing was needed if someone came in contact with anything touched by a woman with a discharge of blood.[85] The healthy, natural function was stigmatized as a filthy, unnatural infection. Menstruants were virtually the only people excluded from all of the courts of the Jerusalem Temple, the place that Isaiah and Jesus thought should be "a house of prayer for all people."[86] Because of menstruation, there was no office of priestess among the Israelites, even though women were not excluded from the prominent public roles of monarch, judge, prophet, or sage.

Rabbis in late antiquity included a whole *Mishnah* chapter, entitled *Niddah* (menstruant), for discussing women's monthly "impurities." Described there were the pollution dangers they posed if they were not isolated. Judaism loaded restrictions on "contaminated" women that were even more burdensome than those in the Mosaic law. Sixty more days a year were added to menstrual defilement, when spouses were to sleep in separate beds to avoid body contact. Menstrual discharge appears to have been regarded as the mark of woman's sin. Introduced in the Jewish oral tradition was a ritual bath requirement at the end of a menstruant's twelve days of "uncleanness."[87]

In defiance of Mosaic law, Jesus rejected the demeaning blood taboo. Although it states of a menstruant, "Whoever touches her shall be unclean,"[88] he disregarded the purification law that declared him contaminated by interacting with such a person. The Judaism of Jesus' day tended to base purity on such externals as avoiding contact with lepers, corpses, and menstruants. But he emphasized internal cleanliness; his list of conditions that make for defilement did not include menstruation and other physical conditions. He rather singled out core evils such as greed, malice, deceit, slander, envy, and arrogance.[89]

In her desperation, the perpetually untouchable hemorrhaging woman thought that a healer who was operating independently of Jewish authorities might help, and in any case Jesus charged no doctor's fee. Concerned that he might shun her, she approached stealthily. Accepting the widespread

---

[85]Leviticus 15:27.

[86]Josephus, *Against Apion* 2.103; Isaiah 56:7; Mark 11:17.

[87]William Phipps, "The Menstrual Taboo in the Judeo-Christian Tradition," *Journal of Religion and Health* (October 1980): 299-300.

[88]Leviticus 15:19.

[89]Mark 7:18-23.

magical notion that a healer's clothing contained potency, she said to herself, "If I touch even his garments, I shall be made well."[90] While mingling among those accompanying Jesus, the poor and smelly pariah sneaked up behind him and made the desired contact. On this occasion, it is the woman, not Jesus, who reaches out and takes the initiative. "She felt in her body that she was healed" before Jesus was aware of who she was and had had an opportunity to speak to her.

According to Mark, Jesus became "immediately aware that power had gone out of him." Expressed here is a main theme of primal cultures, that shamen (holy persons) possess a spiritual force that is discharged to those who touch them, like electricity from a battery. Jesus became aware of the encounter, and stopped to assist the anonymous person. Having been ostracized for twelve years, she had acquired a negative self-image and was chagrined when her brazen scheme was discovered. Mark reports that the woman "came in fear and trembling, fell down before him, and told him the whole truth."[91] However, Jesus was not offended by her brashness in confronting him while he was on an emergency call to a home where the daughter of a synagogue leader was critically ill. When he found the frightened woman he communicated that he did not find her disgusting, or consider her an outcast. Rather, he informed her that healing came from internal confidence, not from external touching, and that her faith had made her "whole"—to use the apt King James Version rendering of *sozo* in Mark 5:34. Her tremendous expectation of improvement in health enabled her to overcome her illness, at least temporarily. For Jesus, faith was not a cerebral assent to credal statements but a bold venturing into new life possibilities. Accordingly, the New Testament provides this definition, "Faith is the assurance of things hoped for."[92]

Strictly speaking, Jesus did not cure people but provided mental therapy to assist healing from within. Here as in other situations he showed himself to be holistically concerned for integrating the psychological personality with the physical organism, linking spiritual holiness with bodily and social wholeness. By affectionately addressing her as "daughter," he diminished her social isolation, enabling her to realize that she was part of his family, a beloved community that transcended biological kin. Jesus was both a

---

[90]Mark 5:28.
[91]Mark 5:33.
[92]Hebrews 11:1.

doctor of divinity and a doctor of psychotherapy. He thought of well-functioning persons as being psychosomatically unified, for humans were intricate composites of soul or mind (Greek, *psyche*) and body (Greek, *soma*). He recognized that mental attitude was a significant factor in the cure of some maladies and that the acceptance of ostracized persons intensifies their healing process. Uta Ranke-Heinemann comments, "Healing is effected not by a supernatural power to work miracles on the part of the healer, but by *the patient's attitude of expectation*."[93]

Throughout Western culture the gospel story of the hemorrhaging woman has been viewed as a classic illustration of the centrality of psychic outlook on the destruction or improvement of life and health. In one of the earliest paintings of Jesus, a third-century Roman catacomb artist shows her anxiously holding onto the fringe of his toga while he turns to assist her.[94] That same century, a Syrian church manual expressed an acceptance of female sexuality in accord with the gospel's rejection of some debilitating purification demands:

> You shall not separate those who have their period. For she also who had the discharge of blood, when she touched the border of our Savior's cloak, was not censured but was even esteemed worthy for the forgiveness of all her sins. And when [your wives have] those issues which are according to nature, take care, as is right, that you cleave to them, for you know that they are your limbs, and love them as yourselves. . . . A woman when she is in the way of woman, and a man when an issue comes forth from him and a man and his wife when they have conjugal intercourse and rise up one from another—let them assemble without restraint, without [ritual] bathing, for they are clean.[95]

Erik Erikson conveys the importance of the hemorrhaging woman episode in the medical field by calling it "the decisive therapeutic event in the Gospels." That famed psychoanalyst commented, "This story is an exalted illustration of that dynamic element, that electric force which has always fascinated the healing professions."[96] From contemporary psychotherapy

---

[93]Uta Ranke-Heinemann, *Putting Away Childish Things* (San Francisco: Harper, 1995) 85.

[94]Gerald Gassiot-Talabot, *Roman and Palaeo-Christian Painting* (New York: Funk & Wagnalls, 1969) 79.

[95]Arthur Voobus, trans., *Didascalia Apostolorum* (Louvain: Corpus Scriptorum Christianorum Orientalium, 1979) 244-45.

[96]Erik Erikson, *Dimensions of a New Identity* (New York: Norton, 1974) 48-49.

comes this insight into the relationship between Jesus and the hemorrhaging woman:

> It seems like the woman was feeling enormous reverence for Jesus and a strong belief that he could heal her. So she was very open to anything that could happen. It helps to have great trust in the healer and it helps even more to trust your own ability to heal. Sometimes trusting the healer can open a pathway to trusting yourself. . . . It's good that Jesus said to her, "Your trust has healed you." . . . He's saying, "Don't think that I actually did anything to you; your own trust is what healed you."[97]

The crucial role of expectation in the improvement of health has now been confirmed. A significant percentage of healing comes through the sick having hope restored for using their own resources in combating illness. Herbert Weiner insists: "Most persons who seek out physicians' ministrations are ill *but do not have a disease*. . . . Their ills are the product of their situation in life, expressed in diverse ways."[98] About one-third of patients who are given placebos instead of drugs show that healing power exists within and is made operative when attitudes are altered by trusting something external to bring about change. From a scientific study of the placebo effect came this conclusion, "Faith, hope, trust . . . can at times heal wounds, alter body chemistry, even change the course of the most relentless diseases."[99]

Brain scans show that the anticipation of healing given by placebos can cause cells to produce dopamine, which relieves physcial pain.[100] Physician Bernie Siegal points out in his widely circulated book, *Love, Medicine, and Miracles*, that disease often can be diminished and the quality of life enhanced by a change in a patient's mental mood. Norman Cousins, while on the staff of a medical school, investigated psychoneuroimmunology, the study of ways in which brain secretions affect the body's immune system. He found numerous scientific studies revealing that a large portion of

---

[97]Quoted in Stephen Mitchell, *The Gospel according to Jesus* (New York: Harper, 1990) 297.

[98]Stanley Cheren, *Psychosomatic Medicine* (Madison WI: International Universities Press, 1989) 22-23.

[99]*Science Digest* (September 1981): 60.

[100]*National Geographic Magazine* (August 2004) 1.

patients seeking medical help are suffering from self-limiting disorders that are within the range of their body's own healing powers.[101]

Paul Tillich, a leading twentieth-century theologian, provided this description of the healing miracles in the Gospels:

> They show the human situation, the relation between bodily and mental disease, between sickness and guilt. . . . Many of our profoundest modern insights into human nature are anticipated in these stories. . . . Becoming healthy means becoming whole, reunited, in one's bodily and psychic functions. . . . We are told how Jesus, knowing this, pronounces to the paralytic first the forgiveness of his sins and then his regained health. . . . These stories also describe the attitude which makes healing possible. They call it faith. Faith here, of course, does not mean the belief in assertions for which there is no evidence. It never meant that in genuine religion. . . . Faith means being grasped by a power that is greater then we are, a power that skakes us and turns us, and transforms us and heals us.[102]

What impression was created by Jesus' work with the sick? After reviewing current research on his miracles, Barry Blackburn reports "the twentieth-century consensus": "Jesus acted neither as an ancient physician, employing contemporary medical knowledge and techniques, nor as a magician, utilizing powerful demons or angels and/or formulas or incantations possessing intrinsic power. Jesus is best described as a charismatic miracle worker."[103]

Accounts of most healings are so brief that one can only speculate as to the contextual situation. Consider the case of Peter's mother-in-law who resided with his family in the fishertown of Capernaum. She had a mild illness when Jesus and his disciples visited in her home, but she responded to his bedside manner. Consequently, her fever subsided and she served them.[104] Her sickness may have been an anxiety attack resulting from her son-in-law's vocational change. From her practical perspective, Peter was probably not providing adequately for her daughter and family because he had left his fishing trade to join up with an itinerant preacher. But after be-

---

[101]Norman Cousins, *Head First* (New York: Dutton, 1989).

[102]Paul Tillich, *The New Being* (New York: Scribner, 1955) 37-38.

[103]Bruce Chilton and Craig Evans, eds., *Studying the Historical Jesus* (Leiden: Brill, 1994) 374-75.

[104]Mark 1:30-31.

coming aware of the dimensions of his gospel, her resentment and illness dissipated.

The story of Zacchaeus, the chief tax collector in Jericho, can best be viewed as another account of healing. He may have heard that Jesus was reputed to be a friend of tax collectors, so he wished to meet him. He may have been both the richest and the loneliest person in the city, because his fellow Jews had no social relations with anyone who had contracted to collect taxes for the despised Romans, the conquerors and occupiers of Palestine. So eager was the pariah to see Jesus when he came to Jericho that he climbed a tree to be above the taller people who had gathered. On spotting him, Jesus invited himself to visit with Zacchaeus in his home. Zacchaeus was delighted but the crowd was shocked. Luke's story continues:

> The bystanders muttered, "He has gone to be the guest of a sinner." Zacchaeus stood up and said to the Lord, "I will now give half of my possessions to the poor; and if I have defrauded anyone, I will make a fourfold restitution." Then Jesus said to him, "Today health has come to this household, because this man too is a son of Abraham. For the Son of Man came to seek out and to heal the lost."[105]

The Greek term *sotepia* is rendered here by "health," following magisterial translator William Tyndale. Its verbal form, *sozein*, is translated as "heal," because in the Gospels it sometimes pertains to someone whom Jesus had made whole. "Salvation" (although derived from *salus*, meaning "health" in Latin) and "save," the usual English translations, have been avoided because they are associated by many with an eschatological deliverance to heaven after death. In contrast to pious Jews who excommunicated Zacchaeus from the synagogue, Jesus called him a true "son of Abraham" because he had been converted to ethical business practices. Part of Jesus' mission was to free those who were obsessed with economic concerns and show them that psychic soundness comes more from giving than from getting.

* * *

In the ancient world there was lore in different cultures about charismatic figures raising the dead that may have been based on instances of

---

[105]Luke 19:7-10.

natural resuscitation. Prior to the advent of scientific diagnosis, mistaken judgment on whether or not a sick person had died was not uncommon. Plato advised a two-day lapse before entombing a body, in order to distinguish between someone who is in a "trance" and one who is really dead.[106] In one story, Apollonius witnessed a bride, who had died the hour of her wedding, being carried out for burial on an undertaker's bier. After he touched her and whispered some words over her, she awakened "just as Alcestis did when she was brought back to life by Hercules." Biographer Philostratus comments, "Whether Apollonius detected some spark of life in her, which those who were nursing her had not noticed . . . or whether life was really extinct and he restored it by his touch, is a mysterious problem which neither I myself nor those who were present could decide."[107]

Other near-contemporaries of Jesus also report that keen perception prevented premature burial.[108] In one account, a physician happened to pass by a large funeral that was being conducted outside the city walls of Rome. Through remarkable power of observation he discovered vital signs in the presumed corpse. As a result the cremation pyre was not lit, which disappointed some heirs.[109] Evidence of body movement in tombs has been found, showing that some individuals who were in a reversible coma have been buried alive. Accordingly, some healers have been alert to prevent such from happening.

In the biblical culture there were also accounts of the reanimation of those presumed dead. Both Elijah and Elisha in separate situations reputedly effected the restoration of breathing by stretching out on children and putting lips to lips.[110] Perhaps some early form of mouth-to-mouth artificial respiration was performed by those Hebrew prophets. Also, a story from ancient Judaism about reviving a servant who had just been declared dead is not completely implausible. After a rabbi asked him, "'Why do you lie prostrate when your master stands?' immediately he stirred and stood up."[111] According to the Jewish Talmud, death was not irrevocable until

---

[106]Plato, *Laws* 959.

[107]Philostratus, *Apollonius* 4.45.

[108]Celsus, *On Medicine* 2.6; Pliny, *Natural History* 7.37.

[109]Apuleius, *Florida* 19.

[110]1 Kings 17:17-23; 2 Kings 4:32-37.

[111]Leviticus Rabbah 16:111d.

three days after breathing ceased; during that period the soul hovered about the deceased as it sought to reinhabit its former body.[112]

Vigils developed in history for the period before burials, in part to make sure that the presumed corpse showed no signs of life. A century ago, James Thompson recorded cases of persons in cataleptic trances who were assumed dead, one being of the Archbishop of Bordeaux who was buried prematurely when a youth.[113] Distinguishing between a dead and a comatose person was difficult prior to the invention of the stethoscope. Occasionally one reads even today accounts of the revival in mortuaries of persons thought to be dead.[114] Some might say that life was detected by a stroke of luck, while others might interpret such happenings as a providential prevention of premature embalming.

Jesus may also have discerned signs of life in some dying individuals. He was asked to heal a girl who was ill, but on arriving at her home he heard wailing from friends who assumed she had already died. Saying, "The child is not dead but sleeping," he held her hand and spoke to her in Aramaic. Mark conveys that this story contains authentic remembrances by recording "*Talitha koum*," words from Jesus' native language.[115] She revived after he said those words, meaning "Arise, little girl." Jairus's daughter may have been among the survivors whom Quadratus had in mind when he wrote to Emperor Hadrian early in the second century:

> Our Savior's works were always there to see, for they were true—the people who had been cured and those raised from the dead, who had not merely been seen at the moment when they were cured or raised, but were always there to see, not only when the Savior was among us, but for a long time after his departure; in fact, some of them survived right up to my own time.[116]

In another story, Jesus encountered, on a road near the town of Nain, a funeral party carrying a body out to bury. In that region, then as well as now, interments took place shortly after death. Jesus commanded the youth on the bier to arise, and he sat up and spoke. Those who witnessed this

---

[112]*Yebamot* 16.

[113]James Thompson, *Miracles in the New Testament* (London: Arnold, 1911) 44.

[114]William Phipps, *Death* (Atlanta: John Knox, 1987) 10-13.

[115]Mark 5:41.

[116]Eusebius, *Church History* 4:3.

exclaimed, "A great prophet has risen among us!"[117] Luke displays a conscious modeling of his story on the one told of Elijah in the Greek version of the Hebrew Bible. In particular, both use the same words to tell of meeting a widow at the gate of her town and returning a restored boy to his mother.

Luke shows an eagerness to give a supernatural interpretation to accounts of those who were presumed dead. He is the only Evangelist who told of the boy at Nain and he alone told of another incident when, in his judgment, a young man is restored to life. One evening, while trying to listen to Paul preach until midnight, Eutychus became drowsy and fell from the window sill on which he sat to the ground three floors below. Luke states that "he was picked up dead," although he may have had a brain concussion that could have been diagnosed otherwise. "Paul hastened down, stooped over him, and embraced him. He said, 'Do not be alarmed, for he is alive.' "[118] Did he give the boy a CPR treatment similar to the manner of Elijah and Elisha?

When in India, Francis Xavier was confronted by a situation that had overtones of Paul's experience with the Ephesian youth. During a church service, the body of a boy who had fallen into a well and was presumed dead was brought to Xavier, who prayed over him. Afterward, when those assembled saw the boy rise up, they assumed that the missionary had performed a miracle. But Xavier discounted that interpretation, saying that the boy had been unconscious and was not raised from the dead.[119]

Mahatma Gandhi read Gospel stories of people restored to life, and compared them with his experience:

> I raised a relative's child from supposed death to life, and but for my presence there she might have been cremated. But I saw that life was not extinct. I gave her an enema and she was restored to life. There was no miracle about it. I do not deny that Jesus had certain psychic powers and he was undoubtedly filled with the love of humanity. But he brought to life no people who were dead but who were believed to be dead. The laws of Nature are changeless, unchange-

---

[117]Luke 7:11-16.

[118]Acts 20:7-12.

[119]Georg Schurhammer, *Francis Xavier* (Rome: Jesuit Historical Institute, 1982) 2:345.

able, and there are no miracles in the sense of infringement or interruption of Nature's laws.[120]

* * *

Jesus healed for the same reason that poets write poems. "Poetry is the spontaneous overflow of powerful feelings," William Wordsworth explained.[121] True poets write because they cannot repress their sentiments, not to prove they are poets. Jesus did not heal to show off, or to attract crowds, or to certify that he was the Son of God. Mark states that Jesus "was moved with compassion" to relieve sufferers who pressed in upon him.[122] Matthew claims that Jesus healed to fulfill this prophecy, "He took our infirmities and bore our diseases."[123] That Evangelist associated Jesus with the "servant of the Lord" in Isaiah 53 because of what he did during his ministry, not because of his suffering in a vicarious way as he died.

Even though Jesus did not seek public acclaim as a healer, both he and his disciples unavoidedly did gain notoriety by attending to those who were ill or presumed dead. Their exorcisms/therapies, more than their preaching, attracted crowds. Mark states that after Jesus' first exorcism "his fame spread at once far and wide throughout Galilee."[124] Whereupon all the possessed and the diseased in the area were brought to him.

A literary device used by Matthew has caused readers of that Gospel to wrongly assume that Jesus' teachings were the main thing that attracted the "multitudes" to him. What is called the Sermon on the Mount is the result of that editor gathering up Jesus' ethical maxims and his brief theological responses to inquiries in a number of settings. Matthew introduced the summary of Jesus' teaching by saying that the crowds, who had come from a distance, sat down on a mountainside to hear his teachings. But it is unlikely that he preached a long sermon or that those attending remembered sayings totaling more than one hundred verses.

The Markan Jesus was a reluctant wonder-worker who attempted to diminish the popularity he was receiving as a health restorer by repeatedly

---

[120]*The Collected Works of Mahatma Gandhi* (Ahmedabad: Government of India, 1976) 65:82.

[121]William Wordsworth, *Lyrical Ballads* (1800) preface.

[122]Mark 1:41.

[123]Matthew 8:17; Isaiah 53:4.

[124]Mark 1:28.

requesting silence from those who felt they had been cured.[125] In an attempt to shake off the healing obsessed crowds, Jesus retreated to a remote area and informed his companions that he was heading elsewhere "so that I may proclaim my message there also, for that is what I came to do."[126] Included in that proclamation was a call to repentance that was generally unwelcomed.[127] Repentance involves a radical change in personal values, resulting in discarding religious legalism, purifying the inner life, and assisting the needy. Mark conveys the difficulty Jesus had in presenting himself as a different type of religious leader than one who made people feel healthier—a role guaranteed to make for success in any culture—while making no demands on moral transformation.

The genuineness of Jesus' healings can be better understood by contrasting him to Oral Roberts's performances. Fifty some years ago I conducted a firsthand investigation of faith healing by talking with followers of that Pentecostal revivalist, then on his way to becoming the most renowned person internationally in the business. He had not yet moved into the lucrative televangelism field and was taking his huge tent to cities of the American South. He made spectacular claims for what he could do with the power that came from the Holy Ghost down his right arm. He pretended to transmit the surge when he seized a defective bodily area, causing what appeared to be an electrical shock in the one hoping to be cured. Were one to listen only to him and his promoters, one might conclude that he could cure cancer and even raise the dead.

But I had an advantage over Roberts's evening audiences, that of being able to observe the procedure for screening those who would appear on the platform with him, and then to follow up on some who allegedly had been miraculously healed. I talked with a simpleminded fellow in a wheelchair who traveled from city to city in his camper to enjoy emotional highs at the tent meetings. Since he could take a few steps with difficulty, a regular feature was placing him in the "healing line" and having him walk unaided after Roberts laid his hands on the cripple's legs. Reveling in the attention given him by the hundreds of witnesses, he was not upset that his condition had not really improved. The desperate cases who could not put on a good show were not only avoided but made to feel guilty. The reason given for

---

[125]Mark 1:44, 7:36, 8:26.
[126]Mark 1:28, 32-39.
[127]Mark 1:15.

their not being selected was that he worked only with those in whom he was able to discern faith. Presumably he could never find it in those who were altogether disabled, so their "demons" could not be exorcised.

The health of some did seem to improve, but whether it was because of, or in spite of, Roberts was impossible to determine. My own research, and my reading of interviews made by journalists, made me aware that illness increased for some from contact with him. In one extreme case a diabetic died not long after being informed that she could discontinue taking insulin. To those who complained about the untruth of being assured that they had been cured, his retort was that continued remission cannot be guaranteed to backsliders in faith. When I began my study of Roberts I presumed that he was a genuine but naive faith healer; I concluded that he was little more than a prestige and profit seeking charlatan who was using age-old tricks of suggestion to exploit those with prodigious gullibility. In the present generation there continue to be prominent "healers," whose manipulation of religion is as reprehensible as that of Roberts. Of course, they could not function without followers who also have a superficial understanding of the gospel. Much of the "faith" frenzy of the self-absorbed is devoted to persuading God and a particular presumed divine agent to cater to their demands.

Jesus resisted making therapeutic work his top priority even though he recognized a relationship between treating the mentally or physically ill and the main theme of his teaching, the sovereign rule of God. Attributed to him is this saying, "If it is by the finger of God that I cast out the demons, then the kingdom of God has come to you."[128] But Jesus realized that there is nothing permanent in individual healings since all who regain their health eventually die. Hence he thought of his healer/exorcist role as secondary to his primary mission. Unlike healing, teaching can be transmitted from person to person and from generation to generation.

In the early church, some Christians treated Gospel accounts of Jesus' miracles as symbols for his healing of the psyche (mind, soul). One wrote: "The Son of the living God, the physician of souls . . . caused the ears of the unhearing soul to hear."[129] Jesus is elsewhere represented as going beyond treating the transitory healing of the temporal body: "Why do you marvel at his cures of the body that are ended by death, especially when you know

---

[128]Luke 11:20.
[129]*Psalm of Heracleides.*

that healing of his that does not pass away? . . . He is a physician of souls, and is different from all other physicians: for all others heal bodies that are dissolved, but he heals souls that are eternal."[130]

Jesus recognized that even spectacular physical miracles tend not to effect changes in basic values. He taught by means of a parable that supernaturalism can engender temporary fright but is impotent to transform a stingy person into a person who habitually shares with the poor. A rich man suffering in hades, as his story goes, requests that he be resurrected in order to warn his brothers of what will happen to them if they persist in an attitude of indifference to the needs of marginalized humans. His request is denied for this reason, "If they do not listen to Moses and the prophets, neither will they be convinced if someone rises from the dead."[131] Jesus did not think that individuals who are unresponsive to the social justice teachings of the Israelite prophets can be amazed into a lifestyle of ethical concern. Neither did he think that authentic faith could be based on miracles, as Lutheran theologian Helmut Thielicke points out:

> He always refuses to perform a miracle where people want to use it to dodge a personal decision. He dispenses with any cheap miracle propaganda because he knows that in the long run you don't win people with this sort of fake advertising. . . . He wants a miracle to be anything but a visual proof which makes the commitment of faith superfluous.[132]

This exchange is recorded in Matthew: "Some of the scribes and Pharisees said, 'Teacher, we wish to see a sign from you.' But he answered, 'An evil and adulterous generation asks for a sign.' "[133] George Bernard Shaw has commented on Jesus' dismay when he was assailed by this clamor for marvels:

> When people who were not ill or in trouble came to him and asked him to exercise his powers as a sign of his mission, he was irritated beyond measure, and refused with an indignation which they . . . must have thought very unreasonable. To be called "an evil and adulterous generation" merely for asking a miracle worker to give an exhibition of his powers, is rather a startling experience. Mahomet, by the way, also lost his temper when people asked him

---

[130]*Acts of Thomas* 78, 95.
[131]Luke 16:19-31.
[132]Helmut Thielicke, *I Believe* (Philadelphia: Fortress, 1968) 61.
[133]Matthew 12:38-39.

to perform miracles. . . . The exercise of such powers would give rise to wild tales of magical feats. . . . Jesus' teaching has nothing to do with miracles. . . . To say "you should love your enemies; and to convince you of this I will now proceed to cure this gentleman of cataract" would have been, to a man of Jesus' intelligence, the proposition of an idiot. If it could be proved today that not one of the miracles of Jesus actually occurred, that proof would not invalidate a single one of his didactic utterances.[134]

George Bernard Shaw is accurate in recognizing that the *Qur'an* tells of a response by Muhammad to his opponents that is similar to a controversy in which Jesus engaged. Meccans challenged him, "Let him show us some sign, as did the apostles of old," and "We will not believe in you until you make a spring gush forth from the earth for us."[135] But Muhammad viewed natural regularities as such a marvelous witness to God that no unnatural portents were needed. The *Qur'an* states: "It was God who gave the sun its radiance and the moon its brightness, ordaining its phases so that you may compute seasons and years. . . . In the alternation of night and day, and in all that He created in the heavens and the earth, there are signs for people who revere Him."[136] A comment of New Testament scholar Günther Bornkamm could apply to both semitic prophets: "Jesus will not allow miracles to be considered a proof of God's working and power, which could be demanded as the prerequisite to faith. Such a demand is a challenging of God. Trust and obedience have both been destroyed at the roots."[137]

Jesus cautioned the faithful about impostors who claim to work miracles. To those who expect divine acceptance because they claimed to perform many powerful deeds in the Lord's name, he would declare, "I never knew you; out of my sight, you evildoers."[138] Jesus warned that "false christs and false prophets will appear and produce signs and omens, to mislead, if possible, even God's chosen."[139] The New Testament also tells elsewhere of impostors who perform "lying wonders" that are devoid of divine

---

[134]George Bernard Shaw, *Complete Plays with Prefaces* (New York: Dodd, 1962) 5:345-46.

[135]*Qur'an* 21:5; 17:90.

[136]*Qur'an* 10:5-6.

[137]Günther Bornkamm, *Jesus of Nazareth* (New York: Harper, 1960) 133.

[138]Matthew 7:22-23.

[139]Mark 13:22.

revelation.[140] The ability to do astonishing things was for Jesus no test of authenticity. Supernaturalism attempts to coerce God to carry out the will of some human individual or group, whereas Jesus submitted to God's will.

Philosopher Immanuel Kant, in treating miracles as superfluous to "moral religion," appealed to a similar comment on "signs" attributed to Jesus. Critical of those who expect additional accreditation of their faith by miracles, he perceived, "Unless you see signs and wonders you will not believe."[141] Kant said, "Belief in miracles . . . bespeaks a culpable degree of moral unbelief not to acknowledge as completely authoritative the commands of duty."[142]

An appeal to signs continues to be found in our own time, even among intellectuals. Positivists, who presuppose that all things real are empirically in evidence, champion what might be called the immaculate perception dogma. They contend that if there are no supernatural signs, there is no God. For example, Bertrand Russell presumed—like Elijah at Sinai,[143] until he learned better—that a convincing God should be revealed in extraordinary rather than in ordinary experiences. Russell asserted, "I think that if I heard a voice from the sky predicting all that was going to happen to me during the next twenty-four hours, including events that would have seemed highly improbable, and if all these events then proceeded to happen, I might perhaps be convinced at least of the existence of some superhuman intelligence."[144]

Russell here discloses that he might be persuaded of the reality of a voice from the blue if a kind of irrational parapsychology could be verified. By contrast, those oriented toward rational religion would find in such precognition *less* evidence for divine "intelligence."

Regarding Jesus' criticism of those who demanded additional legitimation of his teachings, the Kellers write:

> Conviction should rest on what he says and it is on this basis that they should decide whether he is speaking the truth, i. e., whether he is of God or not. Ex-

---

[140]2 Thessalonians 2:9; Revelation 16:14.

[141]John 4:48.

[142]Immanuel Kant, *Religion within the Limits of Reason Alone* (New York: Harper, 1960) 79.

[143]1 Kings 19:11-12.

[144]Leo Rosten, ed., *Religions in America* (New York: Simon & Schuster, 1963) 203.

ternal miracles do not take one any further in this matter; indeed they distract from the real point at issue. Inner conviction through the truth of his words is the only criterion which Jesus has to offer in response to the question as to his credentials. . . . If one describes Jesus' views, as reflected in his rejection of the demand for signs, from the point of view of the history of thought, it may be said that his proclamation liberated man's personal power of judgment by appealing to his personal conviction and individual conscience.[145]

Signs of the Times

All the Gospels tell of religionists who came to Jesus asking for a supernatural sign from heaven, but he refused to satisfy their craving for cosmic validation of whom he claimed to be. "He groaned in his spirit" is Mark's way of conveying Jesus' exasperation with those oriented toward the spectacular.[146]

He called reliance on heavenly signs "adulterous," that is, a display of unfaithfulness to God. Even so, Jesus encouraged people to discern from observable patterns of earthly events what lay ahead:

> The Pharisees and Sadducees came, and to test him they asked him to show them a sign from heaven. He replied, "At sunset you say the weather will be good because the sky is red, and in the morning you say it will be rainy because the sky is red and overcast. You know how to interpret the appearance of the sky, but you cannot interpret the signs of the times!"[147]

From his experience with Galilean fishermen, Jesus was aware that folks take precautions on seeing a red glow in the eastern sky. They accepted the proverbial wisdom, "Red in the morning, sailors take warning." Simple people can discover regularities by examining the sky over a period of time and then make weather prophecies. Jesus excoriated the leaders of his people for not applying their wisdom regarding natural signs to the interpreting of their sociopolitical situation. The same methodology for making intelligent forecasts is used by both physical and social scientists. Analyzing past history and current conditions can signify what is likely to happen in the future if the similar conditions persist.

---

[145]Keller and Keller, *Miracles in Dispute*, 231.
[146]Mark 8:11-13.
[147]Matthew 16:1-3.

The rainbow is the best-known natural sign in the Bible.[148] The Hebrews associated it with God's covenant that continues after the occurrence of destructive natural forces. Of course, they did not have the scientific knowledge to recognize that rainbows are easily explained in a nonsupernatural manner. A psalmist found high waves at sea awesome, but this "wonderous work" of the Lord and the survival of a ship during the storm was not treated as a sign of God's interruption of nature's regularity.[149]

As a boy, Jesus was probably disturbed by a bloody experience that provided him with a lifelong conviction about political realities. At that time a Jewish zealot named Judas, aspiring to restore Israel to a theocracy, stirred up Galileans by instructing them to fight against foreign rule and to refuse to pay taxes to Rome.[150] His guerrilla force sparked an insurrection at Sepphoris, the capital city of Galilee. It was soon crushed, and thousands of the rioters were either crucified or enslaved by the Romans.[151] Growing up in a town only three miles south of Sepphoris, the Nazarene lived near the epicenter of Jewish xenophobia and saw firsthand the devastation it had wrought. Jesus and his father may have provided carpentry assistance during Sepphoris's years of urban reconstruction. Although Jesus had no enthusiasm for Roman control, he appeared to view it as less catastrophic than what had ensued from the revolt of Judas the Galilean. Indeed, he may have considered the Roman government in Palestine a lesser evil than domination by fanatical Jewish patriots who hated pagans. Jesus could read the "signs of the times" and see the toll resulting from centuries of unholy bitterness.

John Riches has plausibly conjectured that the loss of life and property from the Galilean uprising signaled for Jesus throughout his mature years what would be the probable outcome of any subsequent Jewish attempt to throw off Roman colonialism. Riches discusses why Jesus rejected the Armageddon approach of the holy war activists of his time, "The calamities which befell the Jews at Sepphoris and the firm control which [Roman puppet Herod] Antipas exercised over Galilee may well have led Jesus to the conclusion that if God were to vindicate his people, to establish his rule,

---

[148]Genesis 9:13.
[149]Psalm 107:23-29.
[150]Josephus, *Wars* 2.118; Acts 5:37.
[151]*Antiquities* 17.272, 295.

it would not be through military struggle." Over against the popular apocalypticism, Jesus' intention was strikingly different:

> He points to his own ministry of healing and forgiveness, of association with
> sinners as the way of redemption for his people. For his contemporaries the
> way to redemption lay via the destruction of Israel's enemies, not via the
> forgiveness and invitation to the feast of those who wittingly or unwittingly
> were their instruments, i.e. those who collaborated with the foreign powers.[152]

Jesus did not believe that a multitude of angelic warriors would fight on
the side of God's chosen against the Romans, as some compatriots did.[153]
E. P. Sanders contrasts Jesus' style with that of various messianic pre-
tenders who expected the Kingdom of God to come by miraculous intervention, vanquishing the Roman army. In his influential study, Sanders states:

> There are prophetic and symbolic actions, but they are not miracles. . . . Jesus
> saw himself as one who was a servant of all, not their glorious leader in a tri-
> umphal march through parted waters. . . . When he decided to go to Jerusalem
> and to offer symbolic gestures to indicate what was to come (the replacement
> of the Temple) and his own role in it (a king, but one who rides on an ass), it
> is unlikely that he realistically thought that the leaders and aristocrats would
> be convinced that the kingdom was at hand and that he was God's last envoy
> before the end.[154]

Jesus' attitude toward the Roman army is suggested by this saying, "If
anyone compels [*aggareuo*] you to go one mile, go with him two."[155] As is
frequently the case with Jesus' teachings, Thomas Manson best states their
meaning. Alluding to another famous saying of Jesus, the exegete comments, "The first mile renders to Caesar the things that are Caesar's; the
second mile, by meeting oppression with kindness, renders to God the
things that are God's."[156] The Greek verb *aggareuo* is a technical term
pertaining to a soldier's right to require a civilian to carry a load for a
certain distance. Bearing the burdens of aliens for even the mandatory first

---

[152]John Riches, *Jesus and the Transformation of Judaism* (New York: Seabury,
1982) 99-100, 188.

[153]Qumran scroll, *War of the Sons of Light and the Sons of Darkness* 12.8-10.

[154]E. P. Sanders, *Jesus and Judaism* (Philadelphia: Fortress, 1985) 235.

[155]Matthew 5:41.

[156]Mark 12:17; Thomas Manson, *The Sayings of Jesus* (London: SCM, 1949)
160.

mile must have generally caused much resentment. Such work was a bitter reminder to the Jews of the humiliating conquest of their homeland by a succession of foreign powers. Most Jews probably never realized that providing assistance beyond what was demanded could be a way of destroying enemies and that Roman soldiers might be transformed into friends by occasions of unexpected helpfulness.

Out of the crucible of his own experiences Jesus came to this general conclusion, "All who draw the sword will die by the sword."[157] In a study of Jesus' response to the Palestinian political hotbed, Sherman Johnson concludes with this sound judgment:

> He took a highly independent attitude toward the authorities, both political and religious, and, like the Old Testament prophets, was keenly aware of the political situation. On the other hand, while he believed that God alone was king, and men were his free children, he rejected the revolutionary movement entirely. . . . Jesus rejected the way of violence, which his compatriots followed to their own destruction.[158]

John Meier, an expert on the historical Jesus, views his final entry into Jerusalem as "a symbolic action of Jesus carefully staged in the presence of his followers."[159] He decided to show the Passover pilgrims a dramatic personal sign of the type of messianic hope he wished to fulfill. A selection between alternatives was needed, because imbedded in the Hebrew scriptures were two irreconcilable hopes. The popular one was that the Lord's anointed son would become king at Jerusalem, confront national enemies, and "break them with a rod of iron."[160] One prophet, envisioning a holy war led by the Lord against surrounding nations, called for Jews to "beat their pruning hooks into spears."[161] The other hope was of a "Prince of Peace" who would persuade nations to "beat their spears into pruning hooks."[162] In order to signal that his mission was the latter type, Jesus acted out a biblical prophecy.

Küng suggests how Jesus became aware of the signs of what might happen to him in Jerusalem:

---

[157]Matthew 26:52.
[158]Sherman Johnson, *Jesus in His Homeland* (New York: Scribner, 1957) 109.
[159]Doris Donnelly, ed., *Jesus* (New York: Continuum, 2001) 68.
[160]Psalm 2:1-9.
[161]Joel 3:10.
[162]Isaiah 2:4, 9:6; Micah 4:3.

No supernatural knowledge was required to recognize the danger of a violent end, only a sober view of reality. His radical message raised doubts about the . . . traditional religious system. . . . Consequently Jesus was bound to expect serious conflicts and violent reactions on the part of the religious and perhaps also the political authorities, particularly at the center of power.[163]

Prophets in Jerusalem had long used crowd-stopping symbolic actions to draw attention to a message that was counter to popular sentiments. To those prophets, an event was significant if it conveyed God's presence—not if it deviated from the natural order. Thus, Isaiah responded to Judah's foolish alliance with Egypt "by walking naked and barefoot for three years as a sign and a warning."[164] On the basis of historical antecedents, the prophet thought the Assyrian army invading Judah would carry prisoners away naked from towns, even though the Egyptians had guaranteed protection. Also, in the Hebrew Bible particular individuals thought of themselves, or were thought of by others, as signs pointing to the will of God. For example, a prophecy states that "Ezekiel shall be to you [Jews] a sign" because he was a divine spokesman to his generation, not because he was a miracle worker.[165] At the outset of Luke's Gospel, shepherds are told that Jesus "will be a sign for you" and Simeon announces that Jesus is a "sign" whom people will oppose.[166] Supernatural powers are not associated with infant Jesus in those stories.

Recognizing that his fellow Jews treasured stories of the flamboyant acts of earlier prophets, Jesus dramatically proposed an alternative to a future insurrection against Rome. By riding into Jerusalem on what was then the most common beast of burden—rather than on the mount of a military commander—Jesus acted in a highly *sign*ificant manner. He pointed to a radically new kind of reign: one in which majesty is combined with meekness, and one in which international peace replaces national chauvinism.[167] Marcus Borg describes Jesus' procession into the traditional royal capital in this way: "His entry was a planned political demonstration, an appeal to Jerusalem to follow the path of peace, even as it proclaimed

---

[163]Küng, *On Being a Christian*, 320.
[164]Isaiah 20:3.
[165]Ezekiel 3:4; 12:6; 24:24.
[166]Luke 2:12, 34.
[167]Zechariah 9:9-10; Matthew 21:1-9.

that his movement was the peace party in a generation headed for war. It also implied that the alternative of peace was still open."[168]

Jesus' immersion in prophetic history enabled him to extrapolate future scenarios from past happenings. During his last week in Jerusalem, his situation paralleled that of a Hebrew prophet. His method of parading into the city was as unusual as that of Jeremiah, who wore an ox yoke around his neck as he moved though the city streets. That earlier prophet explained to the curious that the burdensome "yoke" of Babylonian rule should be preferred to the alternative of mass destruction by the Babylonian army. Jeremiah believed that Jewish nationalists were inviting war, famine, and pestilence because they aimed at retaining political independence regardless of the cost.[169] He was convinced that submission was the Lord's will, even though many thought of him as subversive to the Judean religious community.[170]

When Jesus obtained a panoramic view of Jerusalem from the Mount of Olives, he lamented that the people did not understand or endorse the vision for the future he shared with some earlier prophets. The city dwellers rested their security on two things: the presumed impregnable walls of the mountaintop fortress and the location of "the house of the Lord" within Jerusalem. Reading the historical signs, Jesus saw parallels between what weeping Jeremiah faced vis-à-vis the Babylonian destruction of Jerusalem six centuries earlier and what might be ahead for those who disregarded the lessons of history. Luke states regarding Jesus: "When he came into full view of the city, he burst into tears, saying, 'If only you knew today the path to peace! But it is hidden from your sight. . . . You and the children within your walls will be dashed to the ground.' "[171] The details of Jerusalem's fall reflect that the Gospels were composed after that devastation was completed.

Like his mentor Jeremiah,[172] Jesus counseled the Jerusalemites to reject the conventional wisdom that patriotism always means warring against the foes of one's nation, presuming that such was God's will. He pointed out that the enemy of the Jewish peasantry was, in considerable part, their own

---

[168]Marcus Borg, *Jesus: A New Vision* (San Francisco: Harper, 1987) 174.
[169]Jeremiah 27:2-13.
[170]Jeremiah 38:4.
[171]Luke 19:41, 44.
[172]Jeremiah 27.

rulers. With that group in mind, Jesus lamented, "Jerusalem, Jerusalem, the city that kills the prophets, and stones those who are sent to it!"[173] At the risk of being called a deserter, he urged: "When you see Jerusalem surrounded by troops, realize that its devastation is near. Then those who are in Judea must run away to the mountains, and those who are inside the city must evacuate."[174] Neither prophet performed any miracle to try to convince the people that it is better to be subject to a foreign power than it is to be buried by them.

Prophets Jeremiah and Jesus both attempted to deflate the presumption that their Temple was indispensable to God. For the Jewish priests it was unthinkable that God would permit the destruction of his presumed earthly dwelling place that they had been commissioned to manage. Jesus infuriated them by supporting Jeremiah's claim that the Temple had become a "den of robbers" and that its destruction was justified.[175] Such rashness led to both prophets being beaten, and caused the Jerusalem elite to demand their deaths.[176] After Jesus instituted the "new covenant" that Jeremiah had announced,[177] he experienced the humiliation of rejection by the Jewish leaders.

The morning following Jesus' cleansing of the Temple, he was confronted by Jewish leaders who demanded to know his authority for attacking the Jerusalem religious establishment. They were probably challenging him to produce some external authenicating sign.[178] He responded by asking them about the authority of John the Baptizer who was accepted by the Jewish people as a credentialed prophet even though he worked no miracles. The discussion ended when Jesus' adversaries refused to answer his question.[179]

In *Discerning the Signs of the Times*, distinguished theologian Reinhold Niebuhr discusses the desire of the Pharisees and Sadducees to have Jesus produce miraculous signs to validate his messianic claims. They had "the egoistic hope that the end of history would give Israel as the chosen nation,

---

[173]Matthew 23:37.
[174]Luke 21:20-21.
[175]Jeremiah 7:11-14; Mark 11:17; 13:1-2.
[176]Jeremiah 26:11; 37:15; Mark 15:14-15.
[177]Jeremiah 31:27-34; 1 Corinthians 11:12.
[178]John 2:18.
[179]Mark 11:27-33.

or the righteous of Israel, victory over their enemies." Over against that expectation, the Gospels describe the true signs:

> Jesus' own conception of history was that all men and nations were involved in rebellion against God and that therefore the Messiah would have to be, not so much a strong and good ruler who would help the righteous to be victorious over the unrighteous, but a "suffering servant" who would symbolize and reveal the mercy of God.[180]

To many Jews in Jerusalem, Jesus must have seemed to be more of a traitorous wimp than a triumphant winner. He advocated paying taxes to Caesar, rejecting the view of Jewish zealots that allegiance to God would be compromised by so doing.[181] On the night he was arrested, according to Matthew, Jesus explained that he had purposely not called on God to rescue him.[182] When Pilate gave his Jewish audience a choice between freeing him or Barabbas, a terrorist and a murderer, they chose the latter.[183] At Golgotha, the unpopular Jesus was taunted by those who equated kingship with militant resistance to alien political powers. Jesting among themselves, the Jewish religious leaders said: "He saved others but he cannot save himself. Let us see the Messiah, the king of Israel, come down from the cross now, and we will believe in him!"[184] Niebuhr comments:

> All this mockery and derision is the natural and inevitable response to the absurdity of weakness and suffering in a royal and divine figure. Common sense assumes that the most significant and necessary attribute of both royalty and divinity is power. . . . The Christian faith has made this absurdity of a suffering Messiah into the very keystone of its arch of faith. . . . "He saved others, himself he cannot save," gives us a clue to the innermost character of a man in history who perished upon the Cross. It also gives us a clue to the mystery of the very character of God.[185]

Discerning Christians have realized that Jesus showed his kinship to God when he was in no way manifesting irresistible physical power. Martin

---

[180]Reinhold Niebuhr, *Discerning the Signs of the Times* (London: SCM, 1946) 11.
[181]Mark 12:13-17.
[182]Matthew 26:53.
[183]Mark 15:7-11.
[184]Mark 15:31-32.
[185]Niebuhr, *Discerning the Signs of the Times*, 116-17, 131.

Luther wrote, "Christ was powerless on the cross; and yet there He performed His mightiest work."[186] New Testament authority C. H. Dodd comments on the central miracle of religious history:

> One might have thought that the spectacle of the undeserved suffering of the best of men would rather have turned men away from God. For the amount of innocent suffering there is in the world has often provided a strong argument for atheism. But those who witnessed the passion of Jesus Christ have left on record that it brought them to God, and their testimony has been corroborated by multitudes in all subsequent ages.[187]

A twentieth-century corroboration of the redemptive effect of vicarious suffering by the innocent can be seen in the life of Martin Luther King. While the civil rights leader had acquired the disdain of racists in the political establishment, it was after he was seen as a obstacle to American imperialism in Viet Nam that he was violently disposed of. The general comment of theologian Luke Johnson is apropos here, "When Christians have most followed the pattern of Jesus' life, they have also come most clearly and painfully into conflict with political rulers and have often followed Jesus not only in manner of life but also in manner of death."[188] Like Jesus, King was an antisuperman but worked with love to bring about reconciliation. Their martyrdom has been a wonderful sign of the nature of God and how social healing can be effected.

---

[186]Jaroslav Pelikan, ed., *Luther's Works* (Saint Louis: Concordia, 1956) 21:340.
[187]C. H. Dodd, *Three Sermons* (London: SCM, 1954) 18.
[188]Luke Johnson, *The Creed* (New York: Doubleday, 2003) 167.

Chapter 5

The Supernatural Jesus

During the earliest period of the church, not much was transmitted among Christians—especially among those living outside Palestine—about what Jesus did. Paul's letters to Gentile congregations relate a little about Jesus' activities and a bit more about his teachings. After the death of the apostles, some second generation Christians made an effort to write down a fuller account of his life. Since most of the eyewitnesses to his life had died during the half-century that had lapsed, scribes searched the Greek version of the Old Testament for information. Convinced that its main purpose was to make forecasts about Christ, they worked over a variety of selected verses with their pious imaginations and recorded it as part of his biography. By this means the Gospel writers filled in to their satisfaction some gaps in the traditions received from his first followers. The miraculous activities of Moses, Elijah, and Elisha were of special interest because they seemed appropriate for a greater prophet to repeat, or upstage, in displaying divine authority.

According to the Evangelists

The four Gospels, dating from the last third of the first Christian century, inconsistently mix traditions of a limited human Jesus, who lived in the first third of that century, with creations of an unlimited supernatural Jesus. More than thirty specific miracles are attributed to him in the months or years prior to the last week of his mortal life. Jesus' suffering (Latin, *passion*) in Jerusalem is set forth in the latter portion of those Gospels and the accounts are generally consistent with the teachings of Paul. This may show that a witness, such as John Mark, who lived in Jerusalem, contributed to the narrative of those events.[1] The person portrayed during those last days in Mark 11-15 is not a superman who tears himself from his cross to frustrate his revilers.[2] On the other hand, about half of the verses in Mark 1-10 are involved with miracles, some of which portray Jesus with superhuman powers. If all references to miracles were cut from Paul's

---

[1] Acts 12:12; in Mark 14:51 the Evangelist may give a veiled indication that he, as a youth, was an observer of events that led up to Jesus' crucifixion.

[2] Mark 15:29-32.

letters, only a few verses would be lost; similar surgery on Mark would remove a large portion of its record of Jesus' Galilean ministry.

The Evangelists evidently shared some of the approach of the "superapostles" whom Paul satirized.[3] J. Christian Beker, in his comprehensive treatment of Paul's theology, exclaims, "It seems as if the Corinthians base their theology on the 'superman Jesus' of Mark 3–9 or his miracle source and omit Mark's passion story!"[4] More broadly, Dennis Duling discerns a basic contrast between Paul's letters and the Gospels, the two main portions of the New Testament, "Paul opposed the divine man approach to Jesus Christ, in which Jesus was pictured as a spirit-filled miracle worker."[5] After a painstaking literary analysis of groups of Mark's miracles, exegete Paul Achtemeier concludes that they were formed from traditions similar to those drawn upon by Paul's opponents in Corinth.[6] Those scholars have brought out a fundamental difference in the outlook on supernaturalism of New Testament writers.

The Evangelists seemed determined to demonstrate how the founder of Christianity was as spectacular as any of the acclaimed Jewish and pagan wonder-workers. Barry Backburn describes the situation:

> The Gospel of Mark is the oldest extant source containing these miracle narratives, but it was probably composed at least thirty years later than the events in question. . . . During this period one would expect various factors to play a role in shaping the stories: the desire to magnify the miraculous, the storyteller's tendency to embellish with folkloristic and novelistic details, and the propensity to assimilate Jesus to famous Jewish, pagan, and even Christian miracle workers.[7]

Mark did not make this miracle oneupmanship explicit, and the writer was probably not fully conscious of what his culture was prompting. Aware that Galileans most associated the prophets Moses and Elijah with extraordinary feats, Burton Mack writes about first-century expectations: "The images for both Moses and Elijah were taken no doubt from the

---

[3]2 Corinthians 12:11.

[4]J. Christian Beker, *Paul the Apostle* (Philadelphia: Fortress, 1980) 300.

[5]Dennis Duling, *Jesus Christ t\Through History* (New York: Harcourt, 1979) 58.

[6]*Journal of Biblical Literature* (June 1972): 198.

[7]Bruce Chilton and Craig Evans, eds., *Studying the Historical Jesus* (Leiden: Brill, 1994) 364.

common stock of lore popular in the north. Elijah was a prophet of the Northern Kingdom . . . about whom rather fantastic stories were still being told, among them some that imagined his reappearance to restore Israel."[8] Moses was remembered as one who, as the Lord's agent, divided a sea in order to accomplish the Israelite exodus.[9] Subsequent Scripture contains echoes of similar power over hindering waters. Elijah is able to divide the Jordan so that he and Elisha can walk through the riverbed to the east bank, and then Elisha accomplishes the same miracle in order to return without the inconvenience of getting wet or using a boat.[10] In the era of Jesus, rabbis Gamaliel and Tanchuma, at different times, were at sea when a tempest threatened to sink their boats, but after they prayed the waters immediately quieted down.[11] In a similar manner, Mark's Jesus calmed a sea so his disciples could cross to the other side in their boat.[12]

Elijah and Elisha, living in the ninth-century BCE, were transformed into wizards by the growth of legends about them, which were written down long after they had died. Elijah's herculean exploits included raising the dead as well as announcing that a drought had begun. He became God's agent to end it years later after drawing down lightning to ignite a pyre.[13] Those mighty marvels were a challenge for any later prophet to match. Jewish New Testament scholar Joseph Klausner writes, "Jesus, who was, in the opinion of his disciples, the greatest of the prophets or even greater than a prophet . . . must do wonders like them and also surpass them."[14] Even as Elisha received a double portion of Elijah's spirit,[15] Jesus appears in the Gospels to have had bestowed on him a generous portion of both of those prophets' spirits.

A fundamental difference between the role of Jesus in Paul's letters and in Mark's Gospel can be seen. Paul never suggests that Jesus is a new Elijah or Elisha but Mark's Jesus fulfills the popular Jewish expectation that a wonder-working Israelite redivivus would establish the messianic era. Jesus

---

[8]Burton Mack, *The Myth of Innocence* (Philadelphia: Fortress, 1988) 92.
[9]Exodus 14:21-22.
[10]2 Kings 2:8, 14.
[11]*Baba Mezia* 59b; *Berakoth* 9, 1.
[12]Mark 4:35-41.
[13]1 Kings 17:1, 17-23; 18:38-45.
[14]Joseph Klausner, *Jesus of Nazareth* (New York: Macmillan, 1925) 267-68.
[15]2 Kings 2:9-12.

ben Sirach, two centuries before the Christian era, had written about the prophet who would come "at the appointed time": "How glorious you were, Elijah, in your miracles! Who else can boast of such deeds? You raised a corpse from death."[16] As a result of the most thorough study of the Gospels by a contemporary scholar, John Meier concludes that miracle-working Elijah is the best single ancient model for Jesus.[17] After Mark's Jesus restored a youth presumed dead, some Jews concluded that Elijah had returned in the person of Jesus.[18]

Elisha is also a model for Jesus' miracles. According to Jewish reckoning, he performed sixteen after receiving the Spirit.[19] Those worked by Mark's Jesus were considerably more than Elisha's,[20] but some were quite similar. Like Elisha, Jesus gains fame by curing a leper, and both prophets miraculously open blind eyes.[21] Also, Elisha's levitation magic in countering the force of gravity by making iron float is trumpeted by Jesus walking on water.[22]

Ancient people cannot be divided between scientific and religious world views, but a separation can be made between those who endorsed a mild versus a wild involvement of divine powers in the world. Mark belonged in the wild and credulous camp. Gerd Theissen argues that "exorcisms and therapies can in essence be traced back to the historical Jesus" but not the nature miracles that Mark also admired.[23] In one story Elisha took a small amount of food and divided it among a number of people, which more than satisfied their hunger. A parallel incident in Mark is the two multitude feedings, except that Mark shows Jesus feeding many

---

[16]Sirach 48:4-5, 10.

[17]Doris Donnelly, ed., *Jesus* (New York: Continuum, 2001) 46; John Meier, *A Marginal Jew* (New York: Doubleday, 2001) 3:623.

[18]Mark 5:35-43; 6:15.

[19]Louis Ginzberg, *The Legends of the Jews* (Philadelphia: Jewish Publication Society, 1910) 3:239.

[20]Mark 1:23-26; 1:29-31; 1:32-34; 1:40-45; 2:1-12; 3:1-6; 3:7-12; 4:35-41; 5:1-20; 5:25-34; 5:35-43; 6:35-44; 6:47-51; 6:53-56; 7:24-30; 7:31-37; 8:1-9; 8:22-26; 9:14-29; 10:46-52; 11:13-14, 20-21.

[21]2 Kings 5:10-14, Mark 1:40-45; 2 Kings 6:20, Mark 10:46-52.

[22]2 Kings 6:4-7; Mark 6:47-51.

[23]Gerd Theissen and Annette Merz, *The Historical Jesus* (Philadelphia: Fortress, 1996) 304.

more people with less original quantity of food.[24] "They all ate and were filled" is the only response here, whereas for a single exorcism—which probably actually happened—Jesus' fame spread throughout Galilee.[25]

In the time lapse between an initial incident and its inclusion in one of the Gospels, a lengthy oral tradition ensued that resulted in modifications of the story. First, eyewitnesses mingled their reports with their own biases, then the resulting story was retold in preachers' sermons to make a theological point. The changes by those unscientific folks were not likely due to deliberate distortions. Milo Connick has comprehensively but succinctly distinguished five stages in the development of miracle material:

> (1) In most cases there was an actual happening in which Jesus participated. (2) The happening was interpreted by those who witnessed it. (3) The story of the happening was used by the church in its teaching and evangelistic endeavors. (4) The story appeared in its first written forms. (5) The story was included in the gospel records.[26]

Recognizing that only the last stage has been preserved, questers of the historical Jesus aim at reconstructing the first step. To illustrate this method, examine the story of Jesus' actions when in a fisherman's boat. While he slept on a cushion, a windstorm arose over the water. Jesus' disciples, worried about the boat capsizing, awakened their teacher and complained about his unconcern. According to Mark, he "rebuked the wind and said to the waves, 'Quiet down!' Then the wind ceased and everything was calm. He said to them, 'Why are you afraid? Have you still no faith?' "[27]

That turbulence on the so-called "Sea" of Galilee—actually an inland lake where one can see from shore to shore—may have been transformed in its retelling. It may be that Jesus instructed the disciples, not the wind, to calm down, but when the wind naturally died down soon afterward, they misinterpreted what he said.[28] It would have been more in keeping with

---

[24]2 Kings 4:42-44; Mark 6:35-44; 8:1-19.

[25]Mark 1:28.

[26]C. Milo Connick, *Jesus, the Man, the Mission, and the Message* (Englewood Cliffs: Prentice-Hall, 1963) 266.

[27]Mark 4:37-39.

[28]This interpretation originated with Karl Bahrdt, an eighteenth-century German scholar; see Ernst and Marie-Luise Keller, *Miracles in Dispute* (Philadelphia: Fortress, 1969) 75.

Jesus' character, determined by what he taught elsewhere about storms,[29] for him to have chided his companions for their lack of courage. Jesus did not attempt to use religion as a means of avoiding adverse natural forces but as a way of living in serenity amid such. It is unlikely that he thought of storms as containing evil demons that needed to be exorcised, but subsequent interpreters did. In this boating episode, religious meaning was replaced by magic, which assumes that utterances by special individuals can control cosmic forces. Also, Mark probably associated the post-Easter nonmaterial Lord Jesus with the Hebrew Lord (a.k.a. Yahweh). A psalmist provides this poetic account of assistance received by voyagers:

> They cried to Yahweh in their trouble,
> and he brought them out from their distress;
> he made the storm be still,
> and the waves of the sea were hushed.[30]

On that Galilean lake surrounded by hills I once swam when no winds were blowing, but later that afternoon a squall caused small waves to break against boats docked at Tiberias. Those waves, which soon subsided, were sufficient to rock a light craft but were minute by big sea standards. My experience was characteristic of the weather phenomena there.[31] As Mack points out in discussing Mark's miracles, "the closer one comes to the spectacular, the less significance there seems to be."[32]

Another episode on the lake is unrelated to anyone in danger. The weary disciples, who had been rowing all night near the shore against an adverse wind, thought they saw a phantom (Greek, *phantasma*) walking on the water. That, according to the Greek text, was their first response on encountering Jesus, whom they had left at the shore.[33] Those fishermen were aware that bodies heavier than water would sink in it. But they were unsophisticated and could have misinterpreted what could have been his walking at dawn on the misty seashore. Again, the Evangelist may have

---

[29]Matthew 7:24-25.
[30]Psalm 107:28-29.
[31]Klausner, *Jesus of Nazareth*, 269.
[32]Mack, *The Myth of Innocence*, 210.
[33]Mark 6:49.

associated the story with a scriptural saying about God "who treads upon the waves of the sea."[34]

"Divine men" were more common in Hellenistic hero cults than in biblical culture. Gentile Christians were more prone than Jewish Christians to transferring pagan motifs of unnatural wonders to Jesus. Before the beginning of the Christian era, legends attributed to philosopher Empedocles the power to raise the dead and to arrest violent wind.[35] In the second century, theologian Justin acknowledged a similarity between the powers of Askepios and Jesus. Askepios was a Greek physician who lived in the fifth century BCE but he was later deified as a healing god. Justin wrote, "When we say that Jesus healed the lame, the paralytic, and those born blind, and raised the dead, we seem to be talking about things like those said to have been done by Askepios."[36] Many inscriptions attributing to Askepios the cure of the lame and blind have been found at Epidaurus in the Peloponnesus.[37] Justin also appealed to a letter of Pontius Pilate to Emperor Claudius, now known to be bogus, that tells of Jesus rebuking the winds and walking on the sea dry-shod.[38]

An ancient biography of Pythagoras contains his teachings along with a collection of miracle stories that are not unlike the Gospel accounts. The word of that Greek philosopher allegedly had power to stop earthquakes and calm tempests. Whereas Jesus was said to have been seen "walking on the sea," Pythagoras "crossed rivers and seas and impassable places, somehow walking in the air.[39] Those tales may have been influenced by stories from India that were becoming known in the Mediterranean region at the time, which have continued in Hinduism until the present day. Sanskrit scholar William Brown observes that "Walking on the water is recognized in India as one of the stages of the psychic power of levitation, of which the highest grade is flying through the air. Accounts of levitation are very old in Hindu

---

[34]Job 9:8.

[35]Diogenes Laertius, *Lives of the Philosophers* 8.59, 67.

[36]Justin, *Apology* 1:22.

[37]Werner Kahl, *New Testament Miracle Stories* (Göttingen: Vandenhoeck, 1994) 59.

[38]Justin, *Apology* 1.48; Johannes Quasten, *Patrology* (Westminster: Newman, 1956) 1:117.

[39]Porphyry, *Life of Pythagoras* 29; cf. Iamblichos, *Life of Pythagoras* 135.

literature, appearing in *Rigveda* 10:136, and therefore being from before 800 BC."[40]

About the time Mark was written, Roman general Vespasian was heralded as having performed miracles in Alexandria before he became emperor. Roman historians Tacitus and Suetonius independently report that two infirmed men informed him that god Serapis had revealed in a dream that the general could cure them by what his saliva and touch could transmit of himself. Vespasian doubted if the procedure would be effective but his advisors convinced him that a powerful person's spittle could do wonders. Also, according to the diagnosis of Alexandrian physicians, the faculty of sight was not completely destroyed in one of the men, and the deformed hand was restorable in the other. While before a large crowd, the Roman spit on the partly blinded eyes and stepped on the hand of the crippled man. To Vespasian's surprise, they claimed they had become instantly healed.[41] The reputation of Vespasian was enhanced by this magic because it appeared to authenticate that he had divine favor. Saliva treatment had been long associated in Egypt with eyesight restoration.

Strikingly similar to one of those accounts of Egyptian cures is the claim that Jesus spit into the eyes of a blind man and placed his saliva on the tongue of a deaf-mute, in addition to inserting his fingers into the ears of the deaf man. By this procedure, healing powers were said to have corrected sight, speech, and hearing impediments.[42] After dealing carefully with stories such as these in Mark, John Hull concludes, "By the time the earliest gospel was written the tradition of the acts of Jesus had already become saturated with the outlook of Hellenistic magic."[43] In ancient times, no country around the Mediterranean basin had a corner on the market of magic and miracles.

German history-of-religions scholar Wilhelm Bousset placed Christianity in the context of Hellenistic religions and showed how stories of wonder-workers were transferred to Jesus. He illustrated "migratory motifs" by comparing accounts of the instantaneous effect of healers on invalids.

---

[40]William Brown, *The Indian and Christian Miracles of Walking on the Water* (Chicago: Open Court, 1928) 13.

[41]Tacitus, *History* 4.81; Suetonius, *Vespasian* 7.

[42]Mark 7:32-35; 8:22-25.

[43]John Hull, *Hellenistic Magic and the Synoptic Tradition* (London: SCM, 1974) 73-86, 142-43.

Lucian reported on a farmer, "Midas took his bed on which he had been carried and went out to the fields."[44] Correspondingly, after Jesus cured a paralytic who had been carried in by helpers, Mark stated, "He stood up, and immediately took his bed and went out in view of them all."[45] Bousset concluded:

> Thus did the community of Jesus' disciples fictionalize and surround the picture of Jesus with the glitter of the miraculous. Or, otherwise expressed, the personal image of Jesus begins to work with magnetic power and to draw to itself all possible materials and narratives which were at hand in his environment. But even where they are quite alien in character, the high power of gospel fabrication so amalgamated them that the process is recognizable only to the more discerning eye.[46]

In Mark's Gospel, Jesus allegedly acted to destroy organic life, which is his only punitive miracle. He is represented as being irritable due to hunger, and vindictive on finding someone else's fig tree without fruit on it for him to pilfer. Mark acknowledges that the tree had put forth leaves but that fruit would not be expected until later. In Palestine, figs ripen during the summer, so it would have been contrary to nature to expect to find mature figs at the Passover season in the spring. Although in no way a defect of the tree, Jesus allegedly pronounced this curse, "May no one ever eat fruit from you again." Assuming animism, the bizarre story states that the hexed tree "withered away to its roots" before the next day. The moral implications of the intended stealing and actual destruction, like Jesus' alleged depriving many swineherds of their property,[47] is as troublesome as the supernaturalism of the event.

Treating the barren tree tale symbolically rather than historically would also be out of character for unrevengeful Jesus. The context lends itself to the tree representing the Jerusalem temple. Could the meaning be that the central Jewish place of worship would be destroyed because the loving Savior had placed a curse on it? Hardly, especially when the story ends with his stipulating that forgiveness of others is prerequisite to God's acceptance of one's prayers.[48]

---

[44]Lucian, *Philopseudes* 11.
[45]Mark 2:12.
[46]Wilhelm Bousset, *Kyrios Christos* (Nashville: Abingdon, 1970) 101, 103.
[47]Mark 5:13.
[48]Mark 11:12-26.

According to the Markan Jesus, the fig tree miracle was intended to teach that uncritical faith can accomplish the most absurd happenings imaginable. Jesus comments on its capricious efficacy:

> Trust in God. I swear to you, if you say to this mountain, "Get up and jump into the sea," and have no inward doubts, but believe that what you say will happen, it will be done for you. So I tell you, everything you ask for in prayer will be yours if you believe that you have received it.[49]

Meier gives good reasons for concluding, "The story of the cursing of the fig tree has no claim to go back to the public ministry of the historical Jesus."[50] Brash Catholic theologian Uta Ranke-Heinemann candidly rates this "the stupidest" of the Gospel miracles, and adds: "This sort of miracle doesn't make one believe in the miracle worker; at most it makes one doubt his sanity. And Jesus surely never deserved to be saddled with such miraculous doings."[51]

* * *

The works of all four Evangelists are anonymous, so the apostolic authorship assigned to the first and fourth Gospels are titles given by later New Testament editors. There is scholarly consensus that Matthew, Luke, and John were written more than a decade after Mark, and about half a century after Jesus' public ministry. Realizing that the apostles lived most or all of their lives in the first half of the first Christian century, and that the Evangelists wrote in the latter part of the century, has contributed to the abandonment by scholars of the traditional assumption that Jesus' apostles wrote any of the Gospels. The time gap between events and written record makes it unlikely that any miracle story in any Gospel was written down by an eyewitness. Anglican bishop Ernest Barnes comments on the writer of even the earliest Gospel, "He was credulous inasmuch as the miracles, as they are narrated, cannot, in the light of our modern knowledge of the uniformity of nature, be accepted as historical facts."[52]

---

[49]Mark 11:22-24.

[50]Meier, *A Marginal Jew* 2:895.

[51]Uta Ranke-Heinemann, *Putting Away Childish Things* (San Francisco: Harper, 1995) 96.

[52]Ernest Barnes, *The Rise of Christianity* (London: Longmans, 1947) 108.

The later Synoptic Gospels borrow heavily from the Gospel attributed to Mark and occasionally heighten its supernaturalism. The appearance that they have fewer miracles than Mark is not due to their total number being diminished but to their being proportionally less. Matthew and Luke are much longer than Mark and the added verses are mostly teachings about the "Kingdom of God." Each of the Synoptics have about twenty miracles of Jesus, but Matthew and Luke omit some of Mark's and add others. Matthew contains nearly all of Mark's verses, and he not only expands on them but frequently revises what he has received from that source. A number of those changes were made in an effort to portray Jesus as the majestic Lord who has been given "all power in heaven and on earth."[53] For example, Mark asserts that when Jesus came to Galilee as a healer "he could do no mighty work there" because of the unbelief of his own people. Matthew, not wanting to admit that Jesus' power was limited by the disposition of the people he encountered, alters Mark's testimony to read, "He did not perform many miracles there."[54]

Matthew had no compunctions in heightening Mark's claim on the supernatural ability of Jesus even though it is unlikely that he had additional sources that pertained to Mark's stories. According to Mark, on one evening in Capernaum Jesus healed *many*, but according to Matthew *all* the sick were healed.[55] Matthew, unlike Mark, states that Jesus and his disciples went about Galilee "curing every disease and every sickness among the people."[56] The one Gerasene demoniac who is cured in Mark becomes two in Matthew.[57] In one of Mark's stories, Jairus informs Jesus that his daughter is dying and requests Jesus' healing touch, but this is contradicted in Matthew. There Jairus affirms that she had died and requests that she be revived.[58] Mark tells of Jesus miraculously feeding "five thousand men" but in Matthew increases that number to "five thousand men, beside women and children."[59]

---

[53]Matthew 28:18.
[54]Mark 6:5-6; Matthew 13:58.
[55]Mark 1:34; Matthew 8:16.
[56]Matthew 4:23; 9:35; 10:1.
[57]Mark 5:1-13; Matthew 8:28.
[58]Mark 5:22-23; Matthew 9:18.
[59]Mark 6:44; Matthew 14:21.

According to Matthew, Jesus immediately healed a centurion's servant sight unseen.[60] Acting from a distance made him as fantastic as Elisha, who treated Naaman's illness without making personal contact with him.[61] These healing stories parallel a Talmudic tale of Rabbi Hanina ben Dosa, another charismatic who lived in Galilee at the time of Jesus. As requested, he prayed for Rabbi Gamaliel's sick son and then assured those who made the request that a cure had been accomplished. When they went to the boy's home they found that his fever subsided at the very hour when the healer made his announcement about the restoration of health.[62]

In the time lapse between the writing of Mark and Matthew, alleged miracles expanded like fermenting dough. Matthew elaborated on Jesus walking on the water story by stating that Peter did the same until a strong wind caused him to lose confidence. Jesus caught him and said, "O you of little faith, why did you doubt?"[63] Faith here involves an unquestioning belief in supernaturalism. According to Mark, Jesus' levitation did not positively affect the disciples' faith, but in Matthew they responded by worshiping him and affirming "Truly you are the Son of God."[64] Matthew's account may have been influenced by a story of Buddha's disciple. In the absence of a ferry boat for transportation, he walked on water as he headed toward his master. All went well so long as he engaged in religious meditation, but he sank when his concentration ceased.[65]

Here is another example of the yeasty rise within legends during the years between the composition of two Gospels. In Mark's account, a day passes before Peter notices the withered condition of the fig tree that Jesus cursed; in Matthew's account, the tree shrivels instantly.[66] In scrutinizing the Gospel miracles, Theissen found seventeen instances where the miraculous is enlarged in the transmission from Mark to Matthew.[67]

---

[60]Matthew 8:5-13.

[61]2 Kings 5:9-11.

[62]*Berakoth* 34b.

[63]Matthew 14:29-31.

[64]Mark 6:52; Matthew 14:33.

[65]*Jataka* 190; Rudolf Bultmann, *The History of the Synoptic Tradition* (Oxford: Blackwell, 1963) 237.

[66]Mark 11:21; Matthew 21:19.

[67]Gerd Theissen, *The Miracle Stories of the Early Christian Tradition* (Philadelphia: Fortress, 1983) 17.

In Matthew, as well as in Luke, John the Baptist asks Jesus, "Are you he who is to come, or are we to wait for another?" John was likely referring to the last prophecy of the Hebrew Bible, that "the coming one" would be like miracle-man Elijah.[68] When the imprisoned John raised his skeptical question, Jesus replied to his messengers, "Go and tell John what you hear and see; the blind recover their sight, the lame walk, the lepers are cleansed, the deaf hear, the dead are raised, and the poor are brought good news."[69] Most of these miraculous works correspond to what Isaiah and some other Jews associated with the future Messiah.[70] The Qumran community, about the time of Jesus, also expressed this hope for God's actions in the messianic era: "The Lord will accomplish glorious things. . . . He will heal the wounded, revive the dead, and bring good news to the poor."[71] The attitude of Jesus is ambiguous; he plays down his miracles and insists that nothing be said about them,[72] yet John is encouraged to find proof of who he is by beholding his miracles, some supernatural and some not.

Matthew viewed Hebrew prophets as supernatural foretellers of the distant future. For example, a pair of stories at the conclusion of a miracle section tell of Jesus opening the eyes of blind men and the ears of a deaf-mute, which corresponds to what Isaiah had forecasted for the messianic age.[73] E. P. Sanders says, "When we find a motif in the gospels that parallels a passage in the Hebrew Bible very precisely, we much always ask whether or not the earlier passage has led to the creation of the later one." Both Sanders and Meier suggest that Matthew created miracle stories to show fulfillment of prophecy when he could find none in the traditions about Jesus to fill that purpose.[74]

Recognizing that the Gospels were to a large extent a record of sermons by preachers who probably never knew the historical Jesus, English biographer Humphrey Carpenter suggests this plausible process by which a miracle story was formed:

[68]Matthew 11:3; Malachi 3:1, 4:5.
[69]Matthew 11:3-5.
[70]Isaiah 29:18-19; 35:5-6; 61:1.
[71]4Q 521, frag. 2.
[72]Matthew 8:4.
[73]Matthew 9:27-33; Isaiah 35:5.
[74]E. P. Sanders, *The Historical Figure of Jesus* (New York: Penguin, 1993) 152; Meier, *A Marginal Jew* 3:657.

In the earliest days of preaching there might merely be generalized statements about Jesus being able to do wonderful things. A little later, more
specific claims might be made, such as "He could do anything: he could even
give sight to the blind and hearing to the deaf." Later still, a real memory of
Jesus giving some sort of help to a beggar at Jericho might become the story
of Jesus curing him of blindness. . . . Anyone who has collected material for
a biography will know how often those close to its subject—his friends and
even his family—will unconsciously depart from the strict historical truth in
their recollections, even a few years after the events, let alone some decades
later. The tendency is to adapt real memories until they are formulated into neat
anecdotes with a beginning and end and a distinct point or moral to them. . . .
The person who still doubts whether such invention really did take place need
only listen to modern sermons. Sooner or later he will hear a preacher making
statements about the life and ministry of Jesus which cannot be borne out word
by word by the Gospels.[75]

Matthew creates a tall tale that is not found in the other Gospels. When
at Capernaum, alongside the Galilean lake, Jesus directs Peter to where a
stater—a coin worth four drachma—can be found to pay collectors the
temple tax of two drachma per person: "Go to the sea and cast a hook; take
the first fish you catch, open its mouth and you will find a stater; take that
and give it to them for both of us."[76] Most Gospel readers assume that Peter
snagged the predicted fish, although no comment is given on the outcome
of the venture. The historical context for this apocryphal story may have
been a tax imposed by Emperor Vespasian for rebuilding the temple of
Jupiter in Rome, which happened after the destruction of the Jewish temple
in Jerusalem.[77]

* * *

Of all the New Testament writers, Luke is the one most fascinated with
wonder-workers. This characteristic is revealed to a lesser extent in his
Gospel narrative and to a greater extent in his Acts of the Apostles. They
contain redactions emerging from the additional years of oral transmission
of the gospel by Christians who felt empowered by the continued presence
of Jesus. The performance of marvels was for Luke the sine qua non of

[75]Humphrey Carpenter, *Jesus* (New York: Oxford, 1980) 72.
[76]Matthew 17:24-27.
[77]Robert Funk et al., *The Acts of Jesus* (San Francisco: Harper, 1998) 222.

apostleship and messiahship. After discussing differences in miracle stories among the Synoptic Gospels, Achtemeier concludes:

> Of all the gospels, Luke appears to have a more unambiguous reliance on the possibility that miracles, and thus miracle stories, can serve as the basis for faith in Jesus. . . . Luke seems to view the miracles with a less critical eye, according them, in a number of subtle ways, a more important role in his account of Jesus. A glance at Acts confirms that impression and shows the extent to which Luke understood the miraculous to play an important, if not, indeed, a central role, in the origins of the Christian church.[78]

Luke spikes some stories he obtained from Mark's Gospel with miracles. According to Mark, Jesus' baptism was an inward experience, "He saw the heavens opened and the Spirit descending upon him like a dove," but Luke gives the impression that the theophany could have been viewed by all present. Also he adds the phrase "in bodily form" to describe the dove, which hinders interpreting the account in only a symbolic manner.[79]

When Jesus speaks in the Nazareth synagogue at the outset of his ministry, Luke portrays him finding models for his ministry in some miracles of Elijah and Elisha. Jesus cites Elijah's assistance to a Gentile widow and Elisha's cleansing of a Syrian leper.[80] Elijah purportedly supplied food for the woman miraculously and revived her dead son.[81] Luke's Jesus, as a greater Elijah, miraculously feeds a multitude and raises two dead youths.[82] In the accounts from both Testaments, revived sons are restored to widowed mothers and the action in Luke provokes this response, "A great prophet has risen among us!"[83]

Several passages in Luke are embellished with miracles involving Jesus' disciples. Mark simply tells of two sets of brothers leaving their fishing nets at the Galilean lake after Jesus invites them to join him.[84] They respond to his call before seeing any miraculous demonstration of his power. But in Luke the fishermen's faith is based on several miraculous

---

[78]*Journal of Biblical Literature* (December 1975): 560.
[79]Mark 1:10; Luke 3:22.
[80]Luke 4:26-27.
[81]1 Kings 17:8-24.
[82]Luke 8:49-56; 9:12-17.
[83]Luke 7:11-16.
[84]Mark 1:16-18.

actions.[85] In the last, Jesus told Peter to cast out his nets again when the seasoned fisherman was convinced no fish were around. Following Jesus' instructions, Peter's nets begin to break because of the enormous catch, and the boat even begins to sink. Again, Mark's Jesus finds Peter's mother-in-law in bed with a fever, takes her hand, and raises her up. In Luke's modification of the story, Jesus appears to exorcize the *high* fever, "He stood over her and rebuked the fever, and it disappeared."[86] Still again, according to Mark, a swashbuckling disciple of Jesus cuts off an ear of the high priest's slave in the Garden of Gethsemane. Luke and John illustrate well how miracles are fabricated and tend to become more specific as they develop. Luke states that the *right* ear was amputated but Jesus "touched the man's ear and healed him." John names Peter as the swordsman and Malchus as the victim.[87]

Some miracles attributed to Jesus are found only in Luke's Gospel. In addition to restoring a widow's son at Nain, another story tells of ten lepers who are healed.[88] Also, passing reference is made to Jesus healing a man on the sabbath who had edema, an abnormal swelling from fluid retention.[89] On another sabbath the Lukan Jesus refers to a cripple, who was unable to stand erect because of a chronic curvature of the spine, as one "whom Satan bound for eighteen long years." But "when he laid his hands on her, immediately she stood up straight."[90]

Luke also indulges in a practice found in Hebrew scriptures that seems to display a supernatural awareness by prophets of details of future events. For example, the book of Isaiah states that the prophet forecasted that God would spare Jerusalem from destruction by the Assyrian army.[91] That oracle was recorded after the invaders withdrew from their siege of the city and could well have been composed by Isaiah's disciples. In a like manner the Lukan Jesus repeatedly foretells how his death and resurrection will occur.[92] Moreover, only Luke tells of Jesus' prophesying the siege and destruction

---

[85]Luke 4:31-41; 5:1-11.
[86]Mark 1:30-31; Luke 4:38-39.
[87]Mark 14:47; Luke 22:51; John 18:10-11.
[88]Luke 17:11-19.
[89]Luke 14:2-4.
[90]Luke 13:11-16.
[91]Isaiah 31:4-8.
[92]Luke 9:22; 18:31-33.

of Jerusalem, which occurred from 66 to 70 CE.[93] Since that Gospel was written after the event took place, it is likely that Luke composed words for Jesus that make it appear that the fall of Jerusalem was the result of divine determinism. Awareness that much of the theologizing in the Gospels is after the historical fact removes the notion that prophets were diviners of specific happenings in the future.

Going beyond Mark's claim that there was darkness over the land during the several hours that Jesus was dying on the cross, which might be interpreted as due to a storm cloud, Luke states that "the sun's light failed" from noon until three in the afternoon.[94] Thallus, a Roman or Samaritan historian in the late first century, dismisses as irrational the Christian claim of a solar eclipse causing a supernatural darkness at the time of Jesus' crucifixion.[95] Historian Edward Gibbon, assuming that reference is made in the passion story to a solar eclipse, notes that "this miraculous event, which ought to have excited the wonder, the curiosity, and the devotion of mankind, passed without notice." He points out that this alleged eclipse, with a duration many times that of any observed elsewhere throughout history, happened during the lifetime of Roman writers Seneca and the elder Pliny, who aimed at recording all the unusual natural events that people of the Mediterranean region had observed. Gibbon sardonically observes that they "omitted to mention the greatest phenomenon to which the mortal eye has been witness since the creation of the globe."[96]

Even though Luke eagerly tells of Jesus as a wonder-worker, he apparently found implausible two accounts in Mark's record. He does not tell of Jesus walking on the water nor of his cursing a barren fig tree. Finding the latter uncharacteristic of his image of Jesus, Luke converts Jesus' alleged action into this parable: a gardener cuts down one of his fig trees after discovering that, in spite of his careful cultivation, it continued to bear no fruit for four years.[97] Confronted with a far-fetched Gospel miracle tale, Luke allegorizes, that is, he transforms the alleged historical happening into a moral story. Biblical interpreters have commonly followed

---

[93]Luke 19:43-44.

[94]Mark 15:33; Luke 23:44-45.

[95]Theissen and Merz, *The Historical Jesus*, 84-85.

[96]Edward Gibbon, *The History of the Decline and Fall of the Roman Empire* (1776) 15.

[97]Luke 13:6-9.

the same procedure when dealing with a passage that they find too gross to be literally accepted by their clientele.

When Luke started on his second volume concerning Christian beginnings, his imagination may have been stimulated by stories circulating in the Greco-Roman culture about the physical ascension of virtuous persons at the end of their mortal life. He probably shared with his contemporary Plutarch an awareness of the well-known story of the ascension into heaven of the body of Romulus, Rome's founder. Plutarch also cited tales of the vanished corpses of other prominent men. That Greek writer commented that they "are told by writers who improbably deify the mortal part of human nature along with the divine."[98] Luke may have known that a Roman official swore he had seen the form of Augustus rise above the emperor's funeral pyre "on its way to heaven."[99] Christian apologist Justin not only alludes to the account of that deified Roman but points out that the story of Jesus' ascension is similar to stories told about Askepios, Bacchus, Hercules, Romulus, and other heroes.[100]

The legend about Elijah's ascension probably influenced Luke more than the pagan Greco-Roman stories. When that prophet ascended, accompanied by fire from heaven, there was a large outpouring of his spirit on Elisha, who had been commissioned to carry on his mentor's work.[101] Correspondingly, in Jerusalem soon after Jesus' body rose and disappeared into a cloud, his disciples beheld tongues like fire from heaven while becoming charged with the Holy Spirit.[102] One outward manifestation of the Spirit experience was "speaking in tongues." Luke interpreted glossolalia as a miraculous ability of Galileans to speak in a variety of languages, enabling them to communicate with the international pilgrims gathered for the Pentecost festival in Jerusalem, whereas Paul treated it as nonsupernatural ecstatic babbling, devoid of intellectual content.[103]

The sermon by the Lukan Peter on that day of Pentecost focuses on "Jesus of Nazareth, a man whom God sent to you with miracles, signs and wonders, as his credentials." Luke may be given the dubious distinction of

---

[98]Plutarch, *Romulus* 28.
[99]Suetonius, *The Deified Augustus* 100.
[100]Justin, *Apology* 1:21.
[101]2 Kings 2:1-18.
[102]Acts 1:9-11; 2:2-34.
[103]Acts 2:5-11; 1 Corinthians 14.

being the first apologist to attempt to prove Jesus' godliness by his alleged miracles. Emphasis is placed in that sermon on Jesus' miracles and resurrection but no mention is made of his teachings. Luke did not refer to "signs and wonders" in his Gospel but he refers to them on numerous occasions in Acts.[104] His outlook is akin to that of the Deuteronomic writer who recalls salvation history in this way, "The Lord brought us out of Egypt with a mighty hand; the Lord displayed before our eyes great and awesome signs and wonders."[105]

A main expression of Spirit activity in Luke's second scroll is the continuation of mighty miracles. A later editor, who was impressed by the supernatural acts contained in the writing, gave it the title "Acts of the Apostles." The sick from towns around Jerusalem were carried on stretchers to streets where at least Peter's shadow might fall on them as he passed by. Luke alleged that all of the great number of those sick or "tormented by unclean spirits" who gathered there were cured.[106] On the Damascus road, Paul is temporarily blinded until scales fall from his eyes days later.[107]

The two parts of Luke's writing contain parallel healings: both Jesus and Peter enable paralytic men to stand up and resume normal activity;[108] Peter as well as Jesus each say "Get up!" to a dead woman, and each one rises.[109] In his doctoral dissertation, Marvin Miller analyzes these Luke-Acts stories and concludes, "The intention of Luke is fairly clear; the miracles of the disciples approximate and continue those of Jesus, just as those of Elisha did Elijah's."[110] Luke was also eager to show that Jesus' actions were Moses redux. After reminding readers that Moses presided over supernatural performances in Egypt, at the Red Sea, and in the Sinai wilderness, he quotes what Moses promised in the Torah, "God will raise up a prophet for you from your own people as he raised me up."[111]

---

[104]Acts 2:22, 43; 4:30; 5:12; 6:8; 14:3; 15:12.

[105]Exodus 6:21-22.

[106]Acts 5:15-16.

[107]Acts 9:8, 18.

[108]Acts 9:33-34; Luke 5:17-25.

[109]Acts 9:36-41; Luke 8:49-55.

[110]Marvin H. Miller, "The Character of Miracles in Luke-Acts" (thesis, Graduate Theological Union, 1971; Ann Arbor MI: University Microfilms, 1971) 126.

[111]Deuteronomy 18:15; Acts 7:37.

Luke believed that miracles legitimize status only if inspired by one whom he identifies as the Holy Spirit. The claim that "signs and wonders happened through the hands of the apostles" who communicated that Spirit caused a Samaritan fraud named Simon the Magician to scheme. He wished to purchase the Spirit that seemed to work like magic and could enable its possessor to perform dazzling tricks. Peter denounced Simon even though he was acclaimed "the power [*dynamis*] of God that is called Great."[112] The apostle preached that such *dynamis* was possessed by Jesus, who "healed all who were oppressed by the devil."[113]

Stories are told in Acts of punitive miracles causing sudden death. Ananias and his wife Sapphira drop dead after Peter confronts them about lying to the church.[114] Also, Luke gives this description of Herod Agrippa's death: "Herod . . . delivered a public address to the people. They kept shouting, 'The voice of a god, and not of a mortal!' Instantly an angel of the Lord struck him down because he had not given the glory to God, and he was eaten by worms and died."[115] By contrast, Josephus reports the death of that Palestinian king in a nonsupernatural and less dramatic manner. He states that Herod did not rebuke impious flatterers, and five days later he died from an illness causing intense internal pains.[116]

Paul is the only Christian who, in Luke's opinion, can hold his own in a miracle competition with Peter, and he also can vanquish a magician who is the devil's agent.[117] In separate episodes, Peter and Paul look intently at lifelong cripples who respond by leaping up, literally fulfilling Isaiah's prophecy that in the new era "the lame shall leap like a deer." On seeing the performances, the crowds view Peter as a thaumaturge (from Greek *thauma*, "wonder" + *ergon*, "worker") and Paul as a god.[118] Also, Peter's resuscitation of Dorcas is balanced by Paul doing the same for Eutychus.[119]

Luke's Paul is released from a prison in Philippi after an earthquake, which parallels nicely Luke's earlier account of Peter's prison break

---

[112]Acts 5:12; 8:10, 18-21.
[113]Acts 10:38.
[114]Acts 5:1-10.
[115]Acts 12:21-23.
[116]Josephus, *Antiquities* 19:346-50.
[117]Acts 13:6-11.
[118]Isaiah 35:6; Acts 3:2-12; 14:8-10.
[119]Acts 9:40-41; 20:10-12.

through divine intervention.[120] Luke's story contains actions reminiscent of a marvel in a drama of Euripides, "Their chains fell off their feet of their own accord, and doors flew open without the help of human hands."[121] But Paul wrote nothing about the miracles that Luke claims happened there. "We had been shamefully mistreated in Philippi" was the limit of the apostle's reference to difficulties in his mission there.[122] In writing the Philippians from a jail cell, he did not suggest that his chains would miraculously be removed; rather, he expressed confidence that God was working through his imprisonment, which might end in death.[123]

Geoffrey Lampe writes:

> The whole mission [of the church], as Luke looks back on its early history . . . is seen in terms of miracle: that is to say, as effected by supernatural power, whether in the guidance given to the missionaries, in their dramatic release from prison or deliverance from enemies or shipwreck, or in the signs of healing and raising from the dead.[124]

Just as Luke embellished the historical Jesus with supernaturalism, so he treated the historical Paul in a parallel manner. Regarding the Lukan Paul, Calvin Roetzel notes, "Within a generation of Paul's death he was already on the way to becoming a wonder-worker of epic proportions."[125] Of the eleven miracles in Acts, seven pertain to Paul. He is first shown to excel over rival religionists, even as Moses triumphed over Egyptian magicians.[126] When Jewish false prophet Elymas opposed Paul, the missionary cast a spell on him that immediately caused blindness. Luke claimed that the Roman proconsul of Cyprus witnessed this astounding hexing and that it caused him to "believe."[127] John Davidson comments pertaining to Luke's Paul, "According to Acts, rather than giving sight to the blind, he robs a man of his sight for disagreeing with him. . . . It is

---

[120]Acts 5:17-19; 16:25-34.

[121]Euripides, *The Bacchantes* 447-48.

[122]1 Thessalonians 2:2.

[123]Philippians 1:7, 20.

[124]Charles Moule, ed., *Miracles* (London: Mowbray, 1965) 171.

[125]Calvin Roetzel, *Paul* (Columbia: University of South Carolina Press, 1998) 165.

[126]Exodus 7:8-13.

[127]Acts 13:6-12.

noteworthy that nowhere in his letters does Paul speak of any such miraculous occurrences."[128]

Although there is no reference in Paul's letters to Christians engaging in exorcism, Luke's Paul was an extraordinary exorcist. In Philippi a slave girl confronted him who was possessed by "a python spirit." In the mythology of her Greek culture, a dragon lurked in a cave near Delphi and some associated it with a snake-induced mania. Similar to the way the priests at the Delphi oracle specialized in spirit manipulation, the girl's owners profited from her proclamations during demonic seizures. But Paul, finding the girl annoying, allegedly cast out her serpentine demon by this incantation, "I order you in the name of Jesus Christ to come out of her."[129] The effectiveness of that formula was recognized at Ephesus, a center of magic. Some Jewish exorcists addressed evil spirits with these words, "I adjure you by Jesus whom Paul proclaims." But the spirits would not acknowledge the non-Christian exorcists, resulting in these copycatters being beaten up by a possessed man.[130] Within a century of the writing of Acts, philosopher Celsus testified, "I have seen these Christian priests use books containing magical formulas and the names of various demons; they surely are up to no good, but only mean to deceive good people by these tricks of theirs."[131]

Topping all of this weird but gripping narrative, Luke tells of how handkerchiefs that Paul touched in Ephesus received power to exorcise and cure. When those blessed cloths were carried away to the sick, "diseases left them and the evil spirits came out of them."[132] Luke would have his readers believe that Ephesus healings were accomplished by magical cloths that extend the personality of holy Paul, and the faith of the recipients is seemingly not relevant. The therapeutic technique of the Lukan Paul is more primitive than what is described in the Gospels. Jesus' healings resulted from a one-to-one personal encounter, and he rejected the magical belief that his clothing had potency to heal.

One of the last wonder stories in Acts provides literal fulfillment for words that Luke attributed to Jesus. To his disciples he declared, "I have

---

[128]John Davidson, *The Gospel of Jesus* (Rockport MA: Element, 1995) 147-48.
[129]Acts 16:16-18.
[130]Acts 19:13-16.
[131]Celsus, *True Doctrine* (New York: Oxford University Press, 1987) 98.
[132]Acts 19:11.

given you authority to tread on snakes and scorpions, and over all the power of the enemy, and nothing will hurt you."[133] Accordingly, after a viper struck Paul on the island of Malta, he cast it into a bonfire. When he did not swell up or drop dead, as the primitive Maltese had expected, they asserted that he was a god.[134] A similar tale is told of Rabbi Hanina ben Dosa who was bitten by a poisonous snake, but it was the reptile that died.[135]

Ernst Haenchen, in his illuminating Acts commentary, points out that a primary discrepancy between Luke's Paul and the epistolary Paul is Luke's portrayal of Paul as a great miracle worker. Haenchen observes, "It is true that the real Paul did on one occasion lay claim to the 'signs of an apostle' (2 Corinthians 12:12) but the exploits in question were so little out of the ordinary that his opponents flatly deny his ability to preform miracles."[136] Paul's letters tell of no particular miracles that he performed, even though he admitted that the gift of healing was a mark of being an apostle. In his doctoral dissertation, Hisao Kayama exposes this contradiction, "The image of Paul portrayed by Luke materially coincides with what the opponents [in Corinth] accused Paul of lacking."[137] Luke certainly did not picture Paul as the apostle viewed himself, a weak instrument of God who could not overcome obstacles by feats of supernaturalism, even if he had so desired. As we have seen, the *dynamis* of Paul like that of his crucified Lord was displayed in ways considered foolish in ancient religions.

* * *

Each Evangelist tells of some stupendous acts by Jesus not found in any other Gospels. Yet, the Jesus of the Synoptics consistently depreciated supernatural "signs" (*semeia*), warning that "impostors will arise claiming to be messiahs or prophets and will show signs and wonders to mislead, if possible, God's chosen."[138] The Matthean Jesus claims that he will declare to false prophets who work miracles in his name, "I never knew you; go

---

[133]Luke 10:19.

[134]Acts 28:3-6.

[135]*Tosefia Berakoth* 3.20.

[136]Ernst Haenchen, *The Acts of the Apostles* (Philadelphia: Westminster, 1971) 113.

[137]Hisao Kayama, *The Image of Paul in the Book of Acts* (Ann Arbor MI, 1971) 154.

[138]Mark 13:22.

away from me, you evildoers."[139] Elsewhere in the New Testament, "signs and wonders" are also interpreted as the lying actions of a wicked person.[140]

In the Gospel of John some criticism of miracle cravers can be also found, as in this comment, "Many believed in Jesus' name because they saw the signs that he was doing, but he did not trust them." But that Gospel, far from associating signs with a false Christ, represents Jesus as giving them high approval.[141] Indeed, "signs" is a principal term in the Fourth Gospel and Jesus' public ministry is organized around a number of signs. They "are all of a stupendously supernatural magnitude," writes historian Michael Grant.[142] Absent in John are parables, even though the Synoptics state that Jesus did not teach without them.[143] To some extent, signs in the Fourth Gospel are acted parables, for they have both a supernatural and a symbolic meaning. The miracles accepted by John appear to be historical "works" witnessed by many bystanders, but their importance is more in the spiritual truth to which they point. According to C. H. Dodd, a sign for John was essentially not a supernatural happening "but a significant act, one which, for the seeing eye and the understanding mind, symbolizes eternal realities."[144]

Jesus' first sign was associated with his turning water into wine.[145] He acts like an alchemist who aims at changing a base metal into a precious one—but here a base compound becomes a more valuable organic one. Consider the chemistry of turning water into wine: hydrogen and/or oxygen atoms would have to produce carbon atoms. Supernaturalists would presumably posit that on this occasion carbon atoms were created from nothing in accord with the way the cosmos was created by God. Bishop Irenaeus stated that Jesus showed his superiority to nature by creating wine, which he could have done without even starting with water.[146]

---

[139]Matthew 7:22-23.

[140]2 Thessalonians 2:9.

[141]John 2:23-24; 6:26.

[142]Michael Grant, *Jesus* (New York: Scribner's, 1977) 37.

[143]Mark 4:34; Matthew 13:34.

[144]C. H. Dodd, *The Interpretation of the Fourth Gospel* (Cambridge: Cambridge University Press, 1953) 90.

[145]John 2:1-11.

[146]Irenaeus, *Against Heresies* 3.11.

That miracle resembles one in which Moses is purported to have transformed water. The Torah states that he poured water on dry ground where it became blood in order to convince the Israelites that he would liberate them. On his behalf, brother Aaron performed this and other "signs" before their own people. After this happened, the text states that the people believed.[147] The causal sequence in John follows those Mosaic stories; faith follows rather than precedes a miracle.

The water metamorphosis story has a traceable literary lineage not only to the Hebrew Bible but to Greek mythology. Folk tales were widely circulated regarding Dionysus, one of which tells of several jugs that filled with wine because of his presence.[148] Jesus may have surpassed the liberality of that Greek god of wine by making more than a hundred gallons of wine for wedding guests in a small town, an incredible amount for those who had already been imbibing! (Embarrassed Christian teetotalers of recent centuries have, without foundation, presumed that unfermented grape juice was served, as in their communion services.) If interpreted literally, the Cana wedding story is without merit religiously and morally, since providing an excessive quantity of wine for celebrators can hardly be defended as supplying a human need. Jesus was noted for aiding people in misery, not for encouraging stupefying binge drinking. It would have been out of character for him to have first "revealed his glory" by producing enough wine to intoxicate every villager in Cana. Sobriety has more sanctity, so a reverse miracle of turning wine into water before the participants became drunk might have been more appropriate!

Both Elisha and the Johannine Jesus restore a son to health, and they cure a cripple by having him wash in a designated place. John treats those healings as Jesus' second and third signs.[149] Johannine authority Raymond Brown observes that there are closer similarities between the miracles of Jesus and Elisha than between Jesus and any miracle man of Gentile Hellenism.[150] The Jesus of the Fourth Gospel has some of the same qualities that made Elisha highly esteemed in Hellenistic Judaism. Indeed, John's Jesus reflects what Sirach wrote of Elisha: "Nothing was too difficult for

[147]Exodus 4:8-9, 30-31.

[148]Pausanias, *Description of Greece* 6.26; Euripides, *The Bacchantes* 704-707; Pliny, *Natural History* 2.231.

[149]2 Kings 4:32-37; 5:1-14; John 4:46-5:9.

[150]Raymond Brown, "Jesus and Elisha," *Perspective* 12 (1971): 85-89.

him; even in death his body kept its prophetic power. In life he worked miracles, and in death his deeds were marvelous."[151] The bodies of both Elisha and Jesus allegedly had supernatural powers after their deaths.[152]

The healing of invalids was widely associated with Askepios, a pagan "savior of all." He is first referred to by Homer as a skilled Greek physician,[153] but subsequently he was worshiped as a god. The central sanctuary for his cult at Epidaurus resembled the shrine Catholics established in the nineteenth century at the French town of Lourdes. In addition to that major center, Askepios healers were found in several cities in the Roman empire. Excavations show that a satellite Askepios shrine was located in Jerusalem at Bethesda near the Sheep Gate pool where a subterranean stream occasionally bubbled up.[154] According to John's Gospel, a man who had been crippled for 38 years came to that spring and was healed. John aimed at showing how no person in antiquity, Israelite or Gentile, surpassed Jesus in the stupendous miracles ascribed to him. Yet, Jesus was not interested in healing at Bethesda the "many invalids—blind, lame, and paralyzed" but inquired of one person, "Do you want to be made well?"[155]

For the fourth sign, the Fourth Gospel writer retold the feeding of the multitude miracle—found five times in the Synoptic Gospels—but he alone explicitly compared the account with the Moses saga. Just as the Israelite savior, seemingly out of nowhere, provided manna for thousands in a place where no other food was available, so Jesus did the same with his "bread from heaven."[156] John had less interest in the facticity of this feeding than in its history of salvation signification. For him, it alluded backward to the divine nourishment given to the Israelite congregation. God supplied what they needed for the continuation of life in the wilderness so they could reach the Promised Land. Also, the sign pointed forward to the eucharistic meal of Jesus with his disciples that empowered the community of his followers to carry on his work after his death.

---

[151]Sirach 48:13-14.
[152]2 Kings 13:21; John 20:26-27.
[153]Homer, *Iliad* 2:731.
[154]Theissen and Merz, *The Historical Jesus*, 113.
[155]John 5:3, 6.
[156]Exodus 16:3, 8, 15, 31; John 6:30-41.

John, similar to Luke, viewed Jesus as the fulfillment of the forecast that a future prophet like Moses would arise.[157] Moses had authenticated that he was God's spokesman by performing miracles. For example, he announced that the rebellious followers of Korah would be killed by falling into the earth when it "opens its mouth." Immediately, according to the Bible, the ground under those rebels split asunder and swallowed them.[158] John stated that Jesus was asked, "What sign are you going to give us then, so that we may see it and believe you?"[159] The miraculous feeding by Jesus evoked this response, "When the people saw the sign that he had done, they began to say, 'This is indeed the prophet who is to come into the world'."[160] Jesus declared that he is greater than Moses because his people not only feed on the physical bread he provided but they also feed on himself, "the bread of life" that will give eternal life. Although John's Gospel contains no narrative about the origination of the Eucharist by the blessing of bread and wine at the final meal of Jesus with his disciples, overtones of that sacramental supper are embedded there. For example, Jesus fed the crowd "after he had given thanks (Greek, *eucharistesas*)."[161] John contains signs pointing to Jesus as both the bread and the wine of life, one who provides essential nourishment that goes beyond biological needs.

In the fifth sign, after a blind man is given sight, John boasts, "It is unheard of since time began that anyone has opened the eyes of someone born blind." In contrast to the Synoptics, John does not admit that others have performed wonders like Jesus.[162] This story probably developed from an incident in Jesus' ministry that had been recorded earlier. They differ in that his spittle was used directly for restoring a man's eyesight in Mark's version but in John it is used to make a mud pack to place on the man's eyes. In Mark, but not in John, the therapy is accomplished in stages; at first there is only a partial restoration of sight.[163] Also, in Mark, as often in the Synoptics, faith is a displayed prior to the healing, but in John's Gospel

---

[157]Deuteronomy 18:15.
[158]Numbers 16:28-31.
[159]John 6:30.
[160]John 6:14.
[161]John 6:32-51.
[162]Mark 3:15; Matthew 12:27; Luke 10:17.
[163]Mark 8:22-25; John 9:1-32.

supernatural feats are done to produce belief.[164] Jesus is represented as saying that a certain person was blind from birth so that "God's power might be displayed in curing him."[165]

The curing of a blind man illustrates that Jesus' therapies are less adorned when they are recorded nearer to the time of the event and that the later records focus more on the nature of Jesus. The healing is a Johannine manifestation that Jesus is "the light of the world."[166] In the Fourth Gospel, the intensification of Jesus' powers in his miracles is described by Theissen in this way: "They are a continuation of God's work of creation, and indeed surpass it. They are unique. No one else can perform them."[167]

At the peak of Jesus' ministry according to John's Gospel, the final and climatic sign is a raising-from-the-dead tale that is even more astounding than those reported in the earlier Gospels. Lazarus had been decomposing for four days and his body "stinketh," as the King James Version indelicately puts it.[168] Gustav Dalman describes the putrefaction caused by the warm Palestinian climate: "A state of death beyond the third day meant, from the popular Jewish point of view, an absolute dissolution of life. At this time the face cannot be recognized with certainty; the body bursts; and the soul, which until then hovered over the body, parts from it."[169] Jesus asserts that he is glad he was not present when his friend Lazarus was dying because he can now accomplish the more demanding work of raising him from the dead.[170] The Fourth Gospel concludes with the claim that "Jesus did many other signs, in the presence of his disciples, which are not written in this book."

A comparison of some Synoptic Gospel teachings with some signs of the Fourth Gospel suggest that the later writer may have transformed them for his purposes. The surface meaning of the first sign is so gross that the Evangelist evidently intended that its importance should lie in its hidden

---

[164]John 9:38; 11:45; 20:30-31.

[165]John 9:3.

[166]John 1:9; 9:5.

[167]Theissen, *The Miracle Stories of the Early Christian Tradition*, 227; John 5:17, 20; 15:24.

[168]John 11:39.

[169]Gustav Dalman, *Jesus-Jeshua* (London: SPCK, 1929) 220; *Semahot* 8.1; Ecclesiastes Rabbah 12:6; Leviticus Rabbah 18:1.

[170]John 11:14.

significance. Since the purpose of any sign, whether along a road or in a scripture, is to give direction toward some destination, to what was Jesus pointing? Many commentators ingeniously interpret the wine story as an allegory, discovering clues in it about the mission and message of Jesus. Those who do not think he worked supernatural miracles assume that the Evangelist made up the story, or transformed a story someone else created, and buried spiritual truths in it. For example, the Cana wedding party "sign" has been interpreted to mean that Jesus sanctioned jovial parties where folks giggle, gabble, gobble, and guzzle. More frequently, commentators claim that the fictional story contrasts water set aside in jars for Jewish ceremonial washing, as described in the story, with the higher quality spiritual nourishment supplied by Jesus. In this regard, the sign may be a subtle way of reinforcing the meaning of one of Jesus' parables in which he contrasted the old wine of the Pharisees' fasting with new wine of the gospel.[171] John reinforces that the superior wine produced by Jesus, and made sacramental by his death, has more vitality than traditional rituals.

Pertaining to the last sign, the only Lazarus who appears in the Synoptics is in a parable Jesus told about the relationship between morality and life after death. In it Abraham refuses to permit Lazarus to return to his earthly existence to warn his brothers to repent of their uncaring conduct and thereby avoid punishment in the afterlife. The patriarch affirms that if earthlings are not persuaded by the teachings of Hebrew prophets to live justly and mercifully, a supernatural happening will not shock them into an abiding change of behavior.[172] John uses not only the same name "Lazarus" as in Luke's parable but also gives the same conclusion that spectaculars do not transform behavior. The reanimation of Lazarus did not cause a lessening of hostility toward Jesus by the Jewish leaders; rather, it made them even more determined to eliminate him.[173]

Helmut Koester, along with some other New Testament scholars, hypothesizes that the Fourth Evangelist is familiar with an earlier "Book of Signs." He comments on the first and last signs in John's Gospel:

> This source is a collection of pieces from the Hellenistic propaganda in which Jesus is proclaimed as divine man. . . . It is characteristic of religious

---

[171]Mark 2:18-22; Matthew 9:14-17; Luke 5:33-38.

[172]Luke 16:27-31.

[173]John 11:53.

syncretism . . . that one of these miracle narratives derived its main feature from the cult of Dionysus. The miraculous power of Jesus is even more emphasized in John's Sign Source than in the Markan parallels. These stories proclaim Jesus as the god who walks the earth. Instead of speaking about God who raised Jesus from the dead, they preach a Jesus with the divine power to call the dead to life from their tombs.[174]

According to Subsequent Christians

The embroidery on the narratives about Jesus and his apostles in some first century writings pales when contrasted to some stories from the following centuries. In the second century a spurious ending was attached to Mark that adds to the types of miracles featured in the original Gospel. Jesus allegedly said that his followers should validate their faith in bizarre ways, "They will pick up snakes in their hands, and if they drink any deadly thing, it will not hurt them."[175] Encouraged by this, several sects have given snakes a prominent place in worship over the course of church history. Fourth-century Bishop Epiphanius told of Ophites who take a snake from a basket during the Eucharist to prove their faith. "Not only do they break the loaves the snake has coiled on and distribute them to the recipients, but they each kiss the snake besides," he reported.[176] In the Appalachian highlands, "holiness" Christians can be found who center their faith in the literal interpretation of Jesus' alleged words about being immune from the effects of poisonous snakes or liquids. I have attended a worship service that climaxed with sect members handling rattlesnakes and drinking a "salvation cocktail" composed of strychnine powder mixed with water. As might be expected, some of the members have died from such testing over the years.

Luke's treatment of the boyhood of Jesus looks like a model of scholarly discrimination when compared with the fantastic stories from the second and later centuries that are found in the New Testament Apocrypha. In contrast to the only Gospel account of Jesus' boyhood, which contains nothing supernatural,[177] the *Infancy Gospel of Thomas* includes fabrications

---

[174]Helmut Koester, *Introduction to the New Testament* (Philadelphia: Fortress, 1982) 2:184.

[175]Mark 16:18.

[176]Epiphanius, *The Panerion* 1:37:5.

[177]Luke 2:41-52.

that misrepresent both Jesus' temperament and actions. The canonical Gospels never portray Jesus as performing a miracle to punish individuals. But in the *Infancy Gospel*, a boy drains off the mud puddle in which Jesus has been playing, causing him to become enraged. He declares: "'You shall wither like a tree and shall bear neither leaves, nor root, nor fruit.' Immediately that youth withered up completely." Again, when irritated by a boy who brushed against him, revengeful Jesus uttered a curse that caused the boy to drop dead. Joseph, on advising Jesus to refrain from such punitive actions, received the curt reply, "Do not vex me." He multiplied a single grain into one hundred measures of wheat. In Joseph's carpentry shop, Jesus showed off by creating out of nothing additional length for boards that had been cut too short.[178] That apocryphal Gospel claims that Jesus made clay birds out of mud and then gave them life, a fiction that reappears in the *Qur'an*. Jesus is there represented as saying, "I bring you a sign from your Lord, in that I will make for you the figure of a bird from clay and breathe into it, and it will become a living bird."[179] Oscar Cullmann has shown how these apocryphal stories "in antiquity, in the Middle Ages and in the Renaissance, exercised a stronger influence on literature and art than the Bible itself."[180]

In medieval folklore, Jesus had powers now associated with Superman. Even as an infant, he assisted his family in their journey across the Sinai desert:

> While they traveled, Joseph said to him, "Lord, we are being roasted by this heat." . . . Jesus replied, "Fear not, Joseph, I will shorten your journey, so that what you were going to traverse in the space of thirty days, you will finish in one day." While this was being said, behold, they began to see the mountains and cities of Egypt.[181]

On arriving in Egypt, Mary desired fruit from the palm tree under which she was resting while Joseph searched for water. Jesus, while on his mother's lap, has the tree to bend over so she can gather its fruit, and has water to spring up from under the tree.[182]

---

[178]*Infancy Gospel of Thomas* 2-5, 12-13.

[179]*Qur'an* 3:49.

[180]Wilhelm Schneemelcher, *New Testament Apocrypha* (Cambridge: Clarke, 1991) 1:418.

[181]*The Gospel of Pseudo-Matthew* 22.

[182]*The Gospel of Pseudo-Matthew* 20.

Some of the stories about Jesus' miracles are claimed to have come from information his mother supplied. She informed church leaders that, while her family lived in Egypt, Jesus turned camels into stones and caused idol temples to collapse. By making a sign with his little hand, a chariot was shattered, killing a magician and her daughter. When Jesus stuck Joseph's olivewood cane in the ground, it immediately grew branches and bore fruit. Once when Mary, Joseph, and Jesus wished to travel by boat, the winds were so turbulent that the sailors refused to take them aboard. Jesus responded not only by stilling the storm but also by causing a rock on which his family was waiting to carry them to their destination.[183]

The license taken with the apostles' lives in the New Testament Apocrypha was no doubt encouraged by biblical legends. After Peter prays for the healing of some blind widows, a beam of light restores their sight. That apostle also takes a smoked fish hanging in a market and asks a pagan crowd, "If you now see this swimming in the water like a fish, will you be able to believe in him whom I preach?" On receiving an affirmative reply, Peter throws the fish in a pond. It comes back to life and many convert to Christianity because of the supernatural display. Again, when archvillain Simon the Magician attempts to demonstrate to a crowd in Rome that he could fly, Peter prays to Jesus; Simon falls to the ground and perishes.[184] Also, Paul saves a companion from being burned alive by efficaciously praying for rain to extinguish the pyre.[185]

Although there are no accounts of animal miracles in the New Testament, naturally fierce animals become harmless to Christians in the apocryphal apostolic acts. Beasts in the arena refuse to attack the bodies of martyrs. In one whimsical tale, a lion intent on attacking Paul is converted; heeding the lion's request, Paul baptizes him.[186] In another such tale, bedbugs follow apostle John's directive, "Behave yourselves bugs, one and all; you must leave your home for tonight and be quiet in one place and keep your distance from the servants of God." The next morning, with John's permission, they come running back to their habitat.[187] Many

---

[183]Ernest Budge, *Legends of our Lady Mary* (Boston: Medici, 1922) 71, 73.
[184]Acts of Peter 3:13, 21, 32.
[185]Acts of Paul 22-24.
[186]Acts of Paul 7, 26.
[187]Acts of John 60.

Christians in the early church apparently had an insatiable appetite for miraculous folklore.

Origen, in the third century, recognized that Jesus, according to John's Gospel, had said to his disciples, "Truly I tell you, those who believe in me will do the works that I do, and will do greater things still."[188] That master of allegorical interpretation applied the text in a nonsupernatural way: "According to the promise of Jesus, the disciples have done even greater works than the physical miracles which Jesus did. For the eyes of people blind in soul are always being opened, and the ears of those who were deaf to any talk of virtue listen eagerly about God and the blessed life with him."[189]

However, a student of Origen took literally Jesus' assurance that his followers would do greater miracles than he did. Bishop Gregory Thaumaturgus ("Wonder-worker") purportedly accomplished not only many exorcisms and healings but also effected the immediate termination of an epidemic by his prayer. His biographer, Gregory of Nyssa, himself a prominent Greek patristic, ranked Thaumaturgus's marvels higher than those of Elijah. The prophet only temporarily blocked the flow of the Jordan but when Gregory thrust his staff in the bank of the Lycus River, destructive periodic floods were permanently dammed. His purported successes caused widespread conversions to Christianity.[190]

Accusations that Christians were causing natural disasters resulted from their boast that Jesus and church leaders could control the weather. This scapegoating of Christians prompted Tertullian to protest, "If the Tiber overflows its banks or the Nile fails to flood the fields, if the sky stands still or the earth moves, if famine has struck or plague killed, the first reaction is 'Let the Christians have it!'"[191] A century later, in Augustine's time, similar sentiments were behind this popular saying among the pagan Romans, "Drought and Christianity go hand in hand."[192] Given traditional Christianity's doctrine of special providence, those who are devastated by

---

[188]John 14:12.

[189]Origen, *Contra Celsum* 2.48.

[190]Gregory of Nyssa, *Life of Gregory Thaumaturgus*, 47, 59, 68, 102, in *Fathers of the Church* (Washington DC: Catholic University of America Press, 1998).

[191]Tertullian, *To the Nations* 8; *Apology* 11.

[192]Augustine, *The City of God* 2.3.

bad happenings have understandably harped on the negative side of the logic of the Omnipotent's preferential treatment.

Athanasius, who is revered as the stellar defender of orthodoxy and the opponent of Arius—another Bishop of Alexandria—contended that the supernatural traditions associated with Jesus proved that he is God. The bishop attributed to him not only changing water into wine and walking on water but also the creation of his own body in the womb of the Virgin Mary, and the resurrection of his dead body. Breaking out of a tomb and soaring to heaven was Jesus' crowning miracle. Neither Askepios nor Heracles, Athanasius claimed, have marvels attributed to them than can compare to those of the Lord of nature.[193]

Ironically, as theologian Norman Robinson points out, Athanasius championed a major heresy: "In the hands of Athanasius the earthly career of Christ virtually disappears from sight and all the emphasis is allowed to fall upon the miracles. . . . This was docetism with a vengeance. . . . The Arians had a far firmer grasp of the concrete personality of Jesus of Nazareth."[194] Likewise, Bishop John Robinson states, "A docetic streak runs through and discredits almost the whole of Alexandrian Christology."[195]

Christians tended to view postbiblical miracles as reinforcing ancient testimony to the almighty God. "The human qualities and human sufferings of Jesus play singularly little part in the propaganda of this period," observes Eric Dodds, a careful student of the early centuries of Christianity.[196] Some fourth-century apologists emphasized the spectacular quality of Jesus' miracles to demonstrate the superiority of the Christian religion to all others. Arnobius claimed that no pagan leader has displayed the ability to utter a word and arrest a storm or to revive a corpse buried for days.[197] Bishop Gregory of Nyssa moved the defense of Christianity down an irrational cul de sac by arguing that "the evidence for Jesus' divinity comes through his miracles."[198] Recognizing the competition in this field

---

[193]Athanasius, *On the Incarnation* 15, 18, 49.

[194]*St. Mary's College Bulletin* (Spring 1972): 10.

[195]John Robinson, *The Human Face of God* (Phildelphia: Westminster, 1973) 39.

[196]Eric Dodds, *Pagan and Christian in an Age of Anxiety* (New York: Norton, 1965) 119.

[197]Arnobius, *Against the Pagans* 1.46.

[198]Gregory of Nyssa, *Catechetical Oration* 34.

even within the Bible, Gregory made this special plea for Jesus, "His walking through the sea was different from Moses' sea miracle that separated waters on either side and made bare its depth for those who passed through, for the surface of the water provided solid support for his feet."[199]

Churches were established on pagan shrine sites and the Christ figure assumed there a supernatural aura even greater than what was prevalent among the vanquished cult figures:

> In the fourth and early fifth centuries, appropriate rituals were established at curative shrines, and candles and incense, once prohibited by the Church as too "pagan," now burned at saints' altars. . . . Although pagan temples and altars were closed down, converted or destroyed, the old cures, visions and miracles of the healing god Aesculapius or Apollonius, still occurred at Christian shrines under the patronage of a new spiritual hierarchy, the martyred saints. . . . The powers of holy bones were recognized by the simplest Christians, innocent of theology, and for a thousand years these beliefs, though sometimes challenged, would dominate much of the folk-Christianity of Europe.[200]

Emphasis on miracles was as prominent in the Latin Church as in the Greek Church. European historian William Lecky wrote:

> If we pass from the Fathers [of the ancient church] into the middle ages, we find ourselves in an atmosphere that was dense and charged with the supernatural. The demand for miracles was almost boundless, and the supply was equal to the demand. . . . Nothing could be more common than for a holy man to be lifted up from the floor in the midst of his devotions. . . . It was somewhat more extraordinary, but not in the least incredible, that the fish should have thronged to the shore to hear St. Antony preach.[201]

Illustrations of the increase in miracle tales come from a variety of medieval sources. Pope Gregory the Great, believing that miracles were still happening in the sixth century like those alleged in the Bible, told of one monk who ran on the surface of water.[202] Following a technique the Evangelists used with respect to Jesus, the Pope adapted stories of Hebrew

---

[199]Gregory of Nyssa, *Catechetical Oration* 23.

[200]Ronald Finucane, *Miracles and Pilgrims* (Totowa NJ: Rowman, 1977) 18-19, 24.

[201]William Lecky, *History of . . . Rationalism in Europe* (London: Longmans, 1870) 1:141.

[202]Gregory I, *Dialogues* 2.7.

prophets to enhance the holiness of Benedict, the founder of a monastic order who had served as a humble administrator before his death a half-century earlier. Elisha, wanting to recover an ax head that had dropped in the Jordan while a riverbank tree was being felled, threw in a stick that caused the iron to float. Accordingly, when a monk was cutting brush along a lake, the blade of his sickle flew off the handle and into deep water. Benedict thrust the handle into the lake and "immediately the iron blade rose from the bottom of the lake and slipped back onto the blade."[203] Just as Elijah and Elisha supernaturally filled jars of oil for needy Israelites, so the abbot prayed during a famine and oil poured into a cask, but it stopped when he ceased praying.[204] Again, not to be outshown by those prophets who restored life to boys, Benedict enabled a boy to regain life and health by praying over his corpse.[205]

In the seventh century, credulous churchman Bede recorded many supernatural tales from his Anglo-Saxon culture. For example, a bishop was beaten during the night by the apostle Peter, the patron of the Canterbury shrine: "Deeply moved by the scourgings and exhortations of St. Peter, Christ's servant Lawrence went to the king as soon as morning had come, drew back his robe and showed him the marks of his stripes."[206]

Much prestige was given the Roman Church by a forged document in the eighth century claiming that Pope Sylvester I cured Constantine of leprosy; in gratitude the Emperor granted the pontiff and his successors sovereignty over the western part of his empire.[207] Legends arose during the century after Francis of Assisi lived regarding his frequent levitations. Brother Leo once saw him raised to treetop height and again when he was exalted almost beyond sight of his companion.[208] Obviously, belief in Jesus' physical ascension was easily accepted by medieval Christians.

Aquinas called Islam "frivolous" because the *Qur'an* admits that their principal prophet worked no miracles. Included in the millions of words written by that premier Christian theologian are these, "Muhammad did not bring forth any signs produced in a supernatural way, which alone fittingly

[203] 2 Kings 6:4-7; Gregory I, *Dialogues* 2.6.
[204] 1 Kings 17:12-16; 2 Kings 4:1-7; Gregory I, *Dialogues* 2.28.
[205] 1 Kings 17:17-23; 2 Kings 4:29-37.
[206] Bede, Ecclesiastical History 2:6.
[207] Kenneth Latourette, *A History of Christianity* (London: Eyre, 1954) 341.
[208] *The Deeds of Blessed Francis and His Companions* 39.

gives witness to divine inspiration."[209] This crass claim of Christianity's superiority over Islam has been continued into modern times. James Mozley, an Oxford divine, faulted Muhammad for performing no miracles to confirm his divine revelation and claimed that the absence of such "unfits his religion for an enlightened age and people."[210] Muhammad was also taunted as an impostor by pagan Meccans when he was establishing himself as a prophet because he admitted his inability to perform supernatural signs. But Muslims argue that he expressed appropriate humility and honesty in rejecting the popular demand that he perform miracles.[211]

Benedicta Ward has described the way belief in miracles occupied a major part of the medieval outlook.[212] The literature of that period was full of stories of saints who "could prophesy the future, control the weather, provide protection against fire and flood, magically transport heavy objects, and bring relief to the sick." There were numerous records of saints walking on water, usually to cross a river where no bridge or boat was available, or to escape from some peril at sea.[213] Church buildings displayed the orientation toward magic, for bells were placed on them not so much to notify the congregation as to dispel the demons.[214]

At the Naples cathedral, chicanery has continued from the Middle Ages until now. Eighteen times a year a priest takes a vial of the dried-up blood of Januarius, a bishop martyred in the fourth century, and exhibits it before the congregation. After turning it up and down, he announces, "The miracle has happened." Allegedly the blood liquifies temporarily, and Catholic authorities accept this performance without criticism.[215] By possessing this relic, so it is claimed, Naples has been preserved from many tragedies.

---

[209]Aquinas, *Summa contra Gentiles* 6.4.

[210]James Mozley, *On Miracles* (London: Rivingtons, 1867) 32.

[211]Rafiq Zakaria, *Muhammand and the Qur'an* (London: Penguin, 1991) 24-26.

[212]Benedicta Ward, *Miracles and the Medieval Mind* (Philadelphia: University of Pennsylvania Press, 1982).

[213]Cobham Brewer, *A Dictionary of Miracles* (Philadelphia: Lippincott, 1889) 330-32.

[214]Keith Thomas, *Religion and the Decline of Magic* (New York: Scribner, 1971) 26, 31.

[215]"Januarius, St." *New Catholic Encyclopedia* (New York: McGraw-Hall) 1966.

Presumably the miraculous transformation is unrelated to the faith of those present when it occurs.

Miracles have had a place in Christian apologetics even after the era of the Renaissance. As we have seen, Francis Xavier was accorded a host of miracles in seventeenth-century Catholicism. In that same century, Italian Franciscan Joseph of Cupertino was allegedly seen by his fellow monks to have levitated dozen of times while in mystical rapture during the Eucharist. A painting of the airborne "Flying Friar" at the high altar can be found in the *New Catholic Encyclopedia*. On visiting Pope Urban VIII he went into ecstasy and rose off the ground until commanded to descend. At his death the physician attending him noted that he floated above the bed, and in 1767 he was made saint.[216]

The shift in the meaning of "saint" in Catholicism illustrates the evolution of supernaturalism in the church. In the New Testament, the term "saint" and "Christian" were synonymous; for Paul, "saint" and "sinner" were not contrasting terms, and he is represented as calling himself "the foremost of sinners" when he was a mature Christian.[217] He wrote to the "saints" of Corinth, some of whom were arrogant, greedy, licentious, quarrelsome, or drunken with communion wine.[218] Centuries later, Christians who were designated "saints" had a reputation for exceptional holiness, and some were martyrs who had died in allegiance to their faith. Then medieval pope Gregory IX decreed that miracles were a prerequisite for sainthood candidates. In that era, Kenneth Woodward writes, "The mass of believers were not interested in saints as moral examples, but as spiritual patrons who protected the populace against storms and plagues." But "only in the last four centuries, with the development of formal predecures for canonization, has the reliance on proven miracles come to be a part of the saint-making process."[219]

The focus upon the human instruments through whom miracles were alleged to have happened deviates from apostolic teaching. Jesus' followers witnessed a healing when Peter and John were present and judged that it resulted from "some power or godliness" those apostles possessed, but they

---

[216]"Joseph of Cupertino," *New Catholic Encyclopedia*.

[217]1 Timothy 1:15.

[218]1 Corinthians 4:18; 6:9-11; 11:17-22; 2 Corinthians 1:1; 12:20-21.

[219]Kenneth Woodward, *Making Saints* (New York: Simon and Schuster, 1990) 70, 214-15.

rejected the attempt to give them credit.[220] Although, in theory, it is God who works miracles, the intricate canonization procedure appears to give more attention to the pious person who was on hand when an alleged breach of the natural order occurred. A saint now needs to be a dead Catholic who led an exemplary life and, except for martyrs, performed at least two supernatural miracles, one to attain the first beatification stage and a second posthumous one to achieve final canonization. Nearly all of the miracles associated with saints in recent centuries pertain to physical healings, so much attention is given to medical case histories. Genuineness is declared when scientific experts, all of whom are Catholics hired by the Vatican, agree that they cannot explain how the cures occurred. Lacking here is an awareness that the so-called miracles under consideration might be natural but inexplicable by current medical knowledge. Pope John Paul II canonized over 400 saints, more than the previous total number of official saints. Although the laity compose more than 95% of Catholics, most of the saints are clergy. Recognition has been mainly given to white, European males who have not come from poverty homes.

The Vatican Council in 1870 affirmed that miracles pertaining to Christian origins are "most certain proofs of God's divine revelation adapted to the intelligence of all men." Excommunication was threatened those who explain such miracles as fables or myths.[221] Nevertheless, a century after that Council's declaration some Catholic biblical interpreters began to question the facticity of those miracles. Meier, one of the most noted contemporary Catholic scholars with New Testament expertise, has analyzed exhaustively the alleged Gospel miracles and rejects the historicity of a number of them.[222]

Martin Luther and John Calvin, the formative Protestant Reformers, had no difficulty accepting biblical supernaturalism but they were disdainful of postbiblical miracles claimed by Catholics. Luther provided this explanation as to why miracles are no longer needed: "In the beginning, when the young trees were still undeveloped and new, they had to be tied to a stake until they became strong. But now that the Word has been disseminated

---

[220]Acts 3:1-12.

[221]Josef Neuner, ed., *The Teaching of the Catholic Church* (New York: Alba, 1967) 33, 39.

[222]Meier, *A Marginal Jew* 2:718, 884, 896, 933, 950.

throughout the world, there is no longer any need to confirm it."[223] Calvin, assuming a geocentric universe, alleged that God intervened to halt the regular movement of the sun in response to Joshua's request and also in having the sun go backward as a sign to Hezekiah.[224] In his commentary on Matthew 12:15-21, he declared that Jesus worked miracles to prove that he was the world's Redeemer, but the reformer stated that "miracles have vanished that the Lord willed to have happened for a time."[225]

Anglican William Paley wrote a text in 1794 that had an enormous impact on English-speaking Protestants. In *Evidences of Christianity* he attempted to reinstate the traditional argument from Gospel miracles to prove the truth of the Christian religion. Of primary importance, he contended, was Jesus' reanimation of Lazarus that displayed Jesus' divinity.[226] Paley believed that it was Jesus' dazzling miracles rather than his sublime message that moved his disciples to die for him. Paley joined Aquinas in claiming that Christianity's superiority over Islam is due to Muhammad's inability to perform supernatural works.[227]

A century ago, Benjamin Warfield, a learned and influential ultra-Calvinist, expressed a viewpoint toward miracles that has been widespread among conservative Protestants. He trumpeted biblical supernaturalism, and said of Jesus, "His was emphatically an otherworld religion."[228] Warfield was convinced that God enhanced true religion by establishing a unique category of miracles for the biblical era. In order to defend every scriptural statement as inerrant, he held that the laws of nature were suspended when assistance was needed for authenicating fledgling Christianity. Miracles were discontinued after the apostolic era, Warfield believed, because no more safeguards were needed to enable the church to flourish. Postbiblical Christians who are looking for the active involvement of God in the world should search the written text, not the current era. There is no basis for expecting even spiritual healing to be a permanent feature of Christianity.[229]

---

[223]Jaroslav Pelikan, ed., *Luther's Works* (St. Louis: Concordia, 1961) 368.

[224]John Calvin, *Institutes of the Christin Religion* 1.16.2; Joshua 10:13; 2 Kings 20:11.

[225]Calvin, *Institutes* 4.19.18.

[226]William Paley, *Works* (Philadelphia: Crissy, 1857) 322; John 11:11-46.

[227]Paley, *Works*, 286-87, 364.

[228]Benjamin Warfield, *Counterfeit Miracles* (New York: Scribner, 1918) 177.

[229]Warfield, *Counterfeit Miracles*, 6, 179-80.

Driven by his anti-Catholicism, Warfield joined skeptical rationalists in attacking claims of miracles over the past nineteen hundred years. While invidiously invalidating all alleged miracles in Catholic history, he uncritically accepted all biblical ones.

Until recent times, Christian apologists assumed without question that supernaturalism was the best means for convincing religious unbelievers of the gospel truth. They are now finding that approach more likely to confirm agnostics. Moreover it imposes an obstacle for many believers who relate better to someone with human limitations than to a superman. Charles Darwin was positively influenced by Paley's writings while studying to become a clergyman but he later rejected supernaturalism as a support for the truth of Christianity. He came to judge the culture of Jesus' time to be "credulous to a degree almost incomprehensible by us" and wondered how "any sane man" could find believable gospel stories that contravene the natural order.[230]

Despite the scientific revolution, a vast number of Christians still believe that the more contrary an event is to the natural pattern, the greater its religious value. Anglican Alan Richardson probably expresses the position of most twentieth-century Christians when he asserts that the supernaturalism of the gospel is a necessary "authentication of the divine mission of Jesus."[231] A sociological survey taken in the United States a generation ago indicated that the majority of Christians accept as "completely true" the statement "Jesus walked on water."[232] James Beverley writes about the contemporary scene, "What is surprising in the vitality of supernatural belief in American religion, Christianity in particular, is the degree to which it has survived centuries of skepticism." He also tells of Korean Sun Moon, the Unification Church founder, who "alleges that he has been to heaven to converse with God directly."[233] The emphasis of much of the "electronic religion" that permeates the air waves is on

---

[230]William Phipps, *Darwin's Religious Odyssey* (Harrisburg: Trinity, 2002) 6, 34.

[231]Alan Richardson, *Christian Apologetics* (London: SCM, 1947) 173.

[232]Charles Glock and Rodney Stark, *Religion and Society in Tension* (Chicago: Rand McNally, 1965) 95; this varies from 19% of United Church of Christ members to 99% of Southern Baptists.

[233]"Miracles," *Contemporary American Religion* (New York: Macmillan, 2000).

supernaturalism. In our so-called scientific age, many people are duped by tales of the Bermuda triangle, the Loch Ness monster, chariots of extraterrestrial gods, and by seances that feign afterlife data.

"Biblical miracles actually happened just as the Bible says they did," is a statement accepted by more than six out of ten American Christians.[234] In another survey taken of Americans a generation ago, with a less specific statement but with a broader group, Gallup reports that eight out of ten American adults "believe in miracles"—86% of women and 71% of men—and that "even today, miracles are performed by the power of God." The surveys found that of those who believe in miracles, most claim that religion is "very important," yet belief in miracles is shared by 42% of the religiously unaffiliated. Even 71% of Americans with postgraduate education believe in miracles, although they are not as likely to believe as those with less education.[235] A Gallup poll also shows that most Americans believe that the Bible contains no scientific errors.[236] Most in that group probably do not realize that biblical writers accepted a geocentric universe that was spread out from Jerusalem to four corners.[237] Also, the Bible presumes that the solid astrodome ("firmament") above the earth provides a track for the sun to move from east to west—unless stopped or moved backward by divine intervention.

Supernatural stories from the Bible are usually read in churches without an explanation to the bewildered that such should not be interpreted as historical. To compound the problem, after a story such as the cursing of a fig tree is read from pulpits, the declaration is often made, "This is the word of God," connoting its absolute truth. As a result, many adults as well as children presume that credulity is favored by God and that faith is in large part believing what seems false to one's reason. Some educated Christians rebel against this situation by abandoning the pews, others by enduring the

---

[234]Rodney Stark and William Bainbridge, *The Future of Religion* (Berkeley: University of California Press, 1985) 55.

[235]George Gallup, *The People's Religion* (New York: Macmillan, 1989) 58, 119; George Gallup and Michael Lindsay, *Surveying the Religious Landscape* (Harrisburg: Morehouse, 1999) 26.

[236]George Gallup, *Religion in America* (Princeton NJ: Religion Research Center, 1990) 50.

[237]William Phipps, "Cultural Commitments and World Maps," *Focus* (Summer 1991): 7-9.

intellectual insult because they like the support they receive from congregational life, and still others by attempting to place their irrational sacred beliefs in a separate mental compartment from their rational secular understandings. The supernatural stories about Jesus and Santa are similar lore, but the way they are presented to children is often quite different. Few parents are reluctant to inform a doubting school-aged child that the aerial sled from the North Pole to their roof is a fantasy created to delight, but many neglect to interpret stories of biblical supernaturalism in a reasonable manner.

In 2000, an animated film for children entitled *The Miracle Maker* was released by BBC television on the life of Jesus. Emphasis is placed on the supernatural, especially on Jesus' ability to restore Jairus's daughter and Lazarus to life. The climax of the film is Jesus' own tangible resurrection from a tomb; he is portrayed as identical to his predeath body. The film illustrates that the craving for superman Jesus by the simpleminded has not abated in the twenty-first century.

* * *

Christians have often not been as perceptive as some of their prominent antagonists who have recognized that one more wonder-working cult leader is nothing momentous. Such a person was presumed to be deceptive, and he had a diminished stature among those who respected the natural order. Lucian, a Greek satirist living in the second century of the Christian era, introduced the term "superman" (*hyperanthropos*) to refer to a pretender who is acclaimed a god. That ancient Voltaire lampooned the credulity of people who are dazzled by a worthless creature who appears to have divine majesty.[238] At that same time, Trypho, a Jewish opponent of Christianity, believed that the upstart religion is centered in "a magician who led the people astray."[239] Also in that period Celsus wrote a treatise attacking Christianity, claiming that Jesus practiced magic and sorcery learned in Egypt. The philosopher believed Askepios was an authenic wonder-worker but Jesus was an impostor.[240]

In the fourth century, Emperor Julian was willing to grant that Jesus "surpassed all the magicians and charlatans of every place and every time."

---

[238]Lucian, *Cataplous* 16.
[239]Justin, *Dialogue with Trypho* 69.
[240]Celsus, *True Doctrine*, 57, 69.

Even though that anti-Christian Roman acknowledged that Jesus "walked on the sea and drove out demons," he judged that "during his lifetime he accomplished nothing of worth."[241] While opponents of Christianity generally did not deny that Jesus worked miracles, they were—in Shakespeare's words—"full of sound and fury, signifying nothing." Classicist Dodds discusses the adoration of divine men in ancient Mediterranean cults who claimed to perform wonders contrary to the natural order. He points out that "miracles were both commonplace and morally suspect" in late antiquity.[242] Historian Robin Fox writes, "Between the Apostolic age and the fourth century AD, we know of no historical case when a miracle or an exorcism turned an individual, let alone a crowd, to the Christian faith."[243]

In contrast to John Crossan,[244] I would argue that interpreters of Jesus, from the first century onward, err in thinking of him as a crowd-mystifying magician. Those stories suggesting that Jesus displayed his power by violating the natural order do not have the ring of authenticity. Jesus appealed to the regularities—not irregularities—of nature. He taught that lessons can be learned from birds, lilies, yeast, and the sown seed.[245] He found "tongues in trees, books in the running brooks,/ Sermons in stones, and good in everything."[246]

The adoring followers of Moses, Elijah, Elisha, Jesus, Peter, Paul, and Muhammad are to blame for the bigger-than-life legends that inflate the status of their heroes. The wonderful qualities of Jesus as a teacher and healer are independent of such incredible stories as his levitating on water, causing a tree to wither, or raising a putrefied corpse to life. The Gospels portray the sunrise of medicine over magic. Found there are some residuals of magical incantations and some declarations of instantaneous cures, but they also show the dawning light of real healing. Hubert Richards writes:

> The God whom Jesus preached is not the God who looks after things we
> cannot ourselves control, the absentee despot who occasionally intervenes to

---

[241]Julian, *Against the Galileans* 99, 191, 213.

[242]Dodds, *Pagan and Christian in an Age of Anxiety*, 125.

[243]Robin Fox, *Pagans and Christians* (New York: Knopf, 1987) 329.

[244]John Crossan, *The Historical Jesus* (San Francisco: Harper, 1991) 137-67, 303-32.

[245]Matthew 6:26, 28; 13:3-33.

[246]William Shakespeare, *As You Like It* 2.1.16-17; Matthew 7:17-19, 24-25; John 7:38.

do superhuman things to inspire a salutary respect for him. He is the mystery of patient and suffering love. . . . Jesus worked miracles, but since he was a man they were the kind of miracles men can work. And so he presumed, quite naturally, that his disciples would work miracles greater than his own.[247]

Why did some early Christians tell of a superman Jesus if, in fact, the historical Jesus functioned as an inspiring leader, an enlightening teaching, a compassionate physician, and a suffering servant? In prescientific cultures, people have generally believed that the more contrary an event is to the perceived natural pattern, the more it indicates the presence of divine power. The Evangelists found themselves in a competitive religious market and they seemed determined to demonstrate—at the expense of consistency—that the founder of Christianity was as spectacular as any of the acclaimed wonder-workers of antiquity. They were especially eager to meet the resistance from Judaism by recording legends displaying that Jesus could match or even surpass the tall stories recorded of the prophets Moses, Elijah, and Elisha. The Evangelists did not perceive that some of the prophets whom Jesus most admired were not associated with contrary-to-nature acts.

This tracing of the growth of the miraculous in Christianity has shown an obvious increase in supernaturalism not only between the generations separating the canonical and the apocryphal New Testament but especially within the crucial first Christian century. Students of Christian origins have long been aware of its growth in the postbiblical church, but few have admitted the rapid inflation that occurred during the decades when the New Testament books were being written. The presumption continues to be widespread that the New Testament is uniform throughout in its theological message, a vestige of the doctrine that everything in it is the infallible word of God. But careful examination discloses that it is far from monolithic and that judgment needs to be made as to its most historical and coherent teaching.

Obviously, a true understanding of a historical person must begin with a study of the earliest relevant records. The figure of Jesus is less likely distorted by Paul in his correspondence than by the sermons about Jesus that later constituted the Gospels. The fact that Paul stated nothing about Jesus as a miracle worker is important, especially since Paul believed that Jesus embodied the most godlike qualities. The apostle accepted the paradox that

---

[247]Hubert Richards, *The Miracles of Jesus* (London: Mowbray, 1983) 112.

the fullness of deity has been expressed in a being who shares the natural limitations of humans. Paul did not accept the gnostic dualism that attempts to superimpose a spiritual nature on a human nature. All authentic portraits of Jesus must rely upon Paul's brief but telling sketch of his Jewish contemporary.

Chapter 6
Visions of Reality

The origin and spread of the Christian church is virtually incomprehensible unless Jesus' disciples experienced in some way the continuity of their leader after his crucifixion. His resurrection was not a deus ex machina, such as an ancient dramatist might attach to remedy the outrageous fate of a hero. Nor was it like the they-lived-happily-ever-after ending of the old-fashioned children's storybook, for it gave validity and vitality to the gospel. Jesus' resurrection expresses hope that the most violent of injustices will not, in the long run, prove victorious. Günther Bornkamm does not exaggerate when he asserts that without the Easter event "there would be no gospel, not one account, no letter in the New Testament, no faith, no Church, no worship, no prayer in Christendom."[1] John Crossan, another distinguished Gospels scholar, also views it as the sine qua non of Christianity:

> If those who accepted Jesus during his earthly life had not continued to follow, believe, and experience his continuing presence after the crucifixion, all would have been over. That is the resurrection, the continuing presence in a continuing community of the past Jesus in a radically new and transcendental mode of present and future existence.[2]

Harvard theologian Gordon Kaufman points to the abiding global effect of the triumphant Jesus: "It was in the conviction of Jesus' resurrection that the church was founded and the Gospel preached to all nations. It was because of this event, therefore, that Christian faith became a powerful force in Western culture and ultimately the whole world, and to this day is a significant and powerful reality in human lives."[3] Recognizing the fundamental significance of Jesus' resurrection for the beginning and the continuance of the church, the way in which it affected the psychic state of three preeminent New Testament figures will be carefully examined.

---

[1] Günther Bornkamm, *Jesus of Nazareth* (New York: Harper, 1961) 181.
[2] John Crossan, *The Historical Jesus* (San Francisco: Harper, 1991) 404.
[3] Gordon Kaufman, *Systematic Theology* (New York: Scribner, 1968) 415.

Of Paul

The apostle Paul introduced *anastasis* into the Christian vocabulary, which is rendered "resurrection" in English Bibles. Compounding the Greek words meaning "up" (*ana*) plus "stand" (*stasis*), or the Latin words meaning "again" (*re*) plus "rise" (*surgere*), "resurrection of the dead" literally means the rising up of bodies that had been recumbent due to death. For example, Apollo observes in the classical drama *Eumenides*, "Once a man is slain and the dust has drunk up his blood, there is no *anastasis*."[4] But Paul did not use *anastasis* to describe corpses literally standing up but, symbolically, to refer to deathless life in the presence of God. That is its import when he inquired of Corinthian Christians, "How can some of you say there is no resurrection of the dead?"[5] In scholarly usage, "resurrection" is reserved for those who have escaped mortality, in contrast to "resuscitation," which describes those who have been revived but who will some day cease breathing again.

No biblical writer placed more emphasis on Jesus' resurrection than Paul. The fullest and most profound New Testament discussion of this subject is in 1 Corinthians 15. There the apostle reasons, "If Christ was not raised, then our [gospel] proclamation and your faith is null and void." That hypothetical would imply that the apostles have been deceived and are even "misrepresenting God."[6] Since the eternal future of Christians is intricately intertwined with Jesus' resurrection, not only is the genuineness of Christians' faith involved but also their hope for life after death. William Sloane Coffin quipped that "Paul puts all his Christian eggs in one Easter basket."[7]

To correct distorted understandings pertaining to Jesus' resurrection and its implications, Paul twice prefaced his comments by noting that he was passing on authoritative oral tradition he had received from those who had been with Jesus prior to his death. The apostle wanted to show that he was not just expressing his own point of view but was undeviatingly presenting the commonly accepted understanding of core happenings in earliest Christianity that antedated his career as a Christian. Accordingly, he provided the first record of the "Lord's Supper" that occurred on the evening

---

[4]Aeschylus, *Eumenides* (458 BCE) 648.
[5]1 Corinthians 15:12.
[6]1 Corinthians 15:14-15.
[7]William Sloane Coffin, *Letters to a Young Doubter* (Louisville: Westminster/ John Knox, 2005) 166.

before Jesus' death.[8] Using the same introductory literary formula, Paul responded to some Corinthians who had expressed doubts about his paradoxical claim that dead persons might continue to live. He wrote down in sequence the official facts pertaining to Jesus' mortal end and immortal beginning that had been conveyed to him. To that he added his personal testimony:

> I passed on to you, as of first importance, what I had received: that Christ died for our sins, in accordance with the scriptures; that he was buried, and was raised three days later, as the scriptures foretold; and that he was seen [ophthe] by Peter and then by the Twelve. After that, he was seen by more than five hundred believers simultaneously, most of whom are still alive, though some have died. Next he was seen by James, and then by all the apostles. Last of all, as to one untimely born, he was seen by me.

Those verses contain several features that give it priority over other New Testament accounts in establishing what really happened in Jesus' resurrection. They contain the earliest tradition pertaining to the event as well as the only record by a witness. What Paul stated there and in other letters was written down more than a decade before the earliest Gospel was composed. The historical significance of this testimony is even greater when it is recognized that Paul was passing on what he received from previous witnesses two decades earlier. He probably learned of the resurrection experiences of Jesus' companions when he journeyed to Jerusalem approximately five years after Jesus was crucified. He wanted to "know" (Greek, historeo) about Jesus and his apostles when with James, the brother of Jesus, and Simon, better known by the nickname "Rocky" (in Aramaic, Cephas; in Greek, Petros) that Jesus gave him.[9] While chronological priority does not in itself prove that an account is more reliable, the likelihood that such is the case increases if its writer is likely to be at least as honest as the later writers. Paul provides the only written source pertaining to the resurrection in first generation Christianity and therefore it deserves the closest scrutiny.

Paul had been informed of two unspecified prophecies in the Hebrew Bible, one of which can be easily discovered. Jesus had been identified with the Suffering Servant of Isaiah who was exalted after "he bore the sin of

---

[8]1 Corinthians 11:20-26.
[9]Galatians 1:18-19; Mark 3:16.

many."[10] The second prophecy, pertaining to his resurrection after three days, is much more difficult to find. The closest source that could possibly have been construed in that manner is Hosea 6:2, which states that "God will raise us up on the third day." But the context of that verse shows that it has nothing to do with an individual resurrection in a future era; rather, it has to do with a hoped for ethical revival of the Israelite people that would soon come in Hosea's time, many centuries before the Christian era. Oxford scholar Frederick Conybeare comments on the Christian presumption that secrets of the gospel were buried in Hebrew scriptures:

> The true explanation of this [Hosea] passage is, of course, to be sought in the immediate circumstances. . . . The Messianic exegetes of the early Church rummaged the Old Testament for passages which even remotely seemed to echo events in a future Messiah's career. These they took out of their context, misunderstood and even garbled, in order to fit them out as prophecies of Christ.[11]

"Three days later" is a biblical idiom for a short while later; it should not be interpreted literally as a precise measurement of time. Subsequently interpreters have attempted to do such, even though it is unusual to think of a period from Friday sunset to Sunday at dawn as composing three days. In Jewish culture, three days after someone appeared dead all doubt ceased that the person was really dead.

Trying to muster the strongest proof possible that Jesus had risen, the apostle went beyond vague scriptural support to present in historical order the names of individuals and groups who had been witnesses. The places where those experiences happened are not given, and the sightings of Christ are not specified as beginning three days after his burial. After Paul related what had been handed down to him, he supplemented that tradition by classifying his sighting with those of the earliest church leaders. His conversion was several years after Jesus' crucifixion, so the normative resurrection sightings were not restricted to a few days or weeks after Jesus' death.[12] Elsewhere Paul rested his claim to be legitimately included in the apostolate on his having seen the risen Christ. That crucial and immensely impressive

---

[10]Isaiah 52:13, 53:12.

[11]Frederick Conybeare, *The Origins of Christianity* (Evanston IL: University Books, 1958) 293-94.

[12]According to the Valentinians (Irenaeus, *Against Heresies* 1.3; 1.30), the risen Jesus remained with his disciples for eighteen months.

experience, he testified, transformed him from a violent persecutor of the Christian church to its principal proclaimer to the Gentiles.[13]

One group of resurrection witnesses that Paul mentioned was composed of the original twelve disciples, although Judas presumably had died and had been replaced by Matthias. Another group contained hundreds of Christians, and still another consisted of male and female missionary apostles such as Andronicus, Junia, Barnabas, Silas, and Timothy.[14] Also, Paul might well have been personally aware that Stephen, the first Christian martyr, had a vision in Jerusalem of the heavenly Jesus.[15] Paula Fredriksen comments on these multiple attestations, "We can draw securely from this evidence only the baldest conclusion: that despite the absolute certainty of Jesus' death, his immediate followers with equal certainty perceived—and then proclaimed—that Jesus lived again."[16]

Paul explicitly referred to Peter and James, who would have been well known, and places his own experience on a par with theirs. He does recognize that he was "untimely born," that is, a late arrival in comparison with the Christian beginnings of Jesus' Galilean companions. The vision of James is only related elsewhere in the second-century *Gospel according to the Hebrews*. It states that Jesus' sibling was fasting when he saw Jesus and heard him say, "My brother, eat your bread, for the Son of Man is risen."[17] James led the church conservatives and Paul the liberals,[18] but both groups were united on the centrality of envisioning the risen Jesus.

Paul used identical language in referring to the Easter event of each individual and group. *Ophthe*, repeated in four clauses, is often translated "appeared," but the Greek is the passive voice as well as the past tense of the irregular verb *horao*, "I see." "Was seen," as found in the King James, the New Century, and the New Living translations, conveys better the nature of the experience because it does not suggest that the apostles' eyes were confronted with an external object for which there was no subjective preparation. Paul never described an ocular experience of the resurrected

---

[13]Galatians 1:12-16; 1 Corinthians 9:1.

[14]Romans 16:7; 1 Corinthians 9:5-6; 1 Thessalonians 1:1, 2:6.

[15]Acts 7:54-56; 8:1.

[16]Paula Fredriksen, *From Jesus to Christ* (New Haven CT: Yale University Press, 2000) 133.

[17]Jerome, *Illustrious Men* 2.

[18]Galatians 2:11-12; Acts 15:12-21.

Jesus. If he received from other Christians a story of Jesus' *physical* resurrection, he did not find it convincing enough to repeat. Bishop John Spong's philological comment is clarifying: "*Ophthe* means to have one's eyes opened to see dimensions beyond the physical. It means to have a revelatory encounter with the holy. It relates to the nature of visions, but not so much subjective hallucinations as seeing into that which is ultimately real, into God or God's inbreaking future."[19]

In a similar way, Loyola philosopher Thomas Sheehan concludes his lengthy discussion of Paul's writing about the resurrection:

> The text from First Corinthians . . . does not tell us how Jesus manifested himself after his death. The verb *ophthe* simply expresses the Christian claim that Jesus "was revealed" . . . in an entirely unspecified way. The manner in which he was made manifest is not mentioned and is not important. The text does not assert that Jesus appeared in any kind of body that the disciples could see or touch, nor does it say that Jesus spoke to the disciples.[20]

In another Corinthian letter, Paul mentions "visions and revelations of the Lord" he had received. His brief comment on the experience suggests why he gave no description of the risen Jesus. He obliquely described himself as "a man in Christ who fourteen years ago was caught up . . . into Paradise and heard things he is not able to explain, words that no mortal is permitted to repeat."[21] Typical of mystics, Paul found the vision to be ineffably sublime. Likewise, he was reticent to say more than that he had seen the risen Jesus, and he called the resurrection metamorphosis "a mystery."[22]

Also in 2 Corinthians, Paul compared the experience of becoming a Christian to having an inward enlightenment. God who created light, he asserted, "has shone in our hearts the light by letting us know God's glory in the face of Jesus Christ."[23] That experience of brightness is similar to the vocational initiations of other outstanding figures in the biblical religion. In discussing those calls, theologians sometime employ the terms "theophany," "angelophany," or "christophany" to label an appearance of God, an angel, or the resurrected Jesus. The undifferentiated word "epiphany," meaning

---

[19]John Spong, *Resurrection* (San Francisco: Harper, 1994) 54.
[20]Thomas Sheehan, *The First Coming* (New York: Random House, 1986) 117.
[21]2 Corinthians 12:1-4.
[22]1 Corinthians 15:51.
[23]2 Corinthians 4:6.

"manifestation," comes from the compound Greek term epiphaneia ("on" plus "appear"), and is used to refer to a revelation.

Throughout the Greek New Testament, *horao*—the verb Paul used for Jesus' resurrection—usually describes revelations occurring within persons. For example, the Gospel of Luke opens with the story of an angel who "was seen" by a priest and closes with an account of women who "had seen a vision of angels."[24] Again, according to Acts, Paul had a "vision" in which a Macedonian man "was seen."[25] The New Testament's use of *horao* follows that of the Septuagint, the Greek translation of the Hebrew Bible. There it is used over 500 times and usually refers to understanding, not sense perception. Consider Moses' burning bush angelophany in the Sinai wilderness, "The angel of the Lord was seen by him in a flame of fire out of the midst of a bush."[26] It is significant that Paul, in writing about the radiant revelation in him of the risen Christ, uses the same verb that he had found in the story of Moses' call. Corporate visionary experiences are also attributed to Moses' associates, for more than seventy elders who were with him saw the God of Israel.[27] The Deuteronomic theologian insisted that "no form" of God was seen when fire accompanied theophanies at holy Mount Sinai. Efforts to express physically the invisible deity were condemned as idolatry.[28]

A broad examination of biblical visions is relevant to understanding Paul's resurrection outlook, especially because of the widespread prejudice against visions in the modern era. On both popular and scientific levels there is a tendency to assume that nothing positive and creative can result from such. But their importance for the Hebrews is captured by their proverb, "Where there is no vision, the people perish."[29] Moses was only the first of Israelites prophets who had encounters with a glorious transcendent reality. While Isaiah was worshiping at the Jerusalem temple he "saw the Lord," even though a physical being was not literally involved.[30] The

---

[24]Luke 1:11; 24:23.
[25]Acts 16:9.
[26]Exodus 3:2.
[27]Exodus 24:9-10.
[28]Deuteronomy 4:1-12.
[29]Proverbs 29:18.
[30]Isaiah 6.

prophets recognized that the Lord was Spirit and not mortal flesh.[31] As
Isaiah grieved over his heroic national king who had recently died as a defiled leper, the image of a holy international King arose. He saw on a
heavenly throne a King who was exalted, yet so intimate that the train of his
robe filled the earthly temple. Isaiah's vision of a thrice-holy God enabled
him to see, by contrast, his personal unholiness as well as his nation's sin.
The young man was imaginatively cleansed when a glowing ember from the
altar of burnt offering touched his lips. He then launched on a thankless
lifetime campaign for justice and peace. Several of the prophet's senses
were involved metaphorically in that supraempirical mystical experience.
Had audiovisual electronic equipment been invented and present in that
temple in 640 BCE, its tape could not have captured a picture of God's
throne nor have recorded the Lord's voice. Moreover, a seismograph could
not have picked up the vibrations of the quaking temple.

Rudolf Otto, in his classic *Idea of the Holy*, tried to convince his readers
that they should reject the "naive supernaturalist" interpretation of mystical
experiences. To that end, he compared the inaugural visions of Isaiah and
Paul:

> Has God a body? Is He really seated upon a throne, or has He any place in a
> physical sense? Do beings such as the Cherubim and Seraphim . . . surround
> Him in visible form? Has He a voice audible to our actual sense of hearing? . . .
> And if we pass on to the Resurrection experience of Paul on the road to
> Damascus, do we not at once recognize the same characteristic features? Have
> we here sense perception or spiritual experience? Paul nowhere describes how
> and in what form he beheld the Risen Christ. . . . The vision would have a
> vesture of outward form just as that of Isaiah did, but this does not, for Paul
> any more than for Isaiah, touch the inmost import of the experience, which is
> here: "He lives; He lives as the accepted of God, the preserved of God, the
> exalted of God, the transfigured of God, as the conqueror of Judgement, of the
> Cross, and of Death."[32]

At the beginning of the prophecy of Ezekiel, a similar theophany is
described:

> The heavens were opened, and I saw visions of God. . . . As I looked, a stormy
> wind came out of the north: a vast cloud with flashes of fire and brilliant light
> around it; and within was something like gleaming brass. . . . Seated above the

---

[31]Hosea 11:9.
[32]Rudolf Otto, *The Idea of the Holy* (New York: Oxford, 1926) 228-29.

likeness of a throne was something that seemed like a human figure. . . . This was the appearance of the likeness of the glory of the Lord.[33]

The setting for Ezekiel's vision was the roaring wind and flashing lightning of a thunderstorm. Afterward the prophet became a minister to the Jewish exiles in Babylon. The reality of such sightings can be tested by the abiding influence they have over the mind and conduct of those receiving such revelations.

There are numerous other biblical accounts of visionary experiences. For example, Daniel envisioned a royal figure, the "Ancient of Days": "His robe was white as snow and his hair was like pure wool. His throne was fiery flames."[34] That visual metaphor has much in common with the christophany experienced by John of Patmos: "His hair was as white as snow-white wool, his eyes were like a flame of fire. . . . His face was like the sun shining in all its brilliance. . . . [The Son of Man] said, 'I was dead, but look, I am alive forever and ever!' "[35] Also, a theophany is described at the baptism of Jesus: "As he was coming up out of the water, he saw the sky open and the Spirit descend on him like a dove. And a voice came from heaven, 'You are my beloved son and I am well pleased with you.' "[36] Jesus subsequently had another heavenly vision, "I saw Satan fall like lightning."[37]

"Apparition" (from Latin *apparere*, "to appear") is a term that has a similar connotation to "vision" and it can involve the auditory as well as the ocular senses. The term is not frequently used in discussing initiating religious experience of pivotal personalities in the Bible, perhaps because it has been sullied by its frequent use in discussing mediums' alleged spirits. The Bible describes one contrived apparition, the performance of the witch of Endor with an Israelite king. The story tells about Saul consulting her in a time of desperation and how she skillfully hoodwicked her client into seeing the ghost of deceased Samuel; she practiced ventriloquism to communicate a forecast of doom from the prophet.[38]

---

[33]Ezekiel 1:1, 4, 26, 29.
[34]Daniel 7:9.
[35]Revelation 1:14, 16, 18.
[36]Mark 1:10-11.
[37]Luke 10:18.
[38]1 Samuel 28:7-19.

The study of visions has been hampered by the pervasive presumption of perennial empiricists that for something to be real it must have visual and auditory components that are literal and objective. In contrast to Paul's account of his Damascus road conversion in the Acts of the Apostles, he did not write about an exchange of words that he had with the resurrected Jesus.[39] Nor did he tell of a miraculous loss of sight and its later restoration when a scale-like substance fell from his eyes.[40] However, he did not regard his encounter with Christ as a fantasy that he had projected. On the contrary, Paul treated his initiating tombless vision as the most real and motivating event of his life. He testified that he was willing to put his life at risk every day, and that he was sustained by his resurrection belief when he fought with wild animals at Ephesus. Were that assurance lacking, the apostle argued, we might as well live by the adage, "Let us eat and drink, for tomorrow we die."[41]

Athenian philosopher Plato, one of the wisest of humans, is helpful in explaining the complexity of religious experience in general, and the type Paul had in particular. He told a profound story to convey his belief that most people tend to be metaphysical materialists. His allegory of the cave shows the plight of the masses for whom reality is what their senses report.[42] The cave prisoners represent percipients who find no validity in statements that cannot be confirmed by stimuli from an external source. They want to kill a Socrates-type individual who insists on leading them to a conceptual realm containing absolute beauty and universal justice. "The psychic eye," suggested the ancient philosopher, is better for seeing the divine than ten thousand visual perceptions, "for by it alone is truth beheld."[43]

Justin, who was a teacher of Platonism before becoming a Christian in the second century, declared that "the vision of God . . . can be grasped only by the mind, as Plato says."[44] Materialists who limit truth is to what can be empirically seen, dismiss this as literal nonsense. For example, Marxist cosmonaut Gherman Titov expressed his inability to comprehend the

---

[39]Acts 26:14-18.
[40]Acts 9:8-18.
[41]1 Corinthians 15:30-32.
[42]Plato, *Republic* 514-18.
[43]Plato, *Republic* 527e, 533d.
[44]Justin, *Dialogue with Trypho* 3.

metaphorical use of "seeing" when he claimed in 1961 that he had not seen God, or even an angel, during his 17 orbits of the earth.

What Paul saw came from behind, not in front of, his eyeballs. If his optic nerve was triggered, it was from what was psychological, not from what was physiological. God is not a thing but a subject, so revelation happens within the minds of personal subjects and hence are necessarily subjective. Paradoxically, faith involves seeing and not seeing. Faith is defined in the New Testament as "a conviction of things not seen."[45] Faith for Paul was based on what was unseen physically and externally but was an indisputable reality spiritually and internally.

The eminent English philosopher John Stuart Mill, in an essay rejecting all supernaturalism, singles out Paul as the only witness in the early years of Christianity who was "competent by character or education to scrutinize the real nature of the appearances which they may have seen." Paul attests to only one miracle, according to Mill, his seeing Jesus at the time of his conversion. "Of all the miracles in the New Testament," that vision, in Mill's opinion "is the one which admits of the easiest explanation from natural causes."[46]

Michael Perry provides an explanation that is both psychological and theological:

> In Paul's case, we can see God working through the operations of the human mind. When Paul had reached the stage at which he was prepared to be intellectually convinced that the Christians were right, God saw to it that the matter was clinched for him and made such that he could not go back upon his new insight. The vision transferred his assent from being merely intellectual to being volitional and effective. His experience coloured the whole of the rest of his theology. He had seen the Risen Christ in inexpressible glory and so he could not do otherwise than write of the Resurrection Body as spiritual, incorruptible, and unimaginably different from the earthly one.[47]

Paul testified to a transcendent dimension of life that cannot be grasped by our commonplace three-dimensional perception. Employing the same verb that he used to tell of various people seeing the risen Jesus, the apostle asserted, "Have I not seen Jesus our Lord?"[48] Paul was referring more to

---

[45]Hebrews 11:1.
[46]John Stuart Mill, *Three Essays on Religion* (New York: Holt, 1874) 239.
[47]Michael Perry, *The Easter Enigma* (London: Faber, 1959) 236.
[48]1 Corinthians 9:1.

insight and conception than to eyesight and perception. To correct the literalist, who confuses metaphor with metaphysics, the Johannine writings make this absolute declaration, "No one has ever seen God."[49] But those writings illustrate the contrasting uses of the verb "see" by also stating: "Whoever has seen me [Jesus] has seen the Father," and "We will see him as he is."[50]

An invaluable help for analyzing the various secondary accounts of Jesus' resurrection in the New Testament is provided by Paul's insistence that Jesus "was seen" by others in a way similar to his own inaugural revelation. The best avenue for understanding the Easter experiences of the earliest Christians is to presume they were like Paul's experience. Since he put his transcendental encounter with Jesus in tandem with that of the previous witnesses, a historical examination of Jesus' resurrection must start with Paul's letters. His firsthand testimony about his initiating Christian experience is free of the legendary material that accumulates in oral transmission. By relying on information written down by the person experiencing what is being described, a basis can be established for judging the historicity of secondhand resurrection accounts about the apostles recorded decades later.

In one of the earlier studies of Paul's christophany, Theodor Keim wrote more than a century ago:

> Paul, in mentioning the resurrection sightings of Jesus, has determinedly excluded the speaking of Jesus, the sitting and walking together, the eating and handling, every gross representation of a restoration of the previous corporeity of Jesus. . . . He conceived the coming of Jesus to them [the apostles] as exactly similar to Jesus' appearance to him, namely as a dazzling disclosure of the Lord who . . . since his resurrection had been exalted to heaven, and momentarily revealed himself from heaven to his followers in the glorified body of the Son of God.[51]

Norman Perrin, although an authority on the Synoptic (first three) Gospels, recognizes that one must go to the letters of Paul for clarity on Jesus' resurrection. Perrin provides this important perspective:

---

[49]John 1:18; 1 John 4:12.
[50]John 14:9; 1 John 3:2.
[51]Theodor Keim, *The History of Jesus of Nazareth* (London: Williams, 1883) 6:290.

The Christian who asks the modern question, what actually happened on that first Easter morning? must come to terms with the apostle Paul. . . . Our assumption has to be that if we could interrogate the other witnesses their claims would be similar to his. In some way they were granted a vision of Jesus which convinced them that God had vindicated Jesus out of his death, and that therefore the death of Jesus was by no means the end of the impact of Jesus upon their lives and upon the world in which they lived.[52]

To understand adequately what Paul meant when he declared that he saw Jesus, it is necessary to draw on disclosures he provides of his religious state before and after that christophany. He was a militant theologian of the pharisaic sect that, as Josephus pointed out, "prided itself on its adherence to ancestral custom and to the laws approved by God."[53] Accordingly, the apostle acknowledged that he had been "faultlessly righteous" in abiding by the law of Moses.[54] What did Paul know of Jesus before his conversion? At minimum he was aware that Jesus was crucified while leading a Jewish band who viewed him as the fulfillment of Scripture's promise of a messianic ruler. In that pre-Christian period, Paul thought it blasphemy to associate God's specially anointed one—called *christos* in Greek—with anyone who had been crucified. That general type of execution was prohibited by the Torah, for, as he pointed out, it declares, "Cursed be everyone who hangs on a tree."[55] That text gave the young zealot sufficient justification for launching a campaign to exterminate Christians.[56]

While he was trying to destroy the church in the Damascus area, Paul had a religious experience similar to that of a Jewish prophet. Jeremiah's initial vision contained this word from the Lord, "Before you were born I selected you to be a prophet to the nations."[57] Paul likewise affirmed, "He who selected me before I was born, and called me through his grace, chose to reveal his Son in me in order that I might proclaim him to the nations."[58] English translations of that sentence have sometimes attempted to objectify

---

[52]Norman Perrin, *The Resurrection according to Matthew, Mark, and Luke* (Philadelphia: Fortress, 1977) 82-83.

[53]Josephus, *Antiquities* 17.41.

[54]Philippians 3:6.

[55]Deuteronomy 21:23; Galatians 3:13.

[56]Galatians 1:13.

[57]Jeremiah 1:5.

[58]Galatians 1:15-16.

Paul's experience by misrepresenting him as asserting that Jesus was revealed *to* him.[59] "By distorting the meaning of a single preposition, traditional Christianity has falsified its premier apostle's own visionary experience," charges Bruce Chilton.[60] Further on in that Galatian letter, Paul clarified that this revelation was not an external phenomenon. Using the same Greek preposition, *en*, basically meaning *within*, he stated this paradox: "I have been crucified with Christ. I no longer live, but Christ lives *en* me."[61] Paul testified that he had "died" to the demands of the Jewish law so that he might "live" for God. He experienced a symbolic reenactment of Jesus' death and resurrection in that mystical union.

In an existential manner, Paul participated *in* Jesus' death and resurrection and was not a spectator *to* it. He viewed himself more as one who lives *in* Christ than as one who lives *after* him. Jesus was a present reality to Paul, and by means of an ego-reorientation he internalized the central values of his "Lord." Robert Grant comments on Paul's encounter with the risen Jesus, "We may well conclude that his experience was primarily subjective; in Acts 26:19 it is called a 'heavenly vision.' "[62] According to Acts, Paul also testifies that he saw Jesus and heard him speak when he fell into a trance while praying in the Jerusalem temple.[63] Presumably what Paul saw was the "man of heaven" to which the historical Jesus had been transformed.[64]

From his perspective as a seasoned Christian, Paul looked back to his previous confidence in a life of legal rectitude and evaluated it as garbage— or something stronger! In his attempt to have the "same mind" as Christ, who "emptied himself" of high status to become a humble servant, Paul relinquished his position in as a blameless Pharisee.[65] He found one type of life by losing another type, and he wrote of "sharing Christ's suffering" and

---

[59]Compare the mistranslation of Galatians 1:16 in the NRSV, NCV (NAB), and TEV ("*to* me") with that of the KJV, NIV, NJB, NASB, and REB ("*in* me").

[60]Bruce Chilton, *Rabbi Jesus* (New York: Doubleday, 2000) 285.

[61]Galatians 2:19-20.

[62]Robert Grant, *A Historical Introduction to the New Testament* (New York: Simon and Schuster, 1972) 372.

[63]Acts 22:17-18.

[64]1 Corinthians 15:49.

[65]Philippians 2:5-8, 3:4-6.

of concomitantly experiencing "the power of his resurrection."[66] That mystical bond became a pearl of superlative value, and he had no regret in exchanging for it his prestigious standing in Judaism.

Gerd Ludemann, director of the Institute of Early Christian Studies at the University of Göttingen, comments on Paul's reference to more than five hundred people at once seeing Jesus. Ludemann plausibly suggests that he could be referring to the collective envisioning of the Holy Spirit descent that happened, according to Luke, in Jerusalem some weeks after Jesus' death.[67] The figure given by Paul was a general way of denoting a large number, such as were present at the first Christian Pentecost. Ludemann cites an example of the way in which an image can stimulate the imagination of a group: "Before St. George appeared to all the crusaders on the walls of Jerusalem he was first certainly perceived by only some of them. Through influence and transference the miracle thus proclaimed was immediately accepted by all." On that earlier day in Jerusalem, the catalyst for the ecstatic pentecostal experience may have been Peter's testimony of his encounter with the risen Jesus.[68]

In the chapter informing Corinthians that the resurrected Jesus was seen by hundreds of people, Paul related the resurrection experience to the "life-giving Spirit."[69] Elsewhere the apostle provided a fuller statement of the relationship between Jesus' resurrection and the Spirit, "God who raised Christ Jesus from the dead will also give new life to your mortal bodies through his indwelling Spirit."[70] John's Gospel also suggests a tie between experiencing the risen Jesus and the Pentecost experience, "He breathed on them [the disciples], saying, 'Receive the Holy Spirit!' "[71]

Paul invited others to join him in imitating Christ's pattern of life.[72] Speaking for Christians generally, he claimed that "our old self has been crucified with Christ." As a consequence, "If we have been unified with him

---

[66]Philippians 3:8-10.

[67]Acts 2:1-4.

[68]Gerd Ludemann, *What Really Happened to Jesus* (Louisville: Westminster/ John Knox, 1995) 99-100.

[69]1 Corinthians 15:6, 45.

[70]Romans 8:11.

[71]John 20:22.

[72]1 Corinthians 11:1.

in his death, we will also be united with him in his resurrection."[73] Charles Wesley's Easter hymn expresses well this theme: "Made like him like him we rise,/ Ours the cross, the grave, the skies."[74] The focal point of Pauline Christianity is a corporate fellowship of those who have become "a new creation"[75] through being intensely identified with the tragedy and triumph of Jesus. A new ethic accompanies this re-creation: "If you have been raised with Christ, seek . . . compassion, kindness, humility, gentleness, patience. . . . Forgive one another. . . . Above all, clothe yourselves with love."[76] For Paul, resurrection is a symbol for a new ethical dimension of life in the here and now. He not only says, "All will be made alive in Christ," but he writes of Christians being resurrected to "walk in newness of life" when they are baptized.[77] Relevant here is the way Homer Dubs, Oxford professor of Chinese, concludes his discussion of miracles in world history: "Christianity depends, not upon an empty tomb, but upon the great truth that underlies even that belief, namely the ever-living Christ, whose transforming influence was felt by St Paul and by millions of others in subsequent centuries. This is no new insight. Luther put the miracle of grace in the heart far above any physical miracle."[78]

* * *

Paul provides another fruitful approach for understanding the nature of the postmortem Christ. Having established to his satisfaction the certainty of Jesus' resurrection, he tackled these difficult questions: "How are the dead raised? With what kind of body do they come?"[79] The apostle encouraged readers of his letters to think realistically about their own life after death and to recognize parallels between their humanity and that of Jesus. He was convinced that resurrection was the same in nature for humans generally and for Christ in particular: "If the dead are not raised, it follows that Christ has not been raised. . . . But Christ has been raised. . . . Just as we were made like the one who was made of dust, so we will bear

---

[73]Romans 6:5-6.
[74]Charles Wesley, "Christ the Lord Is Risen," 5.
[75]2 Corinthians 5:17.
[76]Colossians 3:1, 12-14.
[77]Romans 6:4; 1 Corinthians 15:22.
[78]*The Hibbert Journal* (January 1950) 162.
[79]1 Corinthians 15:35.

the heavenly pattern."[80] Paul believed that Jesus' resurrection confirmed but did not initiate the immortal life, which had been experienced by humans throughout history. That view is simply suggested in a verse pertaining to an antediluvian who allegedly lived for 365 years, "Enoch walked with God, and then he was seen no more because God had taken him away."[81] Since the Genesis chapter omits reference to his death, which is stated of all his ancestors and descendants, the ancient Jews presumed that he is still living with God.

The biological fact that the fleshly organism of humans, like that of all other organisms, decays irretrievably after death was accepted by Paul. He stated that the stomach will be destroyed by death;[82] by extrapolation, all organs of the body will disintegrate. "With the resurrection of the dead," he plainly wrote, "what is sown is perishable; what is raised is imperishable. . . . Our flesh and blood bodies will decay and cannot share in God's kingdom."[83] Paul frankly declared that it is not the case that the buried corpse will be raised. He could not have rejected more clearly the folk belief that "dem bones gonna rise ag'in." Joseph Ratzinger stated, before he became Pope Benedict XVI, "Paul teaches not the resurrection of physical bodies but the resurrection of persons, and this not in the return of the 'fleshly body,' that is, the biological structure, an idea which he expressly describes as impossible."[84]

Paul wrote that mortals can be "raised a spiritual body,"[85] but he was not referring to the physical skeleton and any flesh clinging to it. He did not believe that tomb dust or urn ash would in some miraculous way become the substance of a new material organism. Rather, "spirit" (Greek, *pneuma*), which is God's gift and is not part of the natural composition of the human person, transforms the mortal body (Greek *soma*) into an immortal form. "Spiritual body" means, in modern terminology, the self or the character. Willi Marxsen, a renowned New Testament scholar who has examined

---

[80] 1 Corinthians 15:16, 20, 49.

[81] Genesis 5:24.

[82] 1 Corinthians 6:13.

[83] 1 Corinthians 15:42, 50.

[84] Joseph Ratzinger, *Introduction to Christianity* (San Francisco: Ignatius, 1990) 277.

[85] 1 Corinthians 15:44.

thoroughly what the early Christians meant by resurrection, provides this clarification:

> When we use the word body, we generally understand by it the flesh which decays in the earth. But Paul uses *soma* to mean identity of the personality before and after death. . . . When Paul speaks of the earthly body (it would be better to translate it as the earthly "I"), this earthly "I" can be seen and touched and can eat and drink; it is "flesh and blood." The risen "I" (that is, the spiritual body) exists in a form which is completely separated from this mode of existence.[86]

In a similar manner, John Hick, an authority on eschatology in world religions, comments on the glorified body promised by Paul for those loved by God:

> What has become a widely accepted view in modern times holds that the resurrection body is a new and different body given by God, but expressing the personality within its new environment as the physical body expressed it in the earthly environment. The physical frame decays or is burned, disintegrating and being dispersed into the ground or the air, but God re-embodies the personality elsewhere. . . . A human being is by nature mortal and subject to annihilation at death. But in fact God, by an act of sovereign power, either sometimes or always resurrects or reconstitutes or recreates him—not however as the identical physical organism that he was before death, but as a *soma pneumatikon* embodying the dispositional characteristics and memory traces of the deceased physical organism.[87]

Paul compared the process of a mortal putting on immortality with the growth process of seed.[88] When seed is sown it mingles with the soil in which it lies and will never again be seen in the same form. If the seed is any good it will germinate and the outer husk becomes fertilizer while the inner core or nucleus becomes more alive than ever. Black seed sprouts forth as green plants that are more valuable than what was sown. The seed analogy portrays both transformation and continuity of Christians in the life after death. The corpse is the outer husk that disintegrates in the soil. But the essential kernel, the true self, lives on in a lovelier way.

---

[86]Willi Marxsen, *The Resurrection of Jesus of Nazareth* (Philadelphia: Fortress, 1970) 69.

[87]John Hick, *Death and Eternal Life* (Louisville: Westminster/ John Knox, 1994) 186, 279.

[88]1 Corinthians 15:36-38.

The apostle also thought of Christians' resurrected bodies as having been refashioned like distinct stars. He did not hold the pantheistic view that individuals are absorbed into the infinite Spirit of God after death like drops in an ocean. Rather, he believed that those attaining life after death will retain their psychic histories and continue to be their distinctive selves. Paul drew from the observable heavens an illustration of the continuity of personality. He wrote that as "celestial bodies differ in splendor, so is it with the resurrection of the dead."[89] However, the analogy falls short in that stars are radiating physical bodies whereas Paul claimed there is nothing physical in the spiritual body.

Paul posited that the nonphysical mode of Jesus' life after death is a paradigm for all Christians who have died, "Christ will change our lowly bodies so that they will be like his glorious body."[90] He is the prototype "first fruit" of what can be expected by all who are bound with him.[91] Here and elsewhere the apostle thought of first fruit as representative of the harvest, so the characteristics of one are consistent for all.[92] If resurrected Christians cannot rise up with flesh and bones and leave an empty grave behind, neither was that the case for first fruit Jesus. There is no evidence that Paul thought of the individual sample or the full crop of resurrected Christians as returning to the conditions of earthly life even in a modified body. He wrote that those who have received this first taste of the future harvest await expectantly for liberation from mortality.[93]

Rudolf Bultmann, an outstanding New Testament interpreter in the past century, commented about the tomb of Jesus and the interments of all other creatures, "A corpse cannot become alive again and climb out of the grave."[94] Another noted German, Wolfhart Pannenberg, writes: "For Paul, resurrection means the new life of a new body, not the return of life into a dead but not yet decayed fleshly body. . . . Paul must have had the same conception of the resurrected Jesus, for he always and fully thought of Jesus' resurrection and that of Christians in essential parallel."[95] Subse

---

[89]1 Corinthians 15:41-42.
[90]Philippians 3:21.
[91]1 Corinthians 15:20.
[92]Romans 11:16.
[93]Romans 8:23.
[94]*Christianity and Crisis* (14 November 1966): 255.
[95]Wolfhart Pannenberg, *Jesus, God and Man* (Philadelphia: Westminster, 1968)

quent Christians, in a misguided compulsion to worship a supernatural Jesus unlike others in human substance, have overlooked Paul's claim that Jesus' mode of resurrection is not unique but reveals the pattern for all who are united with him.

For Paul, according to E. P. Sanders, "resurrection means transformed body, not walking corpse or disembodied spirit."[96] Or, as theologian Hans Küng puts it, the resurrected person is not a diminished but a finished being; consequently, "death is not destruction but metamorphosis."[97] That personal transformation to the immortal body was for Paul separable from physique reconstruction. He thought that the living body should be venerated as "a temple of the Holy Spirit,"[98] but he did not find dead flesh of sacred value. Like the assemblage of materials used in a temple's construction, the building might as well be leveled, after reusable parts are salvaged, if there is no more divine worship or other vital activity going on within. Paul believed that all who are resurrected, whether Jesus or other humans, change from physical stuff to incorruptible, immortal beings.

The nonperishable spirit-body that Paul has in mind might be compared to a continuous legislative body. A portion of the physical elements of the United States Senate are subject to change, at least every two years, and every element eventually expires. Yet personal characteristics of the body politic have been transmitted ever since its inception in the eighteenth century. Accordingly, current senators frequently appeal to their Founding Fathers and the traditions built up over the centuries that give a distinctive and defining quality to the living body.

Illustrating the exchange of the old flesh-being for the new spirit-being, Paul writes, "We know that if the earthly tent we live in is destroyed, we have a building from God, a house not made with hands, eternal in the heavens." He will not become a "naked" disembodied soul there.[99] Since the Host of that heavenly home is nonphysical, it is fitting that God's companions should likewise be spiritual beings. At times of unusual personal suffering, the apostle let his preferred abode be known. He stated, "We would rather be away from the [physical] body and at home with the

---

75-76.

[96]E. P. Sanders, *Paul* (New York: Oxford, 1991) 30.

[97]Hans Küng, *On Being a Christian* (Garden City NY: Doubleday, 1976) 351.

[98]1 Corinthians 6:19.

[99]2 Corinthians 5:1-3.

Lord."[100] Elsewhere he expressed his dilemma, "My desire is to depart and be with Christ, for that is much better, but you need me here in the flesh."[101] He apparently expected to become more closely united "with Christ" immediately at death, without an interim purgatory.

For Paul, resurrection was a process already underway in Christians. He wrote that "we were in the flesh" but we serve now "in newness of spirit."[102] Again: "All of us . . . are being transformed into the Lord's likeness with an ever-increasing glory. . . . Though our outer bodies are perishing, our inner spirits are being renewed day by day."[103] During their mortal life, Christians experience the Spirit as a "down payment" on the deathless life to come.[104] The sentiments expressed here are similar to those found in Plato's most influential philosophical essay on immortality ever written. Old Socrates, his spokesperson, observes that though his body is decaying, his *psyche* is growing wiser and thereby is preparing for the deathless mental life of the soul.[105]

Some early Christians comprehended Paul's view that Jesus' resurrection provides a present experience as well as a future expectation. The *Gospel of Philip* quotes what Paul wrote about flesh and blood not inheriting God's kingdom to show that Jesus' resurrection provides a pattern for the spiritual transformation that every Christian should experience at his or her baptism. It states: "While we are in this world it is fitting for us to acquire the resurrection for ourselves. . . . Those who say they will die first and then rise are in error. If they do not first receive the resurrection while they live, when they die they will receive nothing."[106]

* * *

According to Paul, immortality is a quality that *some* "put on" at death.[107] He did not share the characteristic Greek belief that the soul (*psyche*) is naturally immortal. Humans are, however, immort*able*; each has

---

[100]2 Corinthians 5:8.
[101]Philippians 1:23-24.
[102]Romans 7:5-6.
[103]2 Corinthians 3:18; 4:16.
[104]2 Corinthians 5:5.
[105]Plato, *Phaedo* 64-68.
[106]*Gospel of Philip* 56, 66, 73.
[107]1 Corinthians 15:54.

a deathless potentiality that becomes actual by responding to God's gift. The apostle expressed his doctrine of conditional immortality in this way, "To those who keep on doing good and aim at glory, honor, and immortality, God will give eternal life."[108] The eternal or timeless life is therefore not an inherent right but a privilege extended to all whom God finds acceptable. Paul lamented that the unspiritual person rejects what is beyond sight and sound, missing "what God has prepared for those who love him."[109]

Paul balanced his positive hope with a negative forecast, "The wages of sin is death, but the gift of God is eternal life through union with Christ Jesus our Lord."[110] The apostle never wrote that God resurrects the wicked and punishes them in some infernal and eternal hell.[111] Rather, "Their end is destruction, for their god is their appetites; they take pride in what they should be ashamed of, and their minds are absorbed in earthly things."[112] He believed that each person has the option of passing out of existence or of "passing on" to some glorious state. The result of not being united with God is self-destruction, not an everlasting life in a place of horrible physical and mental suffering. Those who do not concern themselves with becoming infused with the immortal Spirit of God, and with accepting the incumbent responsibilities, have nothing within them that can survive biological death. Eschatology authority Robert Charles wrote: "There could be no resurrection of the wicked according to St. Paul. . . . To share in the resurrection . . . is the privilege only of those who are spiritually one with Christ and quickened by the Holy Spirit."[113] Charles acknowledged that a different view is advanced in other parts of the New Testament. For example, the Gospel of John represents Jesus as prophesying: "The time is coming when all who are in their graves will hear the Son of Man's voice and come forth. Those who have done good will rise to live, but those who have done evil will rise to be condemned."[114]

---

[108]Romans 2:7.

[109]1 Corinthians 2:9, 14.

[110]Romans 6:23.

[111]By contrast, Acts 24:15 expresses Luke's theology in a speech he composed for Paul, "There will be a resurrection of both the righteous and the unrighteous."

[112]Philippians 3:19.

[113]Robert Charles, *Hebrew, Jewish, and Christian Eschatology* (London: Black, 1913) 444.

[114]John 5:28-29.

* * *

In no way did Paul think that he had unraveled all the mysteries of death or that he fully understood the nature of the life beyond physical existence. He was convinced that Christians will be with Christ but he lacked knowledge that might satisfy all curiosity about that life. He hoped that Christians, in contrast to Moses, would ultimately have the veil removed that conceals the glory of God.[115] The apostle admits that we now know only partially, seeing only "blurred reflections" of the whole truth of God. He fancied that on the other side of death "we shall understand God as completely as he understands us," enabling us to replace our glimpses of the truth with a complete vision. However, we live at present by "faith, hope, and love"—not by absolute certainty.[116]

There is a grandeur in this dematerialized resurrection way of life that is not dependent on the anticipation of a physical resurrection. Thomas Best comments on the absence of the supernatural in Paul's treatment of the resurrection: "In contrast to the modern tendency to think of the resurrection as the 'biggest' miracle, Paul does not understand it in the conventional category as 'miraculous.' That is, it is not for him a unique event creating a radical disjunction in history and violating the laws of nature."[117]

Paul's lengthy treatment of the resurrection in 1 Corinthians 15 has a significant ending. In effect he urges his readers to turn their primary attention away from their hope for a future resurrection and from the past resurrection of Jesus. They should not seek Jesus behind them in history or above them in heaven. They are encouraged to devote themselves to the Lord's service in the present, with firm assurance that "love's labor" cannot be lost. Thus, Jesus' resurrection is verified and death's sting is removed when Christians shoulder fully their responsibilities toward life, freely and openly sharing in its joys and sorrows.

Of Peter

An understanding of Paul's resurrection views provides a key for interpreting other New Testament references to the risen Jesus. The first letter of Peter supports Paul's outlook on the resurrection. The consensus of

---

[115]Exodus 34:29-33; 2 Corinthians 3:12-18.
[116]1 Corinthians 13:12-13.
[117]Thomas Best, "St. Paul and the Decline of the Miraculous," *Encounter* (Summer 1983): 236.

scholarship throughout church history has held that the epistle contains ideas of the apostle Peter, and now it is recognized that it was probably written by a disciple of Peter after his death in the latter part of the first century.[118] The letter begins with affirming what had been crucial for Peter and others in the church, "We have been born anew to a living hope through the resurrection of Jesus Christ from the dead."[119] Brief though the letter is, it contains telling verses confirming the earliest apostolic testimony of a nonphysical resurrection for both Jesus and his followers. After acknowledging that Jesus' role was that of the innocent sufferer described in Isaiah 53, Peter provides this contrast, "He was put to death in the flesh, but made alive in the spirit."[120] Regarding other resurrected humans, Peter states that "they live in the spirit as God lives."[121] Thus, according to one of the first persons to experience Jesus' resurrection, Christians can confidently look forward to sharing more fully the immortal life of God after their fleshly death. Peter, who contrasts corruptible earthly life with the "incorruptible inheritance in heaven,"[122] is completely in accord with Paul's judgment that "this perishable body must put on imperishability and this mortal body must put on immortality."[123]

The Gospels tell of some sightings of the risen Jesus that may have been in the earliest tradition and were later given externalization in legends. Pertaining to them, Luke and Paul agree that Simon Peter was the one to whom Christ first appeared. "The Lord has really been raised," Luke has some Christians exclaim, "and was seen (*ophthe*) by Simon!"[124] Surprisingly, there is no narrative associated with this first appearance that, according to Luke, happened in the area of Jerusalem. But Mark, followed by Matthew, claims that it will occur after Peter and the other disciples return to Galilee, in accord with Jesus' prediction.[125] John also assumes that Peter returned to Galilee, a three-day journey, for he has Jesus say to his disciples at the last supper in Jerusalem, "The hour is coming, indeed it has

---

[118]John Elliott, *1 Peter* (New York: Doubleday, 2000) 130, 138.

[119]1 Peter 1:3.

[120]1 Peter 3:18.

[121]1 Peter 4:6.

[122]1 Peter 1:4, 23.

[123]1 Corinthians 15:53.

[124]Luke 24:34.

[125]Mark 14:28; 16:7; Matthew 28:10.

come, when you will be scattered, each to his home, leaving me alone."[126]
Peter's home was in Capernaum, alongside the Galilean lake. Yet John
inconsistently has Jesus' disciples first seeing the risen Jesus in Jerusalem
three days after that supper.[127]

Sorbonne professor Charles Guignebert plausibly describes the anxious
expectation that set the stage for visionary experiences in the home area of
Jesus' closest companions:

> The disciples returned to Galilee perplexed, troubled, and afraid; discouraged,
> too, because none of their hopes had been realized and they had sustained a
> crushing blow; but *they did not despair*. They were too deeply attached to the
> person of Jesus and remained too confident in his promises to lose hope
> completely. . . . The promised future which had attracted and bound them to
> Jesus was bound up with his person: to admit that he had disappeared forever
> was to abandon all hope. Their faith was centered in, and, we might say,
> hypnotized by this idea: it is not possible that he should have deceived us, that
> he should have forsaken us, or that he should be irrevocably dead. . . . The
> disciples do not actually conclude from this conviction and the visions which
> authenticate it, that Jesus has come forth from the tomb in flesh and blood, but
> that he has been *glorified*, that all that is still living of him has been transported
> into the *glory* of God.[128]

Peter's encounters with Jesus need to be interpreted in the context of his
traditional understandings. Due to cultural conditioning, he had associated
success, not rejection, with God's messiah.[129] He had a mental block against
accepting Jesus' teaching that he would be killed as a common criminal.
Just prior to Jesus' crucifixion, frightened Peter repeatedly denied having
any connection with an apparently weak person, but then he wept bitterly
over that denial.[130] While Jesus' male disciples despaired over their dashed
hopes that Jesus would inaugurate the promised theocracy, they fled from
Jerusalem on the day of his execution.[131]

The crucifixion was for Peter a kind of shock treatment. Typical of
those suffering from acute grief, he repeatedly found himself recalling

[126]John 16:32.
[127]John 20:19-20.
[128]Charles Guignebert, *Jesus* (London: Trench, 1935) 527.
[129]Mark 8:27-32.
[130]Mark 14:66-72.
[131]Mark 14:50.

pleasant and painful times with the deceased. He probably had a typical fantasy of bereavement grief, imagining what he could have done that might have averted the death of his companion. Peter was no doubt racked with guilt as he reflected on his cowardice, and he probably longed for Jesus to be alive so he could plea to be forgiven for his betrayal.

While bewildered, Peter turned memories of Jesus' teachings over in his mind, and thought about some fresh scriptural interpretations Jesus had given. The apostle attempted to reconcile them with the well-known messianic prophecies of a militant king who would be like David. In searching the Scripture, followers of Jesus found in Psalm 22 and in the suffering servant passages of Isaiah intimations of a man approved by God who had suffered and died but was then vindicated. After mulling over the matter for some days and talking with fellow dispirited disciples, Peter suddenly intuited that defeat is a part of the messiah's mission and that Jesus fulfilled some Jewish expectations. It dawned upon him that Jesus dramatically expressed God's holy love during his last days in Jerusalem and that his teacher's transforming spirit was still with him and his fellows.

The final chapter of John deals imaginatively with Peter finding forgiveness and reconciliation. That appendix by a redactor places him back in Galilee working again at his old trade, along with six other apostles. The routine was to go out before dawn, which was the best time to fish, and bring in a catch to sell at the market. The crew would take from their nets several fish to broil and eat for breakfast, along with the supplies they had brought along. Whenever Peter and his companions shared a meal, their memories of the final meal with Jesus became vivid. They poignantly recalled his words as he passed around the bread and wine. On these occasions they wrestled with their unresolved conflicts on the proper role for a messiah. At one of these gatherings, their vivid memory image gave rise to a vision of Jesus as the host of their common meal. "He showed himself again to the disciples by the sea."[132]

Here is the Johannine story:

Just after daybreak, Jesus stood on the shore, but the disciples did not recognize him. He shouted, "Boys, have you caught anything?" "No," they

---

[132]John 21:1. Incidentally, John 6:19 states that the disciples saw Jesus walking "*epi* the sea"—the same phrase that is translated "by the sea" in 21:1—but translators prone toward supernaturalism have rendered it "on."

answered. He said, "Cast your net to the right side of the boat and you will find some." They did so, and they caught so many fish that they could not haul the net on board. Then the disciple whom Jesus loved said to Peter, "It is the Lord!" When Simon Peter heard him say that, he put on some clothes, for he had stripped, and jumped into the sea. . . . When they came ashore, they saw bread and a charcoal fire with fish on it. . . . Jesus said, "Come and eat." None of the disciples dared ask, "Who are you?" They knew it was the Lord. Jesus came, took the bread and gave it to them, and did the same with the fish. . . . After breakfast, Jesus asked Simon Peter, "Simon son of John, do you love me more than these others?" "Yes, Lord," he replied, "you know that I love you." "Then feed my lambs," said Jesus.[133]

The transforming effect of Peter's lakeside religious experience cannot be attributed to seeing the once expired Jesus now breathing again. Spong gives a plausible reconstruction of the spiritual experience that lay behind the materialized story of Jesus cooking breakfast and eating fish. He finds historical significance in Peter's testimony, recorded elsewhere, that God "allowed Jesus to be seen, not by all the people but to us who were chosen by God as witnesses, who ate and drank with him after he arose from the dead."[134] Unlike a public event such as Jesus' crucifixion, which could have been observed by anybody in the Jerusalem execution area, most people were not privileged to see the risen Jesus. Spong is also aware that, for Peter, seeing Jesus did not stop at identifying him as one he had known before. Even as the great Hebrew prophets' visions resulted in vocations involving difficult service to God, Peter's vision initiated him into a pastoral mission that would consume his talent until his martyrdom. Spong writes insightfully:

Suddenly it all came together for Simon. . . . Jesus' death . . . demonstrated as nothing else could or would that it is in giving life away that we find life, . . . it is in embracing the outcast that we find ourselves embraced as outcasts. . . . Simon saw the meaning of the crucifixion that morning as he had never before seen it. . . . The clouds of his grief, confusion, and depression vanished from his mind, and in that moment he knew that Jesus was part of the very essence of God, and at that moment Simon saw Jesus alive. . . . Jesus appeared to Simon from the realm of God, . . . not bounded by time or space. . . . "Simon, if you love me you will feed my sheep." This was the meaning that Simon

---

[133]John 21:4-7, 9, 12-13, 15.
[134]Acts 10:40-41.

seemed to hear again and again as he tried to make sense out of his experience in Galilee; that is, the risen Christ will be known when his disciples can love as Jesus loved . . . the least of God's children.[135]

Luke told a remarkably similar story to the one in John's Gospel about Jesus' comaraderie with Peter while he fished on the Galilean waters. But since that Evangelist was mistakenly convinced that the apostles did not return to Galilee after Jesus' crucifixion, he appears to have transposed a resurrection episode to a setting during the earthly life of Jesus.[136] The miraculous fish catch in both stories pertains to Peter's missionary potential success in "fishing for humans." His confession, "Have nothing to do with me, Lord, sinful as I am" would have been a more appropriate response after his denial of Jesus in Jerusalem than at the time when they first became acquainted.

The fishing expedition in both John and Luke should be interpreted as symbolic fiction rather than as historical fact. A number of New Testament interpreters find that it makes more sense to treat Luke's story in that manner.[137] For example, Gerd Theissen writes: "Easter experiences have been woven into the text of the miraculous fishing trip. . . . Strictly speaking, Jesus' forgiveness of this sinful man with the words 'Fear not, from now on you will catch men!' was true only after Easter: from then on Peter engaged in independent mission."[138] The story well illustrates the way in which the Evangelists were both editors and authors. They decided which of the oral traditions should be included and how they should be reworded to conform to the aim of their Gospels. Also, they composed passages to make for continuity and to aid their intended readers in understanding situations. They modeled the call of the disciples on Elijah's call of Elisha, which caused him to forsake his regular labor to follow the prophet.[139]

Some scholars also judge the transfiguration account of Jesus in Galilee to be "a resurrection story that was retrojected back to the life of Jesus."[140]

---

[135]Spong 255-56.

[136]Luke 5:1-11.

[137]They are cited in John Meier, *A Marginal Jew* (New York: Doubleday, 1994) 2:899, 990.

[138]Gerd Theissen and Annette Merz, *The Historical Jesus* (Minneapolis: Fortress, 1996) 303.

[139]1 Kings 19:19-21.

[140]Pheme Perkins, *Resurrection* (Garden City NY: Doubleday, 1984) 95.

The Evangelists transfer to Jesus the Torah motif of Moses' shining countenance that was caused by his meeting with God on Mount Sinai.[141] A
Galilean mountain becomes the new setting for Jesus and his disciples to
gather. The Gospel of Matthew ends with a story of the risen Jesus separating from them at that place. Mountains were especially significant in the
biblical culture, for they were presumed to be closer to heaven and God.

On the mount of transfiguration, Peter experienced a luminous epiphany
when sunlight broke through the clouds and Jesus' clothing became
dazzling white. Both Moses and Elijah were seen (*ophthe*) in a "vision."[142]
In Jewish legend, those two prophets were assumed to be still alive because
their manner of departing this life differed from other persons.[143] According
to Mark, the transfiguration story did not become known until after Easter,
which helps to explain the resurrection motifs.[144] Luke can be understood
as describing in his separate volumes a radiant resurrection experience for
both Peter and Paul.[145]

Easter commemorates the revival of what was numb and dormant, but
it was something that happened to the corporate body of disciples, not
something that happened to the body of Jesus. Maurice Goguel, the leading
French authority on the Gospels a century ago, commented:

> There is more truth in the statement, "They saw Jesus because they believed
> and were convinced that he was living," than in that which lies behind the tra-
> dition, "They believed in the resurrection of Jesus because they saw him living
> after his death." The resurrection of Jesus is in reality the resurrection of that
> faith in him which the disciples had had during his ministry.[146]

New Testament specialist Morton Enslin likewise found the significance of Easter in the reanimated disciples, not in the reanimated corpse of
Jesus:

> The change was not in any physical transformation of the body he had
> tenanted, but in the outlook and convictions of the men and women whom he

---

[141]Exodus 34:29.

[142]Matthew 17:2-3, 9.

[143]Deuteronomy 34:5-6; 2 Kings 2:11.

[144]Mark 9:9-10.

[145]Luke 9:29; Acts 9:3.

[146]Maurice Goguel, *The Birth of Christianity* (London: Allen & Unwin, 1953)
61.

had touched. . . . At the time of his arrest the disciples had fled in panic back to Galilee. . . . But a few months before . . . they had found themselves irresistibly drawn to him. . . . They had come to share his conviction that God had finally made known his will. . . . Then had come those awful days. God's prophet of the new day had fallen. His enemies had triumphed. . . . A beautiful dream while it lasted, but now vanished beyond recall? Then something happened. In the place of bleak despair there was a new and victorious confidence. . . . They "saw the Lord" . . . as they sat at table . . . "in the breaking of bread." . . . Had not Jesus built himself . . . into them so completely that he was even then living in them? . . . Upon the solid and unshakable foundation which had been wrought in them through their companionship with him, they eventually returned to Jerusalem to a task they now saw was still unfinished.[147]

Peter's vision, which set in motion the experiences of the other disciples, had both a retrospective and prospective dimension. He remembered his past partial commitment to the gospel and especially recalled Jesus' fellowship at meals. Prospectively, Peter hoped to extend the Jesus movement to fellow Jews. Experiencing the risen Jesus provided him inspiration for the difficult road ahead. Peter's radical shift in outlook was contagious, causing other companions of Jesus to understand that they had been looking for the ultimate disclosure of God in the wrong manner—in political action against Rome or in social segregation from "impure" people. Those who had been Jesus' friends came to the conviction that their leader was still alive and that their band was the body of Christ. They were steeled with the resolve to exemplify in their lives the values of Jesus. Peter exemplifies Gerhard Ebeling's dictum that the "faith of the days after Easter knows itself to be nothing else but the right understanding of the Jesus of the days before Easter."[148]

Awareness of Jesus' resurrection spread from a single person, Peter, to a few disciples who had also been remorseful when their leader died, and hence to hundreds of others who knew Jesus less intimately. Gordon Kaufman observes:

Most of the reports, both in Paul's list of appearances and in the Gospels, involve more than one witness, suggesting that it was when the disciples reassembled as close friends and particularly in the intimate fellowship of a

---

[147]Morton Enslin, *The Prophet from Nazareth* (New York: McGraw-Hill, 1961) 210-13.
[148]Gerhard Ebeling, *Word and Faith* (London: SCM, 1963) 302.

common meal with its undoubted rehearsal of warm but painful memories, especially of the last supper with Jesus, that Jesus was known to them again as raised from the dead. It should not be thought that this quasipublic character of the resurrection appearances distinguished them decisively from what we commonly think of as visions. There are numerous recorded contemporary instances of several persons experiencing the same vision or apparition at the same time.[149]

Of Magdalene

The best known of Jesus' female friends is the Mary who came from a fishing town on the Galilean coast, called Magdala or Magadan.[150] To distinguish her from other biblical Marys, she is called Mary Magdalene in the canonical Gospels, but often simply Magdalene subsequently. Some have plausibly suggested that she might have been the unnamed woman who had an continual flow of blood before encountering Jesus.[151] Beginning with the ministry of Jesus and his disciples in Galilee, and continuing for the rest of his life in Palestine, she and a few other women whom he had successfully treated for illnesses traveled with the itinerating group and took care of their needs.[152]

In the Synoptic Gospels, Magdalene's preeminence is indicated by her first place position in all the listings of women associated with Jesus,[153] even as spokesman Peter heads the lists of male disciples. That order of names suggests that Magdalene was recognized by her contemporaries as a special female companion of Jesus. In *Dialogue of the Savior*, a second-century writing, she is the only woman named and she is frequently the spokesperson for the disciples. In the *Gospel of Thomas*, only five of Jesus' disciples are named and Magdalene is one of them. A third-century writing has Jesus predicting that Magdalene and John will surpass the other disciples.[154]

---

[149]Kaufman, *Systematic Theology*, 421.

[150]Matthew 15:39.

[151]Carolyn and Joseph Grassi, *Mary Magdalene and the Women in Jesus' Life* (Sheed and Ward, 1986) 60-63.

[152]Luke 8:1-3.

[153]Mark 15:40-41; Matthew 27:56; Luke 8:2-3, 24:10.

[154]*Pistis Sophia* 96.

Magdalene has great distinctiveness as the only friend of Jesus who is named in all four Gospels as being with him when he died.[155] In John's Gospel she is named five times even though Jesus' mother is not named once. Whereas his other disciples were uncomprehending and deserted him at the time of his trial and crucifixion,[156] she and some other loyal women were with him until his agony was over. They touched his body for the last time as they lovingly washed it and wrapped it in burial cloth. Having seen where his body was hastily deposited on the eve of a sabbath without completing the customary treatment, they decided to return as soon as they could avoid desecrating the holy day to bring death-masking spices. They came back at the dawn of the first day of the next week, so the passage of time was about half of the often presumed three full days. Due to the occasional burial of someone who might still have been alive, it was customary for family members in denial to check tombs within days of a burial to make sure that a loved one was actually dead.

Although Magdalene had a notable place among Jesus' female followers during his public ministry, she has been most remembered for her role in the Easter event. The Gospels do not tell of any who witnessed Jesus' actually rising from his tomb but they testify to Magdalene being the first to see him after his crucifixion. She is the only woman present in the Easter stories of all four canonical Gospels but her words are recorded only in John. Aquinas, the foremost of Catholic theologians, attributes women's greater capacity to love as the reason why she rather than a male disciple obtained the vision of the resurrected Jesus.[157]

The tradition received from Peter and James, which Paul passed on, named only male apostles as having after-death sightings of Jesus. When Magdalene and her female companions testified to Jesus' living presence, the male disciples initially dismissed their story as nonsense.[158] That prejudiced response is understandable because in the Jewish patriarchal culture a woman's witness was not acceptable as legal evidence.[159] Josephus wrote, "Let not the testimony of women be admitted."[160] Consequently, the

---

[155]Matthew 27:56; Mark 15:40; Luke 23:55, 24:10; John 19:25.
[156]Matthew 26:56.
[157]Aquinas, *Summa Theologica* 3:55:1.
[158]Luke 24:11.
[159]The Mishnah, *Shabuot* 4:1.
[160]*Antiquities* 4.219.

Jerusalem church leaders apparently did not inform Paul about the women's Easter testimony.

The unofficial Magdalene resurrection story is the most intimate one. Even though it dates after Paul's letters, it is implausible that her testimony was fabricated out of whole cloth. Since women's stories were not deemed reliable, why would male Evangelists concoct a tale in which women were featured? A historical kernel can be discerned under the shell of narrative in the Gospel accounts of Magdalene. Just as the stories of the risen Jesus appearing to some male disciples originated in Galilee, so the stories of his appearing to women disciples originated in Jerusalem. Raymond Brown argues that the Easter story in John is independent of the other Gospels and is very early; C. H. Dodd, another Fourth Gospel authority, thinks the story came directly from Magdalene.[161] More recently, Jane Schaberg, in her book devoted to an analysis of resurrection narratives involving Magdalene and Jesus, concludes: "I have tried to mount convincing, coherent arguments that this [story in John's Gospel] is possibly bedrock tradition. . . . Mary Magdalene claimed—or it was claimed by others—that she had a visionary experience of Jesus which empowered her with God's spirit."[162]

What was the nature of Magdalene's experience? The traditional interpretation is that she came before dawn to the garden tomb where Jesus was buried and saw that its vertical sealing circular stone had been rolled aside. Assuming that Jesus' body had been stolen, she ran to tell his disciples the distressing news. Peter and "beloved disciple" John then rushed to the vacated tomb and discovered there only the linen in which Jesus' body had been wrapped. When Magdalene returned, she saw two angels sitting in the tomb where the body of Jesus had been lying. When they asked her why she was weeping, she expressed her dismay that Jesus' body had been removed to some unknown place. She was then asked the same question by someone whom Magdalene supposed was the cemetery caretaker. But when he addressed her by name, she identified as Jesus the one she had seen and heard.

[161]Raymond Brown, *The Gospel According to John (XIII–XXI)* (New York: Doubleday, 1970) 1003; C. H. Dodd, *Historical Tradition in the Fourth Gospel* (Cambridge: University Press, 1963) 148.

[162]Jane Schaberg, *The Resurrection of Mary Magdalene* (New York: Continuum, 2002) 350.

According to the general belief of Christians, the corpse of Jesus was supernaturally reanimated in a somewhat transformed state. And the presence of his risen naked body, which Magdalene could see as plainly as her hands, changed her fear into belief. Most Christians have believed that any who might have been present with Magdalene at that burial site could have perceived with their senses the material form of Jesus.

The main historical problem with interpreting the Magdalene story in the prevailing literalistic manner is that it clashes with Paul's authoritative record of Jesus' postmortem sightings. Yet Magdalene's experience as told in the Fourth Gospel has some qualities that harmonize with Paul's experience. Her exclamation, "I have seen the Lord!" is congruous with his question, "Have I not seen Jesus Christ our Lord?"[163] and the same Greek verb is used in both testimonies. Had Paul been aware of Magdalene and that she had been mesmerized by a vision of a glorified Jesus, he would probably have acknowledged that she shared with him the basic credential for the office of apostle.

Paul's emphasis on resurrection as a present experience rather than a state after death was not completely lost in subsequent Christianity. "Eternal life," a leitmotif of Johannine theology, begins with the acceptance of Jesus' teachings: "Anyone who hears my word and believes him who sent me has eternal life, and does not come under judgment, but has passed from death to life." "Everyone who lives and believes in me will never die."[164] Fourth Gospel expert C. H. Dodd comments: "The 'resurrection' of which Jesus has spoken is something which may take place before bodily death. . . . For John this present enjoyment of eternal life has become the controlling and all-important conception."[165]

The Johannine Jesus engages in a dialogue with Martha, who is grieving over the recent death of her brother. Jesus counsels her to discontinue conceiving of resurrection as a reintegration of relics "at the last day" and think of it as a reintegration of personal values here and now.[166] Hebert Richards comments on the significance of the interchange:

---

[163]John 20:18; 1 Corinthians 9:1.

[164]John 5:24, 11:26.

[165]C. H. Dodd, *The Interpretation of the Fourth Gospel* (Cambridge: University Press, 1953) 148-49.

[166]John 11:24-25.

We are not to think, as the Martha of the story does, that the reality of God is somehow remote from us, something we put our faith in, but which is in another world running parallel to ours and never really meeting until the end. Jesus' contemporaries thought this way, and many Christians continue to do so. "My meeting with God" they tend to say "will cone on the last day. My resurrection into the fullness of God's life is still a long way off. I have my death to worry about first; I'll think about my resurrection later." It is to such people that Jesus says, "I am the resurrection." He is the superabundant life of God made available to us here and now. The divine life has been embodied in a man like ourselves. This means that he is the resurrection of the body, infusing into mankind a life against which death cannot hold out. . . . The deepest meaning of the story, therefore, is not that Jesus has rather more powerful magic than other wonder-workers. It is that through his death and resurrection Jesus is the one source of eternal life.[167]

The focus of the Fourth Gospel is on neither postmortem resurrection nor on final judgment. John demythologizes to some extent the idea of a judgment day *after* death that the Egyptians had introduced into Middle Eastern religions. They believed that god Osiris presided over a trial at which an individual's destination of paradise or destruction was determined by weighing the person's good and bad deeds on a balance scale. But John portrays Jesus as bringing persons to a "crisis" (as the Greek text literally states), a momentous point of decision pertaining to "light" and "darkness" during their lifetime that enables them to determine their own destiny.[168]

According to John, the mission of Jesus was to bring "life in all its fullness."[169] The Greek term used here is *zoa*, an intensive and immortal quality of life resulting from taking within Jesus' spirit. *Bios*, by contrast, a term not used in John's Gospel, pertains to keeping an organism *bio*logically alive by means of healthy habits, and prolonging it endlessly by reproduction. The one who said "I am . . . the life" was more concerned with adding life to one's years than years to one's life. Entering the eternal or timeless life is not the taking up a second life in the future after the first one expires; rather, it is having a fresh mode of life that transcends egocentricism, overcoming the lethargy of humdrum existence by self-giving, finding life by losing it. Magdalene displayed that she had

---

[167]Hubert Richards, *The Miracles of Jesus* (London: Mowbray, 1975) 93-94.
[168]John 3:16-21.
[169]John 10:10.

internalized the "resurrection and the life" by receiving new hope and abiding joy from her Easter experience, which strengthened her to transmit Jesus' spirit to others.

In each account of the Easter legend, the yearning of Magdalene and her companions is significant, as well as where they go for reflection.[170] Seeking precedes the account of Jesus' resurrection in each Gospel, suggesting that the occurrence of the latter happens only after those who desire understanding initiate an inward quest. Mourners characteristically return to places that may spur memories of their loved one, especially to where the body of that person was last seen, hoping for something to fill their psychic emptiness. Magdalene was searching for anything that would stimulate her memory of the man who had given her new life. In the bewilderment following Jesus' death, she was no doubt trying desperately to reconcile his crucifixion with what he taught her about his mission, human sin, and God's will. At the tomb she was not so much looking for a corpse as for the love relationship she formerly had, but was now broken. In spite of her ardent expectation, she did not immediately identify the indistinct image that confronted her. This indicates that she was not seeing the physical body of Jesus she knew so well. Regardless of the "seeing is believing" slogan that is naively applied to physical perception, experiments with optical illusions show that what we see is to some extent dependent on what our mind can accept. Magdalene's belief in Jesus' resurrection was not caused by a visual sighting of an empty tomb where he was buried. Rather, she was stimulated to envision him by becoming aware of his victory over the forces of evil.

John's Gospel, from beginning to end, illustrates Jesus' seek-and-you-will-find teaching of the Sermon on the Mount.[171] In his first words, he asks his disciples, "What are you seeking?" and after his crucifixion he asks Magdalene, "Whom are you seeking?"[172] Those questions are in sync with the usual biblical way of experiencing the presence of God. According to Jeremiah, the Lord said, "If you search wholeheartedly for me, you will find me."[173] Although Magdalene did not dream up the presence of Jesus, neither was the event a "bolt out of the blue" for which there was no inward

---

[170]Mark 16:6; Matthew 28:5; Luke 24:5; John 20:15.
[171]Matthew 7:7.
[172]John 1:39, 20:15.
[173]Jeremiah 29:13.

preparation. Her grief involved pondering the sudden death of a man who was neither old nor ill but was unjustly condemned, and one on whom she owed much for her health and purpose in life. An anonymous hymn suggests the complex interaction of the self and the divine in religious experience:

> I sought the Lord, and afterward I knew
> He moved my soul to seek Him, seeking me;
> It was not I that found, O Savior true,
> No, I was found of Thee.

Lines of an Easter hymn from medieval France capture Magdalene's psychological agony and yearning:

> O Mary, do not weep, look no further. . . . He is with you, he whom you love. You sought Jesus and found him. . . . Why do you moan and cry? You have true joy; the relief of your pain is hidden within you, and you do not know; you have it inside, and you look outside for the remedy to your languor.[174]

Magdalene has often caught the attention of artists over the millennia. One of the earliest extant Christian painting depicts her bringing spices to Jesus' tomb.[175] At the Getty Museum in Los Angeles I have viewed "St. Mary Magdalene at the Sepulcher," a painting by Italian Renaissance artist Giovanni Savoldo that well displays, in my opinion, the externals of her Easter experience. With a tomb and the sunrise in the background, the golden play of light on her cloak seems to reflect Jesus' resurrected radiance. The artist captures the moment when grieving Madalene turns her face and realizes that Jesus is still alive.

Because of the close association of Jesus and Magdalene, some early Christians assumed that she was his wife. Verses in the canonical Gospels can be validly translated to state that Jesus was her spouse. In the Greek New Testament, *gune* can mean "women" in general or, more commonly, "wife" in particular. In Luke's Gospel the word is more often used in reference to spouses of particular husbands.[176] Accompanying Jesus and his male disciples were some *gunai* "who provided for them out of their

---

[174]The Latin text is quoted and translated in Susan Haskins, *Mary Magdalen* (New York: Harcourt, 1994) 218-19.

[175]Haskins, *Mary Magdalen*, 58-59.

[176]Luke 1:13; 3:19; 14:20; 17:32; 20:28.

resources.[177] Magdalene, Susanna, Joanna, the *gune* of a royal steward, and many others not only contributed to support the band but they also traveled with the men as they taught and healed in Palestinian villages.

In John's Easter story, Magdalene says to someone she supposed was the gardner, "Sir, if you carried him away, tell me where you laid him, and I will take him away."[178] Near where the crucifixion took place, Jesus' corpse had been placed in a tomb for what was probably intended by its donor to be a temporary burial site. Unless Magdalene were the next of kin, it would have been inappropriate for her to claim his remains. On the other hand, if Magdalene were Jesus' widow and chief mourner, she would want possession of Jesus' body for proper interment in the family plot. We know that Roman officials, on receiving requests from family members, released bodies of their crucified victims.[179] Discovered near Jerusalem in 1968 were bones of a Jew who had been crucified during that era; his body had been retrieved by relatives and properly buried.[180] Also, Magdalene referred to Jesus as "my lord," a customary way for designating a husband in her culture.[181] In addition, Magdalene desired to clutch him affectionately,[182] which would have been proper in the Jewish culture only if he were her spouse.

According to the *Gospel of Philip*, Magdalene was Jesus' "partner" (Greek, *koinonos*), or "spouse" (Coptic, *hotre*), and he kissed her often.[183] The "mystery of marriage" as it pertains to Jesus is described in this way: "The Lord is the Son of Man and the son of the Son of Man is he who is created through the Son of Man. The Son of Man received from God the capacity to create. He also has the ability to beget."[184] That *Gospel* records a tradition that may be at least as old as the second century.

There is an abundance of data pertaining to subjective experiences resulting from the loss of lovers. For example, the forlorn bride in the Song of Solomon is emotionally exhausted by an imagined search for her

---

[177]Luke 8:3.
[178]John 20:15.
[179]Philo, *In Flaccum* 10.83-84; Cicero, *In Verrem* 2.5.
[180]Crossan, *The Historical Jesus*, 392.
[181]John 20:13; Genesis 18:12; 1 Peter 3:6.
[182]John 20:17.
[183]*Gospel of Philip* 59, 63.
[184]*Gospel of Philip* 73, 81.

beloved. She asks the Jerusalem security guards, "Have you found my true love?" Her fantasy happily concludes with a resumption of the former embracing, "I held him and would not let him go."[185] In the Catholic liturgy, those verses from the erotic Song of Solomon are a reading for the Magdalene feast day. Theologian Jack Lundbom, unwittingly restating what Bishop Hippolytus suggested around 200 CE,[186] maintains that Magdalene may have had in mind those lyrics from the Song that was popular in her day.[187] There is no evidence that those passionate songs had then been denatured by allegorization.[188] Sentiments from the Hebrew song may have contributed to the Easter story in the Gospel of John. Distraught Magdalene frantically inquired about the whereabouts of Jesus, and then the lost loved one is suddenly found. Both the Song and Magdalene's experience have overtones of rekindled love in a renewed Paradise.[189] The Song of Solomon concludes with the affirmation that "love is as strong as death," but Magdalene exemplifies that steadfast love is stronger than death.

The changed nature of the bond between Jesus and Magdalene is expressed in his words to her, "Do not continue to hug me" (*me mou haptou*).[190] The Greek verb *hapto*, meaning "to hold," is used only here in John's Gospel. In the New Testament its meaning ranges from grasping a garment to having intercourse with a partner.[191] The verbal tense here with the negative adverb means to stop a past activity that is still in progress, so "Do not touch me," the harsh prohibition in the traditional Latin and English translations, is erroneous. The imperative, aptly rendered in Moffatt's translation as "Cease clinging to me," graphically conveys the traumatic transformation to which Magdalene was adjusting as her tie with Jesus had become exclusively intangible. No longer could she take hold of him physically, for he was no longer incarnate. Commentator John Marsh offers this explanation, "What Jesus is doing and saying to Mary can be summed up thus: she is to cease from holding him, because the new

---

[185]Song of Solomon 3:3-4.

[186]Haskins, *Mary Magdalen*, 66.

[187]Jack Lundbom, *Interpretation* (April 1995): 172.

[188]William Phipps, "The Plight of the Song of Songs," *Journal of the American Academy of Religion* (March 1974): 82-87.

[189]William Phipps, *Genesis and Gender* (New York: Praeger, 1989) 87-102.

[190]John 20:17.

[191]E.g., Mark 5:28; 1 Corinthians 7:1.

relationship between Lord and worshipper will not be one of physical contact, though it will be a real personal relationship."[192] Magdalene came to realize that her grief could not be quelled until she overcame her desire to cling to the past mode of encounter. What remained was not an anemic emotion but an intense passion for her beloved. She became convinced that Jesus was alive and that her companionship with him was more intimate than had been possible through physical associations. Reginald Fuller adds this broader implication:

> The recognition scene between Mary Magdalene and the Risen One conveys the important insight that Easter faith cannot cling to the early Jesus, the Jesus of history, as a figure of the past. . . . Faith seeks the earthly Jesus not as a dead teacher, but as the living Lord, whose word and work were not merely accomplished once upon a time, but are now made ever present in the community.[193]

Magdalene was among those who refused to allow Jesus' humiliating death to precipitate despair and loss of faith. She should be prominently included among those persons to whom first-century Jewish historian Josephus referred, "When Pilate condemned Jesus to be crucified . . . those who loved him from the first did not cease."[194] Like Paul, Magdalene could have given a negative answer to his rhetorical questions: "Can anything separate us from the love of Christ? Can hardship or distress?" She could likewise have declared with the apostle, "We are completely victorious through him who loved us; for I am certain that nothing in death or life . . . can come between us and his love."[195] Madgalene became convinced that Jesus was alive and that her affection for him was more personal and permanent than ever. She had come to believe what, according to an Evangelist, the risen Jesus said to his disciples, "I am with you always."[196]

In the second-century *Gospel of Mary*, the only one named for a woman, Magdalene tells of how she experienced the resurrected Jesus:

> Peter said to Mary: "Sister, we know the Savior loved you more than all other women. Tell us the words of the Savior that you remember." . . . She said, "I

---

[192]John Marsh, *The Gospel of St. John* (Baltimore: Penguin, 1968) 637.

[193]Reginald Fuller, *The Formation of the Resurrection Narratives* (New York: Macmillan, 1971) 174.

[194]Josephus, *Antiquities* 18.64.

[195]Romans 8:35, 37-39.

[196]Matthew 28:20.

saw the Lord in a vision. . . . He answered me, 'You are wonderful for not wavering at the sight of me. For where the mind is, there is the treasure.' I said to him, 'Lord, does a person who sees a vision see it with the soul or with the spirit?' The Savior answered, 'A person does not see with the soul or with the spirit. Rather the mind, which exists between these two, sees the vision.'" . . . Peter questioned the apostles about the Savior: "Did he really speak privately with a woman without our knowing it? Are we to turn about and all listen to her? Did he prefer her to us?" Then Mary wept and said to Peter: "My brother Peter, what are you imagining? Do you think that I thought this up myself in my heart, or that I am lying about the Savior?" Levi [Matthew] spoke: "Peter, you have always been hot tempered. Now I see you contending against the woman like the adversaries. But if the Savior made her worthy, who are you then to reject her? Surely the Savior knows her very well. That is why he loved her more than us."[197]

According to the tradition transmitted by Matthew and John, in contrast to Luke, the first witness to Jesus' resurrection was Magdalene rather than Peter. The *Gospel of Mary* states that she instructed Peter that seeing Jesus is an inner apprehension that comes through the *nous*—meaning "mind" or "understanding." In another apocryphal Gospel, Peter is represented as saying to his fellow male disciples about Magdalene and her gender, "Let Mary leave us, for women are not worthy of Life."[198] The acrimony between those strong personalities reflects a gender conflict alluded to in the New Testament. Beginning with the second generation of Christians, the patriarchy of Mediterranean cultures returned and soon triumphed over the brief acceptance of women in leadership roles. Not until the past century did this issue again become prominent in the church.

Ernest Renan, the famed nineteenth-century French biblical critic, treated the Easter appearance of Jesus as a product of Magdalene's mental facility, but he was not trying to disparage its significance.[199] He told of the occasion in this romantic way:

Frantic with love, intoxicated with joy, Mary returned to the city. To the first disciples whom she met, she said: "I have seen him; he has spoken to me." Her greatly troubled mind, her broken and disconnected speech, caused some to think she was demented. . . . The glory of the resurrection belongs, then, to

---

[197]*Gospel of Mary* 10, 17-18.
[198]*Gospel of Thomas* 114.
[199]Ernest Renan, *The Life of Jesus* (London: Dent, 1927) 102, 230-231.

Mary of Magdala. After Jesus, it was Mary who has done the most in the founding of Christianity. The image created by her delicate sensibility still hovers before the world. Queen and patroness of idealists, Magdalene knew how to assert the vision of her passionate personality and convince everyone. Her grand feminine affirmation, "He is risen!" has become the basis of the faith of humanity. Away, feeble reason! Apply no cold analysis to this masterpiece of idealism.[200]

Renan summarized the Easter experience tersely, "It was love that raised Jesus."[201] Joseph Klausner, a Jewish expert on the historical Jesus, quoted Renan's treatment of Magdalene and agreed with him that her vision, and those of her male compatriots, had high significance. They help to explain why the memory of Jesus was preserved, in contrast to the memories that were soon lost of other messianic figures of that era.[202]

Over the centuries, the Gospel experiences of the resurrected Jesus have sometimes been classified as "hallucination." Kaufman has defined that term as "a nonpublic but privately extremely significant experience." He thinks of Magdalene as among those early followers of Jesus who have communicated genuine insight on the continuity of God's nature and purposes by means of their hallucinations:

> It is because an event occurred—comprehensible on the human level as a series of "appearances" or "hallucinations" creative of and in the context of a new community of love and forgiveness—through which the earliest disciples came to discern a new and deeper meaning in the life and death of Jesus that here was the definitive manifestation of the unfailing love of almighty God toward man.[203]

"Hallucination" is defined by the *Oxford English Dictionary* as "the apparent perception (usually by sight or by hearing) of an external object when no such object is actually present." Similarly, in medical literature, hallucinatory phenomena pertains to experiencing visual and/or auditory apparitions that have no physical component. A recent parapsychology encyclopedia states that "although hallucination is often associated with various mental and physical diseases, it may nevertheless occur spontaneously while the agent shows no departure from full vigor of body and

---

[200]Ernest Renan, *Les Apotres* (Paris: Levy, 1866) 11-13, 44.

[201]Renan, *Les Apotres*, 70.

[202]Joseph Klausner, *From Jesus to Paul* (Boston: Beacon, 1961) 255-58.

[203]Kaufman, *Systematic Theology*, 425-31.

mind."[204] A hallucination, then, is a vivid perception arising without the stimulus of a corresponding sense impression; it is not necessarily a sign of derangement. Peter McKenzie classifies as hallucinations the visions of mystics in a variety of world religions, but he notes that "this does not exclude the fact that transcendent reality is disclosed to the devout within the framework of these subjective limits.[205]

However, for most people the term "hallucination" does not have the positive meaning that some scholars give it. Commonly it is used pejoratively to describe a delusional state; for example, someone under the influence of drugs who sees pink elephants. Celsus, the first pagan to put in writing his criticisms of Christianity, is dismissive toward its resurrection claim. Aware only of the account of Jesus' appearance to women, he asks Christians about Magdalene's condition:

> But who really saw this? A hysterical woman, as you admit and perhaps one other person—both deluded by his sorcery, or else so wretched with grief at his failure that they hallucinated him risen from the dead by a sort of wishful thinking. This mistaking a fantasy for reality is not at all uncommon; indeed, it has happened to thousands. Just as possible, these deluded women wanted to impress the others—who had already the good sense to have abandoned him—by spreading their hallucinations about as "visions." After getting some few to believe them, it was a small matter for the fire of superstition to spread.[206]

John Cobb finds unsatisfactory the usual meaning of the term "hallucination" in explaining the Gospel resurrection stories because it neglects the consideration of an external cause. He thinks that "Jesus was really present as a cause of the appearances but . . . the sensory content of the visions was contributed by the psychic activity of the percipient."[207] The visions involved a two-way communication, as in prayer. New Testament authority Walter Wink observes: "It is a prejudice of modern thought that events happen only in the outer world. What Christians regard as the most

[204]"Hallucination," *Encyclopedia of Occultism and Parapsychology* (Detroit: Gale, 1991).

[205]Peter McKenzie, *The Christians* (Nashville: Abingdon, 1988) 303-304.

[206]Celsus, *True Doctrine* (New York: Oxford, 1987) 67-68.

[207]John Cobb, *Christ in a Pluralistic Age* (Philadelphia: Westminster, 1975) 253.

significant event in human history happened, according to the Gospels, in
the psychic realm and it altered external history irrevocably."[208]

Jesus biographer Donald Spoto does not find it sociologically plausible
to think that the burgeoning growth of the earliest church could have arisen
from hallucinations as usually defined:

> A hallucination or a hoax, in the final analysis, cannot be reconciled with the
> dramatic and historically remarkable movement that, within twenty-five years
> after Jesus' execution, and under the most agonizing conditions, created Christian
> communities across the Mediterranean world. People do not amalgamate
> and deepen a sense of personal and group purpose without the forceful presence
> of a single charismatic individual and sensational, primal, formative
> events. In other words, if *some* astonishing experience was not at the foundation
> of the Christian movement, then what accounted for the improbable beginning,
> the astonishing expansion and the distinctive writings that reflect its
> origins?[209]

Magdalene's Easter experience should not be interpreted as exclusively
a self-induced hallucination. Her faith that God had raised Jesus from the
dead may well have been produced by more than subjective longing. Her
close ties with Jesus over an extended period gave her a predisposition to
believe that the love she had known could not be permanently lost.
Anglican archbishop William Temple treats Magdalene's resurrection
vision in this way, "It is rather to be supposed that an intense interior
awareness of a divine message leads to the projection of an image which is
then experienced as an occasion of something seen and heard."[210]

A divine disclosure interacting with Magdalene's troubled mind may
have produced her deeply moving Easter experience. After "seeing" Jesus
and "hearing" him call her name,[211] she became convinced that he was not
dead but altogether alive, albeit in a different mode. Her weeping was
mixed with joy as she came to realize that even in this life she could be in
communion with one who is "the resurrection and the life" and who, like a
good shepherd, knows his own and calls them by their individual names.[212]

---

[208]Walter Wink, *The Human Being* (Minneapolis: Fortress, 2002) 152-53.

[209]Donald Spoto, *The Hidden Jesus* (New York: St. Martin's Press, 1998) 245.

[210]William Temple, *Readings in St. John's Gospel* (London: Macmillan, 1945)
380.

[211]John 20:6, 14, 16.

[212]John 10:3; 11:25.

Magdalene felt commissioned by a reimaged Jesus to proclaim his overcoming of death.[213] Rather than hoard privately the revelation that had transformed her sorrow into gladness, she spread the good news to other disciples. She had "enthusiasm" in the etymological sense of the word, for she was filled with the spirit of *theos*, God. In the early centuries of Christianity, some church leaders accepted Magdalene's prominent position as an authoritative witness to the Easter triumph of Jesus. Hippolytus referred to the women at Jesus' tomb as "apostles."[214]

In the Latin church, Magdalene was known as *apostola apostolorum* because she was the first to be "sent forth" (*apostello*) to proclaim to male apostles what the risen Jesus had disclosed to her.[215] Karen King, an authority on the *Gospel of Mary* manuscript, writes, "The historical Mary of Magdala was a prominent Jewish follower of Jesus, a visionary, and a leading apostle."[216] Peter Abelard, an outstanding medieval theologian, gave her this tribute:

> The saint merits to be the first to be consoled by the Savior's resurrection, as his death had been a cause of sorrow and anguish to her. She is also called the apostle to the apostles, that is ambassadress of the ambassadors, as the Lord sent her to the apostles to announce the joy of the resurrection.[217]

Haskins shows how Pope Gregory the Great's erroneous identification of Magdalene with the prostitute who anointed Jesus' feet has had a baneful influence on her reputation.[218] She concludes her careful exploration of the images of Magdalene through patriarchal church history by commenting:

> Mary Magdalen's figure has emerged in bold relief, restored to her New Testament role as chief female disciple, apostle to the apostles, and first witness of the resurrection. The significance of this reevaluation has so far gone mostly unacknowledged by the Church of Rome. From the early centuries of the Christian era, Mary Magdalene has, like the women she represents, been

[213]John 20:17.

[214]Hippolytus, *On Song of Songs* 24-26.

[215]John 20:17-18; J. P. Migne, ed., *Patrologia Latina* (Paris, 1844–1866) 112.1474b, 183.1148.

[216]Karen King, *Gospel of Mary of Magdala* (Santa Rosa, CA: Polebridge, 2003) 154.

[217]Migne, ed., *Patrologia Latina* 178.486.

[218]Luke 7:26-50; Gregory I, *Sermons* 33 (591); Haskins, *Mary Magdalen*, 95-97.

the scapegoat of the ecclesiastical institution, manipulated, controlled and, above all, misrepresented. . . . Mary Magdalen has [now] become . . . the symbol of women's right to resume their place and role in the Church.[219]

Extrabiblical Parallels

Visions are intrinsic to religious figures quite apart from the Bible. In primal cultures, shamen's claim to have had revelatory visions are often the basic criterion for their acceptance as tribal leaders. Muhammad's prophethood was initiated by bright daybreak visions resembling those of semitic prophets who preceded him. At a cave on a mountain near Mecca, he was overwhelmed by envisioning a nearby Person who revealed to him a message to proclaim.[220]

Every culture has its charismatic visionaries who attract adulation; the folks who become charmed often become passionately devoted to the causes of their leaders. After the death of persons with personal magnetism, records of sightings by their followers can sometimes be found in ancient nonbiblical literature. Philostratus's biography of Apollonius, a neo-Pythagorean from the Greek city of Tyana in Cappadocia, concludes with a story of such. That writing provides the closest pagan parallel to the literary history of the Gospels. Stories about the philosopher were based on first-century sources but were recorded several generations later. Philostratus states:

> A young man arrived in Tyana who was quick to argue and did not accept the truth. . . . In the course of denying completely the immortality of the soul, he said, "My friends here, for nine months now I have never stopped praying to Apollonius to reveal the truth about the soul. But he is so thoroughly dead that he has not even appeared in answer to my request, or persuaded me that he is immortal." . . . Four days later, he was discussing the same subject when he fell asleep where he had been talking. . . . The boy jumped up from his sleep like a madman, sweating profusely, and shouted, "I believe you." The others asked what had happened to him, and he said, "Don't you see the wise Apollonius as he stands among us listening to our conversation, and giving his marvellous declamation on the soul?" "Where is he?" they asked. "We can't see him anywhere, though we would give the world to do so." The boy said, "He must

---

[219]Haskins, *Mary Magdalen*, 392-93, 397.

[220]*Qur'an* 53:1-10; Alfred Guillaume, *The Life of Muhammad: A Translation of Ibn Ishaq's Sirat Rasul Allah* (Lahore: Oxford, 1955) 102, 105.

have come to talk to me about what I disbelieved: so let me tell you how he has immortalized the doctrine."

Posthumous apparitions by the bereaved are not uncommon in history. In the second century, Justin defended the Christian belief in Jesus' resurrection by pointing out that ascension sightings of a person who had died are not unique. Aware of reports pertaining to postmortem visions by those who thought the divine Julius and Augustus Caesar had arisen,[221] Justin invites pagans to consider this comparison:

> When we say that . . . Jesus Christ . . . died, rose again, and ascended into heaven we introduce nothing different from what you believe about those whom you call sons of Zeus. . . . What of your deceased emperors, whom you think worthy of being raised to immortality, introducing a witness who swears that he has seen the burned Caesar rise to heaven from the funeral pyre?[222]

Constantine told his biographer, Eusebius, that when he was establishing himself as the Roman emperor he envisioned a cross above the sun. Formed from light, it carried the inscription "By this conquer," and his army also saw the sign. Later "the Christ of God" appeared to urge him to have his soldiers march with banners displaying what had been revealed and thereby achieve victory.[223] Also from the fourth century is an account of the anguish that the distinguished Bishop Ambrose expressed after his brother's death: "I embrace you, gaze upon you, address you. . . . Neither death nor time shall tear you from me. . . . O bitter days . . . unless the likeness of him present offered itself to me, unless the visions of my soul represented him whom my bodily sight shows me no more!"[224]

When an event similar to a biblical story of an extraordinary happening can be identified as having occurred in recent years or centuries in one's own culture then there is some reason for believing that similar events occurred in ancient times. In American history, consider the vision in 1820 by teenager Joseph Smith, who became the founder of Mormonism. While praying in a forest near his family's New York farm, he saw "two Personages, whose brightness and glory defy all description." One pointed to the other and said, "This is my beloved son, hear him." *Joseph Smith's*

---

[221]Suetonius, *Augustus* 100.

[222]Justin, *Apology* 1:21.

[223]Eusebius, *Life of Constantine* 1.28, 29.

[224]Ambrose, *On the Decease of Satyrus* 1.72-74.

Testimony contains more of what was conveyed to him by subsequent visions. Or consider the vision contained in the grief testimony of Gnostic scholar Elaine Pagels. She comments on what happened after the accidental death of her young husband, "I became aware that, like many people who grieve, I was living in the presence of an invisible being."[225] The experiences by Ambrose and Pagels contain crystallized memories they retained of their beloved companions.

William Thompson finds in our experience of the death of loved ones clues for understanding the resurrection stories in the Gospels:

> At such moments we seem to discover the transcendent power of life and love, which sustains our trust and gives us the capacity to "rise" above these deaths. . . . Our human capacity to hope against defeatism and to protest human misery . . . are echoes of the divine gift of life sustaining and renewing us. . . . Like us, in these encounters [of the risen Jesus] early Christian disciples experienced a foretaste of what resurrection life is.[226]

The Harvard Bereavement Study, in which psychiatrist Colin Parkes and others were involved, found three main determinants of acute grief: unexpected sudden death, guilt toward the deceased, and dependency on that person.[227] On the basis of his lengthy clinical research into the experiences of widows, Parkes has documented that postmortem sightings of husbands are common in the early weeks after their deaths, and then they gradually fade away. "In the newly bereaved widow the perceptual element is very strong," Parkes comments. Sometimes the dead husband's presence is sensed internally, and not just nearby, causing the widow to see things through his eyes and adopt his sense of values. Parkes notes that the recipients find the sightings more comforting than disturbing, and he evaluates the experiences as healthy rather than pathological.[228]

Grief counselor William Worden reinforces Parkes's judgment that visions of a deceased loved one are normal and not a sign of mental illness:

---

[225]Elaine Pagels, *Origins of Satan* (New York: Random House, 1995) xv.

[226]William Thompson, *The Jesus Debate* (New York: Paulist, 1985) 228, 234.

[227]Colin Parkes and Robert Weiss, *Recovery from Bereavement* (New York: Basic Books, 1983) 52.

[228]Colin Parkes, *Bereavement* (New York: International Universities Press, 1972) 48, 59, 103, 164.

Hallucinations of both the visual type and the auditory type . . . are a frequent experience of the bereaved. . . . With all the recent interest in mysticism and spirituality, it is interesting to speculate on whether these are really hallucinations or possibly some other kind of metaphysical phenomena.[229]

Psychoanalyst Ana-Maria Rizzuto demonstrates that fantasy can be associated with true reality.[230] Some of those whom secularists describe as having a mental breakdown may be having a theological breakthrough! Renowned psychiatrist Robert Cole concludes that much can be learned of reality from spiritual experiences, and that those who claim to see or hear Jesus may be displaying one way through which divine revelation is given.[231]

Virtual-reality scientist Eric Haseltine demonstrates that there is nothing supernatural about visions. He states:

Electrophysiological studies of the cerebral cortex have uncovered neurons whose main job appears to be that of recognizing faces within the vast visual information sent to the brain. . . . A large concentration of these cells in a section of the visual cortex called the fusiform gyrus . . . are constantly on the lookout for patterns that correspond to facial geometry. . . . Humans are very social animals, for whom recognition of faces and facial expressions is of paramount importance. . . . If you're inclined to look actively for ghosts, your brain will be a willing partner in that adventure.[232]

Over the millennia, many have testified that Jesus lives in them, making them free to share in the joys and sorrows of others. There is nothing involved in this phenomena that is counter to what is known of psychical or physical laws of nature. Eddie Ensley, a theologian and sociologist, surveyed two thousand Christians living in a midwestern American city. He found that thirty percent of them claimed they "had seen dramatic visions, heard heavenly voices, or experienced prophetic dreams." Ensley comments: "Visions are natural. They are not miracles—inexplicable interven-

---

[229]J. William Worden, *Grief Counseling and Grief* Therapy (New York: Springer, 1982) 24.

[230]Ana-Maria Rizzuto, *The Birth of the Living God* (Chicago: University of Chicago Press, 1979) 209.

[231]Robert Cole, *Spiritual Life of Children* (Boston: Houghton Mifflin, 1990) 97.

[232]*Discover* (February 2002): 88.

tions of the supernatural into our workaday natural world. They are natural manifestations of the fullness of reality."[233]

Christian biographers sometime presume that others have had similar visions to their own, and draw on them in telling the life stories of others. Such a transference may explain an alleged episode in George Handel's life. Frequently retold by biographers is a dramatic story of his having a vision while composing the Hallelujah Chorus in 1741.[234] A reference book states this ancedote as fact: "One day his servant opened the door to find Handel at his work, with tears streaming down his face. Handel looked up and cried out, 'I did think I did see all Heaven before me and the great God Himself.' "[235] Although Handel was a sincere Christian, there is no historical substantiation for his ever having such rapture.[236] The anecdote may have been originated by a person who became ecstatic while attending a performance of the oratorical masterpiece Messiah and then told of the experience as though it had happened to the inspiring composer. Likewise, an Evangelist may have similarly adapted his vision, or that of a fellow Christian, to describe what Jesus may have experienced.

Sundar Singh, who became famous as a missionary to Nepal, lived in a culture where visions of Krishna or Buddha were not rare for those engaged in meditation. Jesus appeared to him briefly when he was a young Sikh, and spoke to him in Hindustani. He describes how it happened at night several days after he had expressed his contempt for Christianity by tearing up and burning a Gospel:

> The light increased in intensity and . . . there appeared . . . the living Christ whom I had counted as dead. To all eternity I shall never forget His glorious and loving face, nor the few words which He spoke: "Why do you persecute me? See, I have died on the Cross for you and for the whole world." These words were burned into my heart as by lightning, and I fell on the ground before Him. My heart was filled with inexpressible joy and peace, and my whole life was entirely changed.[237]

---

[233]Eddie Ensley, *Visions* (Chicago: Loyola, 2000) 13-14.

[234]Robert Myers, *Handel's Messiah* (New York: Octagon, 1971) 79.

[235]*The New Encyclopedia of Christian Quotations* (Grand Rapids MI: Baker, 2000) 1091.

[236]Paul Lang, *George Frederic Handel* (New York: Norton, 1966) 336-37.

[237]A. J. Appasamy, *Sundar Singh* (London: Lutterworth, 1958) 21.

Another twentieth-century conversion vision, by a woman convicted of murder in California, also has biblical overtones. As Susan Atkins reflected on her atrocious past conduct, she had intense guilt feelings. She recalled the amazing grace of Jesus and remembered a New Testament verse in which the risen Jesus stands at an entrance with hopes of being welcomed by anyone within.[238] Out of this came an illumination and an awareness of forgiveness that empowered her to make a basic change in her life:

> There in my thoughts was a door. It had a handle. I took hold of it and pulled. It opened. The whitest, most brilliant light I had ever seen poured over me. . . . Vaguely, there was the form of a man. I knew it was Jesus. . . . [He] spoke to me in my nine-by-eleven prison cell, "Susan, I am really here. I'm really coming into your heart to stay." . . . There was no more guilt . . . [or] bitterness.[239]

Even before Sigmund Freud explored depth psychology, William James alerted students of the psyche (mind, soul) to a larger spectrum:

> Our normal waking consciousness, rational consciousness as we call it, is but one special type of consciousness, whilst all about it, parted from it by the filmiest of screens, there lie potential forms of consciousness entirely different. We may go through life without suspecting their existence; but apply the requisite stimulus, and at a touch they are all there in all their completeness, definite types of mentality which probably somewhere have their field of application and adaption. No account of the universe in its totality can be final which leaves these other forms of consciousness quite disregarded. How to regard them is the question—for they are so discontinuous with ordinary consciousness. Yet they may determine attitudes though they cannot furnish formulas, and open a region though they fail to give a map. At any rate, they forbid a premature closing of our accounts with reality.[240]

James applied his view of consciousness to religious biography. He used the term "photisms" to refer to the luminous phenomena of Paul's heavenly vision and Emperor Constantine's vision of a cross in the sky that brought acceptance to the church. To show that photisms were not uncom-

---

[238]Revelation 3:20.

[239]Mary Meadow and Richard Kahoe, *Psychology of Religion* (New York: Harper, 1984) 90.

[240]William James, *The Varieties of Religious Experience* (New York: Doubleday, 1902) 349.

mon in nineteenth-century America, James related this anonymous testimony:

> I had attended a series of revival services for about two weeks off and on. Had been invited to the altar several times, all the time becoming more deeply impressed, when finally I decided I must do this, or I should be lost. Realization of conversion was very vivid, like a ton's weight being lifted from my heart; a strange light which seemed to light up the whole room (for it was dark); a conscious supreme bliss which caused me to repeat "Glory to God" for a long time.[241]

Visions might best be understood by relating them to one of the three psychic states. In addition to the *conscious* mind that handles ordinary perception and reasoning, there is the *subconscious* mind that functions especially when asleep. Then there is the *transconscious* mind that accounts for peak experiences. The ecstatic rapture of religious persons through the ages belongs to the last state. What is called the eighth stage of yoga by Hindus, nirvana by Buddhists, glossolalia by Pentecostals, exemplify nonsustainable trancelike experiences that can be of great personal significance. The psychic experiences of Paul, Peter, and Magdalene that effected their call to mission belong to a category that can be amply illustrated in all living religions, from primal to civilized. John Pilch has related crosscultural data on altered states of consciousness (ASC) to resurrection visions. Ninety percent of 488 global societies report ASC. He suggests, "Since ancient Palestine and neighboring societies such as Ancient Egypt and Greece were included in the data bank, the ASC experience is a highly plausible, cultural explanatory model for Second [New] Testament reports of circum-Mediterranean people seeing the Risen Jesus."[242]

In 1959, in a Pentecostal church in Oakland, California, some two hundred congregational members simultaneously had "Christic visions," seeing a face appearing much like Sallman's "Head of Christ" painting, along with a white robe and nail-pierced hands. That incident interested Phillip Wiebe, whose empirical investigation of religious experience is similar to that of psychologist William James. In 1991 he interviewed some who had been present on the occasion of the visions a generation earlier.[243]

---

[241]James, *The Varieties of Religious Experience*, 231-32.
[242]*Biblical Theology Bulletin* (Summer 1998): 53.
[243]Phillip Wiebe, *Visions of Jesus* (New York: Oxford University Press, 1997) 77-78.

Wiebe found much support for the visions having happened and learned that they had occurred spontaneously in ordinary Christians. He concluded that visions of a transcendent being "generally have great importance for those who experience them."[244] On the basis of Wiebe's research, there is no basis for making a sharp distinction between the postresurrection sightings of Jesus and contemporary visionary experiences. For those California congregants, the visions were the effect, not the cause, of their faith.

In his thorough discussion of resurrection experiences in the New Testament, Anglican archbishop Peter Carnley argues that they are tokens of something real regardless of whether they can be objectively confirmed:

> Only those who devalue the events of their own psychological life or are asleep to this dimension of experience could so misunderstand the importance to the first disciples of the visions, even if they are judged to be "subjective" visions. . . . Even if the visions are today explained as psychological phenomena they are not explained away. . . . There is no doubt that the first disciples interpreted the Easter visions or appearances as signs of the heavenly presence of Christ.[245]

* * *

Several resurrection visions of earliest Christanity have been shown to have in common nonsupernatural elements similar to theophanies or christophanies that have been recorded throughout religious history. The New Testament Peter, Paul, and Mary are like their contemporary namesakes in that they express themselves in harmony. The thought of the deceased Jesus brought them much inner turmoil, even though in the case of Paul the emotion was hateful rather than loving. Each one was then permanently transformed by seeing a risen Jesus who was both near as well as exalted, intimate as well as ultimate. Those three key witnesses were apostles because they were convinced that they had been commissioned to spread abroad the message of Jesus' tragedy and triumph. They have become preeminent in different sectors of Christianity: whereas Peter became the patron saint of the Roman church, and Paul has had a corresponding role in the Protestant church, Magdalene has become a latter-day saint of feminist Christians.[246] A poem of Rudyard Kipling describes the

---

[244]Wiebe, *Visions of Jesus*, 212-13.

[245]Peter Carnley, *The Structure of Resurrection Belief* (Oxford: Clarendon, 1987) 246.

[246]See, e.g., in addition to Haskins's book, Mary Thompson, *Mary of Magdala*

"God of things as they are" encouraging persons in heaven to continue their creative endeavors. Three visionaries there are worthy subjects for artists to paint:

> They'll find real saints to draw from—Magdalene, Peter, and Paul;
> They'll work for an age at a sitting, and never be tired at all![247]

Throughout most of church history, openness to a nonphysical interpretation of Jesus' resurrection cannot be found. Protestant Thomas Woolston may have been the first Christian in European history to argue against a literal interpretation of Jesus' resurrection. He defended the "mystical Resurrection of our *spiritual Jesus*" and said that "the Evangelical Story of the Resurrection of a *carnal Christ* is but mere Type and Shadow."[248] For this and similar judgments on the Gospel miracles he was committed to a prison in England, where he died in 1733.

It is a sellout to the positivist dogma of the immaculate *per*ception to accept the metaphysics that only what is observable by the senses can be true. By that standard, the biblical declaration that God is a rock is literal nonsense and is therefore untrue. But metaphorical language is commonly used, apart from religious discourse, by those who wish to affirm that they have discovered the solution to something that had been puzzling. After struggling with a difficult geometry problem, for example, a student may become enlightened and exclaim, "Now I see it!" In solving what had previously been an enigma, her or his senses may not have supplied any new physical data but s/he has gained real understanding. Likewise, many throughout church history have inwardly seen the risen Jesus and that experience has provided them with his living presence for a lifetime.

Jesus' one beatitude in John's Gospel is a criticism of literalists who crave for visible proof before they make a faith commitment. The story of Thomas's demand for tangible evidence of the risen Jesus concludes in an ironic manner. Jesus declares, "Blessed are those who have not [physically] seen me but have come to believe."[249] Hans Küng remarks: "The Easter

---

(New York: Paulist, 1995) and Esther de Boer, *Mary Magdalene* (Harrisburg: Trinity, 1997).

[247]Rudyard Kipling, "When Earth's Last Picture Is Painted" (1892).

[248]Thomas Woolston, *A Sixth Discourse on the Miracles of our Saviour* (London, 1729) 2.

[249]John 20:29.

faith is oriented neither to the empty tomb nor to the "appearances," but to *the living Jesus himself.* . . . This living Christ and through him the living God, who called him from death to life, are the object of the Easter faith."[250] Most Christians do not have the experience of seeing Jesus like those reported in the New Testament, but they can base their faith on its assurances that the Crucified One really lives and rules with God.

---

[250]Küng, *On Being a Christian*, 371.

Chapter 7
Physical Resurrection

Prior to Christianity

The idea of a postmortem revival of the deceased was introduced into apocalyptic Judaism by the Book of Daniel. "Apocalyptic," meaning "uncovering," pertains to disclosing what will happen to God's people in the future. Daniel, written around 200 BCE at the end of the many centuries of cultural recordings in the Hebrew Bible, appears to have interpreted literally and applied individualistically a poetic oracle by one prophet and a dramatic story by another.

Isaiah, writing about the victory of his kingdom of Judah, forecasts a national rebirth after the departure of enemies:

> Your dead will live,
> > their corpses will rise.
> Those who sleep in the earth
> > will awake and shout for joy.[1]

But more than a century later, the Babylonians destroyed Judah and deported many of their Jewish captives. They had difficulty believing that they would return to their homeland and flourish again. Speaking to this situation, Ezekiel envisioned the revival of his nation from the Israelite remnants: "Suddenly there was a rattling noise and the bones reassembled. . . . Then the Lord said to me, 'Man, these bones are the whole people of Israel.'"[2] That prophet pictured the eventual corporate revival of his religious community in order to encourage the dispirited exiles in Babylon. Several centuries after that prophecy was given, the Jews had returned to their native land but they continued to be under the domination of pagan rulers.

In the absence of a this-worldly restoration of an expired nation, belief in an otherworldly resurrection of individuals emerged. It was assumed that God would provide in the future a just reward for good Jews who had been oppressed, and punishment for the rest. Consequently, Daniel forecasts,

---

[1] Isaiah 26:19.
[2] Ezekiel 37:7, 11.

"Many of those who sleep in the dust of the earth shall awake, some to everlasting life, and some to shame and everlasting contempt."[3]

About that time, a Jewish freedom fighter in the Maccabean war against Greek conquerors affirmed as he was dying, "The King of the universe will resurrect us to an everlasting renewal of life." He and his fellow soldiers were confident of an afterlife in which severed body parts would be restored in a general resurrection at the end of the age. One martyr died by cutting out his bowels with a sword and hurling them at the enemies surrounding him. His last words were a prayer asking the Lord to give his entrails back to him in the future.[4] Prior to the beginning of the Christian era many Jews believed that the righteous will be physically raised, enabling them to participate in the messianic kingdom on a purified earth. The felicity of the blessed will include giving birth to many children and enjoying an abundance of wine produced by bountiful grape harvests.[5]

Jewish notions of life after death developed during the era when they were affected by the religion of the Persians who dominated Western Asia. Persian prophet Zoroaster believed in a resurrection that largely replicated earthly life. He introduced the term *paradise* into religious vocabulary to designate a place beyond death where the righteous enjoy social life in a cool and fragrant garden. An eternity of happy marriage and sensuous pleasures rewards those who do not drop into purgatory because of their iniquities.[6]

Belief in the reanimation of relics on the day of God's final judgment was popular in Judaism during Jesus' time. Unlike the ancient Greeks, many of whom believed in the immortality of the soul, few Jews believed that a soul could survive death without its flesh and bones body. Devout Jews prayed daily, "Blessed art thou, O Lord, who quickenest the dead."[7] One apocalypse affirms, "The earth shall then assuredly restore the dead, which it now receives in order to preserve them, making no change in their form."[8] Some rabbis assumed that even marriage and procreation would

---

[3]Daniel 12:2.

[4]2 Maccabees 7:9-11, 14:41-46.

[5]*First Enoch* 10:17-19, 25:6.

[6]*Bundahish* 30.25; R. C. Zaehner, *The Dawn and Twilight of Zoroastrianism* (New York: Putnam, 1961) 302-308.

[7]*Eighteen Benedictions*, 2.

[8]*Apocalypse of Baruch* 50:2.

continue unchanged in the life after death.[9] An ancient synagogue excavated in Mesopotamia depicts imagery from Ezekiel's dry bones vision. A large fresco on one wall displays severed human heads, hands, and legs reconnecting. Fairy-like souls of the dead flutter down to return to their former fleshly habitations.[10]

* * *

An examination of Jesus' earliest recorded sayings reveal that he apparently said little about life after death. This is surprising since he has had great impact on the conviction that billions of Christians have held on the topic. Also, as Colleen McDannell and Bernhard Lang point out:

> Jesus took no interest in corpses. "Follow me," he said to one [person] he met on the road; "leave the dead to bury their dead." Since the dead body was not the eternal part of the personality, Jesus could comfort those of his followers who suffered persecution and enmity by saying that the enemies can "kill the body but cannot kill the soul [*psyche*]." The body, although obviously essential for earthly life, was not important for eternal life.[11]

Jesus' most insightful teaching on life after death was given in response to a question raised by some Sadducees, the name of the priestly party in Jerusalem. For the sake of argument they posited the notion of an individual life after death in order to expose its inanity. They found no basis for belief in any type of resurrection in the five "books of Moses." According to Josephus, they held that "the soul perishes with the body, and they disregarded the observation of anything except what the [Mosaic] Law enjoins."[12] The conservative Sadducees scorned the newfangled notions that apocalyptic Judaism had imported. Quite accurately, they recognized that the concept of a personal afterlife became accepted by some in the Hebrew culture centuries after the Torah was written.

To ridicule the resurrection doctrine accepted by the rival party of Pharisees, the Sadducees added a stinging question to an old Jewish tale. The book of Tobit tells about seven husbands who died in succession

---

[9]*Sanhedrin* 92b; *Shabbath* 30b; this is denied in *Berakoth* 17a.

[10]Benjamin Mazar, ed., *Views of the Biblical World* (Jerusalem: International Publishing, 1960) 3:195.

[11]Colleen McDannell and Bernhard Lang, *Heaven—A History* (New Haven: Yale University Press, 1988) 29; Matthew 8:22, 10:28.

[12]Josephus, *Antiquities* 13:297, 18:14-16.

shortly after marrying the same bride.[13] The Sadducees asked Jesus which one of the spouses would be married to the widow in an alleged supernatural restoration. Rather than seeking information, they were trying to trap him into advocating a nontraditional idea that they thought was absurd. The Torah sanctioned polygyny but not polyandry, so a wife could not have multiple spouses concurrently.

Jesus' view of the afterlife differed from the prevailing views of his time. In contrast to the Sadducees, he held that there is continuance of life after death because of the nature of God. He twitted them by asking if they had read the "passage about the bush" from a scroll they accepted as the word of God. Jesus then quoted from the burning bush story about God's call to shepherd Moses, "I am . . . the God of Abraham, the God of Isaac, and the God of Jacob."[14] Jesus appeals to the present tense—"I *am*"—to prove that those Hebrew patriarchs, who had physically died centuries before the time of Moses, continue to be in an undying personal relationship with God. To be dead to humans does not necessarily mean to be dead to God. About Abraham and his descendants, Jesus commented, "God is not God of the dead but of the living; for to him all of them are alive."[15] Jesus claimed that God does not permit the covenant he has established to be severed by the physical death of "those who are judged worthy."[16] Perceiving that the Sadducees did not comprehend the way in which the character of the eternal God they professed implied continued life for the faithful, Jesus charged, "You know neither the scriptures nor the power of God."[17]

Contrary to the general outlook of the Pharisees, Jesus did not accept that a postmortem life involved a revival and extension of physical life. He affirmed, "When humans rise from the dead they will not marry but will be like angels in heaven."[18] The reference to "heaven" does not emphasize a physical place, but a nonspatial and nontemporal condition. On the negative side, Jesus asserted that the afterlife is not a biological continuation of assimilating nourishment and generating new life. Reproduction is needed

---

[13]Tobit 3:8.
[14]Exodus 3:6.
[15]Luke 20:38.
[16]Luke 20:35.
[17]Mark 12:24.
[18]Mark 12:25.

only in a mortal society that must replace the perpetually dying in order to avert extinction. The procreative purpose of marriage is removed in a state in which humans "cannot die any more."[19] The exclusive pairings of mortals might well be transformed to inclusive bondings, but the communion of the many would not diminish the love and joy experienced in the present life.

The argument between Jesus and the Sadducees illustrates the way in which our earthbound imaginations pale at intuiting the nonsensory, thus limiting our understanding. His interlocutors presumed that those accepting a resurrection doctrine all think in a literal and supernatural manner. But Jesus treated the "whose wife" question as irrelevant because the social bonding of the physical realm will be transcended in the life after death. Astronomer Carl Sagan observed the mundane way in which scientists rely on forms already known as they try to imagine extraterrestrial life.[20] Imagining intelligent life in another galaxy, or conceiving of fleshless selves among whom there is personal communication, requires a radically different mode of thinking. In a parallel manner, we are often no more able to envisage what is beyond space and time than fetuses, living in darkness and fluid, are able to imagine what it is like to smell stimulating aromas and see colorful sights. Jesus declared that the nature of life after death, like the nature of God, exceeds our fondest imaginings.[21]

Embellishments by the Evangelists

During the first century of Christianity there was a major shift in viewpoint on the nature of the life after death. As we have demonstrated, it was initially believed that God resurrected Jesus spiritually and that such would be the pattern for other righteous humans. Within a few decades, however, the earliest position became transposed into a doctrine of fleshly resurrection for both bad and good people. After Paul's death, his perspective on an altogether nonphysical afterlife was gradually eclipsed by a carnal creed. That heightened supernaturalism has been accepted as basic truth by most Christians and, prior to the past century, pivotal leaders of Catholicism and Protestantism have been in general agreement on the subject.

[19]Luke 20:36.

[20]Carl Sagan, *Cosmos* (New York: Random House, 1980) 40.

[21]See William Phipps, "Jesus on Marriage and the Afterlife," *Christian Century* (3 April 1985): 327-28.

Why has stress been placed on Jesus' physical resurrection from the second generation of Christianity onward? New Testament scholar John Knox explains that the reliance of the first Christians on visions of the risen Jesus encountered "the objection that the evidence, if not faked, was dreamed." "The inevitable effect of this kind of challenge was a tendency toward the materializing of the appearances."[22]

Mark provides the first post-Pauline narrative expansions of the core Easter message. Randel Helms explains:

> Paul did not know the Gospel resurrection stories, for the simple reason that they had not yet been invented, and the four evangelists, who wrote twenty to fifty years after Paul, either did not know his list of appearances or chose to ignore it. Perhaps most surprising of all the differences is Paul's failure to mention the legend of the empty tomb, which was, for the writer of the earliest Gospel, the only public, visible evidence for the resurrection. . . . Indeed, he [Paul] had probably never heard of it; it was a legend that grew up in Christian communities different from his own. . . . Paul would not have agreed with Mark's theology even had he known it; for Paul, resurrection meant not the resuscitation of a corpse involving the removal of a stone and the emptying of a tomb, but a transformation from a dead physical body to a living spiritual one.[23]

The empty tomb stories were not the result of the male disciples reporting on what they had seen. E. P. Sanders explains the situation: "His disciples, reasonably thinking that they would be next, hid. Some of his women followers—who were safer than the men and possibly braver—watched him die and saw Josephus of Arimathea bury his body."[24] According to Mark, the women did not see a postmortem Jesus but a "young man," who happened to be at the tomb and informed Peter and the other disciples: "He [Jesus] is going ahead of you to Galilee; there you will see him, as he told you." Since Peter was in Jerusalem early Friday on the day of crucifixion but then fled, as Mark indicates,[25] then Jesus' appearance in Galilee must have been after Peter had time to walk seventy miles. That would be a several day trip, but there would not have been sufficient time

---

[22]John Knox, *Chapters in a Life of Paul* (Macon GA: Mercer, 1987) 100.

[23]Randel Helms, *Gospel Fictions* (Buffalo NY: Prometheus, 1988) 130.

[24]E. P. Sanders, *The Historical Figure of Jesus* (New York: Penguin, 1993) 276.

[25]Mark 14:50.

for that during the day and a half before Sunday morning, especially if he honored the Jewish Sabbath as a day when extensive travel was not sanctioned.

Mark probably introduced the empty tomb legend as an apologetic device to convince those who required material evidence before accepting something as true. He did not need to fear that the empirical claim might be tested because he was probably writing from Italy about the time Jerusalem was being destroyed by the Romans. Even if someone hearing the story were able to verify where Jesus was buried through a graveyard search, what identifiable remains of a corpse could be found several decades later in a land with a warm climate and limestone geology?

The tomb legend is set in a Jerusalem graveyard and revolves around women who come to anoint Jesus' body with deodorants for obscuring the stench of decaying flesh. It mentions that a large stone sealing the entrance of the borrowed tomb was rolled aside. As the women enter it, they observe that it is vacant. The empty tomb accretion is recorded here for the first time, but it is peripheral because it does not give the women assurance that Jesus is resurrected. Indeed, the women leave in terror rather than in gladness, and do not breathe a word to anyone about what transpired.[26] Mark's comment about the silent women, which is the last sentence of his authentic Gospel, was probably made to explain why the empty tomb story was unknown to the first church leaders and did not emerge until some time later. As a record of what actually happened, it is implausible that women disciples who were courageous enough to remain with Jesus throughout his crucifixion while angry adversaries were gathered around, were fearful to tell others in the Jesus movement that his tomb was empty. Günther Bornkamm compares Mark's Easter story with those that will come in later Gospels: "The wonderful event of the resurrection is not even depicted, such is the reticence and awe. This is very different from later legends, which raise the miracle to the level of the fantastic, elaborate it without restraint, and make even guards and elders its witnesses."[27]

* * *

The Gospel of Matthew, written about a decade after Mark, makes major revisions in the Markan death and resurrection story. According to

---

[26]Mark 16:1-8.

[27]Günther Bornhamm, *Jesus of Nazareth* (New York: Harper, 1960) 182.

Mark, the curtain that closed off the Holy of Holies in the Jewish temple ripped apart when Jesus died.[28] Mark's readers may have understood the torn curtain comment to symbolize that Christians now have unhindered access to God. But Matthew gave the story a literal emphasis by providing a cosmic event to account for the tear. At the hour when Jesus died, Matthew alleges, an earthquake in the region of Jerusalem not only tore that curtain but effected a mystifying supernatural happening: "The earth shook and the rocks split. The tombs opened, and many bodies of the saints who had fallen asleep were raised. After Jesus was raised they came out of the tombs and showed themselves to many in the holy city."[29] Matthew treats literally Daniel's prophecy of dead saints awakening, providing a basis for Christians naming their graveyards "cemeteries," from Latin *coemeteria*, meaning "sleeping places." Those saints of old who were allegedly sighted on the streets of Jerusalem were probably Hebrew prophets and patriarchs. Matthew wished to show that Jesus' revivified body was in accord with the a physical resurrection of devout humans generally. This tale is so bizarre that it has largely received the silent treatment by interpreters of the Gospels. Who has heard an Easter sermon about many resurrected bodies of dead holy people emerging from their tombs and moving about in Jerusalem at the same time as a resurrected Jesus was being seen?

Mark and Matthew differ markedly over what was awesome about Jesus' finale. Mark, written especially to convince Romans of the truth of the gospel, reaches its climax when a Roman centurion in charge of the crucifixion detail declares, "Truly this man was God's son."[30] The soldier came to that conclusion after observing Jesus' human demeanor during his last hours, not after being shaken by an earthquake triggered by the crucifixion. But Matthew states that the terror precipitated by the earthquake at the moment of Jesus' death was what prompted the confession.[31]

The circulation of Mark's story of the empty tomb was the likely cause of some adversaries of the Christians claiming that Jesus' body had been stolen. To counter that charge Matthew apparently invents a story about Pilate assigning a squad of soldiers, at the request of the Jewish authorities, to prevent the opening of the tomb that had been sealed. Because of that

---

[28]Mark 15:38.
[29]Matthew 27:51-53.
[30]Mark 15:39.
[31]Matthew 27:54.

addition, Matthew needed to drop Mark's account about women entering
the unguarded tomb with their spices after finding the stone at its entrance
rolled back. Matthew tells of the women on Sunday at dawn just going to
see the tomb, at which time they are confronted by a divine intervention
into nature: "Suddenly there was a violent earthquake; an angel of the Lord,
descending from heaven, came and rolled back the stone and sat on it. His
[the angel's] face shone like lightning and his clothing was white as snow."
Matthew assumes, as did the composer of the *Gospel of Peter*, that the
physically resurrected Jesus needed an opening in the tomb to get out.
Mark's "young man dressed in a white robe," who announced to the women
that Jesus had been raised from the tomb has been replaced by a luminous
angelophany.[32] When the terrified Roman guards return to the city and tell
the Jewish priests what had happened, they are paid by the Sanhedrin to lie
to their superiors. They testify that they went to sleep while on duty and, at
that time, Jesus' disciples stole his corpse.[33] Matthew would have his
readers believe that the soldiers were so imprudent as to risk being executed
by the Roman command by confessing that they neglected their duty in
exchange for a bribe.

Matthew did recognize that the core of Mark's account is the proclamation in the graveyard, "He is not here; he has been risen." All the rest is an
elaboration and should not be interpreted as description of the event. The
Matthean account features Jesus greeting the women in Jerusalem and states
that they "clasped" the feet of his materialized body and "worshiped him."[34]
Then, on a mountain in Galilee, the eleven male disciples "saw" Jesus, and
they also respond by Jesusolatry. All of them, including some doubters
(*distazo*), are commissioned to make Christian disciples internationally.[35]
Peter may have been among those whom Matthew thought were skeptical,
because the only other New Testament use of the Greek term *distazo* is by
Matthew in reference to that disciple.[36] The concluding paragraph of
Matthew does not indicate that the doubts were relieved, so a questioning
faith seems to have been accepted in nascent Christianity.

---

[32]Mark 16:6; Matthew 28:2-6.
[33]Matthew 28:11-14.
[34]Matthew 28:9.
[35]Matthew 28:16-19.
[36]Matthew 14:31.

* * *

The Lukan redactions display another step in objectifying Jesus' resurrection, making it more real to the unsophisticated. The quantity of Luke's embellishments are striking. Paul, although his experience of the resurrection was firsthand, took what is now six verses to tell about it in 1 Corinthians 15. The Evangelists, all of whom are transmitting second or thirdhand experiences, write more: eight verses are found in Mark, twenty in Matthew, and Luke contains no less than fifty. The number of angels has doubled from Matthew's account. The women, far from remaining silent, "told all."[37] Mark has no account of Jesus sightings, but Luke tells of two on Easter Sunday in Judea.

Luke illustrates what additions are needed when the proclamation of a vision of the risen Jesus is developed into a story. Reginald Fuller comments, "Appearances could be narrated only by borrowing the traits of the earthly Jesus—he must walk, talk, eat, etc., as he had done in his earthly life. These features . . . are now drawn out and emphasized in the interests of apologetic."[38] The resurrected Jesus only speaks in Matthew but in Luke he walks and talks with two of his disciples, who find him physically indistinguishable from others traveling the road to their village.

After the travelers to Emmaus expressed despair over the crucifixion of "the one to redeem Israel," the stranger fanned the embers of their dying hope. He asked them if they did not realize that the Hebrew prophets had declared that it was necessary for the promised messiah to suffer before entering into his "glory," and explained the way in which all of scripture pertained to himself. Possibly considered was a passage from the Wisdom of Solomon that was written about a century before the Gospel of Luke and included in the Greek Bible. There the wicked say:

> Let us lie in wait for the righteous man; . . . the very sight of him is a burden to us, because his manner of life is unlike that of others, . . . and boasts that God is his father. . . . If the righteous man is God's son, he will help him, and rescue him from the clutches of his enemies. Let us test him with insult and torture, so that we may find out how gentle he is, and put his patience to the test. Let us condemn him to a shameful death. . . . They did not know the secret purposes of God, . . . nor discern the prize for blameless souls; for God created

---

[37]Luke 24:9.

[38]Reginald Fuller, *The Formation of the Resurrection Narratives* (New York: Macmillan, 1971) 115.

us for incorruption, and made us in the image of his own eternity. . . . The souls of the righteous are in the hand of God, and no torment will ever touch them. In the eyes of the foolish they seem to have died, and their departure was regarded as a disaster, and their going from us to be their destruction; but they are at peace.[39]

At Emmaus, the two disciples persuade the scriptural interpreter to share with them an evening meal. "Their eyes were opened, and they recognized him" as "he said the blessing, broke the bread, and gave it to them."[40] The mysterious stranger then supernaturally "vanished" into thin air, after which the couple hasten back seven miles to Jerusalem to report what happened. There they find the eleven core disciples and their friends excitedly heralding, "The Lord has really been raised and was seen by Simon [Peter]!"[41] Whereupon Jesus suddenly stood among them and invited them to feel his hands and feet. To suppress the earlier tradition that sightings of him were noncorporeal, the Lukan Jesus proves that he has "flesh and bones" and is not an insubstantial spirit (*pneuma*) by eating a piece of broiled fish in the presence of his disciples.[42] Luke believed that the revivified Jesus had an operative digestive system and fleshly muscles that enabled his bones to move about.

Theodor Keim observes that the Gospel resurrection accounts cater to those who equate real with material, "To meet Jewish mistrust and calumny, as objective and materialistic a colouring was given to the resurrection as was possible."[43] By contrast, Paul had no problem in writing about the risen Christ, the "spirit of Christ," and the "spirit of God" as though the expressions were interchangeable.[44] For him, the term "spirit" (pneuma), which he uses more often than all the Evangelists combined, pertained to what was truly real, although immaterial.

Consistency is of little concern to Luke because his resurrected Jesus walks like other earthlings on the road to Emmaus yet appears and disappears like a ghost. He can dematerialize like magic in one place and

---

[39]Wisdom 2:12, 15-16, 18-20, 22-23; 3:1-3.
[40]Luke 24:13-31.
[41]Luke 24:34.
[42]Luke 24:36-43.
[43]Theodor Keim, *The History of Jesus of Nazareth* (London: Williams, 1883) 6:299-300.
[44]Romans 8:9-10.

rematerialize in another. If Jesus ate and had a healthy body during the alleged forty days he was in the Jerusalem environs after his resurrection, he must have had internal organs functioning and have been seen publicly as he moved about on foot, as previously. Awareness of these problems has influenced Peter Carnley to prefer the way Luke later described the apprehension of the raised Jesus as a "heavenly vision,"[45] and suggests that designation as the best way of interpreting all of them. He rejects the notion "that qualitatively quite different experiences were given to different people, so that some might be said to have seen Jesus in a concrete, material form and others in a more ethereal, visionary or spiritual form."[46]

There is also a basic conflict with the other Synoptic Gospels in that the Lukan Jesus instructs the apostles to stay in Jerusalem, beginning with resurrection day and continuing for the remaining weeks of his earthly physical presence.[47] In order to make the area of Jerusalem exclusively the place of Jesus sightings, Luke omits what his Markan source said about the disciples fleeing at the time of the crucifixion. According to Mark, they would encounter the risen Jesus in Galilee, but Luke makes no allowance for appearances there. The Gospel of Luke ends with Jesus being "carried up into heaven" at the end of the long Easter day.[48]

Maurice Goguel states:

> The growing materialisation of the appearances affected the place where they were thought to have happened. By insisting more and more on the idea that the corpse came to life again, men were bound to tend to place the appearances near the tomb where the corpse had been laid. . . . The Galilean tradition can be said for certain to be the earlier. It is impossible to suppose that it could be formed on the basis of a Judaean tradition while the converse development is easy to explain. . . . Appearances in Galilee . . . were quickly forgotten because so far as we know Christianity did not develop in Galilee in its earliest days to any appreciable extent.[49]

---

[45]Acts 26:19.

[46]Peter Carnley, *The Structure of Resurrection Belief* (Oxford: Clarendon, 1987) 241.

[47]Luke 24:49; Acts 1:3-4.

[48]Luke 24:51; Acts 1:1-2.

[49]Maurice Goguel, *The Birth of Christianity* (London: Allen & Unwin, 1953) 59.

For his second scroll, the anonymous author of Luke/Acts—named "Luke" for convenience of discussion—constructed a story that is inconsistent with his own claim that Jesus had already been taken up to heaven. Acts 1:3-10 differs from his first "book" because Luke wished to provide for several weeks of exposure to Jesus' postmortem corporeal body. The Evangelist then needed a way of getting rid of the "flesh and bones" body, since he recognized at the time when he was writing that Christians had long since ceased to claim that they had witnessed the risen Jesus moving about. Therefore, Luke describes the removal from earth of Jesus' body after he presented himself alive and spoke for forty days about the kingdom of God. This made way for the acts of the Holy Spirit that began a week later on the day of Pentecost.[50] By contrast, it was on Easter day when the Johannine Jesus bestowed the "Holy Spirit" on his followers.[51]

Luke was aware that religions commonly locate in the sky the divine realm and that humans who ascend at death become more godly. He was informed primarily by the story of astronaut Elijah standing in a chariot and being propelled into heaven by fiery horses and a whirlwind. But Jesus, the greater Elijah, does not need that means of transportation, for his body can ascend on its own power. After lifting off from Mount Olivet, "a cloud took him," and two angels, as similarly described in Luke's Easter story, announce that he will return in the same way he went to heaven. The Israelite scribe also states that disciple Elisha, after witnessing Elijah's departure, received a double portion of Elijah's spirit.[52] Accordingly, Jesus' disciples received a bountiful share of the Spirit at Pentecost.

Hebrew scripture was the quarry from which the Evangelists extracted some of their accounts of Jesus' life. By way of legitimizing that literary approach, the Lukan Jesus states, "Everything written about me in the law of Moses, the prophets, and the psalms must be fulfilled."[53] For example, a line from a psalmist's prayer for deliverance alive from his enemies is treated by Luke as a reference to Jesus' last words before dying. Alone among the Evangelists he audaciously places on the lips of Jesus this prayer, "Into your hands I commit my spirit."[54] Luke, wishing to portray a

---

[50]Acts 2:1-42.
[51]John 20:22.
[52]2 Kings 2:9-11.
[53]Luke 24:44.
[54]Psalm 30:5; Luke 23:46.

serene Jesus, substituted those final words for what Mark had taken from another psalm, "My God, my God, why have you forsaken me?"[55]

In his second book on the beginnings of Christianity, Luke has both of his main heroes appealing to an alleged prophecy by King David regarding one of his descendants' physical resurrection. Peter proclaims in his Pentecost sermon, "David foresaw the resurrection of the messiah when he said, 'He was not abandoned to death, nor did his flesh experience corruption.'" But the psalm quoted here, in the original Hebrew text, has no reference to resurrection of any kind. The psalmist actually expressed confidence that God would not permit him to die and that he would again enjoy the pleasures of life. Luke's conviction that Jesus was physically resurrected may have been due to the Septuagint's mistranslation of the Hebrew. Relying again on the Greek misunderstanding of the original text, Luke also attributes to Paul this exposition, "For David, after he had served the purpose of God in his own generation, died, was laid beside his ancestors, and experienced corruption; but he whom God raised up experienced no corruption."[56] This message that Luke composed for Paul is contrary to that of the historical Paul, who believed, as has been shown, that the physical bodies of Jesus and his followers were subjected to the same organic corruption.

Luke has such pronounced differences from Paul in religious outlook that, in all likelihood, they were not missionary companions, as some second-generation Christians claimed.[57] The ascension story satisfies those accepting a physical resurrection of Jesus but Paul needed no two-stage rising of Jesus, first from below to above ground and then from earth to heaven. He considered Jesus' spiritual resurrection and his heavenly exaltation to be parts of one event. He did not allude to Christ returning to Palestine and tarrying there for some days after his resurrection, but he affirmed one "who was raised, who is at the right hand of God."[58]

* * *

[55]Psalm 22:1; Mark 15:34.

[56]Psalm 16:10; Acts 2:27, 31; 13:35-37.

[57]See Gerd Theissen and Annette Merz, *The Historical Jesus* (Philadelphia: Fortress, 1996) 32.

[58]Romans 8:34.

The Fourth Gospel contains an alleged resuscitation of someone who will subsequently be returned to his tomb. The revival is treated as an harbinger of deathless resurrection even though it results in a postponement of eventual physical death. The lengthy story of Lazarus may have been intended to illustrate the convervation between Lazarus' sisters and Jesus in which he asserts that he is the giver of "resurrection and life" that persists beyond death everlasting.[59] The fiction that follows is inept because it confuses resurrection with resusciatation—something categorically different. Although Lazarus is assumed by others to be irrevocably dead because he had been buried for four days, the story climaxes when Jesus shouts at the entrance to his tomb, "Lazarus, come out!" He responds by walking out, even though he is bound from head to toe with strips of cloth.[60] After this restoration, he resumes his previous physical existence by eating food and continuing to live a normal life in his Bethany home.[61] According to John, the performance of this and other supernatural signs caused Jesus' popularity to soar, steeling the resolve of the ruling Jewish council to put him to death.[62] If such a spectacular event had really happened and was accompanied by such dire consequences, why would this story of Lazarus not have been at least mentioned in the earlier Gospels? By contrast, the Synoptics give a plausible reason why Jesus was placed on trial for his life, namely, the Jerusalem priests' retaliation for his disruption of their huckstering in the Temple.[63]

Theologian Rudolf Otto compares the Lazarus story with a nonsupernatural but "genuine miracle" in Mark's Gospel.[64] He comments on the story of Jarius' daughter who had lost consciousness only a short time before Jesus arrived at her home: "There is nothing grandiose or theatrical. . . . The whole incident closes with the soberly practical injunction to give the newly restored child food, and with the direct prohibition to talk further about the event." But Otto notes that in John's Gospel, Jesus expresses pleasure that he was not present when his beloved friend died. This provides him with an occasion for performing a supernatural feat in a dramatic way

---

[59]John 11:17-27.
[60]John 11:39-44.
[61]John 12:1-2.
[62]John 11:45-53.
[63]Mark 11:15-18; Luke 19:45-47.
[64]Mark 5:22-23, 40-43.

that will have a big effect. At the Lazarus's tomb in Bethany, Jesus uses a prayer to inform spectators that God always hears him. He admits, "I have said this for the sake of the crowd standing here."[65]

John concludes with even more embellishments than the other Gospels, which is to be expected in a record that dates two generations after Jesus' death. Peter and the "beloved disciple" race to the tomb; the latter "saw and believed." No object is given for that sighting so there is no way of knowing whether it was intended to be physical or spiritual. The linen wrappings for Jesus' corpse were found left behind in the tomb; they were not unwound, showing that his corpse miraculously passed out of them and escaped from the grave. In that Gospel the resurrected Jesus was ghostlike enough to go through locked doors, yet tangible enough for him to encourage Thomas to feel the crucifixion scars in his hands and side. If persons today saw something like that they would rate it as spectacular magic. But in the same chapter twenty of John there is, as I have discussed, Magdalene's vision of the resurrected Jesus that needs not be given a supernatural interpretation.

The New Testament displays a shift in epistemology, resulting in an increasing tendency to flesh out the picture of Jesus' resurrection held by the earliest Christians. In the course of a few decades, striking modifications were made to the earliest tradition of Jesus' resurrection. We know that Paul, the first to record what the apostolic authorities had conveyed to him, did not testify to an empty tomb, attending angels and guards, or an earthquake removing its sealing stone. Nor did he tell of disciples touching his resurrected body. Had that apostle known, surely he would have communicated to the Corinthians all the proof Peter and James had given him of that crucial event, even the negative witness of a vacated place where Jesus was buried. Paul declared with total certainty that Jesus had risen but gave no attention to providing *objective* proof. Whereas Paul, and probably the other apostles, did not accept that Jesus' flesh and bones had been resurrected, a half-century later when the Third and Fourth Gospels were being written, Jesus' body is portrayed as able to assimilate food in a life after death. The supernatural evidence offered in Luke and John is directed toward empiricists such as Thomas. He had said, "Unless I see the mark of the nails in his hands, and put my finger in the mark of the nails

---

[65]John 11:11-15, 42; Rudolf Otto, *The Idea of the Holy* (London: Oxford University Press, 1926) 215-16.

and my hand in his side, I will not believe."[66] Each Evangelist seems to want to outdo previous accounts in providing documentation of Jesus' alleged physical resurrection that would satisfy the common, naive empiricist. Poorly educated people in every age and many modern physical scientists tend to accept only what is perceivable as true and real, which causes a basic problem for those who claim that the most real experiences in life are intangible. This would include not only the religious worshiper, but also the theoretical mathematician and the musical listener.

Lutheran theologian Wolfhart Pannenberg has concluded:

> The [resurrection] appearances reported in the Gospels, which are not mentioned by Paul, have such a strongly legendary character that one can scarcely find a historical kernel of their own in them. Even the Gospels' reports that correspond to Paul's statements are heavily colored by legendary elements, particularly by the tendency toward underlining the corporeality of the appearances.[67]

Nag Hammadi documents expert James Robinson, in his presidential address to the Society of Biblical Literature, adroitly showed how the ancient Christian texts discovered during the past century support the assumption that the physicality of Jesus' resurrection in the canonical Gospels "reflects a secondary stage in the transmission of resurrection appearances." His analysis of early Christian writings demonstrates that what came to be accepted as orthodox Easter doctrine was established on a misinterpretation of the primary stage of Christianity. The church was launched not by the physical resurrection of Christ but by visions of a luminous spiritual body to which Paul refers. After those visionary experiences faded, apologists wrote of alleged objective happenings in an attempt to prove the Easter event.[68]

Postbiblical Views

Within a few years of Luke's and John's writing about the risen Jesus proving that he was not a bodiless ghost, normative doctrine molder Ignatius, convinced by that record, affirmed, "I believe that even after the

---

[66]John 20:25.

[67]Wolfhart Pannenberg, *Jesus, God and Man* (Philadelphia: Westminster, 1968) 89.

[68]*Journal of Biblical Literature* 101 (January 1982): 12-16.

resurrection he was in the flesh."[69] Moreover, he stated that Christian believers will be raised just as God raised Jesus.[70] Albert Schweitzer contrasts Ignatius with Paul, who thought of the flesh "as something doomed by its nature to perish." "For Paul," Schweitzer continues, "the Spirit [of God] unites [in the resurrection] with the spiritual part of man's personality; for Ignatius, with his fleshly corporeity."[71]

In his *History of Christian Thought*, Arthur McGiffert observes that, other than some Gnostics who were judged unorthodox, Christians living after the New Testament era held a doctrine of the resurrection that was essentially opposed to Paul's. He stated, "Most of the early Christians interpreted it in materialistic terms as the resurrection of the present fleshly body."[72] McGiffert illustrates this outlook by quoting from a second-century sermon, "Let none of you say that this flesh is not judged and does not rise again."[73]

Doctrine pertaining to the resurrection affects the treatment of corpses. During the first Christian century, neither the burial sites nor the relics of church leaders were hallowed. The veneration of the remains of martyrs began after the death of Bishop Polycarp, a second-century defender of orthodoxy. In his dying prayer he affirmed his belief in "the resurrection to eternal life of both soul and body, made incorruptible by the Holy Spirit." He was burned alive on a pyre by adversaries who believed they were thereby destroying his possibility for resurrection. Polycarp's biographer, from his diocese of Smyrna, wrote that his bones were annually celebrated on "the birthday of his martyrdom, making them "more valuable than precious stones and more splendid than gold."[74] Church historian Eusebius also reports that executioners of martyrs in Gaul thought they were making doubly sure that God could not restore martyrs to eternal life by throwing their charred remains into the Rhone River. They said mockingly, "Now let's see if they'll rise again, and if their god can help them and save them

---

[69]Ignatius, *Smyrna* 3.

[70]Ignatius, *Trillians* 9.

[71]Albert Schweitzer, *The Mysticism of Paul the Apostle* (New York: Holt, 1931) 342.

[72]Arthur McGiffert, *A History of Christian Thought* (New York: Scribner's, 1932–1933) 1:88-89, 142.

[73]2 Clement 9:1.

[74]Eusebius, *Church History* 4.15.

from our hands."[75] Gaius, writing around 200, is the first to refer to Peter's burial monument on Vatican hill.[76] Even though his bones would be the most prestigious of all remains, none have been confirmed by archeologists who have spent years searching for them under St. Peter's Cathedral.[77]

Apocryphal gospels, written during the century after the canonical Gospels, satisfied the growing hunger for more detailed information about physical resurrection. Nowhere in the New Testament is this question asked or answered: how did Jesus rise? No one in the first century claimed to have witnessed Jesus' exit from the tomb. That gap was partly filled by a fantastic story in the *Gospel of Peter*. Two shining beings descend from heaven to the sepulcher where Jesus was buried and enter it on "the Lord's day" after the sealing stone rolled itself back. Presently, the Roman soldiers and Jewish elders guarding the tomb see three beings come out, "two of them sustaining the other, and a cross following them, and the heads of the two reaching to heaven, but that of him who was led of them by the hand overpassing the heavens." The soldiers, on reporting to Pilate what they witnessed happening to Jesus, confess, "Truly he was the Son of God."[78]

According to the *Gospel of the Hebrews*, Jesus verifies his physical resurrection to the Jerusalem authorities by giving his burial shroud to the servant of the high priest, and then he searches for his brother James.[79] Another apocryphal account attempts to confirm the doctrine that there was a physical resurrection for Jesus and that consequently there will be the same for all humans. These words are put into the mouth of the risen Jesus: "That you may know that it is I, lay your finger, Peter, in the nail print of my hands; and you, Thomas, in my side; and also you, Andrew, see whether my foot steps on the ground and leaves a footprint. For it is written in the prophet, 'A ghost, a demon, leaves no print on the ground.'" The apostles respond, "Now we felt him, that he had truly risen in the flesh."[80] The *Gospel of Nicodemus* tells of Jesus' descent into hell after his crucifixion,

---

[75]Eusebius, *Church History* 5.1.

[76]Gaius, *Dialogues* quoted in Eusebius, *Church History* 2.25.

[77]*Atlantic Monthly* (October 2003): 141-43.

[78]*Gospel of Peter* 9-11.

[79]Wilhelm Schneemelcher, ed., *New Testament Apocrypha* (Philadelphia: 1965) 1:165.

[80]*Epistula Apostolorum* 11; in Schneemelcher 1:197.

and before his resurrection, to break down its gates, to seize Satan, and to release Adam and others.[81]

In subsequent apocryphal acts of the apostles, Paul states: "As for those who tell you that there is no resurrection of the flesh, for them there is no resurrection. . . . You know that Jonah . . . was swallowed by a whale, and after three days and three nights God heard Jonah's prayer out of deepest hell, and no part of him was corrupted, not even a hair or an eyelid."[82] Paul restores life to a boy in Antioch, to a man called Dion in Myra, and to a woman named Frontina who had been thrown from a rock.[83] The *Acts of Paul* concludes with the apostle before Nero predicting the consequences of his decapitation, "If you behead me, I will arise and show you that I am not dead." As he died, milk rather than blood spurted on the executioner's clothing. Then he returns to the emperor and announces: "Caesar, here I am—Paul, God's soldier. I am not dead, but alive in my God. But for you, unhappy man, there shall be many evils and great punishment." Apostle Andrew is alleged to have raised nine persons from the dead resulting in many who witnessed these separate events being converted to Christianity.[84] The *Acts of John* tells of that apostle raising several people who had died, and the *Acts of Peter* tells of that apostle doing the same.[85]

Most second-century Christians accepted a theme of the last book of the New Testament in believing that their dead will enjoy a millennial reign with Christ.[86] John the Seer had described a first resurrection for 144,000 martyred male virgins followed by a second resurrection after the final judgment.[87] An Eden-like creation renewal will ensue: "I saw the holy city, the new Jerusalem, coming down out of heaven from God. . . . I heard a loud voice proclaiming from the throne: 'Now the home of God is among

[81]*Gospel of Nicodemus* 22, 24; in Schneemelcher 1:474.

[82]*Acts of Paul* 24; in Schneemelcher 2:376-77.

[83]*Acts of Paul* 4, 8; in Schneemelcher 2:365, 378.

[84]Gregory of Tours, *Epitome* 3, 7, 14, 18-19, 23-24.

[85]*Acts of John* 23, 51-52, 75, 80; *Acts of Peter* 27-28; in Schneemelcher 2:219, 240, 249, 251, 309-10.

[86]Revelation 20:4; J. G. Davies, "Factors Leading to the Emergence of Belief in the Resurrection of the Flesh," *Journal of Theological Studies* (October 1972): 449.

[87]Revelation 14:1-4.

mortals. He will dwell with them and they shall be his people.' "[88] According to Papias, Bishop of Phrygia, "After the resurrection of the dead there will be a period of a thousand years, when Christ's kingdom will be set up on this earth in material form."[89] Soon afterward Justin declared, "Christians who hold the true faith in all things know that there will be a resurrection of the flesh, and that a thousand year period will come in the restored, adorned, and greater Jerusalem of which the prophets Ezekiel, Isaiah, and the rest speak."[90] Justin was the first to use the phrase "resurrection of the flesh" that was featured in later creedal statements. He believed that the mundane body of Christians will be exactly replicated in the life after death.[91] Jesus performed miracles on bodies, according to Justin, as a sign of their eventual imperishable physical restoration. His healings were "to arouse the belief that, at the resurrection, the flesh as a whole will rise again; for, if he healed the weaknesses of the flesh and made the body whole on earth, he will do that still more so at the resurrection, so that the flesh also rises uninjured and whole."[92]

Following Justin, but in the Latin culture, Tertullian described the millennial rule by saints, which would be followed by the last judgment:

> What a spectacle is that fast approaching advent of our Lord! . . . What glory of the saints as they rise again! What a kingdom of the righteous thereafter! What a city, the new Jerusalem! Judgment Day is another sight to come. . . . What causes me to rejoice? I see mighty emperors, whose ascent to heaven used to be announced, . . . groaning in the depths of darkness, and governors of provinces melting in flames fiercer than those they kindled against the Christians. Whom else shall I behold? Those philosophers blushing as they burn together with their disciples, . . . whom they assured that their souls would never return to their former bodies.[93]

Millennialism continued to impact European Christianity, replacing Paul's view of the resurrection with a belief in the fleshly restoration of the dead. McGiffert, in explaining why the clause "resurrection of the flesh" is in the so-called "Apostles' Creed," states: "The church at large was not

---

[88]Revelation 21:2-3.
[89]Eusebius, *Church History* 3:39.
[90]Justin, *Dialogue with Trypho* 80.
[91]Justin, *Apology* 1:8.
[92]Justin, *On Resurrection* 4.
[93]Tertullian, *Spectacles* 30.

satisfied with Paul's doctrine of a spiritual body . . . but insisted upon the resurrection of this very flesh, with all its particles intact and unchanged, in order to prepare the believer for the earthly millennial kingdom [to] which Christ was to return and establish."[94]

Influential church father Tertullian could not have been more explicit in insisting that Jesus' resurrection pertained to "this flesh, suffused with blood, built up with bones, interwoven with nerves, entwined with veins." For a proof text he quoted words that Luke put in the mouth of the resurrected Jesus, "Feel me and see that it is I myself, for a ghost does not have flesh and bones as you see I have."[95] The church father readily admitted that belief in the physical resurrection of Jesus was irrational, "He rose again; the fact is certain because it is impossible."[96]

Paul's logic that the resurrection for Christians is of the same type as the resurrection of Christ was accepted by Tertullian.[97] He said: "For a dead man to be raised again amounts to nothing short of his being restored to his entire condition. . . . God is quite able to remake what he once made. . . . The flesh shall arise again, wholly and entire in every person."[98] Tertullian tortured Paul's declaration that "flesh and blood cannot inherit the kingdom of God" by claiming that the apostle meant that all humans will rise physically, but only those who have been spiritually sanctified will become members of God's kingdom.[99] Christ will return with this mission, "He will come again to take the saints to the enjoyment of everlasting life . . . and to condemn the wicked to everlasting fire, after the resurrection of both these classes shall have happened, together with the restoration of their flesh."[100] All will stand on judgment day with limbs restored that were amputated and teeth that were extracted. Dental renewal will be especially needed by the damned. Without such, asks Tertullian, how can Jesus' prophecy be fulfilled that there will be "gnashing of teeth" by those in hell?[101]

---

[94]Arthur McGiffert, *The Apostles' Creed* (New York: Scribner's, 1902) 20-21.
[95]Luke 24:39.
[96]Tertullian, *On the Flesh of Christ* 5.
[97]Tertullian, *On the Resurrection of the Flesh* 48.
[98]Tertullian, *On the Resurrection of the Flesh* 57, 63.
[99]Tertullian, *On the Resurrection of the Flesh* 50.
[100]Tertullian, *On Prescription against Heresies* 13.
[101]Tertullian, *On the Resurrection of the Flesh* 35, 57, 60.

Tertullian also cited the preservation of Jonah while submerged for days in the digestive tract of a whale as biblical proof that buried bodies retain their integrity.[102] His appeal to Jonah may have influenced the late addition to Matthew's Gospel of these words attributed to Jesus, "Just as Jonah was three days and nights in the belly of the sea monster, so for three days and nights the Son of Man will be in the bowels of the earth."[103] But Tertullian looked to John's Gospel for his conclusive proof, "In the case of Lazarus, the preeminent instance of resurrection, . . . the flesh stank in corruption, and yet as flesh Lazarus rose again."[104] Tertullian offered extrabiblical data to support his corporeality position: some corpses that had been interred at Carthage for five centuries were found to be in a remarkable state of preservation, even to the extent of the hair retaining its perfume.[105] His literalism set the pattern for resurrection doctrine in Latin orthodoxy.[106]

The Greek and Latin antecedents of "the Apostles' Creed" date back as early as Tertullian in the third century. They affirm, "I believe . . . in the resurrection of the flesh (*carnis* in Latin)."[107] In the English translation, "body" replaced "flesh," but a similar change has not been made in all modern languages. The creed was not even formulated by an ecumenical council of church leaders, as was the Nicene Creed. Countless millions of Christians across the centuries have recited this most used creed that contains a clause about corporeal revivification, and wrongly presume that it was formulated by the apostles. Encouraged by this deceptive identification of the creed with Jesus' right-hand men, Christians have believed, or think they ought to believe, that scattered bits of dust will, in some supernatural manner, again become one's own personal organism when they move into heavenly mansions where Jesus sits, or into a fiery subterranean place of physical torture. "He descended into hell (*inferna* in Latin)," the traditional translation of a sentence of that creed, is still much more used

---

[102]Tertullian, *On the Resurrection of the Flesh* 32.

[103]Matthew 12:40; Matthew and Luke both use the Q source that associates Jonah only with Ninevah's repentance, and Justin's quotation of that passage from Matthew in the mid-second century (*Dialogue with Trypho*, 107) shows that he was not aware of that teaching.

[104]Tertullian, *On the Resurrection of the Flesh* 53.

[105]Tertullian, *On the Resurrection of the Flesh* 42.

[106]John Kelly, *Early Christian Creeds* (London: Longman, 1950) 165.

[107]John Leith, ed., *Creeds of the Churches* (New York: Anchor, 1963) 21-25.

than the ecumenical version, "He descended to the dead." That Creed, which became foundational for the theology of Western Christianity, also contains statements about other interruptions of natural processes.

Tertullian was the first Christian to denounce cremation on the assumption that dead bodies can be affected by what would have been excruciating if inflicted on them when they were alive. Only the heathen, he contended, "burn up their dead with harshest inhumanity."[108] He also thought that God needed skeletal remains for guiding in the restoration of the predeath body. Like potsherds, they require the skilled hands of the master Craftsman in order to be reconstructed with the bodily integrity they previously had.

Cremation had been the normal Roman method for corpse disposal before Christianity became influential, but after Christianity became the official religion of the Roman empire in the fourth century, cremation practically ceased, and catacombs for inhumation were common.[109] Most Christians were confident that their corpses would arise again, in a somewhat changed form, to receive reward or punishment. Intense fire became identified with hell to such an extent that the thought of cremation was horrifying. Pope Gregory the Great illustrates how flame became associated with Satan's torments. He tells of an Italian official who seduced a virgin: "After his burial, tongues of fire were seen issuing from his grave. These continued to burn for a long time, feeding on his remains until they had consumed them entirely, causing the mound of earth over the burial place to cave in."[110] The fiery eruptions from volcanos were presumed to be a means of relieving the overcrowding of hell.[111]

Although hell was not part of Paul's doctrine, the third-century *Apocalypse of Paul* claims to reveal what he was not permitted to disclose after envisioning the afterlife.[112] On his journey to the underworld he saw grisly scenes of torment: fornicators immersed up to their navels in "a river boiling with fire," adulterers suspended by their eyebrows and hair, an unfaithful priest pierced by a pitchfork in his intestines, and other wicked

---

[108]Tertullian, *On the Resurrection of the Flesh* 1.

[109]William Phipps, *Cremation Concerns* (Springfield IL: Thomas, 1989) 12-13, 22-23.

[110]Gregory the Great, *Dialogues* 4:33.

[111]William Inge, *Outspoken Essays* (London: Longmans, 1922) 36.

[112]2 Corinthians 12:1-4.

individuals torn apart by wild animals.[113] Such descriptions supplied imagery for poet Dante's *Inferno* and for the Muslim treatments of an otherworldly dream-vision of Muhammad.[114]

Irenaeus, the influential Bishop of Lyons, gave much attention to arguing against Gnostics who rejected a physical resurrection. Astutely basing their authority on Paul's assertion that "flesh and blood cannot inherit the kingdom of God,"[115] they held that Christians err if they imagine that the rising up of a corpse occurred for Jesus or for any of his followers. Irenaeus interpreted Paul's doctrine to mean only that those who are devoted to "the lusts of the flesh" will not qualify for citizenship in the heavenly kingdom. He insisted that Christians will be raised "in the same manner as Christ rose in the substance of flesh and pointed out to the disciples the marks of his nails and the opening in his side." To buttress what was crystallizing as orthodoxy, the bishop found in Ezekiel's dry bones sermon a prophecy of God breathing life into rejoined skeletal parts. Irenaeus claimed that Jesus restored crippled limbs and diseased eyes in order to guarantee his clients sound bodies for immortal life. He asserted that the Nain widow's son, the daughter of Jairus, and Lazarus of Bethany "rose in the identical bodies, their limbs and bodies receiving health" to prefigure the future resurrection of the dead.[116]

Historian Edward Gibbon has noted how ancient philosophers responded to orthodoxy's focus on physical resurrection:

> In the days of Irenaeus, about the end of the second century, the resurrection of the dead was far from being esteemed an uncommon event. . . . At such a period, when faith could boast of so many wonderful victories over death, it seems difficult to account for the scepticism of those philosphers who still rejected and derided the doctrine of the resurrection. A noble Grecian . . . promised Theophilus, bishop of Antioch, that, if he could be gratified with the sight of a single person who had been actually raised from the dead, he would immediately embrace the Christian religion. It is somewhat remarkable that the prelate . . . thought proper to decline this fair and reasonable challenge.[117]

---

[113]*Apocalypse of Paul* 31, 33, 39, 40.

[114]William Phipps, *Muhammad and Jesus* (New York: Continuum, 1996) 197-98.

[115]1 Corinthians 15:50.

[116]Irenaeus, *Against Heresies* 1:30; 5:7, 9, 11-15.

[117]Edward Gibbon, *The History of the Decline and Fall of the Roman Empire*

Celsus, the first of the cultured despisers of Christianity, commented sardonically in the second century on the prevailing Christian eschatology. He discerned that Christians generally presume that Jesus' resurrection was physical, which served as a paradigm both for those destined for heaven or hell. Christians say, he observed, that "those long since dead will rise up from the earth possessing the same bodies as they did before." Celsus, in adherence to Greek philosophy, believed in the divine Logos and in the immortality of the human spirit, but he queried tauntingly about the dominant Christian doctrine of the resurrection:

> What sort of body is it that could return to its original nature or become the same as it was before it rotted away? . . . They take cover by saying, "Nothing is impossible with God." . . . But the fact is, God cannot do what is shameful; and God does not do what is contrary to nature. . . . He may, as Heracleitus says, be able to provide everlasting life for a soul; but the same philosopher notes that "corpses should be disposed of like dung." . . . As for the body—so full of corruption and other sorts of nastiness—God could not (and would not) make it everlasting, as this is contrary to reason. For he himself is the Logos— the reason—behind everything that exists, and he is not able to do anything that violates or contradicts his own character.[118]

Celsus appears to have been unaware of Paul's letters, but he gave a telling criticism of a theological proposition that Mark repeatedly attributed to Jesus, "For God all things are possible."[119] That pagan's assault on Christian doctrine in the second century prompted a response from Origen, the first outstanding scholar of the patristic era. He separated himself from the prevailing Christian doctrine and accepted much of Paul's doctrine of the resurrection. Origen correctly pointed out that the apostle championed a "spiritual body" resurrection.[120] He commented on what Paul had written about "flesh and blood" not being part of God's incorruptible kingdom, "We would be simpleminded and flesh-loving to say that these bones and this blood and flesh—that is, the whole complex structure of the body—will rise again in the last day, enabling us to walk with feet, work with hands, see with eyes, hear with ears, . . . and digest food with stomachs."[121]

(1776) 15:3.

[118]Celsus, *True Doctrine* (New York: Oxford, 1987) 86.

[119]Mark 10:27; 14:36.

[120]1 Corinthians 15:44; Origen, *First Principles* 2:10.

[121]Quoted in Jerome, *To Pammachius against John of Jerusalem* 25.

Appropriating Paul's grain analogy, Origen replied to Celsus that he and his followers did not maintain that a rotted body resumes its original nature any more than a planted grain of wheat returns to its former condition.[122] Origen also quoted Paul's comparison of the earthly body's death to a razed tabernacle that has been replaced by an eternal form without a material construction.[123] According to McGiffert, Origen's denial of a fleshly resurrection was for Christians the most offensive aspect of his theology, "for to many the necessary consequence seemed to be that the life beyond the grave is without reality."[124] In the sixth century, Pope Vigilius condemned Origen for his views on the resurrection, along with some other doctrinal deviations.[125]

Around 300 CE, Christian apologist Athenagoras asserted, "It is impossible for the same persons to be reconstituted unless the same bodies are restored to the same souls." That common view gave rise to this difficult question: how will there be full resurrection of the flesh for martyrs who have been consumed by beasts? For example, Ignatius had been eaten by lions in the Roman Colosseum. Athenagoras alleged that organisms cannot assimilate food that is not a part of their regular diet. Human flesh can thus never become part of other bodies, so it is either vomited or excreted undigested. In the resurrection, God will fuse together the fragmented and decomposed human bodies.[126] Athenagoras's argument can be interpreted as, in effect, a reductio ad absurdum of the doctrine that he was trying to defend!

The raising of Lazarus by miracle worker Jesus was a prominent motif in Christian art prior to the fourth century even though there was no portrayal of Jesus' resurrection in that period.[127] Neither did early Christian art display Jesus on a cross, but it often depicted him with a magical wand

---

[122]1 Corinthians 15:35-38; Henry Chadwick, *Origen: Contra Celsum* (Cambridge: University Press, 1953) 281.

[123]2 Corinthians 5:1; Chadwick, *Origen: Contra Celsum*, 421. 125

[124]McGiffert, *A History of Christian Thought*, 1:228.

[125]Henry Denzinger, *The Sources of Catholic Dogma* (St. Louis: Herder, 1957) 84.

[126]Athenagoras, *On the Resurrection of the Dead* 8, 25.

[127]Graydon Snyder, *Inculturation of the Jesus Tradition* (Harrisburg: Trinity, 1999) 104.

raising Lazarus.[128] The attempt to draw a parallel between the resuscitation of Lazarus and Jesus is defective even if the Lazarus story is accepted as having literally happened. Lazarus made only a temporary return to life in Bethany before his subsequent death. By contrast, as Paul put it, "Christ being raised from the dead will never die again."[129]

In the fourth century, the influential Bible translator and interpreter Jerome opposed Origen's position and classified him among those heretics who claim that "the bodies that we shall have in heaven will be subtle and spiritual according to the words of the apostle: 'It is sown a natural body; it is raised a spiritual body.' "[130] Jerome believed that Enoch, Elijah, and Jesus ascended to heaven physically, showing that "a resurrection without flesh and bones, without blood and members, is unintelligible."[131] The resurrected body must have a stomach, Jerome reasons; otherwise, how can the Gospels presume that Lazarus and Jairus's daughter ate food after being raised? Jerome declared that no physical parts will be lacking, "As our Lord rose in the body, which lay among us in the holy sepulcher, so we also shall rise again on Judgment Day in the very bodies in which we are now clothed and buried."[132] Jerome alleged that Jesus left his tomb with his teeth, tongue, palate, arms, chest, stomach, legs, and feet.[133]

Jerome wrote a diatribe against a priest named Vigilantius who was critical of those who paid idolatrous homage to relics, believing that they contained miraculous powers.[134] The pious believed that a saint's efficacious soul was present in every body part, so supernatural power could be transmitted by viewing even a holy toe. This is in accord with the principle of contagious magic, which anthropologists use to describe a widespread feature of primitive cultures. Any body part that had been closely associated with a hero was believed to have continuous potency.

Bishop Ambrose inaugurated the practice of using the relics of saints in consecrating churches.[135] Ironically, the veneration of saints often

---

[128]Ian Wilson, *Jesus: the Evidence* (London: Weidenfeld, 1984) 99, 110.

[129]Romans 6:9.

[130]Jerome, *Letters* 108:23; *To Pammachius against John of Jerusalem* 23.

[131]Jerome, *To Pammachius* 29, 31.

[132]Jerome, *To Pammachius* 24.

[133]Jerome, *Letters* 108.24.

[134]Jerome, *Against Vigilantius* 8-9.

[135]Paulinus, *Life of Ambrose* 14.

involved exhuming their corpses and ghoulishly dismembering them for wide distribution to church reliquaries. At that time some believed that the bones of Stephen, the first Christian martyr, had been found in Jerusalem and brought to North Africa, where dozens of Christians had been cured by viewing them, and three resuscitations had been effected by them.[136] Although the New Testament does not suggest that the historical Stephen performed miracles, centuries later any bone fragment from his alleged corpse was considered magical.

The Palestine pilgrimage of Helena, the mother of Emperor Constantine, stimulated legends about the supernatural effects of Jesus' cross. After allegedly finding the remnants of several crosses in the Jerusalem area, she imposed a supernatural test to ascertain the one on which Jesus was crucified. She found that wood from two excavated crosses did not effect healing, but the relics of a third one discovered between the other two caused an invalid "to spring from her bed immediately." Helena further confirmed that she had located Jesus' cross by touching a dead person with a fragment of the relic, resulting in resusitation. "The cross was said to have been made of the wood of the Tree of Life, taken belatedly from the Garden of Eden."[137] Pieces of the "True Cross" were placed in silver caskets for placement in churches. The nails found with the cross were also considered to have holy potency.[138]

Gibbon argued that the conqueror was conquered:

> The sublime and simple theology of the primitive Christians was gradually corrupted. . . . The Christians frequented the tombs of the martyrs in the hope of obtaining, from their powerful intercession, every sort of spiritual, but more especially of temporal, blessings. . . . The most respectable bishops had persuaded themselves that the ignorant rustics would more cheerfully renounce the superstitions of Paganism if they found some resemblance, some compensation, in the bosom of Christianity. The religion of Constantine achieved, in less than a century, the final conquest of the Roman empire: but the victors themselves were insensibly subdued by the arts of their vanquished rivals.[139]

Emperor Julian, who was educated by Christian teachers in the fourth century, became disgusted with his boyhood religion in part because "the

---

[136] Augustine, *City of God* 22:8.
[137] "Relics," *The Encyclopedia of Religion* (New York: Macmillan, 1987).
[138] Sozomen, *Church History* 2:1.
[139] Gibbon 28:3.

tombs of Peter and Paul were being worshiped." He pointed out to
Christians, "In your scriptures it is nowhere said that you must grovel
among tombs and pay them honor."[140] Those giving homage to the apostles
were usually seeking supernatural benefits for themselves. Classicist Edith
Hamilton comments on this postapostolic development:

> Christianity soon after Paul's death was given over to the cult of the miracu-
> lous. The proof of a saintly life was not so much what a man did when he was
> alive as the wonders he worked when he was dead. . . . Paul had no responsibil-
> ity whatever for this unfortunate development. He did not believe in Christ
> because of miracles.[141]

Relics included anything alleged to have been in contact with Jesus or
a saint, including clothes, hair, breast milk, or a crown of thorns, and they
assumed a supernatural potency. In contagious magic, personal possessions
are equivalent to a person's whole self and convey power to those within
their aura. The biblical accounts of dead Elijah's cloak having power to
divide a river and Elisha's bones being potent enough to revive the dead,[142]
gave encouragement to the preservation of the remains of prominent holy
persons. A reliquary at the Vatican allegedly contains Jesus' foreskin, saved
after his circumcision, believed by Catholics to be the only flesh he left on
earth.[143]

Venerating relics was prompted by the belief that they provided the
faithful with cures for their earthly bodies and a guarantee of everlasting
life. The craving for relics was so intense that some devotees were crushed
to death in the press of the crowds wanting to touch the "holy body" of
Basil. It was considered meritorious to die at shrines while in this holy
pursuit.[144] In the sixth century, Bishop Gregory of Tours wrote about the
power emanating from dead holy men. His eight books on miracles contain
stories of more than a hundred supernatural happenings connected with
saints' tombs in Gaul. He recommended dust from sacred tombs, consumed
with a water mixture or carried in a box, as a healing remedy.

[140]Julian, *Against the Galileans* 327, 335.
[141]Edith Hamilton, *Witness to the Truth* (New York: Norton, 1957) 165.
[142]2 Kings 2:13-14, 13:20-21.
[143]*Time* (29 December 1975): 44.
[144]Gregory of Nazianzen, *Funeral Orations* 80.

A martyr's tomb usually became an altar over which mass was celebrated. This often resulted in the construction of a church around the altar, and in a community growing up around the sanctuary. At St. Andrews Scotland, where I once studied, the alleged relics of apostle Andrew were deposited by a monk at a place along the North Sea coast. On that site a cathedral was consecrated in 1318; the commerce from pilgrims visiting there in search of magical protection resulted in the formation of a town and a seminary. Andrew also became the patron saint at Mediterranean area sites because some of his relics were believed to have been brought there.

Historian Richard Southern describes the prime medieval craving:

> Throughout these centuries relics were the most important feature in the religious landscape. . . . Every church, every altar, every nobleman, every king, every monastery, had relics, sometimes in great quantity. . . . They were carried out with the armies; they were borne in procession to encourage the drooping crops . . . [and] were necessary for every important undertaking. . . . Relics were the main channel through which supernatural power was available for the needs of ordinary life.[145]

The ultimate and most powerful church relic resulted from the Eucharist doctrine of the Fourth Lateran Council in 1215.[146] The earlier view that Jesus was only spiritually present in the consecrated bread and wine was augmented with a carnal understanding. The "transubstantiation" term introduced by the Council has been accepted ever since in Roman Catholicism to affirm that the communion elements were supernaturally transformed by the priest into the actual body and blood of Jesus that worshipers consume.

Relics are what students of primal religions call fetishes. Their presumed power to assure health and prosperity is derived from their having once belonged to shamen who had been charged with mana, an invisible spiritual power. A saint cult, involving pilgrimages on feast days to relic enshrinements, was a central feature of religious life and regional tourism throughout the thousand years of the Middle Ages.[147] The revering of holy

---

[145]Richard Southern, *Western Society and the Church in the Middle Ages* (Grand Rapids MI: Eerdmans, 1970) 30-31.

[146]Davud Chidester, *Christianity* (San Francisco: Harper, 2000) 210-13.

[147]Peter Brown, *The Cult of the Saints* (Chicago: University of Chicago Press, 1981) 1-4, 76-78, 83-84.

bones gave a mystique to skeletons, especially on the eve of All Saints' Day, which continues to be recalled in some Halloween costumes and lore.

Receptacles for the bones of the dead, called ossuaries, were prominent in the Middle Ages. The gathering up of physical remains, after about a year of corpse decay, was a practice begun by Jews in the first century BCE.[148] It resulted from synagogue leaders interpreting Ezekiel's famous vision of the rejoining of human relics as a forecast of God's revivification of the worthy dead at the end of time. In order to guarantee such reconstruction it was believed that God needed at least the tip of a person's coccyx at the lower extreme of the spinal column to provide individuality.[149] Orthodox rabbis recognize now that such procedure prodided an individual's unique DNA. Graveyard supervisors realized that by consolidating remains in a small bone box, the burial spaces could be reused frequently without jeoparizing the doctrine of physical resurrection. The placement of ossuaries in "charnel houses" has continued in some cemeteries to the present era.

Since relics were considered essential for resurrection, the medieval Catholic inquisitionists thought that heretics could be eternally eliminated by burning them to ashes, preferably while they were alive. At the Council of Constance in 1415, Czech church leader John Hus was burned at the stake and his remains were cast into the Rhine to prevent them from being treated as sacred relics by his followers. The Council also ordered that the remains of John Wyclif, another Protestant Reformation forerunner, be dug up and treated in a similar manner. Accordingly, Pope Martin V issued this directive to Bishop Fleming, "Proceed in person to the place where John Wyclif is buried, cause his body and bones to be exhumed, cast far from ecclesiastical burial and publicly burnt, and his ashes to be disposed so that no trace of him shall be seen again."[150]

No miracle in hagiography is more revered than accounts of raising the dead,[151] and sometimes church records describe them in a more spectacular manner than does the Bible. For example, Pope Gregory told how Benedict, the famous sixth-century abbot of the Mount Cassino monastery, restored the life of a novice who had been crushed when a wall fell on him. His body

---

[148]Roland de Vaux, *Ancient Israel* (New York: McGraw-Hill, 1:57).

[149]George Foot Moore, *Judaism* (New York: Schocken, 1971) 2:385.

[150]Herbert Workman, *John Wyclif* (Oxford: Clarendon, 1923) 2:319-20.

[151]Cobham Brewer, *A Dictionary of Miracles* (Philadelphia: Lippincott, 1889) 78-88.

parts were gathered up and taken to Benedict's cell. By means of his prayers, the pieces joined together and the youth's body was totally restored to normality. Also, Gregory related how saintly Libertinus always carried with him a sandal of his revered deceased teacher Honoratus and when a mother begged him to restore life to her child he accomplished such by praying while placing the sandal on the dead son's chest.[152]

Fantastic stories were told of French saints. Denis, the apostle to Gaul, became the first bishop of Paris and the patron saint of France. After he was decapitated on what is now called *Montmartre* (martyr's hill) in his honor, he rose up, placed his severed head under his arm, and walked miles in the company of angels to the site of the present church dedicated to him.[153] Thirteenth-century Bishop Louis of Anjou was said to have raised twelve individuals from the dead, more than the total number of alleged biblical resurrections by Israelite prophets, Jesus, and his apostles. This is cited by Calvin Miller, a contemporary professor at an evangelical seminary, who has written a book on miracles with the subtitle "How God Changes His Natural Laws to Benefit You." Accepting uncritically purported supernatural acts by the French saint, Miller uses them to support his contention that God raised Jesus bodily from his tomb and will eventually physically resurrect author Miller.[154]

No object in Christendom has received more veneration than the alleged shroud of Jesus that has been periodically exhibited ever since 1578 at the cathedral in Turin, Italy. Its creator may have been motivated by the legend of Veronica's handkerchief that captured the image of his bloody face shortly before his crucifixion. Enlarging upon that, a French knight claimed that he possessed a burial cloth containing an impression of Jesus' entire crucified body. Pierre d'Arcis, Bishop of Troyes, wrote Pope Clement VII about it, which he judged to be inauthentic after it was displayed in 1389 at a church in the town of Lirey. He reported that Henry of Poitiers, the Troyes bishop who preceded him, had interviewed an artist who confessed making the forgery in the 1350s. D'Arcis stated that the purpose of the hoax was "to attract the multitude so that money might cunningly be wrung from them. Pretended miracles were worked, certain men being hired to represent

[152]Gregory the Great, *Dialogues* 1:2, 2:7.

[153]Stephen Wilson, ed., *Saints and Their Cults* (Cambridge: University Press, 1983) 143.

[154]Calvin Miller, *Miracles and Wonders* (New York: Time Warner, 2003) 68.

themselves as healed at the moment of the exhibition of the shroud."[155] The Pope ordered that an announcement be given when the shroud was displayed that it "is not the true burial cloth of our Lord Jesus Christ but only a kind of painting or picture made as a form or representation of the burial cloth."

In 1988 fragments of the Turin cloth were tested independently in three European and American laboratories for radiocarbon dating, establishing for all who accept standard scientific procedures that the so-called shroud was made of fibers dating thirteen centuries after Jesus died. Moreover, the alleged blood stains on the fraud have been found to be pigments of paint used by the hoodwinker. Robert Wild, President of Marquette University, concludes that "it is most unlikely that this object is the authentic burial shroud of Jesus."[156] All that is historically known of Jesus' burial wrappings is contained in the Gospels, which describe typical Jewish funeral procedures. But many books have been written to prove the genuineness of this famous fake, showing that many are willing to believe what even the Vatican, on the basis of sound investigation, declared centuries ago to be unauthentic.

The accomplishments of Thomas Aquinas, the preeminent medieval Catholic theologian, were so well known during his lifetime that competition for his holy corpse began immediately after his death.[157] Monastic communities mangled his corpse to obtain relics: one taking his head, another a hand, and then the flesh was boiled off his bones so that they could be placed in a reliquary.[158]

Aquinas had accepted the resurrection doctrine of medieval Christianity. He retained the Pauline judgment that "Christ's resurrection is the exemplar of ours," but he gave this non-Pauline definition, "We cannot call it resurrection unless the soul returns to the same body." Our imitation of Christ will extend even to our arising before daybreak from the grave in bodies that are about thirty years old![159] Aquinas also wrote about the

---

[155]*Collection de Champage* (Paris: Bibliotheque Nationale) 154:138.

[156]"Shroud of Turin," *New Catholic Encyclopedia* (Detroit: Gale, 2003).

[157]Jean-Pierre Torrell, *Saint Thomas Aquinas* (Washington DC: Catholic University of America Press, 1996) 1:297-98.

[158]Kenneth Woodward, *Making Saints* (New York: Simon and Schuster, 1990) 373.

[159]Thomas Aquinas, *Summa Theologica* 3a.77.3, 79.1, 81.1.

inhabitants of heaven gazing down at those being tortured in hell, "In order that the happiness of the saints may be more delightful to them and that they may render more copious thanks to God for it, they are allowed to see perfectly the sufferings of the damned." His authority for this attitude comes from a psalmist who said, "The just shall rejoice at the sight of revenge."[160] Subsequently, Jonathan Edwards, the outstanding colonial American theologian, stressed that the sight of those being tortured heighens the enjoyment of the saved.[161] The pleasure that Aquinas and Edwards express toward retaliation provides an egregious example of reverting to a teaching of the Hebrew Bible that is contrary to a teaching of Jesus and his apostles.[162]

In the Middle Ages, a Gospel parable about social ethics was also given an interpretation that was never intended by Jesus. For his story, Jesus took picturesque images of Gehenna and Paradise that would have been familiar to his listeners. A Jewish writing of that era gave this description of two compartments of Hades, the abode of the dead, "The furnace of Gehenna shall be made manifest and over against it the Paradise of delight."[163] Jesus first pictured the scene of a man named Lazarus who begged for leftovers at the gate of an unnamed rich man who feasted daily. The second scene, in the life after death, reverses the first: the rich man, who is in the hot side of Hades, begs for cooling water from Lazarus. He can be seen across a chasm, banqueting in Paradise as an equal with Abraham, the foremost Hebrew patriarch.[164]

Jesus was trying to get the affluent to accept a leading motif of the Israelite prophets.[165] They should share their wealth if they wished to get right with God, but during medieval history more attention was given to the nonessential background setting. A favorite motif of cathedral art was to use Jesus' fictional story to picture the topography of the places where resurrected people lived after Judgment Day. Angels were depicted as bringing restored bodies of the elect to rest on "Abraham's bosom" while

---

[160] Aquinas, *Summa Theologica* 94.1.3; Psalm 58:10.

[161] *The Works of President Edwards* (New York: Carter, 1879) 4:292.

[162] Matthew 5:38-39; Romans 12:17; 1 Peter 3:9.

[163] 2 Esdras 7:36.

[164] Luke 16:19-26.

[165] Luke 16:29-31.

devils were throwing bodies of the damned into the fiery jaws of hell.[166] In contrast to that otherworldly treatment, the this-worldly intended meaning of the Lazarus parable is well illustrated by the life of Albert Schweitzer. When he was an acclaimed musician and theologian in Europe, this disturbing teaching of Jesus contributed to his becoming a medical missionary in tropical Africa. He identified himself with the man who lived in luxury from wealth obtained from "wretched Lazarus," the African native who was being ruthlessly exploited by European colonists.[167]

Islam, which arose during the medieval era of European Christianity, echoes some of the notions of physical resurrection shared by Judaism and Christianity. The *Qur'an* asserts, "We [God] will reassemble bones even to the fingertips,"[168] and "We will raise the bones and cover them with flesh,"[169] which are needed to enjoy the sensuous Paradise. Providing a contrast to the hot Arabian desert, it is graphically described in the *Qur'an* as a place of abundant cool water, fruitful vegetation, and bodily pleasures for those whom God has judged to be worthy.[170] Jane Smith and Yvonne Haddad, in their thorough study of resurrection views in classical Islam, state that "the vast majority of believers" interpret eschatology literally rather than metaphorically.[171]

Belief in physical resurrection also continues to be the official doctrine of Roman Catholicism, and therefore of a billion of the world's Christians. After affirming the physical resurrection of Christ, its latest catechism states that "we shall rise like Christ." More specifically it affirms, "We believe in the true resurrection of this flesh that we now possess."[172] "Perpetual punishment with the devil" is also an integral part of Catholic teachings.[173]

---

[166]T. S. Boase, *Death in the Middle Ages* (New York: McGraw-Hill, 1974) 28-46.

[167]Albert Schweitzer, *On the Edge of the Primeval Forest* (London: Black, 1928) 1-2.

[168]*Qur'an* 75:3-4.

[169]*Qur'an* 2:259.

[170]*Qur'an* 56:12-36.

[171]Jane Smith and Yvonne Haddad, *The Islamic Understanding of Death and Resurrection* (Albany NY: SUNY, 1981) 84.

[172]*Catechism of the Catholic Church* (Washington DC: Catholic Conference, 2000) 260, 265.

[173]Richard P. McBrien, *Catholicism* (San Francisco: Harper, 1994) 1175-76.

That doctrine helps to explain why a 1997 survey by Opinion Dynamics of American registered voters found that 71% believe in hell.[174]

The Dogma of the Assumption of the Virgin Mary, proclaimed by Pius XII in 1950 to be infallible truth, reinforces the Catholic belief in physical resurrection by providing a similar supernatural ascension for both Jesus and his mother. The dogma is based on this reasoning: since the bodies of Mary and Jesus were undefiled by sex on earth they deserved to be raised forever uncorrupted into heaven. Alleging the authority of Jesus and his apostles, the Pope declared that Mary, without mortal decay, "was assumed body and soul into heavenly glory" at the end of her life, enabling her to sit enthroned as queen beside her son. The faithful are instructed to find in this compulsory doctrine a magnificent affirmation of the "lofty goal to which our bodies and souls are destined." Whereas the bodies of ordinary Christians temporarily remain in "the corruption of the grave, sinless Mary did not have to wait until the end of time for the redemption of her body." This dogma is actually based historically on no more than the absence of reference to Mary's death in the earliest Christian traditions. An unanswered question by the Church is, why would anyone need a physical body in heaven to be in communion with God, the fleshless Spirit?

The Catholic Church's inflexible doctrine of physical resurrection precipitated a clash with the modern cremation movement. Canons were enacted to prohibit Catholics from allowing the burning of corpses and to deprive church rites to those requesting cremation.[175] The Church feared that the acceptance of cremation would diminish belief in fleshly resurrection and in hallowed relics. In the twentieth century Paul VI eased up on the old restrictions by permitting church rites for those opting for cremation while urging the faithful to abstain from the practice.[176] That pontiff's relaxation on strictures against one method of corpse disposal has not signaled a shift in traditional Roman Catholic resurrection dogma. He reaffirmed that "souls will be reunited with their bodies" on the resurrection day regardless of whether the remains have been reduced to ashes or to dust.[177] Current canon law expresses preference for corpse burial, but cremation is permitted. Those who have chosen cremation are not deprived

---

[174]*Public Perspective* (May 2000): 27.

[175]*Code of Canon Law* (1917) 1203, 1240.

[176]Paul VI, *Instructio: De cadaverum crematione* (8 May 1963).

[177]Paul VI, "The Divine Truth," *Vital Speeches* 34 (1 August 1968): 612.

of church funerals unless they are thereby expressing disbelief in the physical resurrection.[178]

In spite of differences on other points of doctrine, the two principal leaders of the Protestant Reformation accepted without question the medieval Catholic doctrine of physical resurrection. Martin Luther taught that "our bodies, the same bodies that have died, shall be made alive."[179] John Calvin followed Paul in holding that the resurrection of all humans will be of the same nature as that of Christ, but he substituted the outlook of Tertullian for that of Paul in claiming that the bodies will be raised with the same elements of matter as constituted them before.[180]

Calvinists likewise professed that Christ was resurrected "with the same body in which he suffered," meaning that his body did not undergo any of the usual process of decay while in the tomb, and that "all the dead shall be raised up with the selfsame bodies" in spite of temporary corruption.[181] Charles Hodge, the most influential nineteenth-century American Calvinist, affirmed:

> The whole Christian world, in all ages, has understood it [the Bible] to teach . . . the literal rising from the dead of the body deposited in the grave. . . . Our resurrection is to be analogous to that of Christ: . . . there can be no doubt that the very body which hung upon the cross, and which laid in the tomb, rose again from the dead.[182]

The Church of Jesus Christ of Latter-day Saints (aka the Mormons), a nineteenth-century spinoff of apocalyptic Protestantism, interprets the resurrection literally. That popular doctrine among the masses may contribute to its being one of the most rapidly growing religions in the world. The *Book of Mormon* describes the final state: "The spirit and the body shall be reunited again in its perfect form; both limb and joint shall be restored to its proper frame, even as we now are at this time. . . . This

----

[178]*Code of Canon Law* (1983) 1176:3, 1184:2.

[179]Martin Luther, *Small Catechism*, 165.

[180]John Calvin, *Institutes of the Christian Religion* 3.25.7-8; *Theological Treatises* (Philadelphia: Westminster, 1954) 43.

[181]*Westminster Confession of Faith* 8.3; 34.2.

[182]Charles Hodge, *Systematic Theology* (New York: Scribner's, 1895) 3:774-75. Ironically, I found a denial of physical resurrection on Hodge's tombstone in Princeton NJ. Inscribed there are these words of Paul, "To be absent from the body is to be present with the Lord" (2 Corinthians 5:8).

restoration shall come to all. . . . and even there shall not so much as a hair of their heads be lost."[183] The wicked (fornicators and the lustful are explicitly mentioned) as well as the righteous will be physically raised, and the former will "be cast into that lake of fire and brimstone."[184]

Mormons claim confirmation for their doctrine in the Gospels. Following Matthew, the *Book of Mormon* states that "many saints did arise and appear unto many."[185] Also, the corporeal resurrection of Jesus is cited by President Joseph F. Smith as the prototype of what all corpses will become:

> He lived again in his own person and being, bearing even the marks of the wounds in his flesh, after his resurrection from the dead—so also a testimony has been given to you, in later days, through the Prophet Smith, and others who have been blessed with knowledge, that the same individual Being still lives and will always live. . . . We will meet the same identical being that we associated with here in the flesh.[186]

Mormon corporeal theology exceeds anything previously held in church history. According to revelations received by church founder Joseph Smith and preserved in one of the Mormon books of scripture, both the heavenly Father and the heavenly Jesus have bodies "of flesh and bones."[187] Eternal physical marriage will be provided for those who have been sealed by a special ceremony on earth. In the Celestial Kingdom, males will attain godhood and, with at least one wife, engage in everlasting propagation.[188] The innumerable heavenly children who are procreated might engage in missionary work on other planets.

During the American Civil War, American undertakers restored a commercial venture that began with the Egyptians. Those ancient embalmers integrated mythology with mummification. Egyptians believed that divine King Osiris was murdered and dismembered, but magically his fragmented parts were reassembled in a mummy and his winged soul returned to give it vitality. Osiris then presided over the final judgment and afterlife

---

[183] Alma 11:43-44.

[184] Jacob 3:11.

[185] 3 Nephi 23:11; Matthew 27:52-53; "Resurrection," *Encyclopedia of Mormonism* (New York: Macmillan, 1992).

[186] Joseph F. Smith, *Gospel Doctrine* (Salt Lake City: Deseret, 1969) 22-23.

[187] Joseph Smith, *Doctrine and Covenants* (1843) 131:2.

[188] Smith, *Doctrine and Covenants* 132:19-20, 63.

for humans. Pious Egyptians hoped for a psychosomatic renewal like that of the resurrected sovereign whom they worshiped. Priests chanted assurances from the *Book of the Dead* over embalmed bodies: "You live again, you live again forever. Here you are young once more forever."[189] Hieroglyphs on a mummy-bearing coffin read, "Besenmut is alive and strong again, resurrected without blemish or fault."[190]

American morticians profit from encouraging clients to believe that bodies can be preserved for a future rising. Embalmers replace body fluids with chemicals that temporarily retard decay. That procedure masks reality long enough to prevent mourners from being confronted with the putrid odors of an open coffin. Some of them seem to feel that death's sting is lessened when they gaze at cosmetic covered corpses that have been placed in expensive "caskets." The success of this modern funeral industry is due, in large part, to a residual belief in physical resurrection. The slowness of Americans, in comparison to people from other developed countries, to cremate human corpses has resulted from the funeral industry subtly promoting the fantasy that human bodies, if prepared by its techniques, will not decompose before they are raised at the end of the world.[191]

Mark Twain was both amused and disgusted by the revival of practices that participants in Western civilization had not missed for millennia. Based on his observations of newfangled "embamming," the American humorist commented:

> I encountered a man in the street whom I had not seen for six or seven years; and something like this talk followed. I said: "But you used to look sad and oldish; you don't now. Where did you get all this youth and bubbling cheerfulness? . . . "
>
> He chuckled blithely, took off his shining tile, pointed to a notched pink circlet of paper pasted into its crown, with something lettered on it, and went on chuckling while I read, "J.B., UNDERTAKER." . . .
>
> " . . . Undertaking?—why it's the dead-surest business in Christendom. . . .
>
> " . . . You take a family that's able to embam, and you've got a soft thing. You can mention sixteen different ways to do it—though there *ain't* only one or two ways, when you come down to the bottom facts of it—and they'll take

---

[189]Christiane Desroches-Noblecourt, *Tutankhamen* (London: Rainbird, 1963) 221.

[190]Michael Davison, *The Splendors of Egypt* (New York: Crown, 1979) 92.

[191]Phipps, *Cremation Concerns*, 45-52.

the highest priced way, every time. . . . All it wants is physical immortality for deceased, and they're willing to pay for it."[192]

* * *

In tracing interpretations of the resurrection in Christian thought from ancient to modern times, it has been shown that the doctrine has tended to become more materialistic with the passage of time. Initially some of Jesus' disciples were transformed through experiencing visionary phenomena, coupled with some fresh insights on his mission. From this certainty of an exalted Christ who was not defeated by his crucifixion, there arose stories of his revitalized corpse and his temporary physical return to legitimate his new status. His resurrected body allegedly could digest food and presumably eliminate it. Those stories were probably innocent creations by simple folks to give material support for a reality independent of such verification. Those Christians, living after the first years of the church's beginning, evidently found that skeptics could easily dismiss apostolic testimonies of a spiritual resurrection as ghost tales invented by deluded persons. Church leaders discovered that apologetics seemed to be strengthened when materialistic metaphysics was mixed with accounts of visionary experiences. Hence, some Christians began to transmit stories of a sealed and guarded sepulcher and of a supernatural rolling away of Jesus' gravestone. They believed that this appeal to alleged objective facts would overwhelm unbelievers.

Throughout church history the best known and most adored accounts of Jesus' resurrection have been found in the Gospels of Luke and John. Those stories, written down more than a generation after the events they purport to describe, have been cited as proof of the dogma that Jesus appeared to his disciples in substantially the same body he had prior to his crucifixion. As has been demonstrated, that dominant view of Jesus' resurrection clashes with the earliest New Testament record written by Paul. For him the decisive evidence that Jesus had risen from the dead was not material. His letters give no basis for believing that Jesus returned to conditions of his earthly life.

---

[192]Mark Twain, *Life on the Mississippi* (repr.: New York: Harper, 1903) 323-25: chap. 43, "The Art of Inhumation."

The classic theologians of Roman Catholicism and Protestantism have followed Paul in claiming that God-man Jesus is the model human and therefore the general resurrection for all Christians will be like his. However, other than Origen, churchmen prior to modern times have disregarded Paul's adamant rejection of a physical resurrection. Rank and file church members have tended to interpret in a literal manner what is written in the Gospels on this topic.

Occasionally there is even a contemporary scholar who champions the historicity of Jesus' physical resurrection. Philosopher Stephen Davis contends in recent books that the postmortem Jesus continued to be a material object and that "a camera could have taken a snapshot of the risen Jesus, say, feeding the seven disciples beside the Sea of Tiberius."[193] He caters to the metaphysical materialists of every age who expect divine beings to credential themselves by observable phenomena. Hans Küng has such interpreters in mind when he writes: "The raising of Jesus is not a miracle violating the laws of nature, verifiable within the present world, not a supernatural intervention which can be located and dated in space and time. There was nothing to photograph or to record."[194]

N. T. Wright, a prominent Anglican New Testament interpreter, thinks that Paul's letters, as well as the Gospels, affirm that Jesus' resurrection was a physical happening that was witnessed by normal perception. He claims that a camcorder—had such a devise been available then—could have recorded not only the empty tomb where his body had lain but also his resurrected body interacting with his friends on Easter. Wright declares, "I know this sounds ridiculous and extraordinary, but this is actually what happened."[195] Here we have a current expression of Tertullian's irrational brand of religion.[196] How incongruous that stance is with the church's belief that Jesus incarnates the Logos, the voice of divine reason![197]

In recent generations, many Christians who are not critical scholars continue to believe that the *physical* resurrection is an essential "fact" of

---

[193]Stephen Davis, *The Resurrection* (New York: Oxford, 1997) 142; idem, *Risen Indeed* (Grand Rapids: Eerdmans, 1993), 24.

[194]Hans Küng, *On Being a Christian* (Garden City NY: Doubleday, 1976) 349.

[195]Marcus Borg and N. T. Wright, *The Meaning of Jesus* (San Francisco: Harper, 1999) 123, 125.

[196]See p. 264.

[197]John 1:14.

Christianity. When the term "fundamentalism" was coined a century ago, one of the five fundamentals was that human immortality is inseparable from an objective rising of buried physical remains. After a mid-century decline, the last quarter of the twentieth century brought a resurgence of American fundamentalism.[198] This can be illustrated by the leadership of the Southern Baptist Convention, the largest Protestant denomination, shifting to fundamentalism during that period. Christian fundamentalists number about 25 million in the United States, according to American church historian Martin Marty.[199]

Warren Vanhetloo of Minneapolis's Conservative Baptist Seminary, and William Craig illustrate fundamentalism as it relates to physical resurrection. Vanhetloo claims that words of Job, as found in the King James Version and expressed in an aria of Handel's *Messiah*, show that the bodies of believers will be physically resurrected. Job allegedly testified that disease will destroy his body, "yet in my flesh shall I see God."[200] But Job's outlook should not be equated with divine revelation; moreover, the Hebrew text here is uncertain and Job may have said "without my flesh I shall see God." William Craig argues that "the empty tomb [of Jesus] is a sine qua non of the resurrection and that even Paul accepted it."[201]

Even though the writer of Book of Revelation states at the outset that he expected his forecasts to become fulfilled when the Roman empire would soon collapse, a *Time*/CNN poll indicates that 59% of Americans believe that the prophecies in Revelation pertain to the end of the world in our future. A *Time* magazine cover story tells how many millions of Americans have been frighten by a *Left Behind* series of books published by Tim LaHaye and Jerry Jenkins, which are based on a literal interpretation of biblical visions. They write about the Antichrist dying but returning from the dead as Satan incarnate, whom Jesus defeats at the battle of Armageddon. Following this, the "rapture" comes when Jesus physically lifts up true believers to heaven while the rest are damned for eternity. By

[198]"Fundamentalist Christianity," *Contemporary American Religion* (New York: Macmillan, 2000).

[199]Martin Marty and Scott Appleby, eds., *Fundamentalism Observed* (Chicago: University of Chicago Press, 1991) 38-56.

[200]Job 19:26; James Fraser, *Cremation* (Neptune NJ: Loizeaux, 1985) 5.

[201]Michael Wilkins and J. P. Moreland, eds., *Jesus under Fire* (Grand Rapids MI: Zondervan, 1995) 151.

calling Catholicism a "false religion" and describing the many pernicious traits of gays, one can discover who LaHaye thinks are headed for hell's torment.[202]

Jesus' physical resurrection is also affirmed by most nonfundamentalistic Christians. They believe that Jesus' dead body began to breath again many hours after its burial at Jerusalem and that it continued to have at least some of its former physical qualities for a few weeks before ascending. Novelist John Updike expresses this outlook in a dire manner when he writes that if, for Jesus, "the cells' dissolution did not reverse, the molecules reknit, the amino acids rekindle, the Church will fall."[203]

Christians tend to be more supernaturally inclined with regard to Jesus' afterlife body than to their own bodies.[204] Unless they has been tricked by the funeral home industry, a decreasing number of Christians seriously believe that what is deposited in the grave will be the skeleton and soft tissue that will someday arise and "walk all over God's heaven." The prevailing tendency is to endorse what Paul says about the general resurrection. A typical example of this position can be found in a widely circulated book that contains an article entitled "What is a Presbyterian?" by John Bonnell. He states that nearly all members of his denomination follow Paul in believing that bodies of believers decay irretrievably, but for them there is a spiritual resurrection. Yet "our Lord's sinless body did not see corruption," he declares, and "retained certain physical properties" when resurrected.[205]

Bonnell's interpretation is much wider than one denomination; Jesus is viewed as an exception to the general rule, not a model for what believers can expect. Although an unintelligible nonsequitur, many Easter sermons now assert that Jesus' physical resurrection and the empty tomb are the basis for a nonphysical resurrection of Christians. For logical consistency, the assertion should be either that the resurrection of Jesus was physical and therefore the resurrection of his followers will also be physical, or that Jesus' resurrection was spiritual and therefore Christians will likewise have a spiritual resurrection. To accept the position stated in the authentic

---

[202]*Time* (1 July 2002): 41-53.

[203]*Christian Century* (22 February 1961): 236.

[204]Leo Rosten, ed., *Religions of America* (New York: Simon and Schuster, 1975) 99, 103, 205.

[205]Rosten, ed., *Religions of America*, 205.

accounts in the letters of Paul and Peter is to combine the historical truth of Jesus' spiritual resurrection with a valid deduction pertaining to the destiny of Christians.

Most biblical scholars who continue to state that "Jesus arose from the grave" can be compared to those who say "the sun arose over the mountains." To use this pre-Copernican expression is not a sign of delusional thinking because nearly all people recognize that the locution is about appearance, not reality. Metaphors have their place in describing complex theological and scientific ideas as long as recognition is given that they are not to be taken literally. Like Jesus' fictional parables, his teaching on life after death contains profound religious and psychological truth.

Chapter 8

Curative Interpretations

The heavy association of religion with the supernatural over the centuries has made it appear that the realm of the normal is not God's concern. Church leaders have frequently been a hindrance to rational religion by advocating that faith should be based on presumed infractions in the order of nature. Ambrose Bierce satirized that outlook in his *Devil's Dictionary*:

> PRAY, v. To ask that the laws of the universe be annulled in behalf of a single petitioner confessedly unworthy.

But some major theologians and philosophers across church history have been convinced that regular nature is the arena in which God works and that he does not tamper with natural causality to benefit particular individuals or nations.

Augustine on Nature

Orthodoxy has not always been constricted by a doctrine of supernaturalism. Bishop Augustine of Algeria, who ranks next to Paul in theological impact on the church, asked in the fifth century: "How can anything be contrary to nature that happens by the will of God, since the will of so mighty a Creator is the nature of each thing? A miracle (*portentum*), therefore, happens not contrary to nature, but to what we know as nature."[1] Although humans often perceive events as abnormal, Augustine writes that they actually "happen in a continuous river of everflowing succession, passing along a regular course."[2] He developed this idea of Origen, "Things done by God, which may be or may *appear* to some to be incredible, are not contrary to nature."[3]

Augustine criticized the commonplace assumption that God is best manifested in disruptions of nature:

> We cannot listen to those who maintain that the invisible God works no visible miracles; for even they believe that he made the world, which surely they will not deny to be visible. Whatever marvel happens in this world, it is certainly less marvelous than the whole world itself—I mean the sky and earth and all that is in them—and these God certainly made. But as the Creator himself is

---

[1] Augustine, *City of God* 21.8.
[2] Augustine, *The Trinity* 3.11.
[3] Origen, *Against Celsus* 5.23.

hidden and incomprehensible to man, so also is the manner of creation. Although, therefore, the standing miracle of this visible world is little thought of, because always before us, yet, when we arouse ourselves to contemplate it, it is a greater miracle than the rarest and most unheard-of marvels. For man himself is a greater miracle than any marvel done through his instrumentality.[4]

To focus on occasional interventions by God wrongly implies, Augustine realized, his usual absence from what transpires on earth. Constant natural recurrence, he observed, dulls one's amazement at the ordinary course of God's creation: "How many common things are trodden under foot that, if examined carefully, awaken our astonishment! Take, for example, the property of seeds; who can either comprehend or declare the variety of species, the vitality, vigor, and secret power by which from within small compass evolve great things?"[5] Peter McKenzie comments:

> For Augustine the daily wonders of nature are greater than those related in the Bible. The sprouting of the wheat out of the insignificant seed . . . is a greater miracle for him than the feeding of the five thousand. Indeed, the creation of mankind is a greater miracle than the resurrection and that of the cosmos a greater miracle than all the biblical miracles put together. Similarly the spiritual miracle of the awakening of numerous sinners to new life is a greater miracle than the awakening of the dead in the gospel stories.[6]

In his book on Augustine's view of nature and miracle, Thomas Lacey notes the absence in his thought "of that distinction of nature and supernature which afterwards invaded theology." Lacey clarifies: "According to the mind of St. Augustine, a miracle can no more be *supra naturam* than *contra naturam*. All things that happen are within the natural order."[7] Augustine's appreciation of natural regularity is reflected in Voltaire's dictionary, "It is impossible for the infinitely wise Being to make laws in order to violate them."[8]

---

[4]Augustine, *City of God* 10.12.

[5]Augustine, *Letters* 137.3.

[6]Peter McKenzie, *The Christians* (Nashville: Abingdon, 1988) 266. Augustine wrote: "It is a greater miracle for one to be created who did not exist before than for one who was created to come back to life" (*Sermons on the Gospel of John* 8.2).

[7]Thomas Lacey, *Nature, Miracle, and Sin* (London: Longmans, 1916) 75, 86.

[8]Francois Voltaire, *Philosophical Dictionary* (New York: Basic Books, 1962) 2:392.

Augustine safeguarded divine consistency by maintaining that laws of nature describe God's permanent mode of action. He recognized that thinking of God working against his established order to prove his greatness is absurd and would encourage atheism among rational people. Whereas the atheist believes that interventions into the natural order cannot happen because there is no deity, Augustine argues that they do not happen because there *is* a God. Ernst and Marie-Luise Keller explicate Augustine's thought: "God cannot contradict himself—that is a cogent argument, both logically and theologically. If, then, the contradiction cannot be either real or ultimate, it must be merely superficial and apparent. It may possibly be based on a false subjective impression, or perhaps on man's imperfect knowledge."[9] Augustine admired the predictability of a constant God and recognized the monumental problems if God's mode of acting fluctuated. Would it not be unfair for a game creator to temporarily change the rules during the play to assure that his favorite team or individual won? Natural law, which rejects what is arbitrary and capricious, is in synch with viewing God, along with one New Testament writer, as one "with whom is no variableness, nor shadow due to change."[10]

The occurrence of wonderments inexplicable to a person gives no basis for concluding that some miracle has happened. Such labeling of extraordinary events, Augustine reasoned, is provoked by our lack of understanding God's mode of operating. He suggested that there is a more complete perspective than the one possessed by mortals. Phenomena that astonish us are called miracles because of our ignorance of God's establishment of nature's ordinary causality. Augustine humbly championed the biblical recognition that human knowledge of reality is limited. As God's spokesperson, Isaiah proclaimed, "As the heavens are higher than the earth, so are my ways higher than your ways and my thoughts than your thoughts."[11] Similarly,, Paul exclaims: "How deep the riches and wisdom and knowledge of God! How unsearchable are his judgments and how inscrutable his ways! Who knows the mind of the Lord?"[12] Even though many pages of the Bible are filled with what Isaiah and Paul understood to be God's will, they

---

[9]Ernst Keller and Marie-Luise Keller, *Miracles in Dispute* (Philadelphia: Fortress, 1969) 20.

[10]James 1:17.

[11]Isaiah 55:9.

[12]Romans 11:33-34.

were under no illusion that they had fully comprehended the deity whom they worshiped.

Augustine cited Paul's calling something "contrary to nature" that was really in accord with nature. The apostle described a graft made "contrary to nature" on a limb of an olive tree to obtain nurishment from its roots.[13] Augustine explained that "'contrary to nature' is here used in the sense of contrary to the ordinary course of human experience." He reiterated:

> God, the Author and Creator of all natures, does nothing contrary to nature; for whatever is done by him who appoints all natural order and measure and proportion must be natural in every case. Whatever God does contrary to the usual course of nature we call a miracle. But against the supreme law of nature, which is beyond the knowledge both of the ungodly and of weak believers, God never acts, any more than he acts against himself. As regards spiritual and rational beings, to which class the human soul belongs, the more they partake of this unchangeable law and light, the more clearly they see what is possible, and what impossible; and again, the greater their distance from it, the less their perception of the future, and the more frequent their surprise at strange occurrences.[14]

Augustine recalled his childhood exposure to a magnet, "When I first saw it I was thunderstruck," and he went on to describe its strange behavior.[15] Since he never understood electricity, he viewed magnets as miraculous throughout life. When five-year-old Albert Einstein was shown a compass, the determined movement of its needle caused him to exclaim, "This is a miracle."[16] The only physical force in nature he had previously been aware of was gravity. Einstein spent the rest of his life relating the force of falling bodies to the mysterious electromagnetic force, and he discovered some previously unknown ways in which these forces were an basic part of the natural order. Like Augustine, he acknowledged that the Creator is not arbitrary but is difficult to comprehend. "God does not play dice with the world," he quipped.[17]

---

[13]Romans 11:24.

[14]Augustine, *Against Faustus* 26.3.

[15]Augustine, *City of God*, 21.4.

[16]Abraham Pais, *Subtle Is the Lord* (New York: Oxford University Press, 1982) 37; Paul Schilpp, ed., *Albert Einstein* (London: Cambridge University Press, 1952) 9.

[17]Philipp Frank, *Einstein* (New York: Knopf, 1947) 285.

Augustine acknowledged that it was from reading about astronomy that he came to realize the constancy of nature.[18] He was aware that "the ignorant multitude" believed that Romulus, one of the two mythic founders of the city of Rome, caused solar eclipses by his divine power. Roman ignorance was due to their not knowing that eclipses are "brought about by the fixed regularity of the sun's course."[19] Galileo recognized that Augustine, like virtually all ancient writers, thought that the sun moved relative to the earth and not vice versa. Even so, he appreciated Augustine's stace on the regularity of nature and quoted him in defending himself from charges by the Catholic church that he was blasphemously countering established theology.[20] Augustine had said that sacred writers wisely omitted discussing theories about "the form and shape of the heavens," so theologians should not demand that biblical opinions on scientific matters be accepted as the truth.[21]

"Providence is an unchangeable law," said Augustine,[22] which became a way of integrating Christian theology with science. But theologians have two contrary ways of using the word "providence." *Special* providence assumes that God directly intervenes in the lives of individuals, often as the result of prayer, to protect the righteous and punish the unrighteous. *General* providence pertains to God creating and providing for the universe in an orderly way. For example, as Protestant reformer John Calvin wrote, "Although it is by the operation of natural causes that infants come into the world . . . yet therein the wonderful providence of God brightly shines forth."[23] A birth is immediately caused by the natural activity of sexual partners but that in no way excludes recognizing their child as an awesome gift of God. Those who, with a psalmist, say of God, "You knit me together in my mother's womb,"[24] are not denying the facts of life. Similarly, to say God created organic species should not require a rejection of the evolutionary method by which it happened. In an Augustinian manner, William

---

[18]Augustine, *Confessions* 4.4-6, 5.6.

[19]Augustine, *City of God* 3:15.

[20]Galileo, Letter to Grand Duchess Christina of Lorraine.

[21]Augustine, *The Literal Meaning of Genesis* 2.20.

[22]Augustine, *On Diverse Questions* 27.

[23]John Calvin, *Commentary on the Book of Psalms* (Grand Rapids MI; Baker, 1981) 1:369.

[24]Psalm 139:13.

James writes: "The God whom science recognizes must be a God of universal laws exclusively, a God who does a wholesale, not a retail business. He cannot accommodate his processes to the convenience of individuals."[25]

It appears that Augustine shared the outlook expressed in the first sentence of the Bible's opening chapter. "When God began to create heaven and earth" (as translated by the New Jewish Publication Society) implies that divine creativity has continued henceforth. For Augustine, creation was not limited to unique events in the course of one primeval week but encompasses extended temporal periods.[26] He believed that God created matter at the beginning of time but gave the earth power to generate various forms over the ages by gradual natural processes. Prior to the appearance of plants yielding seeds, as described in Genesis, a germinal principle was created that would cause organic development. The dormant seeds did not burst forth when matter was created because "conditions suitable for their proper development were lacking." Augustine used this analogy, "As mothers are pregnant with unborn offspring, so the world itself is pregnant with the causes of unborn beings, which are not created in it except from that highest essence."[27]

* * *

There was no understanding of Augustine's creation doctrine during the era of Christianity that followed him, appropriately designated as the Dark Ages. Attention was then focused on presumed unnatural happenings, as church historian Kenneth Latourette notes, "In the years after 500, miracles loom more prominently in the writings of the educated leaders of the church in the West than in the centuries before that dividing line."[28] But Renaissance philosopher Michel Montaigne revived Augustine's insight by asking: "How many things do we name miraculous and contrary to nature? . . . All do it according to the measure of their ignorance."[29]

In that same sixteenth century, Calvin appealed to the New Testament and to Augustine in support of his criticism of supernaturalism in church

[25]William James, *The Varieties of Religious Experience* (New York: Doubleday, 1902) 442.
[26]Augustine, *Against the Manichees* 1.23.
[27]Augustine, *On the Trinity* 3.8-9.
[28]Kenneth Latourette, *A History of Christianity* (New York: Harper, 1953) 369.
[29]Michel Montaigne, *Essays* 2.12.

history. The preface of his *Institutes of the Christian Religion* contains a letter to the reigning French king in which he expressed skepticism toward the so-called miracles attributed to "saints" as designated by Catholicism. Calvin believed that their "miracles" have misled the simpleminded, and referred to the Pauline warning against those who use "all power, signs, lying wonders, and every kind of wicked deception."[30] Then he told how Augustine had denounced the Donatist sectarians of North Africa, comparing them to the tricksters who appeared to work miracles before Pharoah at the time of Moses, and to the false prophets who boasted about performing "signs and wonders" that Jesus found offensive.[31] According to Paul, Augustine pointed out, if Christian love is absent, miracles are of no value.[32] Scornful of the Donatists' credulity, he said, "If anyone brings them a lump of earth [from Palestiine], they will worship it."[33]

Philosophers on Miracles

In the seventeenth-century, Benedict Spinoza, a Dutch Jew, studied with Jewish and Christian teachers who enabled him to acquire a thorough knowledge of Judeo-Christian texts. He decided that Moses was not the author of the Torah and that judgment caused him to be excommunicated by leaders of his synagogue. Christians also generally abhorred him, but he found acceptance in a family of Mennonites whom other Protestants had cast out. Defending himself from the accusation of teaching "sheer atheism," Spinoza wrote: "I maintain that God is the immanent cause [of nature]. . . . All things, I say, are in God and move in God, and this I affirm together with Paul." He went on to state that those who accuse him of identifying God with physical nature are completely mistaken.[34] However, Spinoza's God does not intervene from outside nature because there is no outside.

The sixth chapter of Spinoza's *Tractatus Theologica-Politicus* contains his philosophizing on the relationship of God to the natural order, from which the following excerpts are taken:

---

[30]2 Thessalonians 2:9-10.

[31]Mark 13:22-23; Augustine, *Sermons on the Gospel of John* 13.17.

[32]1 Corinthians 13:2; Augustine, *To Petilian, the Donatist* 55.

[33]Augustine, *Letters* 52.

[34]Spinoza, *The Letters* (Indianapolis: Hackett, 1995) 236-39, 332; Acts 17:25.

The universal laws of Nature are merely God's decrees, following from the necessity and perfection of the divine nature. . . . If anyone were to maintain that God performs some act contrary to the laws of Nature, he would at the same time have to maintain that God acts contrary to his own nature—than which nothing could be more absurd.

Spinoza recognized that God cannot engage in self-contradiction, even though few devotees to religion concern themselves with such logic. Although most of them are inspired by supernatural stories, "to call an event a miracle is merely to baptise human ignorance."[35] Sharing Augustine's reasoning, Spinoza also wrote:

The common people are accustomed to call . . . the work of God any work whose cause is generally unknown. For they suppose that God's power and providence are most clearly displayed when some unusual event occurs in nature contrary to their habitual beliefs concerning nature, particularly if such an event is to their profit and advantage. . . . Therefore they believe that all those who explain phenomena and miracles through natural causes . . . are doing away with God, or at least God's providence. They consider that God is inactive all the while that nature pursues her normal course, and, conversely, that nature's power and natural causes are suspended as long as God is acting. . . . Therefore unusual works of nature are termed miracles, or works of God, by the common people. Partly from piety, partly for the sake of opposing those who cultivate the natural sciences, they prefer to remain in ignorance of natural causes, and are eager to hear only about what is least comprehensible to them and consequently evokes their greatest wonder.

The Dutch philosopher showed that the Hebrews, who thought God decreed all things for the sole benefit of their tribe, established a doctrine of special providence for Bible believers. Accordingly, "they have not ceased to this day to invent miracles with view to convincing people that they are more beloved of God than others, and are the final cause of God's creation." The masses find this prejudice so satisfying that they have no desire to investigate their traditions in an intelligent manner. For Spinoza, the conflict is not between science and true religion but between science and ego/ethnocentricity.

Spinoza recognized that the Bible is not a book of science, written to inform humans about the nature of the universe, but a book of religion, con-

---

[35]Robert Larmer, ed., *Questions of Miracle* (Montreal: McGill, 1996) xvi.

taining stories that can inspire its readers to lead better lives. He introduced a basic principle of modern biblical exegesis:

> To interpret scriptural miracles and to understand from their accounts how they really took place, one must know the beliefs of those who originally related them and left us written records of them, and one must distinguish between these beliefs and what could have been presented to their senses. . . . Many things are related in Scripture as real, and were also believed to be real, but were nevertheless merely symbolical and imaginary; as that. . . . Elijah ascended to heaven in a chariot of fire and with horses of fire.

A good example of Spinoza's perspicacity can be found in what he wrote about Paul's treatment of Jesus' resurrection, anticipating by several centuries the interpretation that now prevails among scholars:

> Christ's resurrection from the dead was in fact of a spiritual kind, and was revealed only to the faithful according to their understanding, indicating that Christ was endowed with eternity and rose from the dead, and also by his life and death he provided an example of surpassing holiness, and that he raises his disciples from the dead in so far as they follow the example of his own life and death. . . . It is only on this hypothesis that 1 Corinthians 15 can be explained.[36]

Einstein disclosed his philosophical alignment when he cabled: "I believe in the God of Spinoza, who reveals himself in the orderly harmony of the universe. . . . I believe that intelligence is manifested throughout all nature."[37] Other sayings of his include: "A spirit is manifest in the laws of the universe—a spirit vastly superior to that of man, and one in the face of which we, with our modest powers, must feel humble."[38] "To know that what is impenetrable to us really exists, manifesting itself as the highest wisdom and the most radiant beauty which our dull faculties can comprehend only in their most primitive forms—this knowledge, this feeling, is at the center of true religiousness."[39] Einstein's worldview can be found in Vernon McCasland's comments on the way Spinoza viewed God's manifestation in the cosmos:

---

[36]Spinoza, *The Letters*, 338-39.

[37]*New York Times* (25 April 1929): 30.

[38]Helen Dukas, *Albert Einstein* (New York: Viking, 1972) 33.

[39]Henry Leach, ed., *Living Philosophies* (New York: Simon and Schuster, 1931) 6.

Spinoza never ceased to wonder at the marvelous things of the natural world. So his reverence for the processes revealed by chemistry, physics, biology, and the other sciences took the place of awe with respect to miracles in traditional religion. . . . His view shows how it is possible for one to retain a feeling of deep reverence although he doubts the occurrence of some of the miraculous events related in the Bible. . . . Naturalism in theology is deeply indebted to Spinoza. . . . God is like a dynamo which generates electricity that keeps a current going to all the motors, machines, and light globes throughout all the system supplied by the power plant. But we must not be misled by this simple analogy to think of God merely in terms of the physical energy of the world. The analogy must apply also to life in all its forms, to mind, and to all aspects of truth, goodness, and beauty.[40]

Spinoza was at a watershed in biblical interpretation. Prior to him, as Steven Smith observes, the Bible was used to understand natural phenomena but Spinoza used nature to interpret the Bible.[41] For example, Martin Luther, on dismissing Copernicus as a fool who wished to throw astronomy into disorder by arguing that the earth revolves around the sun, gave this authority for his cosmology, "I believe the Holy Scriptures, for Joshua commanded the sun to stand still, and not the earth."[42] Joshua had prayed that the sun halt its presumed regular daily journey across the sky so his army could complete defeating the Amorites before dark.[43] In 1616, the Vatican also condemned Copernicus's theory, declaring that it "runs completely counter to the divine Scriptures."[44] But after Spinoza's ideas were expressed a generation later, few churchmen have attempted to prove geocentrism by appealing to the biblical record of God temporarily stopping the sun's arching movement along the firmament.

* * *

In Britain, Spinoza's contemporary, Thomas Hobbes, had a similar approach to purported miracles. After citing the biblical claim that Moses'

---

[40]"Miracle," *The Interpreter's Dictionary of the Bible* (Nashville: Abingdon, 1962).

[41]Steven Smith, *Spinoza, Liberalism, and the Question of Jewish Identity* (New Haven: Yale Univeristy Press, 1997) 60.

[42]Helmut Lehmann, ed., *Luther's Works* (Philadelphia: Fortress, 1967) 54:359.

[43]Joshua 10:12-14.

[44]Hermann Kesten, *Copernicus* (New York: Roy, 1945) 375.

staff became a snake, and the Catholic priests' claim that sacramental bread becomes transformed into the body of Christ, he commented, "In these times I do not know one man that ever saw any such wondrous work, done by the charm or at the word or prayer of a man, that a man endued but with a mediocrity of reason would think supernatural."[45] Following Hobbes, Isaac Newton expressed well the view that the totality of truth about God and about the universe is far beyond human grasp. That devout Christian and astrophysics genius testified shortly before his death, "I do not know what I may appear to the world, but to myself I seem to have been only like a boy playing on the seashore, and diverting myself in now and then finding a smoother pebble or a prettier shell than ordinary, whilst the great ocean of truth lay all undiscovered before me."[46]

Subsequent scientists have joined Newton in recognizing that humility is needed to open the door to intellectual illumination and religious understanding. For example, twentieth-century geneticist John Haldane concluded: "The universe is not only queerer than we suppose, but queerer than we *can* suppose. . . . I suspect that there are more things in heaven and earth than are dreamed of, or can be dreamed of, in any philosophy."[47] Increasing the diameter of one's knowledge enlarges even more the circumference of one's ignorance. That is true in comprehending the processes of the physical sciences as well as of the human psyche, which is now slowly becoming understood. Whenever events seem to happen that are incompatible with how we believe things normally happen, then our understanding is inadequate. Either our perception is faulty or our accepted criteria for regular happenings—called natural law—is deficient.

A law of nature is ideally an absolute and universal principle known only to God. But what we know of a law of nature is a description of what has been perceived to be stable physical behavior. If current observations do not conform to an established law, then it is modified to include the presumed irregularity so it can more accurately be used for predictions. Consider, for example, the historical formulations of gravitational law. Galileo demonstrated that Aristotle was faulty in stating that heavier solid objects fall faster than lighter solid objects. After several more centuries,

---

[45]Thomas Hobbes, *Leviathan* 3.37.

[46]David Brewster, *Memoirs of Sir Isaac Newton* (Edinburgh: Constable, 1855) 2:407.

[47]John Haldane, *Possible Worlds* (London: Chatto, 1927) 286.

Einstein's relativity theory effected a slight change in Newton's law. Scientific progress results from revisions in such generalizations.

In the eighteenth century, Scottish empiricist David Hume's challenge to traditional ways of viewing miracles became the most influential philosophical writing on the subject. While avoiding a discussion of biblical miracles, Hume indirectly considered basic issues in interpreting them. His views are tersely expressed in the tenth chapter of his famous *Enquiry concerning Human Understanding*. The crux of his position is contained in this excerpt:

> A miracle is a violation of the laws of nature. . . . Nothing is esteemed a miracle if it ever happens in the common course of nature. It is no miracle that a man, seemingly in good health, should suddenly die; because such a kind of death, though more unusual than any other, has yet been frequently observed to happen. But it is a miracle, that a dead man should come to life; because that has never been observed in any age or country. . . . When anyone tells me that he saw a dead man restored to life, I immediately consider with myself whether it be more probable that this person should either deceive or be deceived, or that the fact which he relates should really have happened. . . . Suppose that all the historians who treat of England should agree that, on the first of January 1600, Queen Elizabeth died . . . and that, after being interred a month, she again appeared, resumed the throne, and governed England for three years. . . . I should only assert it to have been pretended, and that it neither was, nor possibly could be real. . . . The knavery and folly of men are such common phenomena that I should rather believe the most extraordinary events to arise from their concurrence, than admit of so signal a violation of the laws of nature.

The hypothetical case of a monarch's physical resurrection and postmortem reign substantially parallels accounts of Jesus' engaging in physical activity after rising from the dead. It would be implausible to think that either of those virtuous persons faked being dead in order to overwhelm people by a feigned resurrection. The issue then is the credibility of the those writing about the seemingly anomalous phenomena. Hume recognized the tendency, especially of people living in prescientific cultures, to accept uncritically what is told them and to prefer stories that fill them with emotional excitement. For example, if sailors were to attest that they had seen a mermaid, no rational modern person would accept their testimony that a half-human, half-fish creature actually exists. Miracle assessment involves weighing two types of evidence: the reliability of the historical witnesses and the laws of nature that are based on careful observations over time as to what happens without exception. It is possible that what has been designated as a law of nature is faulty, such as the ancient general assumption that the sun rotates around the earth.

Hume's approach to alleged miracles explains why modern scriptural interpreters usually place healing stories in a separate category from the rest. There are enough documented current instances of rapid remission from serious illnesses to recognize that no law of nature has been violated when health returns to victims. Allowing for exaggeration by recorders in gravity of sickness and in speed of recovery, stories of Jesus' assistance in the restoration of mental health or in the healing of certain physical maladies is no miracle as defined by Hume. The stories that he dismisses are those that have been classified as nature miracles, such as iron floating and the reanimation of a corpse that had been decomposing for days.[48]

Antony Flew, one of the more prominent twentieth-century critics of Christian orthodoxy, actually holds much in common with Augustine's view of miracles. After quoting Augustine's definition of a miracle, the philosopher commented, "The occurrence of events which are merely inexplicable *to us*, and *at present*, provides no good ground at all for believing that doctrine associated with these occurrences embody an authentic revelation of the transcendent."[49] Science aims at making extraordinary happenings understandable, but what it has conceptualized up to the present time is probably a small part of reality. If an event is incomprehensible by what scientists now know, then the scope of the natural order as currently understood lacks universality. Flew further explains:

> Suppose, for instance, that all previous observation and experiment had suggested that some performance was beyond human power; and suppose then we find, to our amazemeent, that after all some people can do it. . . . This . . . is a reason, not for postulating a series of infusions of supernatural grace, but for shaking up the psychological assumptions which these discoveries have discredited. . . . If something occurs inconsistent with some proposition previously believed to express such a [natural] law, this occurrence is not an occasion for proclaiming a miraculous violation, but a reason for confessing the error of the former belief, and for resolving to search for the law which does hold.[50]

---

[48]2 Kings 6:6; John 39-44.
[49]"Miracles," *The Encyclopedia of Philosophy* (New York: Macmillan, 1967).
[50]Antony Flew, *God and Philosophy* (London: Hutchinson, 1966) 149-50.

Modern Theologians

Although some of Augustine's thought is quite antiquated,[51] appreciation of his outlook on miracles has increased in recent centuries. Eighteenth-century Anglican Bishop Joseph Butler recognized that we speak of such because our knowledge is imperfect; consequently, "persons' notions of what is natural will be enlarged in proportion to their greater knowledge of the works of God."[52] According to Robert Mullin, in his book on Christian treatments of the miraculous in the nineteenth and twentieth centuries, "no person was more influential than Augustine."[53]

Albert Schweitzer, in his landmark book on the ways in which Jesus has been interpreted by European critical scholars, treats Karl Bahrdt as one of the first to attempt to explain away supernaturalism in the Gospels. Belonging to the eighteenth-century Age of Enlightenment, he accepted the Evangelists' accounts as factual but incomplete, and proceeded to give rational explanations of how Jesus allegedly operated a secret society. Consider Bahrdt's interpretation of the multitude feeding and the water walking episodes: "The Order had collected a great quantity of bread in a cave and this was gradually handed out [by his disciples] to Jesus, who stood at the concealed entrance. . . . Jesus walked towards the disciples over the surface of a great floating raft." Also, after Jesus' body was removed from the cross and taken to a cave, Joseph of Arimathea commenced measures of resuscitation, and after three days of therapy Jesus was able to walk again. At intervals he left his place of hiding to make appearances in the Jerusalem area and on the Damascus road.[54]

To those who found such deceptions ridiculous, Bahrdt queried, "You do not find it impossible that God should cast aside the laws of Nature, which he has made in his wisdom, and should transform the hunger-stilling property of five loaves into that of two thousand?"[55] Regarding miracles,

---

[51]William Phipps, *Influential Theologians on Wo/man* (Washington DC: University Press of America, 1980) 61-80.

[52]Joseph Butler, *The Analogy of Religion* (New York: Eaton, 1875) 65.

[53]Robert Mullin, *Miracles and the Modern Religious Imagination* (New Haven CT: Yale University Press, 1996) 10.

[54]Albert Schweitzer, *The Quest of the Historical Jesus* (repr.: Minneapolis: Fortress, 2001) 37, 40-42.

[55]Karl Bahrdt, *Explanatory Letters* (1784) 68.

Bahrdt said, "Instead of establishing us in our faith, they entangle us in dangerous superstition and accustom men to hold as true things which rest merely on strange witnesses and which not only lack the support of reason but are directly contrary to it." He insinuated about those who reported Jesus' actions:

> Healings of the sick only owe the name of miracle to the ignorant narrators. . . . If one remembers the ruling Jewish tendency to ascribe everything new, rare, inexplicable to an invisible divine power or to a demon; it then becomes highly understandable that the disciples of Jesus . . . related everything in such a way that the only circumstances which appeared were those which gave the matter a strange and marvellous aspect, while the natural features were entirely lost.[56]

A generation after Bahrdt, another attempt to explain how the miracle stories of the Gospels arose was made by David Strauss, a tutor at Tubingen University. While agreeing with Bahrdt on the implausibility of some of those stories, he did not view Jesus or the Evangelists as intentional deceivers. Strauss's ideas became much better known than those of his fellow German, in part because his lengthy *Leben Jesu kritisch bearbeitet* was translated into English (*Life of Jesus, Critically Examined*) by Mary Evans (aka George Eliot) in 1848.

Strauss was a student of Friedrich Schleiermacher, the most influential of nineteenth-century German theologians. That teacher had rejected supernaturalism, arguing that interference with the established natural order would display imperfection in the works of God.[57] Schleiermacher's emphasis on divine immanence motivated him to detect the wondrous presence of God throughout the natural order. He favored the philosophy of Spinoza, whom he eulogized as "full of religion, full of the Holy Spirit."[58] Schleiermacher realized that biblical writers spoke of God clothing lilies, growing grass, and fashioning limbs in a mother's womb, but they did not imply by such language that natural processes are obliterated. He wrote, "The more religious you would be the more you would see miracles everywhere."[59] Miracles, then are in the mind of the devout beholder.

---

[56]Bahrdt, *Explanatory Letters*, 66.

[57]Friedrich Schleiermacher, *The Christian Faith* (Edinburgh: Clark, 1928) 179.

[58]Friedrich Schleiermacher, *On Religion* (New York: Harper, 1958) 40.

[59]Friedrich Schleiermacher, *On Miracles* (New York: Ugar, 1955) 73.

Frederick Conybeare, who was among the first theologians to express
appreciation for Strauss's radical criticism, comments on the man and his
contribution:

> His *Leben Jesu* . . . was a gigantic success. He woke up to find himself famous,
> but an outcast. . . . He was deprived of his modest appointment in the univer-
> sity. . . . His enemies complained that he might at least have concealed his
> thoughts from the general public by writing in Latin. . . . Strauss summarily
> eliminated the supernatural element. . . . Strauss understood far better than the
> reactionaries of 1835 the conditions under which the gospels took shape, and
> the influences which molded their narratives. His critics argued that, since the
> first and fourth evangelists were eyewitnesses and took part in the miraculous
> episodes, their narratives cannot be myths in any sense whatever. . . . Strauss
> . . . declared that the single generation which elapsed between the death of
> Jesus and the date of the earliest gospel was amply long enough time for such
> mythical accretions as we find to gather about the memory of Jesus.[60]

Gregory Dawes, the leading contemporary interpreter of Strauss,
explains the specialized meaning of his key term "myth":

> It is a narrative which is historical in *form*, but fictitious as regards its *content*.
> . . . Myth "relinquishes the historical reality" of the biblical stories, [but] it
> does so only "in order to preserve to them an absolute inherent truth." . . . Myth
> is to be regarded as the product, not so much of the creative genius of an indi-
> vidual, but of the religious imagination of a community. . . . If the interpreter
> of myth is to understand its origins and meaning, he ought to seek out "the
> spirit and modes of thought of the people and of the age" in which it was pro-
> duced. . . . The New Testament myths . . . arose out of the Old Testament and
> out of the Jewish messianic expectations of the time immediately before the
> birth of Jesus. . . . Strauss did not argue that *all* the contents of the Gospels
> were "mythical." Rather he studied each incident on its own terms.[61]

Unlike Bahrdt, Strauss thought that the Evangelists had little interest in
writing a factual history of what Jesus actually did but a strong desire to
relate him to particular prophetic forecasts. They presumed that anything
that appeared to be predicted of a future messianic leader of the Jews must
have happened, so Hebrew scripture became the main quarry from which

---

[60]Frederick Conybeare, *History of New Testament Criticism* (London: Watts,
1910) 103-106.

[61]Gregory Dawes, *The Historical Jesus Question* (Louisville: Westminster/
John Knox, 2001) 86-88.

they dug up expectations for Jesus to fulfill. The purported miracles in the Gospels were mostly the product of what the religious imagination of the Evangelists did with their readings of their Bible. Prior to Strauss the common assumption was that the Israelite prophets were preternaturally able to see facts of the distant future, especially pertaining to the life and mission of the promised Messiah. But Strauss launched what he called a mythical interpretation that contends that the Evangelists looked at the prophets retrojectively. They searched texts written in the distant past to find wonderous happenings and appropriated them in telling about activities of Jesus. For example, they found that Isaiah described the messianic age as a time when the deaf will hear, the blind will see, and the lame will be restored; hence, dramatic stories were woven to convey that Jesus fulfilled that expectation.[62]

In the preface to his *Life of Jesus*, Strauss declares that his aim is to supplant the dominant biblical interpretations of his day, namely the "antiquated system of supernaturalism and rationalism." He then plunges into a critical examination of Jesus' birth stories that are found only in Matthew and Luke. Convinced that the stated birthplace in those Gospels was unrelated to historical fact, Strauss discusses the improbability of Joseph and Mary going to Bethlehem to be registered for a census. Placement of the nativity in that town originated in the mind of a Christian who read verses from the Hebrew Bible with the perspective that prescient writers living centuries earlier had received details of Jesus' biography.[63] Matthew quoted from Micah's prophecy of a king who would be born in Bethlehem, and declared its fulfillment in Jesus.[64]

In spite of the claim of two Evangelists that Jesus was born in Bethlehem, scholars now tend to accept Strauss. They find more plausible what Mark and John suggest, that Nazareth was Jesus' town of origin.[65] Those two Gospels refer to Nazareth as Jesus' native place or fatherland (*patris*).[66]

---

[62]Isaiah 35:5-6; Luke 7: 22; David Strauss, *A New Life of Jesus* (London: Williams, 1879) 1:202.

[63]David Strauss, *The Life of Jesus Critically Examined* (Philadelphia: Fortress, 1973) 152-56.

[64]Micah 5:2; Matthew 2:5-6.

[65]Mark 1:24; John 1:45-46; Theissen and Merz, 164-65; John Meier, *A Marginal Jew* (New York: Doubleday, 1991) 1:407.

[66]Mark 6:1; John 4:44.

In John's Gospel, some critics asked about Jesus: "Surely the Messiah does not come from Galilee, does he? Has not the scripture said that the Messiah is descended from David and comes from Bethlehem, the village where David lived?"[67] No attempt is made to inform the questioners that Jesus indeed was born in Bethlehem, probably because that was not John's understanding. The unimportance of Nazareth is displayed by its not being mentioned either in the Hebrew Bible or by Josephus, even though his historical writings tell of numerous Galilean towns in Jesus' day. Apparently Bethlehem was preferred by Matthew and Luke as the site of Jesus' birth because it was a more prestigious place; it was the birthplace of David, the most noted of the earlier anointed Jewish rulers, and it was where Ruth lived, David's famous ancestress. As the Kellers point out, prophecy fulfillment was the determining factor, "Jesus' actual birthplace is replaced . . . by a theological one."[68] Multiple references are made to "Jesus of Nazareth" in all the Gospels, and a total of twenty in the New Testament, but none to "Jesus of Bethlehem."

Strauss may have provided the best key for understanding the way supernatural feats are imbedded in the Gospels. He stated about Jesus: "He must be transfigured on a mountain, even as his prototype Moses had descended from his Mount Sinai with shining countenance. It was necessary that he should have raised the dead, that he should have multiplied insufficient food, else would he have lagged behind Elijah and Elisha."[69]

Traditionalists were shocked by Strauss even though he accepted the theist's doctrine of a personal God.[70] While skeptical of biblical miracles, he did not think of the Evangelists as cunning. He accepted stories of healings as historical if they could be duplicated in reliable therapeutic literature apart from the Bible. Regarding Jesus saying to the woman with an irregular menstrual flow, Strauss quoted and commented: "'Your faith has made you whole.' He could not have expressed himself more truly, more modestly, more correctly, or more precisely."[71]

Pertaining to the period following Jesus' death, Strauss wrote, "It was from renewed and profounder study of the sacred writings of the Old

---

[67]John 7:41-42.
[68]Keller, *Miracles in Dispute*, 218.
[69]David Strauss, *The Old Faith and the New* (New York: Holt, 1873) 59.
[70]Strauss, *A New Life of Jesus* 1:198.
[71]Strauss, *A New Life of Jesus* 1:365.

Testament that the certainty arose that their Jesus, in spite of suffering and death, had been the Messiah, that his suffering and death had been for him only the passage to the glory of the Messiah." Strauss perceived that the Emmaus narrative shows that a new comprehension of Jesus' suffering—combined with elevated memories of his past companionship in travel and at meals—resulted in an unforgettable awareness of his abiding presence. The subsequent resurrection experience by Paul was understood by Strauss as "a vision which . . . took place in his own mind."[72]

Strauss wanted to banish the "supernatural religion of mysteries" contained in the New Testament in order to recover the "patience, gentleness, and charity" of Jesus' "religion of humanity."[73] He ended his *New Life of Jesus* with a colossal sentence, part of which follows:

> The critic is convinced that he is committing no offence against what is sacred, nay rather that he doing a good and necessary work, when he sweeps away all that makes Jesus a supernatural Being, as well meant and perhaps even at first sight beneficial, but in the long run mischievous and now absolutely destructive, and restores . . . that moral pattern in which the historical Jesus did indeed first bring to light many principal features.

Schweitzer gives this tribute to Strauss:

> He was not the greatest, and not the deepest, of theologians, but he was the most truthful. . . . Disappointment and suffering gave his life its consecration. It unrolls itself before us like a tragedy, in which, in the end, everything is transfigured by the gentle radiance which shines forth from the nobility of the sufferer.[74]

In 1864, as a young scholar, Friedrich Nietzsche "savored the work of the incomparable Strauss" who maintained that Jesus was an extraordinary personality but was not to be identified with the supernatural figure of the Gospels. Although Nietzsche later attacked some of Strauss's ideas, he continued to share the view that the real Jesus should be critically extracted from the untrustworthy interpretations of the Evangelists. The German philosopher wrote: "What concerns me is the psychological type of the Redeemer. This *could* be contained in the Gospels despite the Gospels,

---

[72]Strauss, *A New Life of Jesus* 1:423, 429, 430-31, 436-37, 414.
[73]Strauss, *A New Life of Jesus* 1:xvi; 2:436-37.
[74]Schweitzer, *The Quest of the Historical Jesus*, 65.

however mutilated or embroidered with alien features: as that of Francis of Assisi is contained in the legends about him despite the legends."[75]

Like Strauss, Nietzsche presumed that "Christianity can be understood only by referring to the soil out of which it grew."[76] He accepted Strauss's argument that the Gospel portrayals of Jesus have come from early admirers who were convinced that Jesus must have done more marvels than any Israelite hero. Hence they told stories of Jesus raising the dead, creating a meal, and ascending into heaven—as in the Elijah-Elisha legends. Nietzsche attributed "faith in unbelievable things" to Jesus' followers.[77] But the man hidden under the literary accretions did not claim to have power to intervene in nature's orderliness, according to that philosopher. He stated:

> Jesus' faith does not prove itself, either by miracles or by rewards and promises, and certainly not "by scriptures": it is every moment its own miracle, its own reward, its own proof, its own "kingdom of God." . . . The idea is lacking that a faith, a "truth" could be proved by reasons (his proofs are inner "lights," inner feelings of pleasure and self-affirmations).[78]

Nietzsche is appropriately remembered widely for this aphorism, "There has truly been only one Christian, and he died on the cross."[79] His understanding was that Jesus did not resort to rational arguments or to supernatural wonders; the only validation of his teaching was the integrity he exhibited through a life climaxed by crucifixion.[80] Displaying considerable acumen, Nietzsche argued that falsifications about the real Jesus have abounded from the earliest Christians onward. Most church leaders have imaged Jesus as a miracle worker, and have accepted as historical even such "a dreadful corruption" as his cursing a fig tree.[81] Such crudities were due to proselyters who vulgarized the noble message of Jesus in order to win converts from uncouth pagan cults.[82]

Ernest Renan, a contemporary of Nietzsche, likewise followed Strauss in rejecting supernaturalism:

---

[75]Friedrich Nietzsche, *The Antichrist* 28-29.
[76]Nietzsche, *The Antichrist*, 24.
[77]Nietzsche, *The Will to Power*, 169.
[78]Nietzsche, *The Antichrist*, 32.
[79]Nietzsche, *The Antichrist*, 39.
[80]Nietzsche, *The Antichrist*, 40.
[81]Nietzsche, *The Will to Power*, 164.
[82]Niezsche, *The Antichrist*, 37.

Those who admit the supernatural believe in something that is outside the province of science and accept an explanation that is set aside by the astronomer, the physicist, the chemist, the geologist, the physiologist, and also the historian. We reject the existence of supernatural occurrences for the same reason that we reject the existence of centaurs and hippogriffes. . . . I say, "the Gospels are legends; they may contain history, but certainly, all that they set forth is not historical."[83]

Renan, a French Catholic, joined Spinoza, Strauss, and Nietzsche in receiving hostility from the theological establishment. As a result of challenging traditional doctrine, they were ostracized and had difficulty making a living. Renan's charming books on the New Testament—in particular his *Vie de Jesus*—shocked Catholics especially, for they had previously had little awareness of critical studies of Jesus' life.

* * *

Some Anglicans were open to receiving ideas from the European continent that could reconcile Christian tradition with Britain's newly developing sciences of geology and biology. Oxford theologian Baden Powell, who was influential in forming Charles Darwin's worldview, and one of the first scholars to accept his evolutionary theory,[84] wrote regarding miracles, "The enlarged critical and inductive study of the natural world cannot but tend powerfully to evince the inconceivableness of imagined interruptions of natural order."[85] Powell was aware of the theological sea change, "If miracles were in the estimation of a former age among the chief *supports* of Christianity, they are at present among the main *difficulties*, and hindrances to its acceptance."[86] He urged Christians to look for evidence of the divine in moral changes within people rather than in physical changes in the order of nature.[87]

In 1869 zoologist Thomas Huxley introduced "agnosticism" into English. According to the *Oxford English Dictionary*, he coined the term to express that God cannot be known by human empirical and rational facul-

---

[83]Ernest Renan, *Vie de Jesus* (1867) preface.

[84]William Phipps, *Darwin's Religious Odyssey* (Harrisburg PA: Trinity, 2002) 50, 86.

[85]*Essays and Reviews* (London: Parker, 1860) 110.

[86]*Essays and Reviews*, 140.

[87]*Essays and Reviews*, 127.

ties. "Agnosticism" (*a*, "no" + *gnosis*, "knowledge" in Greek) was used by Huxley and Darwin to label their own outlook, but it has been subsequently often misused to refer to atheism, the belief of those who claim to have knowledge that there is no God. Huxley was informed by the epistemology of Immanuel Kant who argued that our knowledge is restricted to the "phenomenal world," the realm humans construct in accord with patterns provided by their minds. Accordingly, we can have belief in, but no certain knowledge of, the external world as it really is, whether considering matter, God, or immortality of the soul. According to Kant, absolute proof of the existence *or* nonexistence of God is not possible. Huxley accepted the New Testament definition of faith as "the assurance of things hoped for."[88] Yet he pointed out that one may have absolute faith in the honesty of a friend but that provides no evidence that he did not commit a crime. One's subjective faith has little bearing on objective reality.[89]

Huxley explained, "[My outlook is] antithetic to the 'gnostic' of Church history, who professed to know so much about the very things of which I was ignorant."[90] A group known as Gnostics, who were declared by the majority group of early Christians to be heretical, were disdainful of those who did not claim to have received esoteric knowledge from God.[91] Huxley endorsed the advice of the apostle Paul, "Prove all things; hold fast to what is good."[92]

Philosopher of religion Geddes MacGregor appropriates "agnostic" to express his own perspective and accepts a fifth-century creed, mistakenly attributed to Bishop Athanasius, in which God is acknowledged as "incomprehensible":

There is a profound agnosticism in all authentic religion, perhaps most vividly in Christianity. . . . No religious revelation worthy of serious attention has ever purported to "solve" mysteries, least of all the mystery of divine Being. On the contrary, . . . we are to rejoice if we get as much as a glimmer of light shrouded

---

[88]Hebrews 11:1.
[89]Thomas Huxley et al., *Christianity and Agnosticism* (New York: Appleton, 1889) 18-19, 41-42.
[90]Huxley, *Christianity and Agnosticism*, 38.
[91]1 Timothy 6:20.
[92]Huxley, *Christianity and Agnosticism*, 43; 1 Thessalonians 5:21.

in a cloud of puzzlement. . . . The paradox that God is unknown yet known is expounded in medieval Christian Scholasticism by St. Thomas.[93]

Scorned by Huxley were theologians who pretended to be completely certain about the nature of God and uncritically accepting of biblical supernaturalism. In examining the story of Jesus' cure of the Gerasene demoniac, he expressed doubt that "unclean spirits" were cast out of the man and then entered a large herd of swine, causing them to stampede and drown in the sea.[94] He compared that alleged demonology to the "wicked nonsense" in European history of believing that witches were possessed by the devil.

But Huxley also opposed atheists who were immodest about the limits of human cognition. He said that agnosticism undermined "not only the greater part of popular theology but also the greater part of popular anti-theology."[95] In his day, atheism was especially associated with the dialectical materialism of Marx and Engels. Huxley declared, "I, individually, am no materialist, but on the contrary believe materialism to involve grave philosophical error."[96]

Aubrey Moore and Matthew Arnold, outstanding Oxford scholars in the Victorian era, believed that Christianity would be better off with a gospel sans supernaturalism. Moore asserted: "A theory of 'supernatural interferences' is as fatal to theology as to science" because "God cannot interfere with Himself. His creative activity is present everywhere."[97] Arnold thought that those who interpret biblical miracles figuratively gain more true religious insights. He described the apostle Paul as having a scientific outlook and as understanding Jesus' resurrection as a spiritual experience arising out of those who identified with what preceded and followed his death.[98] Another Victorian, Episcopalian Richard Newton, viewed Jesus' miracles from this perspective: "Those unusual gifts [of Jesus] are not

---

[93]Geddes MacGregor, *God Beyond Doubt* (New York: Lippincott, 1966) 183-85.

[94]Mark 5:1-20.

[95]Quoted in Adrian Desmond, *Huxley* (Reading PA: Addison-Wesley, 1997) 528.

[96]Thomas Huxley, *Methods and Results* (New York: Appleton, 1896) 155.

[97]Aubrey Moore, *Science and the Faith* (London: Kegan Paul, 1892) 225.

[98]Matthew Arnold, *St. Paul and Protestantism* (New York: Macmillan, 1883) 71-76.

supernatural. They are all natural, orderly, under the reign of law. . . . They are the marvels of a marvelous personality."[99]

Cardinal John Henry Newman helped Catholics accept scientific evolution by providing them with a modified theology. He rejected the traditional thought of God vis a vis nature as more of an interferer than a cooperator. Newman also championed the Augustinian conception of a being who operates more from within the processes of nature than by triggering abnormal events from outside the cosmos. He admitted to his fellow Victorians, "I frankly confess that the present advance of science tends to make it probable that various facts take place, and have taken place, in the order of nature, which hiterto have been considered by Catholics as simply supernatural."[100]

* * *

Leading twentieth-century theologians continued an assault on supernaturalism. Late in life, Oxford exegete William Sanday brought fresh notions of scholarship to conservative Christianity. He quoted the "golden words" of Augustine on miracles to express his changed position, and explained:

> In popular usage the word 'miracle' is often used . . . to imply real contradiction or violation of the accustomed order of nature. . . . But I do not think that they [New Testament miracles] involve any real breach of the order of nature.[101]

Anglican Dean Inge of St. Paul's Cathedral criticized the Catholic search for miracles to determine the worthiness of a candidate for sainthood:

> There are few among our ecclesiastics and theologians who would spend five minutes in investigating any alleged supernatural occurrence in our own time. It would be assumed that, if true, it must be ascribed to some obscure natural cause. . . . Supernaturalism . . . is the most unsatisfactory of all theories,

---

[99]Richard Newton, *Christian Science* (New York: 1898) 30.

[100]John Henry Newman, *Apologia pro Vita Sua* (London: Longmans, 1890) 303.

[101]William Sanday, *Divine Overruling* (Edinburgh: Clark, 1920) 66; idem, *Miracle* (London: Longmans, 1911) 8.

traversing as it does the first article in the creed of science—the uniformity of nature.[102]

Writing later, in 1929, Inge shared some of Augustine's perspective when describing the worldview of those who accept modern science:

No one says dogmatically that miracles are impossible; that is more than anyone can know. But whereas in the dark ages it was considered the most natural explanation of a strange occurrence to assume that it was a miracle, we now expect to find either that it was not a miracle or that it did not happen. We do not call telegraphs, telephones and broadcasting miraculous, though they would have seemed so two hundred years ago; they are not miraculous, because their mechanism is understood. If something apparently inexplicable happens, we assume that there is a natural explanation, and sooner or later we find it.[103]

German theologian Ernst Troeltsch emphasized principle of analogy. Similar to the approach of Hume, he stated that we reconstruct history by using parallels to contemporary events known to be genuine after careful scrutiny.[104] We understand the past by presuming that the fundamental natural regularities currently experienced have always been present. Only if the interference of supernatural powers into natural processes are found in the present can they be postulated for ancient times. Accordingly, Gospels specialist Gerd Theissen insists that for an event reported in the past to merit consideration for historicity it should resonate with our own experience and understanding:

Miracle only becomes a problem where one's own experience knows no analogies to miracles. We . . . tend to regard the elements in them that contradict our own experience as unhistorical. We cannot imagine anyone walking on the water or multiplying loaves in a miraculous way and are therefore rightly sceptical about these reports. But the same principle of analogy which is the basis of our scepticism obliges us to recognize the possibility of healings and exorcisms. For in many cultures there is an abundance of well-documented analogies to them.[105]

---

[102]William Inge, *Outspoken Essays* (London: Longmans, 1919) 123-24.

[103]Dean Inge, *Labels and Libels* (New York: Harper, 1929) 70.

[104]"Historiography," *Encyclopedia of Religion and Ethics* (New York: Scribner's, 1928).

[105]Gerd Theissen and Annette Merz, *The Historical Jesus* (Philadelphia: Fortress, 1996) 310.

Harry Emerson Fosdick, a twentieth-century bellwether of liberal Protestantism, exclaimed, "If the church had followed Augustine's lead, how different the course of subsequent thought would have been!" But many churchmen after Augustine theorized that the established cosmic order is ruptured when a miracle is performed, and the scientific implications of that outlook in our scientific era have been, in Fosdick's opinion, "disastrous."[106] Reginald Fuller, another leading twentieth-century New Testament scholar, begins his book on biblical miracles by quoting the way Augustine defined them, and then he acknowledges that it contains religious virtue, "This formula is attractive both for its scientific and theological humility."[107]

Thoughtful persons are now recognizing that the presumption of supernatural intervention tends to undermine rather than bolster theism. Theologian George Hedley tells of conversing with a woman who adamantly claimed she was an atheist. He discovered what she meant by the deity she was denying, "She didn''t think there was a grandfatherly gentleman sitting on a heavenly throne, watching mankind through a supernatural telescope, and now and then interfering to direct matters more nearly to his own satisfaction." But she thought that the orderly universe "may have been planned and set going by a conscious intelligence."[108] The issue here is well stated by philosopher Christine Overall:

> If order, regularity, and harmony constitute evidence for God, then miracles cannot also be accepted as evidence for his existence, for they are, to follow the metaphor, dissonances in the harmony. . . . Hence, a Christian believer cannot have it both ways. A miracle, a violation of natural law or a permanently inexplicable event, is a moment of chaos, a gap in the spatiotemporal structure. If one were to occur, it would therefore have to constitute evidence against the Christian God's existence.[109]

---

[106]Harry Emerson Fosdick, *The Modern Use of the Bible* (New York: Macmillan, 1934) 139-41.

[107]Reginald Fuller, *Interpreting the Miracles* (Philadelphia: Westminster, 1963) 8.

[108]George Hedley, *The Symbol of the Faith* (New York: Macmillan, 1948) 20-21.

[109]"Miracles as Evidence against the Existence of God," in Larmer, ed., *Questions of Miracle*, 135-36.

Miracles depend on the perspective from which one views nature. Helmut Thielicke confesses: "If I speak of . . . miracles of earth's beauty, then I do not say, 'Here we have a supernatural intervention by God.' More probably, I only want to say, 'Here we have something quite ordinary, yet I see something extraordinary in it.'"[110] Elizabeth Browning gave poetic expression to that immanence theology. She mused on the burning bush story pertaining to Moses' call to become a prophet, which traditionally has been interpreted supernaturally. Browning indelibly expressed how a natural phenomenon can convey a divine message, if an individual is properly attuned:

> . . . Earth's crammed with heaven,
> And every common bush afire with God:
> But only he who sees, takes off his shoes,
> The rest sit round it, and pluck blackberries.[111]

Rudolf Bultmann, one of the most influential New Testament interpreters of the past century, encouraged Christians to "demythologize," that is, to discard the obsolete, supernatural worldview. But he did not wish to leave only scientific secularism to fill the void. Rather, Bultmann's aim was positive; he used Paul's language to express the hope that Christians would "eliminate a false stumbling block and bring into sharp focus the real stumbling block, the word of the cross."[112] Bultmann urged that miracles should only be associated with one's internal awareness of, and gratitude for, God's natural activity in creation:

> The very idea of miracle in the sense of an event contrary to nature has become untenable and *must be abandoned*. . . . The Christian really has the possibility *of seeing ever new miracles*. The operation of the universe which to the eye of unfaith must appear as a sequence of events subject to law, acquires for him the character of a universe in which God acts.[113]

In his lengthy discussion of biblical miracles, Jesuit theologian Piet Schoonberg indicates that he shares much of the outlook of Augustine and Bultmann:

---

[110]Helmut Thielicke, *I Believe* (Philadelphia: Fortress, 1963) 45.

[111]Elizabeth Browning, *Aurora Leigh* bk. VII, ll. 20-23.

[112]Rudolf Bultmann, *Jesus Christ and Mythology* (New York: Scribner's, 1958) 36; see 1 Corinthians 1:23.

[113]*Religion in Life* (Winter 1957): 65, 69, 74.

Once we have purified our idea of the miracle of all thoughts of an additioinal creation or an intervention from without, an exclusion of created causes, a cancellation of laws, we are left with an expectation, and that a limited one, concerning encounter with a miracle. . . . The extraordinary is at all times to be expected from God. For he is the one "who by the power [*dynamis*] at work within us is able to do far more abundantly than all that we ask or think" (Eph. 3:20). . . . On the other hand, this same conception of the miracle will also limit our expectation. . . . We expect God . . . to remain faithful to the laws of his own creation, which are revealed primarily in the normal course of things. . . . An exclusion does not follow from the fact that God is active. . . . It is therefore not at all rationalism, rather healthy theology, to attempt to point out such forces at play in miraculous events.[114]

Paul Tillich brought to America developments in German scholarship pertaining to an existential way for perceiving religious testimony. He wrote: "Miracles cannot be interpreted in terms of a supranatural interference in natural processes. . . . A genuine miracle is first of all an event which is astonishing, unusual, shaking, without contradicting the rational structure of reality."[115] Tillich argued that an "antisupernaturalistic attitude" is needed for an indepth understanding of Christianity. To define a miracle—as C. S. Lewis[116] and others have—as "an interference with nature by supernatural power" was, for Tillich, "distorted because it means that God has to destroy his creation in order to produce his salvation. . . . God is then split in himself." He continued: "Miracles operate in terms of ordinary causality. To think of them as involving an objective breaking of the structure of reality, or suspending the laws of nature, is superstition."[117]

Tillich's separation of God's transcendence from supernaturalism was his "great contribution to theology," according to Bishop John Robinson.[118] His antisupernaturalism was judged to be so central to his thought that it is singled out in the Indiana park where he is memorialized. These words of his are carved there on a stone, "Today we know what the New Testament

---

[114]Piet Schoonberg, *Covenant and Creation* (Notre Dame IN: University of Notre Dame Press, 1969) 208-209.

[115]Paul Tillich, *Systematic Theology* (Chicago: University of Chicago Press, 1951) 1:116.

[116]C. S. Lewis, *Miracles* (New York: Macmillan, 1947) 15.

[117]Paul Tillich, *Ultimate Concern* (New York: Harper, 1965) 158-59, 161.

[118]John Robinson, *Honest to God* (Philadelphia: Westminster, 1963) 56.

always knew—that miracles are signs pointing to the presence of a divine power in nature and history, and that they are in no way negations of natural laws."[119]

American theologian John Macquarrie shared Tillich's view of miracles. He rejected the idea of otherworldly irruptions to explicate events, because such causation cannot be correlated with analogous scientific or historical happenings:

> Science proceeds on the assumption that whatever events occur in the world can be accounted for in terms of other events that also belong within the world; and if on some occasions we are unable to give a complete account of some happening—and presumably all our accounts fall short of completeness—the scientific conviction is that further research will bring to light further factors in the situation, but factors that will turn out to be just as immanent and this-worldly as those already known. . . . The event may still be regarded as a miracle in the sense of an event that excites wonder and in which God's presence and activity become known, but this is quite independent of any attempt to represent the event as a supernatural intervention.[120]

In the present generation, fellows of the Jesus Seminar rank Strauss high because of his "monumental" book on Jesus. They recognize his distinction of the "mythical" from the historical in the Gospels. Generations passed after his death before his seminal study of the Gospels made its impact in transforming New Testament scholarship. Now, due to the general acceptance of Strauss's approach by those not shackled by commitments to church dogma, "the gospels are now assumed to be narratives in which the memory of Jesus is embellished by mythic elements that express the church's faith in him, and by plausible fictions that enhance the telling of the gospel story for first-century listeners who knew about divine men and miracle workers firsthand."[121]

Marcus Borg, one of the more moderate Seminar fellows, explains:

> Prior to Strauss, scholars generally agreed that the miracle stories were to be read as historical narratives, and differed on the question of whether a super-natural or natural explanation of the story was to be sought. . . . Strauss cut through this preoccupation with treating the miracle stories as historical and

---

[119]Paul Tillich, *The New Being* (New York: Scribner's, 1955) 44.

[120]John Macquarrie, *Principles of Christian Theology* (New York: Scribner's, 1966) 227-28.

[121]Robert Funk et al., *The Five Gospels* (New York: Macmillan, 1993) 3-5.

suggested instead that many of the miracle stories are to be understood as literary creations of the early church which draw upon the rich imagery of the Old Testament: their meaning lies in their symbolism. Strauss's book was radical in his day; a review called it the most pestilential book ever vomited out of the bowels of hell, and he was blackballed from the universities of Europe. With modification, his approach has now become the position of mainstream scholarship.[122]

The miracle stories that have continued through the course of church history should be treated similarly. About these, Jeffrey Eaton comments:

> The reports are varied and legion, sometimes investigated by scientific methods, but usually not. The stories are also of varying quality; some are instances of palpable charlatanry, some are the product of superstitious credulousness, some are matters of abnormal psychology, and some are genuinely mysterious and deserve serious consideration. But it seems to me neither necessary nor desirable to interpret any of them an instances of supernatural intervention, intervention from *above* what nature permits. . . . The fact that an occurrence is extraordinary is no guarantee that it is a miraculous overriding of nature by God.[123]

Nature can be viewed as the Creator's "handiwork"[124] sans freedom. Scientists are motivated to probe nature because they are confident of its regularity. The unscientific, by contrast, have an anthropomorphizing tendency and try to project onto nature human-like voluntary conduct. Astrologers, for example, assume that certain astral bodies have wills and foresight as well as the power to effect such. The Greek word for God, *theos*, may have originally meant "wonder," in accord with the common primitive belief that the wind, sea, and heavenly luminaries have the liberty to accomplish supernatural marvels. But those natural forces are impersonal and should not be associated with the making and executing of choices.

In his exploration of Jesus' miracles, E. P. Sanders comments on the outlook of those who appreciate both scientific and religious approaches to understanding:

> When people today look back on miracles in the ancient world (not just those in the Bible), they naturally wish to explain them rationally, since Cicero's view that nothing unnatural can happen, and that whatever happens is natural

---

[122]Marcus Borg, *Jesus, a New Vision* (San Francisco: Harper, 1987) 74.
[123] *Modern Theology* (April 1985): 215.
[124]Psalm 19:1.

has become the dominant opinion, even though a lot of people do not share it. . . . Ancient people attributed to supernatural powers (good or evil spirits) what modern people explain in other ways. It is perfectly reasonable for us to explain ancient events in our own terms. In my opinion, it is plausible to explain an exorcism as a psychosomatic cure. It is, however, an error to think that rational explanations of the miracles can establish that the gospels are entirely factual. Some of the miracle stories cannot be explained on the basis of today's scientific knowledge.[125]

Most people who live in any generation would not be open to Sanders' approach because they take testimonies of miracles as truth without scrutinizing the evidence. Russian novelist Fyodor Dostoevsky commented on a perennial human craving: "Man seeks not so much God as the miraculous. And as man cannot bear to be without the miraculous, he will create new miracles of his own for himself, and will worship deeds of sorcery and witchcraft." Dostoevsky pointed to the human obsession with those who claim to be able to suspend natural causality in order to set in bolder relief the intention of the founder of Christianity. The Grand Inquisitor, in *The Brothers Karamazov*, says to Jesus, "You did not want to bring man to you by miracles, because you wanted their freely given love rather than the servile rapture of slaves subdued forever by a display of power."[126] That summing up of Jesus' values was drawn from a strand of New Testament thought. The Jesus of Paul's letters is awesome not because he intervenes in the natural process, but because he inaugurates a community bearing these nourishing "fruits of the Spirit": "love, joy, peace, patience, kindness, generosity, faithfulness, gentleness, and self-control."[127]

---

[125]E. P. Sanders, *The Historical Figure of Jesus* (New York: Penguin, 1993) 158-59.

[126]Fyodor Dostoevsky, *The Brothers Karamazov* 1:5.

[127]Galatians 5:22-23.

Chapter 9

Paul and the Historical Jesus

The Gospel according to Paul

Paul's letters have been foundational for this study. Because of their re-vealing quality, no personality is better known from the ancient era than the self-designated "man in Christ."[1] That contemporary of Jesus stood near the headwater of the river of Christianity. Paul described and to some extent directed its flow during the crucial first generation of the church. From his perspective at the beginning of Christianity, he was unable to discern his importance in his own generation, much less the preeminent role he would be playing in subsequent generations. His self-evaluation that he was "the least of the apostles"[2] shows how unreliable individuals are in estimating their own abiding significance. Jesus' paradox that "the last will become first" is well illustrated by the chief persecutor of Christianity becoming metamorphosed into its seminal theologian. As the author of a quarter of the New Testament books, Paul provides the only firsthand source of earliest Christianity written by a main leader. Moreover, Acts of the Apostles, the first book of church history, deals in large part with his career.

The writings of the rest of what came to be the New Testament belong to the second and third generations of Christians, beginning about thirty years after the death of Jesus. The pristine fountain of God's spirit, as expressed in Jesus, became polluted as it moved downstream among later generations of followers who had pagan backgrounds in which the occult was prominent. Typical of religions generally, Christianity has been impacted by historical developments and its practice has become in part a following the followers of the followers of Jesus who are far removed from the pure source. Paul may give a clearer picture of the core teachings of Jesus than the later Gospels; for example, Romans 12–14 arguably provides more clarity on Jesus' ethics than the Sermon on the Mount in Matthew 5–7. Paul's succinct dictum, "Rejoice with those who rejoice, weep with those who weep," is well illustrated by Luke, who represents Jesus as

---

[1]2 Corinthians 12:2.
[2]1 Corinthians 15:9.

celebrating with Levi when he became a disciple, and as grieving with a widow at the death of her son.[3]

Paul's letters contain the gospel in its least adulterated form and thereby lead us closer to the essence of earliest Christianity. His undisputed letters are the only writings with undoubted apostolic authority. Indeed, there is only one gospel in the New Testament that is explicitly associated with an apostolic author. "According to my gospel"[4] was a phrase used by Paul before the Gospels were written and, in two cases, later attributed to apostolic authors. Most of the uses of "gospel" (Greek, *euaggelion*) in the New Testament are not in the Gospels, but in Paul's letters. For example, Paul announces at the beginning of Romans, his magnum opus, that his main theme is the "power of the gospel." He uses the noun "gospel" dozens of times and the verb "to proclaim the good news" is frequently found. For understanding the New Testament, it cannot be overemphasized that Paul's message was the gospel before the Gospels.

Although Paul is probably the most reliable source for the learning about Jesus, his letters have generally been neglected over the centuries by those engaged in that biographical search. James Charlesworth, typical of historical Jesus questers, boldly asserts that the New Testament Gospels "always take precedence over all other sources."[5] Historian Donald Akenson is amazed to find that "almost nobody" starts a search for the Jesus of history by examining Paul's letters. His book on that apostle is intriguingly subtitled, "A Skeleton Key to the Historical Jesus." Alkenson shows that factual information garnered about Jesus from those letters is more trustworthy than what is found in the Gospels.[6] Jerome Murphy-O'Connor, in a scholarly probe of Paul's life, is also convinced that accounts of what Jesus said and did undergirded Paul's theology.[7]

Unfortunately, the parts of the New Testament were not arranged, as were the three parts of the Hebrew Scriptures, according to the time when they received community acceptance as authoritative. For Paul's letters

---

[3]Romans 12:15; Luke 5:27-29; 7:11-13.

[4]Romans 2:16, 16:25.

[5]James Charlesworth and Walter Weaver, eds., *Jesus Two Thousand Years Later* (Harrisburg: Trinity, 2000) 88.

[6]Donald Akenson, *Saint Saul* (New York: 2000) 122, 228.

[7]Jerome Murphy-O'Connor, *Paul: a Critical Life* (Oxford: Clarendon, 1996) 91.

would then have the priority in the New Testament that the Pentateuch has in the Old. Over the centuries the Torah has been exalted in the synagogue as being the sine qua non of Hebrew scriptures. The authentic letters of Paul were the first Christian writings to attain a status equal to the Hebrew scriptures.[8] Within several decades of Paul's death they were gathered from the churches to whom they were addressed.[9] The letters were then circulated together, enabling Christians to quote from them before the end of the first century. At that time Clement referred frequently to Paul's letters, but he hardly alluded to Peter even though Clement was his legendary successor as bishop of Rome. The Pauline epistolary corpus became the nucleus of what emerged several centuries later as the New Testament.

* * *

What did Paul include in writing about the historic Jesus? Significance can be found in both what he did and did not mention. He did not begin by alluding to a heavenly figure who became incarnate. Bishop John Robinson soundly wrote,

> Jesus was not . . . for Paul, as he became for later dogmatics, a divine being veiled in flesh or one who stripped himself of supernatural attributes to become human; he was a man who by total surrender of his own gain or glory was able to reveal or "unveil" the glory of God (2 Cor. 3:12-18) as utterly gracious, self-giving love (Rom. 5:6-8).[10]

Paul's commitment to a human Jesus is displayed in his emphasis upon "the word [*logos*] of the cross."[11] Greeks, who viewed their gods as "the immortals," were repelled by Paul's focus on Jesus' mortality and on his execution as a common criminal.

Although neither Paul nor any other ancient writer composed a biography of Jesus, he crafted a cameo depicting his essential qualities. In the holy family of *Abba* (Aramaic for "Father"), Jesus is the unique elder brother amid many other siblings.[12] In him, the apostle saw the true image

---

[8]2 Peter 3:15-16.

[9]Leslie Mitton, *The Formation of the Pauline Corpus of Letters* (London: Epworth, 1955) 76.

[10]John Robinson, *The Human Face of God* (Philadelphia: Westminster, 1973) 166.

[11]1 Corinthians 1:18.

[12]Romans 8:14-29.

of God in the role of a lowly human (Greek, *anthropos*).[13] A virginal mother of Jesus would have made no sense to Paul. In commenting on the goods of God's creation, he affirmed that nothing is unclean. Hence, the notion that sexual intercourse is defiling and that a completely holy person must be conceived in an asexual manner would have been viewed by him as both blasphemous and absurd.[14] The apostle would have perceived that such supernaturalism is incongruous with his conviction that Jesus embodied ideal humanity. Since Paul recognized him as the promised messiah with davidic ancestry, he would have been supportive of the geneologies subsequently generated in which Jesus' forefathers are traced through Joseph to King David.[15]

As Paul viewed Jesus, the miracle of his life pertains to the way in which he lived rather than to the manner in which he was conceived. Paul's Jesus was the righteous one who did not experience sin.[16] Stated more positively, he embodied "the image and reflection of God" that humans were created to display.[17] The apostle appealed to Christians "on the basis of the gentleness and kindness of Christ."[18] Following that servant example, Christians should build up their neighbors and not arrogate themselves.[19] Paul introduced the term *koinonia*, traditionally translated "communion," to refer to church suppers where the shared cup and bread stimulated a "remembrance" of the Lord's death.[20]

The apostle referred to Jesus as born under Jewish law,[21] implying that he was raised according the traditions of the synagogue. Early Judaism specified five principal responsibilities for a father toward his son, which were recorded in this sequential manner, "He must circumcise him, redeem

---

[13]Philippians 2:6-7.

[14]Romans 14:14; 1 Corinthians 6:19; 10:25-26; see William Phipps, "Is Paul's Attitude toward Sexual Relations Contained in 1 Cor. 7:1?" *New Testament Studies* (January 1982): 125-31.

[15]Romans 1:3, 9:5; Matthew 1:6-16; Luke 3:23-31.

[16]Romans 5:18; 2 Corinthians 5:21.

[17]Romans 3:23; 1 Corinthians 11:7.

[18]2 Corinthians 10:1.

[19]Philippians 2:5-8; Romans 15:2-3.

[20]1 Corinthians 10:16, 11:25.

[21]Galatians 4:4.

him, teach him Torah, teach him a trade, and find him a wife."[22] An adult
Jew was expected to inculcate the prophetic emphasis upon mercy and
social justice as well as to live by the "golden rule."[23] He ministered to his
fellow Jews to confirm God's faithfulness to promises given the patriarchs,
yet some of those Jews bore responsibility for his death on a cross.[24]

Paul's stress on Jesus' example, in letters to Gentile congregations that
he established, presupposes that he had taught them about Jesus' ministry.
Consider, for instance, Paul's advocacy for humble helpfulness, "Let each
of us please our neighbor . . . for Christ did not please himself. . . . Live in
harmony with one another after the manner of Christ Jesus."[25] Another letter
contains the same theme, "Bear one another's burdens and so fulfill the law
of Christ."[26]

Jesus' teachings as well as his lifestyle influenced Paul. He pointed out
that Christ instructed that support should be given for those who proclaim
the gospel by the communities that they serve.[27] The apostle's letters
contain a number of references to Jesus' ideas on a variety of subjects, even
though attribution to him is not explicitly acknowledged.[28] Moreover, Paul
was aware of sayings of Jesus that the Evangelists overlooked.[29] The apostle
alluded to Jesus' sayings in about two dozen places, and Seyoon Kim
tabulates over forty possible echoes of those sayings.[30]

Some important historical information pertaining to Jesus is provided
by Paul that is not found in any Gospel. James of Nazareth was an apostle

---

[22]George Foot Moore, *Judaism in the First Centuries of the Christian Era*
(New York: Schocken, 1971) 2:127; *Kiddushin* 29a.

[23]William Phipps, *The Wisdom and Wit of Rabbi Jesus* (Louisville: Westmin-
ster/John Knox, 1993) 13-15, 189-90.

[24]Romans 15:8; 1 Thessalonians 2:15; Philippians 2:8.

[25]Romans 15:2-3, 5.

[26]Galatians 6:2.

[27]1 Corinthians 9:14.

[28]E.g., 1 Thessalonians 5:2, cp. Matthew 24:43; 1 Thessalonians 5:13, cp. Mark
9:50; 1 Thessalonians 5:15, cp. Luke 6:27-28; Galatians 2:11-12, cf. Mark 2:16;
Romans 12:14, cp. Matthew 5:44; Romans 13:7, cp. Mark 12:17; Romans 14:13,
cp. Matthew 7:1; Romans 14:14, cp. Mark 7:15-23; Romans 16:19, cp. Matthew
10:16.

[29]1 Thessalonians 4:15; Acts 20:35.

[30]Seyoon Kim, Paul and the New Perspective (Grand Rapids MI: Eerdmans,
2002) 259-90.

who witnessed Jesus' resurrection, and he was among the brothers of Jesus who were married.[31] The apostle also acknowledged that the other apostles were married and that he unaware of Jesus' attitude toward celibacy.[32] Moreover, Paul indicated that Jesus rejected the Torah's law that made di vorce a husband's prerogative for anything obnoxious he found in his wife.[33]

In this study, Paul's interpretation of Christianity has been treated as normative and has been used to measure the writings later produced by the church, the most important of which are contained in the New Testament. He provides the only glimpse of the human Jesus before legendary trappings had much chance to develop. As has been shown, Paul did not present Jesus as involved in supernatural miracles or accept such claims that were beginning to be circulated by the apostle's opponents. Unlike most other New Testament writers, he had no interest in attempting to authenticate Christianity by unnatural occurrences, and he was critical of those who claimed that such miracles added grandeur to Christianity. I have attempted to explain the anomaly that Paul recorded no miracles of the man who soon would exceed all persons in ancient history in the number of miracles attributed to him.

In 1946, the long lost *Gospel of Thomas* was found in Egypt. It contains no miracles, so it is similar to Paul's letters in at least one respect. Scholars speculate that it may have originated as early as the first century. It was discarded along with some other ancient Christian texts because they contained some perspectives on Jesus and his ministry that the church of late antiquity wished to suppress. Some distinctive sayings of Jesus found there may have been authentic.

In the chapters devoted to two parts of church doctrine that have been traditionally exalted and are still basic to Christian fundamentalism—namely, Jesus' alleged *virginal* conception and *physical* resurrection—it was demonstrated that Paul did not support either. He had died before stories were created by Matthew about Mary fulfilling an alleged virgin prophecy, and by Mark about Jesus' body exiting the tomb where it had been buried.

---

[31]Galatians 1:19; 1 Corinthians 9:5; 15:7.
[32]1 Corinthians 7:25, 9:5.
[33]Deuteronomy 24:1; 1 Corinthians 7:10-11.

Paul's Christology stands in sharp contrast to magical views of the universe that have been perennially popular. In spite of attestation by all four Evangelists to a story of Jesus multiplying lunches out of nothing to provide a multitude with a free meal, one will search Paul's writings in vain for even an allusion to such. But one can find there the more important teaching on economic equality, which pertains to providing basic assistance to any who are hungry.[34]

The gospel according to Paul features the historical Jesus as a moral teacher and as a companionable leader. It conveys some of Jesus' practical judgments, and it transmits immortal words spoken at "the Lord's Supper." At the end of a life of loving service, Jesus presided "on the night when he was betrayed" over a meal with his disciples.[35] The bread did not become heavenly manna and the wine did not change its substance to Jesus' blood; his body was *at* the table but not *on* the table. Ordinary food and drink was consumed, for Paul's Jesus was not a master magician who attempted to gain the confidence of people by unnatural performances. He acted contrary to establishment morality, but not contrary to established physical regularities. There is no evidence that Paul thought of Jesus as one who could suspend the force of gravity, conjure food from nowhere, convert water to wine, or reverse the putrefaction of a corpse. Paul stressed the centrality of Jesus' resurrection while explicitly rejecting that it involved a blood and bones reanimation. He thought of the physical body as a fragile "earthenware jar" that is shattered irretrievably by death. However, being animated by the undying "life of Jesus" is the redeeming quality for Christians.[36]

The glorious cosmic sovereignty of Jesus eclipsed for Paul the perennial ancient preoccupation with stellar powers and angelic mediators. Greco-Roman religions specialist Shirley Case writes:

> As interpreted by Paul, Christ assumed responsibility for insuring every type of salvation that had previously been credited to any or all Gentile saviors. . . . He had met "the principalities and the powers" in deadly conflict and had despoiled them of their authority. No sinister astral divinities, however cruelly they turned the wheel of fate, held any power over the destiny of the soul that had experienced union with Christ.[37]

---

[34] 2 Corinthians 8:13-15.

[35] 1 Corinthians 7:10-11; 11:20, 23-25.

[36] 2 Corinthians 4:7-12.

[37] Shirley Case, *The Origins of Christian Supernaturalism* (Chicago: University

The force by which Jesus ruled was not that of an amoral Homeric demigod, drunk with the power to do magic. In condemning astrological "cosmic elements" and the "worship of angels," Paul advocated allegiance to the one cosmic ruler and to the moral principles of his rule. He wrote of Christ and the Christian life in this manner:

> In him the fullness of God lives in a human body, and in union with him you have been brought to fullness of life. Every power and authority in the universe is under his rule. . . . As God's chosen, consecrated, and beloved people, clothe yourselves with compassion, kindness, humility, gentleness, and patience. Bear with one another and if anyone has a complaint against another, forgive as the Lord has forgiven you. Above all, clothe yourselves with love, which ties everything completely together.[38]

* * *

If science oriented persons were to begin to read the New Testament according to the traditional arrangement of its books, they might quickly lose motivation to venture beyond a few pages. On the basis of its opening chapters they might judge that Christianity is based on irrationality and supernaturalism. Matthew begins with a genealogy tracing Joseph's ancestors through Hebrew history but that is immediately made irrelevant by an angel's declaration that Mary, his betrothed, had become pregnant without receiving human sperm. Those chapters presume that divine guidance is mainly communicated through dreams. By means of five dreams, Joseph and some magi receive directives on what they should do.[39] The second chapter of Matthew reads like bizarre fantasy for it tells of Mesopotamian horoscope devotees, whom translators have approvingly called "wise men." The moving star they follow was so close to the earth that it guides magi as they travel the few miles from Jerusalem to Bethlehem, and then it stops over the house where the infant king of the Jews lies. That chapter also contains unrelated prophetic forecasts to events claimed in Jesus' life. One pertains to a sojourn in Egypt by Jesus and his parents because the Israelite exodus was from there. Another one refers to a nonexistent prophecy in which there is a similarity of sound, but not of meaning, between the words "Nazorean" and "Nazarene."

---

of Chicago Press, 1946) 172-73.
[38]Colossians 2:8-10, 18; 3:12-14.
[39]Matthew 1:20; 2:12, 13, 19, 22.

The incredible supernaturalism of Matthew's nativity story—virginal conception, dream revelations, astrological portents, and preposterous fulfillments—might well cause modern readers to conclude that one must deny science and reason in order to accept the gospel message. Matthew's prologue to the story of the adult Jesus sets the stage for the dozens of miracles to follow. They portray a deity with a split personality: on the one hand there is a Creator who is responsible for the orderly cosmos, but on the other hand there is a Supermagician who operates outside of the established framework so as to make people marvel.

If those persons with a scientific disposition were to investigate the New Testament in the approximate chronological order of its composition, a different understanding might emerge. By starting with Paul's letters, they could realize that it is altogether possible to accept Christian theology without sacrificing intellectual integrity. He stressed that Christianity should engage one's whole self, brains included. To the Corinthian glossolaliacs who babbled when they worshiped, he admonished that "both spirit and mind" are needed.[40] Paul also urged Roman Christians to renew their mind (Greek, nous) and honor "rationality" (Greek, *logos*) in religion.[41] "Change of mind" (Greek, *metanoia*) is usually poorly translated as "repentance." For example, Paul writes Roman Christians about their scornfulness toward pagan immorality, "God's kindness is meant to lead you to repentance."[42] But the apostle, echoing Jesus' teachings, was advising a mental transformation and not merely that his readers would have emotional sorrow for sins. *Logos* and *nous* had long been favorite terms of Greek scientists and philosophers.

Paul's Jesus is mainly an enfleshment of *agape*, which is usually translated as "love," but the Evangelists' Jesus is also a supernatural thaumaturge. With the passage of time, his human limitations were increasingly muted and his divine nature was accentuated. Most Christians do not recognize the disparate strands in the tangled skein of early Christian literature, so they presume that all sectors of the early church believed the founder of Christianity did miracles to prove his divine qualities. Christian apologetics developed this circular logic: since Jesus is divine he performed miracles, but conversely since he performed miracles he was divine.

---

[40]1 Corinthians 14:19.
[41]Romans 12:1-2.
[42]Romans 2:4.

In 1 Corinthians 13, Paul exalted *agape*, an infrequent word in the Gospels and in Greek literature apart from the Bible. To stress its centrality he posed this hypothetical hyperbole, "If I have all faith, so as to remove mountains, but have not love [*agape*], I am nothing."[43] The apostle boldly contrasts *agape* with "faith to move mountains" that is commended by Mark's Jesus.[44] Reference in the New Testament to mountains moving was probably prompted by poetry in the Hebrew hymnbook. A psalmist wrote of God causing mountains to "skip like rams," evoking an image of supernatural power.[45] But Paul's outlook is conveyed by an African-American spiritual, "Lord, don't move the mountain; just give me strength to climb it." The apostle also placed a zero value on the arbitrary fanaticism contained in a saying of Luke's Jesus, that a person of faith "could say to this mulberry tree, 'Be uprooted and planted in the sea,' and it would obey you."[46]

After devaluating supernaturalism in his famous ode to *agape*, Paul goes on to describe the true miracle of God. Unlike the perspective of the Gospels, Jesus in Paul's letters is more the message than the messenger. Since the Crucified One was for the apostle the quintessential personification of *agape*, sentences of 1 Corinthians 13 may be read with this subject substitution: "Jesus is patient and kind; he is not envious, boastful, arrogant, or rude. Jesus is not selfish, irritable, or resentful; he does not gloat when others go wrong, but is gladdened by the truth. There is nothing Jesus cannot face; his faith, hope and endurance is limitless."

In discussing the effect of *agape* Paul penned, "When I became an adult, I put away childish things." Catholic scholar Uta Ranke-Heinemann selected *Putting Away Childish Things* for the title of one of her books. In a chapter entitled "Miraculous Fairy Tales" she appropriately commented on Paul having said nothing about Jesus preforming any supernatural miracles.[47] Paul thought that attention to alleged miracles were an obstruction to understanding in a mature way the *agape* that Jesus embodied. He would have treated as foolishness, not faithfulness, the fantasy that a loved

---

[43] 1 Corinthians 13:2.
[44] Mark 11:23.
[45] Psalm 114:4.
[46] Luke 17:6.
[47] Uta Ranke-Heinemann, *Putting Away Childish Things* (San Francisco: Harper, 1995) 80.

one who had died could return from the grave in a tangible physical body. Had he heard of John's tale of a decomposing Lazarus being reanimated, he would probably have dismissed it as ghoulish superstition. Paul believed that a main purpose of religion is to change the attitude of participants toward natural happenings rather than to change external conditions that religionists find personally malevolent.

Paul would surely have found it counter to "the mind of Christ" to ask for a supernatural spectacle that would aggrandize one's importance. The Jesus whom Paul followed fulfills Isaiah's prophecy of a coming servant of the Lord who figuratively would "not break a bruised reed."[48] The humble Christian sufferer, in imitation of Christ, would express no vengeance or selfishness; he would not curse a fruit tree—interpreted either literally or symbolically—that was just awakening from dormancy to produce fruit in due season.[49]

Spinoza contrasted Paul's appreciation of reasoned discourse with the prophets of his Hebrew religion. Unlike those who were continually proclaiming that they were spokespersons for the "word of God," Paul occasionally acknowledged that he was uttering his own opinions. To illustrate that he thought of himself as a teacher, and preferred intellectual argumentation to authoritarian prophesying, Spinoza quoted from a Corinthian letter, "I speak to you as sensible people; judge for yourselves what I say."[50] Spinoza concluded with this hope for the modern age: "None of the apostles philosophized more than did Paul. . . . How happy our age would be if we were to see religion freed from all superstition!"[51]

Albert Schweitzer, whose genius was expressed in masterful interpretations of Bach's music and Jesus' religion, joined Spinoze in admiring Paul's interest in reasonable religion. He commented on the way that the apostle integrated the dissonance between faith and reason into a symphony:

> Christianity can only become the living truth for successive generations if thinkers constantly arise within it who, in the Spirit of Jesus, make belief in Him capable of intellectual apprehension in the thought-forms of the worldview proper to their time. . . . Paul is the patron saint of thought in

---

[48]Isaiah 42:3; 53:3-7.
[49]Mark 11:11-14; Philippians 2:5-8.
[50]1 Corinthians 10:15.
[51]Spinoza, *Tractatus Theologico-Politicus* (1670) 11.

Christianity. And all those who think to serve the faith in Jesus by destroying freedom of thought would do well to keep out of his way.[52]

Schweitzer began another book on Paul with this sentence, "The Reformation fought and conquered in the name of Paul."[53] The Protestant Reformation later became mired in dogmatism, Schweitzer thought, but he was hopeful that continual intellectual reform would again be characteristic of the church. But he recognized, as did Paul, the need to go beyond rational comprehension that Gnostic cultists were emphasizing, because "knowledge [*gnosis*] puffs up, but *agape* builds up" the Christian community.[54] Consequently, Paul forsook a career as a learned rabbi to form communities of simple Christians and Schweitzer gave up his scholarly fame in Europe to become a missionary physician to exploited Africans.

Contemporary philosopher Frederick Ferre also maintains that Paul placed "unequivocal priority on the use of intellect" when he said: "I would rather speak five intelligible words in order to instruct others than thousands of ecstatic words. Friends, stop being childish in your understanding. Be as infants in evil but be mature in your thinking."[55] Ferre is convinced that it has been Paul's interpreters rather than the apostle who have created an impasse between religion and reason by associating the intellect with "cold lovelessness."[56]

If Paul were able to compare our familiar fantasies, he might place one about Elijah soaring skyward in a chariot drawn by fiery horses on a par with lore about Saint Nicholas sailing from roof to roof in a sleigh drawn by reindeer. Marvelous stories such as these have always delighted the credulous, but the apostle expected adults to be wary of kindergarten fantasy. Although he patiently nursed some "babes in Christ" with "milk," he longed for Christians who could chew and digest "solid food."[57] He wanted people who could analyze the dilemmas of life in a reasonable and Christlike manner, and then act on their understandings in responsible ways.

---

[52]Albert Schweitzer, *The Mysticism of Paul the Apostle* (New York: Holt, 1931) 377.

[53]Albert Schweitzer, *Paul and His Interpreters* (London: Black, 1912) 2.

[54]1 Corinthians 8:1.

[55]1 Corinthians 14:19-20.

[56]Frederick Ferre, "Ecstasy and Intelligence," *Christian Century* (21 October 1981): 1059.

[57]1 Corinthians 3:1-2.

Paul's incisive mentality, combined with his urbane upbringing, explains why he was uninterested in miracle stories. Gerd Theissen has shown that the "primitive Christian miracle stories are rooted in the predominantly rural world of Galilee."[58] They appealed to simple peasants and fisherfolk who shared the naivete of the uneducated. The sociocultural dimension of Paul's life was quite different. He was city oriented and received the best education that could be obtained in a culture noted for its literacy.[59]

Along with other ancient Jews, Paul was aware of the regularities of nature. Hebrew scriptures refer to the sequencing of "seedtime and harvest . . . summer and winter, and day and night."[60] A psalmist praises the Lord for establishing heavenly bodies with an everlasting law.[61] Without some recognition of how things normally happen, exceptions cannot be detected and people cannot be awestruck at the extraordinariness of any particular event. Paul found the natural order dependable enough to draw a parallel between predictability in the physical and moral realms. He taught that divine judgment operates through consequential causality similar to the way that a farmer generally reaps in accord with what he plants and cultivates.[62]

Those who are biased toward modern notions of progress presume that all ancient people were uncritical of supernaturalism and that scientific understanding is only now dispelling miracle mania. But in every century some people are skeptical of alleged miracles and others are credulous, even though the latter tendency was more pronounced in primal cultures. Cicero, a Roman statesman with religious convictions, reasoned: "Nothing can happen without cause; . . . when what was capable of happening has happened, it may not be interpreted as a miracle. Consequently, there are no miracles."[63] Paul, like Plutarch, Polybius, and Herodotus,[64] was cautious in accepting accounts widely believed by the masses. While many yokels would have had no difficulty in believing that a person could walk on water,

---

[58]Gerd Theissen, *The Miracle Stories of the Early Christian Tradition* (Philadelphia: Fortress, 1983) 246.

[59]Galatians 1:14; Acts 22:3.

[60]Genesis 8:22.

[61]Psalm 148:6.

[62]Galatians 6:7.

[63]Cicero, *On Divination* 2.28.

[64]Plutarch, *Camillus*, 6; *Coriolanus*, 38; Polybius, *History* 16.12; Herodotus, *History* 2.55-57, 73, 156; 4.94-96, 105.

no doubt some of the sophisticated among them would question a report of such. Possible explanations they might suggest include mistaken perception of the reporter, or that the water was frozen, or that the walker was on a sand bar extending into the lake slightly below the surface. Had Paul encountered someone walking on water, he would more likely have empirically inquired, "How do you do that?" than to have confessed, "You must be divine." But one Gospel, after telling of Jesus walking on a lake, states that his disciples responded by worshiping him as the Son of God.[65]

Paul's outlook can be clarified by contrasting it with Tertullian's uncompromising stance. Living two centuries after Paul, he did much, as we have seen, to establish orthodoxy in Western Catholicism. "We have no more need for curiosity since Jesus Christ has come," he asserted; "nor for inquiry since the gospel."[66] Presuming that the Bible contains all truth, Tertullian believed that further religious questioning and research is futile. Since God has finally revealed the only way of salvation, affirmation of and obedience to Christian doctrine is all that is needed. Some of his rigid positions, such as that of physical resurrection, have held sway throughout most of church history. Tertullian exemplifies the unreasonableness that Celsus, his contemporary, found in Christianity. According to that pagan philosopher, its slogan was, "Do not ask questions, just believe!"[67] In the present generation there are many, both inside and outside of fundamentalism, who share Tertullian's rigid separation of revelation from reason. For example, liberal media essayist Roger Rosenblatt agrees with Tertullian that scholarly Athens and holy Jerusalem are opposing cultures.[68]

The scientific habit of Paul's mind is well expressed in his correspondence with the Christians at Thessalonia. "Test everything," he advocated; "hold fast to what is good."[69] Like Jesus, he was aware that false pronouncements abound, so only substantiated assertions should be accepted. The educated apostle was concerned that all Christians, regardless of how well their minds were trained, should beware of authoritarian figures. In his advocacy of religious criticism, he set the standard for both the scholarly and the simple. He realized that the congregations he was addressing were

---

[65]Matthew 14:33.
[66]Tertullian, *On Prescription against Heretics*, 7.
[67]Celsus, *True Doctrine* (New York: Oxford University Press, 1987) 54.
[68]*Time* (12 November 1984): 112.
[69]1 Thessalonians 5:21.

predominantly uneducated.[70] About one-tenth of those living in the Roman empire were literate and the membership of the church may have had an even lower literacy rate.

Paul's skepticism was akin to that of medieval theologian Abelard, who said, "By doubting we are led to inquire, and by inquiring we perceive the truth."[71] Far from confusing credulity with faith, Paul hoped that a Christian would not believe unsupportable claims. Armed then with his respect for critical judgment and with his understanding of the essence of the gospel, the inquirer can attempt to distinguish what Jesus actually did and said from the out-of-character accretions in later writings about him by churchmen.

The apostle acknowledged that throughout history humans have learned of God by understanding natural phenomena. "Ever since the creation of the world, God's everlasting power and nature have been visible in what has been made," he asserted.[72] In line with Paul's philosophical theology, Renaissance scholar Francis Bacon held that "God never wrought miracles to convince atheism, because his ordinary works convince it."[73] That outlook has been reiterated in our time by Jewish novelist Isaac Singer: "The most wonderful miracle is what Spinoza called the natural order of things. To me, causality is more than a category of pure reason. It is the essence of creation."[74]

Scientific and religion modes of perception were subtly balanced by Blaise Pascal, the pioneering French physicist. One of his aphorisms expresses Paul's outlook, "Two extremes: to exclude reason, to admit reason only." He also said, "Faith indeed tells what the senses do not tell, but not the contrary of what they see. It is above them and not contrary to them."[75] Paul found among the Greeks some who thought they could solve all problems through reason. To them he said, "If anyone fancies that he is in the know, he does not have true knowledge."[76] The apostle was con-

---

[70]1 Corinthians 1:26.
[71]Abelard, *Yes and No*, preface.
[72]Romans 1:20.
[73]Francis Bacon, *Essays*, "Of Atheism."
[74]*The Boston Globe* (9 November 1984) 2.
[75]Blaise Pascal, *Pensees*, 253, 265.
[76]1 Corinthians 8:2.

vinced that modesty toward knowledge was the disposition needed for dealing with every mystery.[77]

* * *

Mark's Jesus taught that "all things are possible to the one who believes,"[78] but Paul confessed from his own experience that all things are not possible to a believer. He learned of the perimeters of religion's effectiveness after praying repeatedly to be relieved of "a thorn in the flesh" that was tormenting him. "The Lord" provided a response that became the core of his religion, "My grace is all you need, for power [*dynamis*] is made perfect in weakness."[79] The apostle's faith enabled him to cope with intense pain, even though it was not removed. Absent from his letters are stories of dramatic healings from physical disabilities, but here is a moving account of a continual pain from some unspecified cause. Paul found resources in his religion that enabled him to interpret personal suffering constructively. Regarding the paradox that divine dynamism comes to fulfillment in weakness, the famous German New Testament interpreter Martin Dibelius comments that the apostle discovered what many Christian mystics have known: when the human vessel is fragile, spiritual strength seems to be a "divine miracle." The apostle learned to understand all his travel trials in a similar way.[80]

The piety of Jesus and Paul was unlike that of Jacob, the scheming patriarch, who vowed that he would serve God if personal success were granted.[81] Paul followed Jesus in maintaining that religious depth is measured by trust in God when things do not turn out to an individual's personal advantage. Joy amid suffering was the theme of his letter to the Philippians that was written while he was inprisoned, facing possible execution. In the midst of physical and/or emotional suffering, Paul poured out prayers, acknowledging the benefits he had received from God's grace. In those circumstances he could say, "Rejoice in the Lord always."[82] Like Dietrich Bonhoeffer before he was hanged by Nazis, he gained satisfaction

---

[77]Romans 11:33.
[78]Mark 9:23.
[79]2 Corinthians 12:9.
[80]Martin Dibelius, *Paul* (London: Longmans, 1953) 106.
[81]Genesis 28:20-21.
[82]Philippians 4:4.

by spreading the gospel to the guards who were with him inside the prison, and by correspondance with friends outside. Elsewhere the apostle reiterates the paradox, "We rejoice in our sufferings."[83]

In some ways Paul's situation paralleled that of Job who felt he was being unjustly destroyed by the arrows of adversity. Job, as expressed at the end of the dramatic poem that fills most of the book entitled with his name, came to realize that a personal relationship with God was sufficient even though his desires were unfulfilled.

Paul's predicament was also somewhat similar to that of Jesus who "offered up prayers and requests, with loud cries and tears to God, who could save him from death," yet "he learned through his suffering to be obedient."[84] Richard MacKenna comments on the relationship between what Paul suffered and Jesus' passion:

> Jesus' loyalty to his truth led him on to the cross and to this strange Christian paradox: that we believe that it was precisely when he was at his most broken, most defeated, most empty, most helpless, that he accomplished the most—the supreme example of God's words to Paul, "My power comes to its full strength in weakness." The Christian symbol of triumph is an instrument of defeat and torture . . . stripped of everything except love; wrists nailed to wood, as helpless as a baby, unable even to grasp anything.[85]

In his Romans letter, Paul told of a figurative festering thorn that gave him "unceasing anguish." He was distressed that only a few of his fellow Jews viewed Christianity as a fulfillment of the ancient Hebrew religion.[86] In discussing his failings in witnessing to other Jews, the apostle identified with an episode in Elijah's life. That prophet had two encounters with the government of Israel that involved mountain settings. The first encounter pertained to the cause of a drought. Elijah challenged the prophets of Baal, who had been accepted by the royal family, to a gather on Mount Carmel to learn whether the Lord (Hebrew, *YHWH*) of Israel or the Canaanite storm god controlled weather phenomena. The dramatic story alleges that only Elijah's God could miraculously ignite the wood beneath a sacrificial animal and then cause the rainfall.[87]

---

[83]Romans 5:3 .
[84]Hebrews 5:7-8.
[85]Richard MacKenna, *God for Nothing* (Worthing: Churchman, 1985) 92.
[86]Romans 9:1-5.
[87]1 Kings 18.

Paul related his situation to the contrasting second encounter of Elijah with Israelite royalty. The prophet's elation was short lived after the Mount Carmel victory because Queen Jezebel threatened his life. On realizing that winning an alleged nature manipulation competition did not improve Israelite faithfulness to Yahweh, he fled to Mount Sinai. While there, the despairing prophet hoped to receive reassurances through an extraordinary storm to stifle his doubts that Yahweh was more powerful than Baal. The prophet was listening for a revelation that a psalmist claimed to have had:

> Yahweh's voice kindles flashing fire;
> Yahweh's voice causes upheaval in the wilderness. . . .
> Yahweh's voice twists the trees and strips the forests.[88]

At Sinai, however, Elijah did not hear Yahweh speak in the expected manner. Even though Israelite tradition claimed that he descended on Sinai in fire, causing the mountain to shake violently before speaking to Moses,[89] Elijah's experience was different. The story conveys that Yahweh was not found in the hurricane, earthquake, and lightning. But in the stillness afterward, Elijah's confidence is restored, enabling him to make courageous plans for subsequent activity to carry out the will of God. Facing up to his self-righteous presumption that he was the only one left on the "God squad," he comes to understand that many have remained loyal to Yahweh and that he should leave his wilderness retreat to appoint new political and religious leaders, as well as to work with others who shared his convictions. He realizes that the revelation of God is best found in changes in the social order rather than in terrifying displays of amoral omnipotence.[90]

Judging from Paul's letters, the apostle was not at all interested in Elijah the miracle worker, even though that role was prominent in the scriptural stories about the prophet, and it was what the Judaism of Paul's day tended to focus upon when remembering him. The apostle's only reference to Elijah tells of his learning, during a period of despondency on Mount Sinai, that God works in a quiet unsupernatural manner. Paul writes: "What does the divine voice say to him? 'I have kept for myself seven thousand persons who have not worshiped Baal.' So too at the present time

---

[88]Psalm 29:7-9.
[89]Exodus 19:18.
[90]1 Kings 19.

there is a remnant left of those whom God had chosen by grace."[91] When the apostle was dejected over many of his fellow Jews rejecting Jesus as the promised messiah, he was encouraged by the story of important but overlooked Israelites who were faithful to God.

Paul may have found in that portion of the Elijah saga what some interpreters regard as a landmark development in the Hebrew religion. It graphically reveals a transcending of the primitive tendency to think that the power and presence of God is best found in the apparent irregular convulsions of nature. God is disclosed in calm, nonsensational activities rather than by the flamboyant ways expected by some religionists. The crucial discovery made by Elijah and transmitted to Paul is that God is not a fitful, coercive force but a persistent, persuasive agent. The apostle learned that divine revelation can be found in everyday happenings that hallow one's work. He recognized that a frantic search for supernatural Christ above or below the earth is unnecessary, for "the word of faith" is within the believer.[92] To attain it demands no exacting obedience to religious rules but rather to become aware of the divine presence in the temporal present.

"God moves in a mysterious way," but not, as hymnwriter William Cowper would have it, by riding upon the storm clouds—the way in which Baalists said that their god traveled.[93] Phillips Brooks grasped Elijah's new understanding and expressed it in his Christmas carol:

> How silently, how silently, the wondrous gift is given!
> So God imparts to human hearts the blessing of his heaven.
> No ear may hear his coming, but in this world of sin,
> Where meek souls will receive him, still the dear Christ enters in.[94]

Although Paul wrote nothing about the way Jesus was generated, he was existentially longing for human regeneration, which occurs when the spirit of Christ becomes alive within a person in any time or place. Like a mother, the apostle once wrote people in one of his mission areas, "I am in the pain of childbirth until Christ is formed in you."[95]

---

[91]Romans 11:4-5.

[92]Romans 10:6-8.

[93]James Pritchard, ed., *Ancient Near Eastern Texts* (Princeton NJ: Princeton University Press, 1955) 130.

[94]Phillips Brooks, "O Little Town of Bethlehem" (1868) 3.

[95]Galatians 4:19.

Habakkuk is another Hebrew prophet who had an impact on Paul's gospel. That prophet raised skeptical questions about why God would use the tyrannical Babylonians to punish the Judeans. But he became convinced that, in spite of his inability to understand the way divine justice was working internationally, he should be patient and trustful. In composing a theological essay for the Roman Christians, Paul borrowed from Habakkuk this main theme, "The righteous will live by faith."[96] The best expression of faith in the prophecy is contained in Habakkuk's concluding affirmation:

> Though the fig trees and the vines bear no fruit,
>   the olive crop fails and the fields produce no grain,
>   the sheep die and the stalls lodge no cattle,
> I will still rejoice in the Lord,
>   and exult in the God of my salvation.[97]

Characteristic of the Hebrew prophetic books, Habakkuk did not extol supernaturalism. Faithfulness to God is in no way based on the expectation that God would miraculously liquidate national enemies or that the Creator would satisfy Jews by bringing them the right amount of rain and healthy flocks. For Paul, as for Habakkuk, religion was separated from the arrogant assumption that nature's productivity must cater to localized human needs, if God is to be worshiped. Habakkuk and Paul did not think of religion as a device for getting what one wants any more than did the agonizing Jesus in the Garden of Gethsemane who prayed: "Remove this cup [of suffering] from me. Yet not what I want, but what you will."[98]

In the Middle Ages, one occasion of Paul's physical suffering was transformed into a supernatural spectacle. In his Galatian letter, Paul figuratively referred to the effect of a hot iron singed on a slave or domestic animal to show ownership. As "the slave of Christ," the apostle testified, "The marks [*stigmata*] of Jesus are branded on my body."[99] Paul may have been referring to the scars left from persecution when he was nearly killed while on a missionary journey in Galatia.[100] But many centuries later, that stigmata metaphor was interpreted literally and applied to other saints.

---

[96]Habakkuk 2:4; Romans 1:17.
[97]Habakkuk 3:17-18.
[98]Mark 14:36.
[99]Galatians 1:10; 6:17.
[100]Galatians 4:13-15; Acts 13:50; 14:19.

Francis of Assisi's ministry was centered in humility and nonviolence that resulted from his attempt to imitate the life of Jesus. But hagiographers, years after Francis's death, told of a reputed imprint upon his body of Jesus' pierced side, hands, and feet when crucified, which they called stigmata. They claimed that blood would often flow from those wounds on Francis's body.[101] For centuries afterward, sainthood was often related to believing that certain persons had received similar stigmata.[102]

More in accord with Paul's stigmata is a testimony of Martin Luther King, Jr. He told of painful situations similar to those of the apostle, which had a profound spiritual effect but no supernatural component:

> Due to my involvement in the struggle for the freedom of my people, I have known very few quiet days in the last few years. I have been arrested five times and put in Alabama jails. My home has been bombed twice. A day seldom passes that my family and I are not the recipients of threats of death. I have been the victim of a near-fatal stabbing. . . . There are some who still find the cross a stumbling block, and others consider it foolishness, but I am more convinced than ever before that it is the power of God unto social and individual salvation. So, like the Apostle Paul, I can now humbly yet proudly say, "I bear in my body the marks of the Lord Jesus."[103]

Judging from a letter attributed to Peter, other apostles dealt with afflictions in much the same way as Paul did. Appealing to Jesus' undeserved sufferings, Peter encouraged innocent Christians who were undergoing the "fiery ordeal" of persecution. The power expressed by that letter writer, in contrast to the Lukan Peter, did not come by doing wonders that intervene in the natural order to avert bad happenings, nor did the letter mention Jesus' alleged miracles. Rather, Peter found power in the bloody cross, and urged Christians to follow in the steps of the Crucified One.[104] By participating gladly in the sufferings of Jesus and holding unfailing *agape* for one another, Christians live in hope of sharing the everlasting life of God.[105]

---

[101]Raphael Brown, ed., *The Little Flowers of St. Francis* (New York: Doubleday, 1958) 192-93.

[102]Cobham Brewer, *A Dictionary of Miracles* (Philadelphia: Lippincott, 1889) 423-27.

[103]*Christian Century* (27 April 1960): 510.

[104]1 Peter 1:19; 2:21-24; 4:11.

[105]1 Peter 4:6, 8, 13.

The brave and submissive dispositions of Job, Habakkuk, Peter, Paul, and Jesus have been exquisitely expressed in this testimony of an unknown soldier who was on the losing side in the American Civil War:

> I asked God for strength, that I might achieve,
> I was made weak, that I might learn humbly to obey.
> I asked for health, that I might do great things,
> I was given infirmity, that I might do better things.
> I asked for riches, that I might be happy,
> I was given poverty, that I might be wise.
> I asked for power, that I might have the praise of men,
> I was given weakness, that I might feel the need of God.
> I asked for all things, that I might enjoy life,
> I was given life, that I might enjoy all things.
> I got nothing that I asked for—but everything I had hoped for.
> Almost despite myself, my unspoken prayers were answered.
> I am, among all men, most richly blessed.

* * *

Suppose Paul had decided to compose a brief creed that would condense the basic theology and practice of Christianity. From his writings, what would he accept and what would he reject? Part of it would come from Philippians 2:5-11, which is more creed-like than anything he wrote. That passage contrasts Christ with the representative first human, *adam* in Hebrew, who tried to grab divine status.[106] Both were intended by God to express his likeness, but only the second *adam* accepted servanthood and a humiliating death resulting from that obedience. As a result, universal honor was bestowed on him and worshipers confess "Jesus Christ is Lord." In other letters Paul also discusses the "living being" who came from and returned to "dust" because of his disobedience.[107] That symbolic human preceded the spiritual "last Adam," who has enabled those who are incorporated in him to transcend death.[108]

Paul would not mention a mythological conception of Jesus by the Holy Spirit or his descent to an underworld after death. The *exclusive* divine sonship of Jesus and the resurrection of the *flesh* would not be accepted. In later life he probably would not have referred to Jesus' return to this earthly

---

[106]Genesis 3:5.
[107]Genesis 2:7, 3:19; Romams 5:19.
[108]1 Corinthians 15:45-49.

realm after ascending to heaven. A creed based on the letters of that apostle would be along this line:

> I believe in the God of grace and power who is revealed in the continuing crea-
> tion, and in Christ Jesus.[109] He was the true image of God, but he did not snatch
> at divine equality.[110] Jesus was born into a particular human community and
> grew up under Jewish law. While his teachings sometimes went against that
> law,[111] he accepted "Love your neighbor as yourself" as its quintessence and
> extended "neighbor" to include other ethnics.[112] He instructed adroitly, served
> humbly, loved sacrifically, and suffered joyfully.[113] He transformed Jewish no-
> tions of a miracle-working deliverer, and perfectly revealed the wisdom of
> God.[114] By being crucified for our sins he overcame our alienation from God
> and established a new covenant based on freedom and responsibility.[115] God
> has highly exalted Jesus as Lord and has likewise spiritually resurrected all
> who are part of his forgiving and trusting fellowship.[116] I believe in the Holy
> Spirit, the living presence of Jesus who inspires a life of consecration and
> prayer.[117] By participating in baptism and the Lord's Supper we share eternally
> in God's inclusive family, with Christ as elder brother.[118]

Paul's affirmation can be contrasted with the so-called "Apostles' Creed," which can be traced to fourth-century European Catholicism.[119] Leaders of the Protestant Reformation approved of the Creed, and it still plays a central part of the doctrine and ritual of most Christian congregations.[120] The Creed eviscerates much of the gospel teaching about Jesus. Alleged supernatural events pertaining to Jesus are singled out, beginning with his unnatural conception and ending with his ascension to a place above the sky. There he sits beside God until the day for his reentry to the

---

[109]2 Corinthians 4:6; 5:17-19; Romans 3:24; 8:19-23; 1 Corinthians 1:24.

[110]Colossians 1:15; Philippians 2:6.

[111]Galatians 4:4; 1 Corinthians 7:10-11; cf. Deuteronomy 24:1.

[112]Leviticus 19:18; Galatians 5:6, 14.

[113]2 Corinthians 10:1; Galatians 2:20; 1 Thessalonians 1:6; Philippians 2:7-8.

[114]1 Corinthians 1:23-24.

[115]Colossians 2:13-14; 2 Corinthians 5:18; 1 Corinthians 11:25; Galatians 5:1, 6:2.

[116]Philippians 2:9-11; Romans 6:5; Colossians 3:13; 1 Corinthians 4:2.

[117]Romans 8:9-11, 26-27.

[118]1 Corinthians 11:17-26; Romans 6:4; 8:22-29;; 9:24.

[119]Rufinus, *Commentary of the Apostles' Creed*, 2.

[120]Brian Gerrish, *The Faith of Christendom* (New York: Meridian, 1963) 53-55.

earth, when he will judge all humans. The formulation suggests a completely passive Jesus who initiated nothing while on earth; indeed, only a comma separates the beginning from the ending of his life. Attention is given to three days when he is alleged to have descended into the "inferno," but passed over in silence are the three decades when he grew up, taught, healed, and exemplified the godly life. The Creed does not allude to the disturbing things Jesus did to the status quo as a messianic figure. Hundreds of Jews were crucified during the Roman period of Palestinian occupation, so it was the quality of Jesus' life that distinguished him from those forgotten executed men. He insisted that faith should be centered in the love of God and neighbor, as is declared in the Torah,[121] but the Apostles' Creed contains no reference to love or mercy. Jesus asserted that his followers should be known by their "fruits,"[122] but the Creed conveys that the test for being a Christian is correct doctrine, not moral action.

Significantly, the letters of Paul never mention Gehenna or Hades, usually translated as "hell," so the later Creed is contrary to the apostle's belief when it affirms that Jesus "descended into hell." Gehenna refers to the Valley of Hinnom outside Jerusalem that had been associated with fiery torment. A Jewish prophet described the dead bodies of those who rebel against God in this way, "Their maggots shall not die, their fire shall not be quenched."[123] Several Gospel writers used the image of that ravine to denote an alleged place in the underworld for punishment of the wicked after death. The absence of such eschatological supernaturalism in Paul casts doubt on whether Jesus ever used harsh words such as this: "If your eye gets you into trouble, tear it out! It is better to enter the kingdom of God with one eye than to keep both and to be thrown into hell, where the devouring worm never dies and the fire is never extinguished."[124]

This examination of the core of Paul's doctrine gives grounds for rejecting a position some influential European scholars took a century ago. William Wrede claimed that Paul was determined to "crush out the man Jesus" and replace him by "a superhuman . . . celestial being."[125] Heinrich Weinel expressed a similar outlook, "Jesus can scarcely be said to have

---

[121]Deuteronomy 6:5; Leviticus 19:18; Mark 12:30.
[122]Matthew 9:20.
[123]Isaiah 66:24.
[124]Mark 9:47-48.
[125]William Wrede, *Paul* (Boston: Unitarian Association, 1908) 87, 182.

existed for him [Paul] as a human being."[126] Subsequent noted scholars have endorsed that erroneous interpretation, including Wilhelm Bousset who held that Paul transformed the down-to-earth gospel of the historical Jesus into an otherworldly salvation scheme of a supernatural Christ.[127]

Some New Testament interpreters continue to allege that Paul exalted his "Christ of faith" while depreciating the "Jesus of history." This misrepresentation may be due in part to Paul's showing no apparent awareness of numerous stories of Jesus' sayings and actions that were later published in the Gospels. Also, the apostle may have judged untrustworthy some of those stories that were being circulated. His knowledge of what Jesus did and said consisted of events in Jerusalem that led to the crucifixion as well as to the beginning of the Christian church. He learned of this shortly after his conversion through conversations with prominent apostolic eyewitnesses who had known Jesus for a long time. But the Evangelists, writing about Jesus after Paul died, used stories that in many instances probably exceeded secondhandedness in remoteness from the actual happenings.

The false dichotomy between the resurrected Christ and the historical Jesus has been encouraged by a misunderstanding of this comment by Paul, "Though we once understood Christ from a human point of view, we do so no longer."[128] In 1912, New Testament professor Wilhelm Heitmuller commented on that verse, "Quite decisively Paul says here that the earthly Jesus, the human personality Jesus, has no meaning whatever for his religious life."[129] But the apostle probably meant that in his pre-Christian days he shared his culture's standards and judged the shamefully crucified Jesus to deserve rejection by Judaism, but subsequently he knew better. He did not intend to say with the docetics that the life and work of the earthly Jesus was no importance.

The conventional wisdom that Paul had little interest in Jesus' ministry is preposterous. Is it plausible to think that a student of religion would persecute the Christian movement in the region where Jesus had lived when he was uninformed about its leader? Would that keen-minded person have spent fifteen days after his conversion with Jesus' companion Peter and

---

[126]Heinrich Weinel, *St. Paul* (New York: Putnam, 1906) 314.

[127]Wilhelm Bousset, *Kyrios Christos* (Nashville: Abingdon, 1970) 172-87; Hans Schoeps, *Paul* (Philadelphia: Westminster, 1961) 58.

[128]2 Corinthians 5:16.

[129]Wayne Meeks, ed., *The Writings of St. Paul* (New York: Norton, 1972) 309.

Jesus' brother James in Jerusalem, as well as a subsequent visit with them and apostle John, without learning a lot about the Nazarene's life and ministry?[130] After making a careful data analysis, John Macquarrie concludes, "The historical material about Jesus in Paul, scanty though it seems, is very similar to what a modern critical historian will take to be the basic reliable historical facts about Jesus."[131]

In deed as well as in doctrine, the focus of Paul's religion was God as manifested in the human Jesus. In the apostle's life, the rhythms of liberty and service, anger and forgiveness, joy and compassion—that also pulsated through Jesus—were ended with his execution by the Roman government. Those who wish to get back to Jesus must go through that martyr's understandings for, as Hans Küng has also concluded, "Paul succeeded more clearly than anyone in expressing what is *the ultimately distinguishing feature* of Christianity: . . . *the Christ who is identical with the real, historical Jesus of Nazareth*."[132] Paul did not see Jesus through supernatural lenses and would probably have agreed with Küng's forthright judgment: "A supernatural intervention by God in the world would be nonsense. Physically, the consequences would be unthinkable if God were to suspend even for a moment the rules of that system which he himself laid down."[133] If events on our planet were based on a divine Puppeteer who accomplishes his or her will by jerking strings lowered to the earth, no science could exist.

According to Paul, even though many crave for wonderous happenings that go against nature, the true miracle of God is seen in the life and death of the lowly, loving Jesus. The apostle's central doctrine is succinctly expressed in two sentences from his letters: "God was in Christ reconciling the world to himself; and "God shows his love [*agape*] for us in that while we were sinners, Christ died for us."[134] That essence remains after all supernaturalism is jettisoned from the New Testament. When listing human hardships, the apostle did not promise that God will miraculously replace famine and war with abundance and peace, but rather that no deprivation "will be able to separate us from the love of God in Christ Jesus our Lord."[135]

---

[130]Galatians 1:18-19; 2:1, 9.

[131]John Macquarrie, *Jesus Christ in Modern Thought* (London: SCM, 1990) 54.

[132]Hans Küng, *On Being a Christian* (New York: Doubleday, 1976) 409.

[133]Hans Küng, *Does God Exist?* (New York: Doubleday, 1980) 653.

[134]2 Corinthians 5:19; Romans 5:8.

[135]Romans 8:39.

The role of God in the midst of detrimental natural events is different from what many expect. Paul wrote about the synergism (Greek, *synergeo*) operative between God and those who love him that can effect a good outcome from any situation.[136] That theology can be illustrated by this myth about divine-human relationships. When a flood threatened a city, a police officer visited one still occupied home to urge the owner to drive away before a river began to overflow. But the man said, "My trust is in the Lord who will save me." The next day a neighbor came by boat to his door to take him to safety, but the same conviction was expressed. A day later a helicopter pilot lowered a ladder to the man on his rooftop to airlift him away from the still rising waters. The man shouted, "The Lord will save me." After drowning, he comes into the presence of God. "Why didn't you rescue me?" the man plaintively asks. With exacerbation, God replies, "Day after day loving people cooperated with me to save you. What were you expecting, something supernatural?"

There are other natural ways of working with God to avoid some of the catastrophic results of flooding. One obvious example it to avoid building where hurricanes and swollen rivers are likely to hit. Likewise, death from tsunamis could be greatly lowered by establishing detectors in oceans to warn those in their paths. Again, the future flooding of coastal plains that would come from massive melting of polar ice might be avoided by the establishment of environmental regulations that could prevent global warming.

At pivotal periods in church history, Paul's influence has been heavy. If Peter is excepted, Paul's impact has been greater than that of all the other apostles combined. Augustine's monumental *Confessions* and *City of God* are filled with hundreds of quotations from Paul's letters—many times the citations from any other writer. That church father struggled to comprehend the apostle even though he often misinterpreted him.[137] A millennium later the Protestant Reformation was ignited by Marter Luther's study of Paul's letters. That rediscovery continued with John Calvin, who quoted from Paul's writings in his *Institutes of the Christian Religion* more often than from all four Gospels. The Methodist movement in England began when

---

[136]Romans 8:28.

[137]William Phipps, "The Heresiarch: Pelagius or Augustine?" *Anglican Theological Review* (April 1980): 124-33; *Influential Theologians on Wo/Man* (Washington DC: University Press of America, 1980) 71-76.

John Wesley was "strangely warmed" by the reading of Luther's commentary on Romans. In the contemporary era, theologian Wayne Meeks accepts church historian Sydney Ahlstrom's assessment that "Christian theology is a series of footnotes to St. Paul."[138] Again and again the letters of St. Paul have been shown to be no more extinct than the St. Helens volcano; his ideas have repeatedly blazed forth to transform the theological landscape and to provide a dazzling glimpse of what is at the core of historic Christianity.

The Human Jesus

How different are our superman fantasies from the way the earliest Christians portrayed the human Jesus! Even in the two Gospels that tell of God's presence in Mary's conception, Joseph is, without qualification, called Jesus' father. The only biblical description of Jesus as a youth shows him not as a bionic boy but as a curious student who listened to teachers and asked them questions. Like the boy Samuel who became an Israelite prophet, his growth was in a normal fourfold pattern: intellectual, physical, social, and spiritual.[139] He was probably taught Hebrew and was informed about his religious heritage in the Nazareth synagogue. It is likely that he worked as a carpenter, joined in the folk dancing of his culture, and loved friends of both sexes.

The New Testament affirms that Jesus was "tempted in every respect as we are."[140] Since sexual desire is powerful in humans, he probably dealt with lustful impulses in the sanctioned manner of ancient Judaism—by becoming married not long after reaching puberty. Jesus is frequently referred to as a rabbi in the Gospels, and marriage was required for Jewish teachers as it had been for Hebrew priests. In absence of evidence that he was criticized for not marrying, it is likely that Jesus became married as a young man.[141] Had he been celibate it is amazing that this abstention would have had so little impact on those contemporaries who aimed at patterning

---

[138]Meeks, ed., *The Writings of St. Paul*, 435.

[139]1 Samuel 2:26; Luke 2:52.

[140]Hebrews 4:15.

[141]William Phipps, *The Sexuality of Jesus* (Cleveland OH: Pilgrim, 1996) 39-109.

their lives after his. Moreover, church leaders in the second generation of Christianity were expected to marry.[142]

A pre-Gospel written source, called *Quelle* (German for "source") by scholars and abbreviated "Q," shows that some Christians who lived in the first decades after his death remembered him primarily because of teachings, not miracles. Although the original Q is not extant, it can be reconstructed by determining what non-Markan material is quoted by both Matthew and Luke. Like Paul's letters, which were composed about the same time, it belonged to a time before rampant supernaturalism had developed in Christianity. Q specialist John Verbin writes, "Like prophetic books, Q shows no interest in miracle stories."[143] In that source, Jesus criticizes those whose faith rests on alleged miracles:

> This is an evil generation: it demands a sign, but none will be given it except the sign of Jonah. For just as Jonah was a sign to the Ninevites, so will the Son of Man be to this generation. When the judgment comes, the queen from the south [Sheba] will appear in court and condemn it; for she traveled a long way to hear the wisdom of Solomon, yet someone greater than Solomon is here. The Ninevites will also appear in court and condemn it; for they repented at the proclamation of Jonah, yet someone greater than Jonah is here.[144]

In that passage, some Gentiles are commended for being open to non-supernatural expressions of power and wisdom. Ninevah, the capital of militaristic Assyria, is alleged to have repented because of Jonah's "sign," that is, his demonstration of God's power through preaching.[145] Jesus thought his fellow Jews should also attend to changing their lives rather than demanding supernatural signs. Likewise, the Queen of Sheba was attracted by Solomon's sagacity.[146] Neither Jonah nor Solomon performed supernatural wonders. Jesus lamented that some adversarial Jews resisted his self-authenticating teaching and insisted that he give miraculous proof of his legitimacy as a divine spokesperson. The opening of that teaching in Q has been given this contemporary paraphrase:

---

[142]1 Timothy 3:2, 12; Titus 1:6.
[143]John Verbin, *Excavating Q* (Minneapolis: Fortress, 2000) 141.
[144]Luke 11:29-32.
[145]Jonah 3:4-5.
[146]1 Kings 10:6-7.

Later a few religion scholars and Pharisees got on him. "Teacher, we want to see your credentials. Give us some hard evidence that God is in this. How about a miracle?" Jesus said, "You're looking for proof, but you're looking for the wrong kind. All you want is something to titillate your curiosity, satisfy your lust for miracles."[147]

Mark also records that Jesus declared, "No sign will be given,"[148] but it had little impact because it was counter to the assumptions of the prevailing apocalypticism of his age. Although Jesus refused to perform a miracle to confirm who he was, the editor of Matthew distorted his teaching about "the sign of Jonah." That Gospel added to the words of Jesus quoted from the Q source, "As Jonah was in a sea monster's belly of three days and nights, so will the Son of Man be deep in the earth for three days and nights."[149] That addition reverses Jesus' teaching about no miraculous proofs and utilizes the story about supernatural preservation in a big fish to signify the unnatural release of Jesus' crucified body from the depths of the grave. Like most scripture readers for two thousand years, Matthew associated Jonah only with a sea monster in which he survived for days. The fish in that story was even then a red herring, obscuring the symbolic purpose of the Book of Jonah, which aims at comparing the wideness of God's mercy on warring people who repent with a Jew's unrepentant hatred toward a nation located where Iraq is now.

* * *

Jesus' overcoming of devilish impulses to perform supernatural signs might be cited as "Q 4" because the story of this victory is coincidentally found in the fourth chapter of both Matthew and Luke. It tells about his struggle to decide on his mode of operation after becoming fully convinced of his call to be God's special agent. Walter Wink comments:

However this narrative may have been produced—and it is one of the most profound in all literature—only Jesus seems capable of having been its source, or someone else who had a very accurate and equally profound grasp of Jesus' self-understanding. . . . The category of historicity yields to the question of

---

[147]Eugene Peterson, *The Message* (Colorado Springs: Navpress, 1993) 34.
[148]Mark 8:12.
[149]Matthew 12:40.

truth: this story is true, whether it happened or not, whether Jesus told it or not.[150]

The form of this story reflects what was circulated about Greek hero Heracles. On becoming mature he retreated to a solitary region to contemplate what his vocation should be. There he had an apparition of an evil person who assured him of sensuous indulgences, and an apparition of a good person who challenged him to accomplish difficult feats through serving others. Hercules chose the virtuous way and was successful in rescuing people from difficulties.[151]

The setting for Q's imaginative testing account was at the time when Jesus retreated to the wilderness near the Jordan River for a few weeks after his baptismal experience. There he fasted and meditated in seclusion on his mission ahead. For sensitive Semites, the desert was a stimulating place for contemplating God's will for their lives. Sinai had earlier been the setting for the transforming religious experiences of Moses and Elijah. Also, Paul meditated in Arabia after his conversion, and a cave near Mecca would later become a place for Muhammad to reflect on a change in vocation.[152] After Jesus withdrew to a secluded place, several vocational possibilities for the future appear to have crossed his mind. One was this: should I aim at satisfying the material needs of hungry folk? Another was: should I choose any effective means for achieving control over others? The third was: will attempting a supernatural stunt promote my cause?

The temptation story expresses ancient Jewish psychology in a picturesque manner. Each person has within, so it was thought, an evil and a good inclination (Hebrew, *yetzer*) which could be personified as a devil and an angel in battle.[153] The ancient Jews did not interpret Satan or devils in a literal manner, with hell as their home address. European folklore, not biblical tradition, is responsible for imagining the devil to have a horned skull and a forked tail, wearing scarlet leotards and carrying a pitchfork. The Jews did not believe in an uncreated rival to God who existed from all

---

[150]Walter Wink, *The Human Being* (Minneapolis: Fortress, 2002) 122.

[151]Gustav Schwab, *Gods and Heroes* (New York: Random House, 1974) 158-61.

[152]Galatians 1:15-17; Alfred Guillaume, trans. *Ibn Ishaq's Sirat Rasul Allah* (Lahore: Oxford University Press, 1955) 102, 105.

[153]Genesis 6:5; *Berakoth* 9.5; Moore, *Judaism in the First Centuries of the Christian Era* 1:478-93.

eternity. One of their ancient sages, Jesus ben Sirach, made this demythologizing clarification, "When a godless person curses Satan, he really curses
himself."[154] Subsequently, Jesus ben Joseph likewise affirmed that evil does
not come from outside an individual but "from within, out of the human
heart."[155] The stories of Eve arguing with a serpent, and of Jacob wrestling
with an angel, are examples of what Freudian psychology expresses more
prosaically and secularly as the ego's confrontation with id and superego.

The first temptation suggests that Jesus may have thought of attempting
to become a new Moses, delivering his people from latter-day pharoahs
while providing physical sustenance. Through a weary wilderness similar
to the one where he was meditating, Moses had led his people toward the
land of their ancestors. The Exodus saga tells of water, manna, and quail
miraculously appearing along the way for Israelite consumption. Is the role
of a savior, Jesus pondered, inseparable from feeding down-and-out people?
He may have memorized sentences from a scroll of Deuteronomy because
his cogitation over this and other career possibilities show awareness of that
source. Jesus reflected on a principle relevant to his situation that allegedly
was said by Moses, "Bread is not the only human need."[156]

In the second temptation—following the order in Luke's Gospel—Jesus
is shown, in his mind's eye, all the world's kingdoms from a mountain. For
all who accept the sphericity of the earth, this temptation is especially
absurd if taken literally. If Jesus had had unlimited human vision, he could
not have seen all the "inhabited earth" even at the summit of Mt. Everest.
The symbolic meaning here is that Jesus contemplated obtaining authority
over people internationally by using devilish tactics. In human history,
before and after Jesus, conquest by war or military threat has been the most
common means that leaders have used to gain international power. While
Jesus desired to promote God's transcultural kingdom, he rejected the
principle that a good goal justifies any evil means for achieving it.

Jesus' final wilderness temptation deserves a more thorough consideration because it involves his rejecting the theology contained in a chapter
of scripture. The testing appears to have occurred while he was meditating
on a theme from his favorite anthology of poetry. One psalmist claims that
the person who trusts in God will remain unscathed by disaster:

---

[154]Sirach 21:27.
[155]Mark 7:21.
[156]Deuteronomy 8:3; Luke 4:3.

You will not fear the terrors of the night,
    nor the dangers of the day;
Neither the plague that stalks in the dark,
    nor the calamity that spreads havoc at midday.
Though hundreds die at your side
    and thousands close at hand,
    the pestilence will not harm you.
You will look about you and see
    how the wicked are punished.[157]

Here scripture clearly promises safety during an epidemic to those who worship God. They can gaze with satisfaction at those who are dying all around them in recompense for their sins. A bold declaration is then made regarding immunity from future injury:

God has charged his angels
to guard you wherever you go.
They will carry you in their arms
to keep you from hitting your foot against a stone.[158]

The psalmist encourages the devout to be fearless, assuring them that their divine Protector will in some supernatural manner rescue them from trouble and reward them with longevity.

While reflecting on the brazen sentiments of this perennially favorite psalm, an idea seems to have entered Jesus' imagination: could he, as one with strong religious convictions, jump off the highest building in his nation and be rescued in midair by guardian angels? Had not John the Baptist called him a mighty man?[159] The Temple in Jerusalem rose hundreds of feet above the ravine below. Josephus said that one could not look down from its pinnacle without becoming overcome with dizziness.[160] Although the psalmist promises the devout a kind of angelic parachute for protecting devout persons who physically fall, Jesus pondered the implications of special providence. He may well have asked himself, would a person who jumps from the Temple be a praiseworthy believer or a foolhardy exhibi-

---

[157]Psalm 91:5-8.
[158]Psalm 91:11-12 .
[159]Luke 3:16.
[160]Josephus, *Antiquities* 15.411-12.

tionist? Should a person expect God to counter dependable natural forces and selectively save life and limb in a supernatural manner?

Jesus did not accept the psalmist's fantasy of God's agents hovering over the righteous and making emergency rescues by contravening the natural order. Rejecting such sensationalism, Jesus realized early in his public ministry that, regardless of what his scripture may have claimed, it is ridiculous to aim at making a religious witness by attempting to defy the force of gravity. That force is not confounded, but confirmed, by simpletons who rely on presumed guardian angels to exempt them from the universal rule.

Although reference to such angels was a common motif in Jewish writings of Jesus' era, they had little role in his public ministry. This is understandable because their alleged function is incongruous with the story of Jesus. If angels really rescue the innocent from death, why were the hands of the crucifiers not stayed? Why did an angel not save him, as the Bible alleges to have happened for Isaac at a mountain altar, and for Peter in a Jerusalem prison?[161]

Jesus appears to have associated the testimony in Psalm 91 with the evil inclination in humans who confuse courageousness with zealotry. He found the wiles of Satan in that scripture, but he discovered the will of God in this proclamation attributed to Moses, "You shall not put God to the test as you did at Massah."[162] During the exodus from Egypt, thirsty Israelites withheld their trust in God until Moses allegedly followed Yahweh's instruction and produced water by striking a rock at Massah with his magical rod.[163] While in another wilderness, Jesus decided that he should not attempt to test God by expecting special providence as the Israelites had done.

Shakespeare discerned from Q's account of the dialogue between Jesus and Satan that biblical passages can be used as proof texts for sinister schemes. His character Shylock cites a story from Genesis to justify an unscrupulous monetary venture. Antonio, the Venice merchant with whom he is dealing, responds: "The devil can cite Scripture for his purpose. An evil soul producing holy witness is like a villain with a smiling cheek, a goodly apple rotten at the heart."[164] A line from a musical expresses Jesus'

---

[161]Genesis 22:11; Acts 5:19.

[162]Deuteronomy 6:16.

[163]Exodus 17:2-7.

[164]William Shakespeare, *The Merchant of Venice* 1.3.

attitude toward devilish interpreters, "The things that you're liable to read in the Bible—they ain't necessarily so."[165] Confusing evil impulses with divine directives is now illustrated by the suicidal jihad terrorists, because their Muslim holy book condemns both the taking of one's life and the attacking of nonaggressors.[166] Apropos here is Jesus' warning to his peaceful disciples, "The time is coming when those who kill you will suppose that they are serving God."[167]

The evaluation of Psalm 91 by Thomas Manson and Reinhold Niebuhr follows that of Jesus. Exegete Manson offers this sound comment, "To thrust oneself into peril, merely to provide God with the occasion for a miracle, is not faith but presumption."[168] Niebuhr finds that psalm "a perfect illustration of all the illusions which may arise from an ultimate religious faith." The distinguished theologian explains:

> It is easy to be tempted to the illusion that the child of God will be accorded special protection from the capricious forces of the natural world, or special immunity from the vindictive passions of angry men. Any such faith is bound to suffer disillusionment. Nor does it deserve moral respect. Stoic indifference toward the varying vicissitudes of mortal existence is preferable to lobbying, with whining entreaties, in the courts of the Almighty, hoping for special favours which are not granted to ordinary mortals or to godless men.[169]

Macquarrie comments on the wider implication of the testing story of Jesus under consideration:

> One of his temptations is said to have been to throw himself down from the pinnacle of the Temple and so, presumably, convince the people by a spectacular display in which he would be saved from harm by angelic intervention. He firmly rejects any approach to his ministry that would involve this kind of marvel and magic. He condemns the kind of mentality that looks for such "signs." Moreover, he points out that such signs will not convince anyone in whom more sober approaches have failed to awaken faith. . . . The true meaning of a miracle does not lie in some extraordinary publicly observable event, but in God's presence and self-manifestation in the event.[170]

---

[165]Ira Gershwin, *Porgy and Bess* (1935).

[166]*Qur'an* 2:190; 4:29.

[167]John 16:2.

[168]Thomas Manson, *The Sayings of Jesus* (London: SCM, 1949) 45.

[169]Reinhold Niebuhr, *Beyond Tragedy* (New York: Scribner, 1937) 97.

[170]John Macquarrie, *Principles of Christian Theology* (New York: Scribner,

Jesus must have been ambivalent in his evaluation of the sentiments expressed in psalms, whose ostensive purpose is to praise God. In contrast to Psalm 91, Psalm 23 conveys the faith that Jesus found genuine. In that best known devotional poem in world literature, the Shepherd's goodness and mercy is present with those who walk through the darkest valley. Jesus recognized that the devout person whose prayer is recorded as Psalm 22 was not saved by God from torture and premature death. The God of suffering servants does not protect them from adversity but dwells within them in spite of it. Theologian Shirley Guthrie asks, "Could it be that we spend too much time looking up to the heavenly heights, expecting miraculous help 'from above,' when we should be looking around us, ready to recognize the sovereign power of God's love and justice at work in the everyday events of our lives, even in the depths of the worst that can happen to us?"[171]

The temptation stories of Jesus were deliberately placed at the beginning of his public ministry, not for the purpose of showing the final vanquishing of sinister forces but to dramatize what he would continually have to confront. Robert Funk writes about the way the entire temptation account graphically depicts Jesus' rejection of any fantasy to become a supernatural redeemer:

> He reviews all the possibilities associated with the messianic and prophetic tradition and rejects all the standard features: turning stones into bread like Moses in the wilderness; assuming the role of divine magician by surviving a fall from the temple, offering allegiance to Satan as the means of coming to world power as a new caesar. After rejecting these options, the visionary returns to embrace the everyday world and endeavors to anoint every village and marketplace with touches of the divine, asking nothing for himself but daily bread. A true savior incarnate . . . must submit to the same limitations imposed on the rest of us.[172]

According to conventional wisdom, God is keen to protect his favorites, supernaturally delivering them from danger. The Hebrew proverb states, "Nothing bad happens to good people."[173] The first Psalm concisely

1966) 228.

[171]Shirley Guthrie, *Christian Doctrine* (Louisville: Westminster/John Knox, 1994) 112.

[172]Robert Funk, *Honest to Jesus* (San Francisco: Harper, 1996) 308.

[173]Proverbs 12:21.

captures that sentiment in declaring that the wicked perish but the righteous prosper in all that they do. That doctrine caused some Jews to wonder if the eighteen people who were killed by the collapse of a tower on the wall of Jerusalem were more evil than those who escaped injury. On asking Jesus for his opinion, he affirmed that disaster victims and survivors are generally no worse or better than anyone else.[174] Therefore, the accidental death of individuals should not be attributed to divine intervention.

Jesus and the writer of the prologue of the Book of Job thought picturesquely as they worked through issues in the psychology of religion. The creator of Job pictured Satan as attempting to prove his assumption that God has established a bribery scheme whereby immunity from personal tragedy is exchanged for worship. But the fictional Job and the historical Jesus illustrate that piety unbiased by selfish interest does occasionally exist. Their trust in God was not dependent on being insulated from horrendous personal suffering. They rejected the simpleminded belief that the righteous can rest assured that their health and lives will be miraculously preserved by divine intervention. Josiah, the most righteous of all kings of Judah, was killed at the age of thirty-nine, while his grandfather Manasseh, the most wicked of all those kings, had the longest reign.[175] Also, the depraved Jewish monarch who began the Herodian dynasty acquired enormous wealth and power before dying at a ripe old age.[176] The dictum of Job's friends that special providence assures that the righteous are rewarded with longevity and the unrighteous die young is shown by Job and Jesus to be false. They also witness that in-depth religious commitment is not motivated by a desire to achieve worldly success.

* * *

In Jesus' day it was popularly believed that pious persons could accomplish supernatural wonders by imitating an Israelite prophet. Elijah had allegedly called "fire down from heaven" several times, enabling him to kill many adversaries.[177] But Jesus rebuked some of his disciples who requested that he also cause lightning to strike a town of unhospitable Samaritans.[178]

---

[174]Luke 13:4.
[175]2 Kings 21:1–23:29.
[176]Josephus, *Antiquities* 18.190-92.
[177]2 Kings 1:9-12.
[178]Luke 9:52-55.

Even so, one New Testament writer believed in the effectiveness of Elijah's petitions pertaining to elements in the sky: "He [Elijah] prayed earnestly that there should be no rain, and no rain fell on the land for three and a half years. When he prayed again, the rain poured down and the earth yielded its harvest."[179] A century before the Christian era began, the Jews associated another rainmaker with Elijah.[180] During a drought a man called Honi drew a circle on the ground and informed God that he would stand inside it and persist in prayer until rain came. According to the *Mishnah*, a violent rainstorm followed, causing Honi to pray successfully for a more gentle rain.[181] Also, Hanina ben Dosa, a Galilean contemporary of Jesus, allegedly caused showers to fall for the sake of his own convenience. When that holy man was caught in a downpour while walking home, he prayed that he not get soaked, and the rain stopped at once. On arriving home dry, he prayed and the rain began again.[182] The theology of those popular Jewish figures was similar to that expressed in a twentieth-century drama. In *The Green Pastures* "de Lawd" proclaims, "I'll jest r'ar back an' pass a miracle."[183] Then, when folks complain over too much rain falling, he passes another miracle to cause it to cease. Aware of quantity of precipitation problems, but continuing to accept special providence, the Episcopal *Book of Common Prayer* has a prudent prayer for "moderate rain."

By contrast, Jesus did not believe that the forces of nature were subject to personal manipulation. Rejecting the supernaturalism of folk religion that is as long as history in every land, he realized that the natural order established by the Creator does not favor the good guys. Rather, "he makes his sun rise on the evil and on the good, and sends rain on the just and on the unjust." Jesus' comment on ethics and the elements was given to explain why we, like God, should love our enemies.[184] "The impartiality of nature is made the symbol of divine grace," Niebuhr explains.[185] Contrary to

[179]James 5:16-18; 1 Kings 17:1; 18:36-45.

[180]Josephus, *Antiquities* 14.22; Genesis Rabbah 13:7.

[181]*Taanith* 3.8.

[182]*Taanith* 24b; *Yoma* 53b.

[183]Marc Connelly, *The Green Pastures* (New York: Rinehart, 1929) 25.

[184]Matthew 5:44-45.

[185]Reinhold Niebuhr, *An Interpretation of Christian Ethics* (New York, Meredian, 1956) 46.

believers in special providence, Jesus found no correlation between holiness and harvests.

Jesus referred to floods and hurricanes as witnesses to the absence of favoritism by nature's Creator; the intensity with which they hit all in their path is unrelated to the morality of those living there. To cope with the turbulence that confronts everyone, Jesus advocated faith that is founded on the divine Rock.[186] Serenity comes to those who avoid living on flood plains; instead, they erect structures that can endure the stress of high winds. Those who risk living in harm's way and who lose their faith because God did not intervene to deliver them from storms, probably had little faith to lose. The God whom Jesus affirmed was active in the regular processes of nature, but not to give preferences to some. Nature operates impersonally, independent of human "just deserts," so life-sustaining and life-destructive forces are no respecters of persons.

Noticing that nature is careless of human deserts, church leader Henry Sloane Coffin asked, "Why is a universe, over which a God . . . is supposed to reign, utterly indifferent to moral distinctions?" In responding to that troublesome question raised by many, Coffin pointed out that God bears no grudges: "There is nothing vindictive or vengeful in Him. If His children sin, the sun will still shine and the rain fall on them, as though nothing had occurred."[187] Jesus, imaging God as a good parent, realized that showing preferential concern for certain children in a family violates true love.

The saga of Jesus' earliest Hebrew ancestors illustrates the proper way to live within the constraints of nature. When Abraham and Sarah were confronted by famine they did not remain stationary and pray for rain to replenish the land God had promised them. Rather, they moved temporarily to Egypt where surplus food was available. When Jacob encountered a similar drought, he had the foresight to buy grain from the Egyptians. His son Joseph was in charge of their economic planning, enabling them to increase grain storage during years of abundance and thereby avert starvation when the Nile failed to inundate and irrigate their farms.[188] Divine providence was accomplished when humans operated prudentially within the natural fluctuations of Canaanite and Egyptian weather.

---

[186]Matthew 7:24-27.

[187]Henry Sloane Coffin, *The Creed of Jesus* (New York: Scribner, 1907) 247-49.

[188]Genesis 12:10; 41:15–42:5.

Significantly, Jesus' outlook on the relation between human needs and weather phenomena coincides with that of eminent men of scientific orientation who lived centuries before and after him. Aristotle observed that rain falls without regard either to giving growth to a farmer's grain or to spoiling it on the threshing floor.[189] Sigmund Freud, apparently unaware of Jesus' view on natural forces, held that all religions are doomed because they cannot stand up against the scientific spirit, which holds that "earthquakes, tidal waves, conflagrations, make no distinction between the virtuous and pious and the scoundrel or unbeliever."[190] Jesus, while having a religious outlook sharply different from the pagan Athenian philosopher and the atheistic Viennese psychologist, nevertheless shared their observation on the indiscriminate operation of natural processes.

* * *

The early Christians believed that Jesus was at his best during his last hours. Some Jewish leaders, who assumed that power was best displayed in supernatural interventions, shouted this challenge to Jesus, "Save yourself, and come down from the cross!" Unwittingly expressing the gospel truth, they mockingly said, "He saved others; he cannot save himself." Jesus responded with cries of agony and abandonment. The bloody victim was not, even emotionally, a "man of steel." Even so, a pagan centurion who witnessed this death scene exclaimed, "Truly this man was God's son!"[191] As Augustine judiciously put it, "Through Christ as human you come to Christ as God."[192]

A poem of Frederic Myers relates in an exquisite manner the paradoxical qualities of Jesus:

Not as one blind and deaf to our beseeching,
    neither forgetful that we are but dust,
not as from heavens too high for our up-reaching,
    coldly sublime, intolerably just:—
nay but thou knewest us, Lord Christ, thou knowest,
    well thou rememberest our feeble frame,

---

[189]Aristotle, *Physics* 198b, 17-23.

[190]Sigmund Freud, *Introductory Lectures on Psychoanalysis* (New York: Norton, 1964) 146.

[191]Mark 15:29-39.

[192]Augustine, *Sermons* 261.7.

thou canst conceive our highest and our lowest,
   pulses of nobleness and aches of shame. . . .
Jesus, divinest when thou most art man![193]

Jesus was a *super, natural* person; "super" as in *super*lative but not as in *super*natural. He was unlike the American Superman with power over natural forces or the Wonder Woman with telepathic ability. He was not a half-God, half-man hybrid; he was even more of a full-fledged person than his followers. He was abnormal only in the sense that a person with clear vision would stand out in a community in which all had deficient sight. Religious and moral facilities were completely developed in that archetype of authentic humanity. Holy Jesus, like the Holy Bible, was a product of human environment and divine inspiration. To diminish Jesus' humanity is to diminish his greatness. His human qualities include a superlative example of compassion, wisdom, and courage.

Had Jesus been a superman, ascending over cities, the apostles could not have realistically advised, "You should follow in his steps."[194] Such an Omnipotence may be marveled at but not imitated. Jesus was the superlative model of holy suffering *agape* to neighbors far and near. All of his followers should aspire to be super earth beings, loving God, neighbors, and nature even as they love themselves. Mouths agape at alleged supernatural feats have been characteristic of folk religion throughout history, but the more demanding regulation of life by *agape* has been shunned. To become like Jesus is to discover what being human really means.

Gifford lecturer Charles Raven observed that Christians in his day—the mid-twentieth century—tended to focus more on the continued presence of the unique Jesus and less on some supernatural way by which he was conceived or by which he arose from his tomb. According to Raven, "We associate miracles rather with the love of God than with His power, rather with His encounter with us and response to our need than with such events as we cannot otherwise explain."[195] If Christians of this century continue that movement, then Pauline Christianity will have had a resurgence, and the authentic gospel will become better known. Paul thought of the mighty acts of God as going beyond, but not against, nature. Among those acts are

---

[193]Frederic Myers, *Saint Paul* (New York: Macmillan, 1896) 15-16.

[194]1 Peter 2:21; 1 Corinthians 11:1.

[195]Charles Raven, *Natural Religion and Christian Theology* (Cambridge: University Press, 1953) 80.

divine creation, prayer, visions of reality, calls to service, and life with Christ before and after death. Although they cannot be accounted for in the space-time categories of science, they contain vital theological truth. Jesus expresses the power of love not the love of power.

The subtitle of this study of supernaturalism, "its growth and cure," intentionally uses medical terms. My approach has been similar to that of an epidemiologist who investigates the historical development of a disease. Consider, for example, the smallpox virus. Its ancient source may be impossible to find but much data is available on its prevalence in large populations. The search for the international outbreaks of the pandemic is motivated by a desire to reduce, and even eliminate, the infection. Our tracing of the supernaturalism virus has revealed that the Israelite religion contributed to its stoppage through identifying its creator deity with regular natural functioning. Sexual intercourse was viewed as a holy practice for pair bonding and baby production, even though some cultures lauded virginity as holier. The Hebrew Bible denounces astrology that was widespread among pagans. That Bible shows that individual physical resurrection was almost completely rejected. But the records about several prophets—principally Moses, Elijah, and Elisha—allege their performance of miracles that temporarily suspended the regular natural order. The best vaccination for supernaturalism is Pauline Christianity. Although Christianity and other religions have been scarred and even blinded by that pox, those who have been guided by Paul have made strides in isolating religion from supernaturalism. Recognizing that information is the crucial first step in halting an epidemic, this book has been devoted to that effort.

Selected Bibliography

Akenson, Donald. *Saint Saul: A Skeleton Key to the Historical Jesus*. New York: Oxford, 2000.

Aquinas. *Summa Theologica*.

Augustine. *City of God*.

Borg, Marcus. *Jesus, a New Vision*. San Francisco: Harper, 1987.

Bornkamm, Günther. *Jesus of Nazareth*. New York: Harper, 1960.

Bultmann, Rudolf. *Jesus*. Tubingen: Mohr, 1926.

Case, Shirley. *The Origins of Christian Supernaturalism*. Chicago: University of Chicago Press, 1946.

Chadwick, Henry. *Origen: Contra Celsum*. Cambridge: University Press, 1953.

Connick, C. Milo. *Jesus, the Man, the Mission, and the Message*. Englewood Cliffs NJ: Prentice-Hall, 1963.

Crossan, John. *The Historical Jesus*. San Francisco: Harper, 1991.

Dodds, Eric. *Pagan and Christian in an Age of Anxiety*. New York: Norton, 1965.

Ferguson, John. *The Religion of the Roman Empire*. Ithaca: Cornell University Press, 1970.

Fuller, Reginald. *The Formation of the Resurrection Narratives*. New York: Macmillan, 1971.

Funk, Robert et al. *The Acts of Jesus*. San Francisco: Harper, 1998.

Haskins, Susan. *Mary Magdalen*. New York: Harcourt Brace, 1994.

Josephus. *Jewish Antiquities*.

Justin. *Dialogue with Trypho*.

Kaufman, Gordon. *Systematic Theology*. New York: Scribner's, 1968.

Kee, Howard Clark. *Miracle in the Early Christian World*. New Haven: Yale University Press, 1983.

Keller, Ernst and Marie-Luise. *Miracles in Dispute*. Philadelphia: Fortress, 1969.

Küng, Hans. *On Being a Christian*. New York: Doubleday, 1976.

Macquarrie, John. *Principles of Christian Theology*. New York: Scribner, 1966.

Meier, John. *A Marginal Jew*. Three volumes. New York: Doubleday, 1991–2001.

Pannenberg, Wolfhart. *Jesus, God and Man*. Philadelphia: Westminster, 1968.

Philostratus. *Apollonius*.

Renan, Ernest. *Vie de Jesus*. 1867.

Sanders, E. P. *The Historical Figure of Jesus*. New York: Penguin, 1993.

Schneemelcher, Wilhelm, editor. *New Testament Apocrypha*. Philadelphia: 1965.

Schweitzer, Albert. *The Mysticism of Paul the Apostle*. New York: Holt, 1931.

Spinoza, Baruch. *Tractatus Theologico-Politicus*. 1670.

Spoto, Donald. *The Hidden Jesus*. New York: St. Martin's Press, 1998.

Strauss, David. *The Life of Jesus Critically Examined*. Philadelphia: Fortress, 1973.

Theissen, Gerd, and Annette Merz. *The Historical Jesus*. Minneapolis: Fortress, 1996.

Indexes

Biblical Index

General Index

*Limited to cross-references of names and subjects
used at least twice on different pages.*